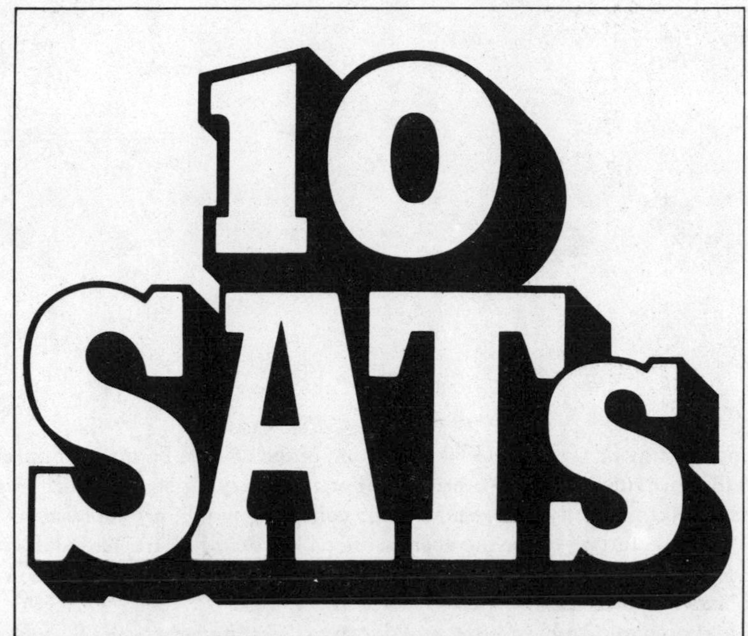

SCHOLASTIC APTITUDE TESTS OF THE COLLEGE BOARD

COLLEGE ENTRANCE EXAMINATION BOARD
NEW YORK

The Admissions Testing Program (ATP) is a program of the College Board, a nonprofit membership organization that provides tests and other educational services for students, schools, and colleges. The membership is composed of more than 2,500 colleges, schools, school systems, and education associations. Representatives of the members serve on the Board of Trustees and advisory councils and committees that consider the programs of the College Board and participate in the determination of its policies and activities.

This book was prepared and produced by Educational Testing Service (ETS), which develops and administers the tests of the Admissions Testing Program for the College Board. The text of this book is adapted from *Taking the SAT,* a booklet that is shipped at the beginning of each academic year to secondary schools for free distribution to students who plan to register for the SAT. (Copies of *Taking the SAT* are available for purchase at $4.00 each, or in quantities of 50 or more at $2.00 each.)

The College Board and Educational Testing Service are dedicated to the principle of equal opportunity, and their programs, services, and employment policies are guided by that principle.

Cover design by Bob Silverman.

Library of Congress Catalog Card Number: 83-71936

Printed in the United States of America
9 8 7 6 5 4 3 2 1

Contents

Class #1

Introduction

The College Board knows that some people are uncomfortable when they are faced with the prospect of taking any test, but that there is even greater uneasiness before taking national standardized tests such as the Scholastic Aptitude Test (SAT). One of the reasons that people tend to worry so much about how they will do on the SAT is their lack of understanding about what will be on the test, what it measures, and how the results will be used.

This book attempts to help students get better acquainted with the SAT and, in the process, alleviate some of that anxiety. The College Board believes that everyone who takes the SAT should be fully familiar with the test beforehand and thus be able to demonstrate their abilities. Before taking the SAT, every student should know:

- What the SAT is designed to measure
- The format of the test as a whole
- The kinds of questions on the test
- How to mark the answer sheet and how each question is scored
- Rules of good test-taking practice
- How scores are reported and used
- How to use sample tests for practice and self-scoring

The College Board provides this information free of charge to all students planning to take the SAT. Before taking the test, students receive through their schools a copy of *Taking the SAT*, which provides directions, examples, and explanations of the test, as well as a sample SAT and answer sheet. All the information in *Taking the SAT* is included in this book.

In addition, the College Board currently makes public an average of five editions of the SAT per year as part of its ongoing program to insure full public information about these tests. Ten of these editions, all of which have been administered in the past few years, are included in this book.

Except to help students become familiar with the overall format of the SAT, the use of all ten tests in preparing for the SAT probably will be of extremely limited value. These tests are provided to give examples of the range of questions and topics on any SAT test; however, there is no evidence that extensive drill or practice on these particular tests will increase scores. Students are encouraged not to allow any sample tests to distract them from the kind of general academic study that will help them develop the verbal and mathematical reasoning skills that the SAT measures and that are important for college. Research on the relative effectiveness of activities and materials intended to prepare students to take the SAT indicates that short-term efforts to cram or drill with sample questions have little effect on test performance. The soundest preparation for the SAT continues to be serious application to regular school studies, with emphasis on academic courses and plenty of outside reading.

Although this book has been written for students and others who are planning to take the SAT, it also may be useful to parents, teachers, and individuals who have an interest in the SAT and who use its results.

How the Tests Are Developed

Many people are involved in the development of every new edition of the Scholastic Aptitude Test (SAT) and the Test of Standard Written English (TSWE). Questions are written by high school and college teachers and by test specialists at Educational Testing Service. Questions then are placed in one of the experimental sections of the SAT. In this way, new questions are tried out under standard testing conditions by representative samples of students taking the SAT. Each question then is analyzed statistically for its usefulness and may be revised, if necessary. Satisfactory questions become part of a pool of questions from which new editions of the SAT are assembled.

In developing a new edition of the SAT, several test specialists and a test editor review each question and reading selections on which questions are based for accuracy and to ensure balanced content of the test as a whole. Each reviewer prepares a list of answers that is compared with other reviewers' lists to verify agreement on the correct answer for each question. In addition, specially trained "sensitivity" reviewers read the test material and eliminate any references that might be unfair or offensive to some student groups because of stereotyping, sex bias, or meaning that could produce negative emotional feelings.

After the new edition has been assembled, the SAT and TSWE Committees, composed of high school teachers, college faculty, and educational administrators, review the test a final time before it is given to students. In addition to reviewing all new tests, these committees also are responsible for overall test specification, recommending related research, and advising the College Board on policy matters related to the tests.

SAT Committee 1982-83

Willie May, Wendell Phillips High School, Chicago, Illinois, *Chairman*

James R. Buch, University of Oregon, Eugene, Oregon

Nancy S. Cole, University of Pittsburgh, Pittsburgh, Pennsylvania

William Controvillas, Farmington High School, Farmington, Connecticut

Margaret Fleming, Cleveland Public Schools, Cleveland, Ohio

Lynn H. Fox, Johns Hopkins University, Baltimore, Maryland

Jeanette B. Hersey, Connecticut College, New London, Connecticut

Robert S. Moore, South Carolina State Department of Education, Columbia, South Carolina

Allen Parducci, University of California — Los Angeles, Los Angeles, California

Hammett Worthington-Smith, Albright College, Reading, Pennsylvania

TSWE Committee 1982-83

Ronald B. Newman, University of Miami, Coral Gables, Florida, *Chairman*

Carlota Cárdenas de Dwyer, University of Texas, Austin, Texas

Michael C. Flanigan, University of Oklahoma, Norman, Oklahoma

Maurice Lee, Bard College, Annandale-on-Hudson, New York

Marjorie G. Roemer, Brookline High School, Brookline, Massachusetts

About the Tests

The Scholastic Aptitude Test (SAT)

The SAT is a multiple-choice test made up of verbal and mathematical sections. The verbal questions test your vocabulary, verbal reasoning, and understanding of what you read. The mathematical questions test your ability to solve problems involving arithmetic, elementary algebra, and geometry. These verbal and mathematical abilities are related to how well you will do academically in college. The SAT does not measure other factors and abilities — such as creativity, special talents, and motivation — that also may help you do well in college.

SAT scores are useful to college admissions officers in comparing the preparation and ability of applicants from different high schools, which may vary widely in courses and grading standards. Colleges also consider your high school record and other information about you in making admissions decisions. Your high school record is probably the best single indicator of how you will do in college, but a combination of your high school grades and test scores is an even better indicator.

The Test of Standard Written English (TSWE)

The TSWE is a multiple-choice test given at the same time as the SAT, but it has a different purpose. The TSWE is intended to be used to help the college you attend choose an English course appropriate for your ability. The questions in it measure your ability to recognize standard written English, the language that is used in most college textbooks and that you probably will be expected to use in the papers you write in college.

How the Tests Are Organized

The SAT and TSWE are included in the same test book. Each test book is divided into six sections:

- 2 SAT-verbal sections,
- 2 SAT-math sections,
- 1 TSWE section, and
- 1 section of experimental verbal, mathematical, or TSWE questions.

The questions in the experimental section do not count toward your score. They are used to maintain the quality of the tests and to provide essential information for future editions.

You will be given 30 minutes to work on each section. The six sections are not in the same order in every test book. Later in this book you will find detailed explanations of each type of question as well as tips on how to make the best use of the testing time.

How to Register

The *Student Bulletin* for the SAT and the Achievement Tests contains a registration form and all the information you will need on how to register for these tests and how to have your score reported. The *Bulletin* also describes the other tests and services of the Admissions Testing Program (ATP), such as the Achievement Tests, the Student Descriptive Questionnaire (SDQ), and the Student Search Service (SSS).

The SAT is administered on a regular schedule (six times a year in most states) at thousands of test centers throughout the world. To avoid late fees, you must send in your registration form at least five weeks before the test date you have chosen.

A supply of the *Student Bulletin* is sent to all high schools each year. High school students should be able to pick up a copy of the *Bulletin* at their school guidance or counseling office. Test candidates who are not currently in high school may obtain a copy by writing to the address below.

Address
College Board ATP
Box 592
Princeton, NJ 08541

Phone Numbers (Monday-Friday)

Princeton, NJ	Berkeley, CA
(609) 771-7600	**(415) 849-0950**
8:30 a.m. to 9:30 p.m.	8:15 a.m. to 4:30 p.m.

How to Prepare for the Tests

Know What to Expect

The best way to prepare for the tests is to familiarize yourself with their organization, the types of questions that will appear on them, and what will be expected of you on the actual test day. To make sure you are prepared for the actual test administration, you should:

- **Read this book or *Taking the SAT* carefully.** Be sure you understand how each test is organized and how it will be scored. The information in these books will help you learn the answers to such questions as "Should I guess?" "Do difficult questions get more credit than easy ones?" "Should I memorize mathematical formulas?"

- **Study the sample questions and explanations.** The sample questions and explanations that begin on page 12 will give you a good idea of the kinds of questions that actually appear on the tests. The more familiar you are with the sample questions, the more comfortable you'll feel when you see the questions in your test book on the day of the tests.

- **Study and understand the test directions.** The directions for answering the questions are printed here exactly as they appear in the test book. Study them now so you will understand them when you take the test. The less time you need to spend reading and figuring out the directions on the test day, the more time you'll have for answering the questions.

- **Take at least one sample test.** Included in this book are 10 complete SATs (and one TSWE) together with copies of answer sheets. Try to take a test for practice under conditions as similar as possible to those of the actual test day. (Suggestions for doing so appear on page 34, just before the practice test.) Make sure that you use one of the answer sheets provided. That way you'll already have been through a "dry run" before you actually take the SAT.

The Day Before the Tests

Learning as much as you can about the tests is something you'll want to do several weeks before the day you plan to take the tests. Following are some suggestions for what to do on the day or evening before the tests:

- **Spend an hour or so reviewing the sample questions and explanations in this book.** Hours of intense study the night before the test day probably will not help your performance on the tests and might even make you more anxious. But a short review of the information you studied earlier probably will make you feel more comfortable and prepared.

- **Get your testing materials together and put them in a place that will be convenient for you in the morning.** Use this checklist:
  - ✓ Admission ticket
  - ✓ Positive identification (You won't be admitted to the test center without it. See the *Student Bulletin*.)
  - ✓ Two No. 2 pencils with erasers
  - ✓ Directions to the test center if you need them
  - ✓ All the materials you will need to register as a standby, if you have not preregistered (See the *Student Bulletin*.)

- **Spend the rest of the evening relaxing**. You'll accomplish little by worrying about the next day. Read a book, watch a television program you enjoy, or do anything you find relaxing.

- **Get a good night's sleep**. You'll want to feel your best when you take the tests, so try to be well rested and refreshed. Get to bed early, set your alarm early enough to avoid having to rush, and feel satisfied that you've prepared yourself well for the test day.

Special Preparation

If you or your parents have been thinking about special preparation for the SAT outside your regular classroom activities, consider the following points:

- This book (or *Taking the SAT)* and the *Student Bulletin* are the best sources of information about the SAT. All the questions in these books are taken from actual SATs that have been administered during the past few years.

- The SAT measures developed verbal and mathematical reasoning abilities that are involved in successful academic work in college; it is not a test of some inborn and unchanging capacity.

- Scores on the SAT can change as you develop your verbal and mathematical abilities both in and out of school.

- Your abilities are related to the time and effort spent. Short-term drill and cramming are likely to have little effect; longer-term preparation that develops skills and abilities can have greater effect. One kind of longer-term preparation is the study of challenging academic courses.

- While drill and practice on sample test questions generally result in little effect on test scores, preparation of this kind can familiarize you with different question types and may help to reduce anxiety about what to expect. You can help yourself to become familiar with the test by using the explanations and a full sample test in this book.

- Whether longer preparation, apart from that available to you in your regular high school courses, is worth the time, effort, and money is a decision you and your parents must make for yourselves; results seem to vary considerably from program to program, and for each person within any one program. Studies of special preparation programs carried on in many high schools show various results, averaging about 10 points for the verbal section and 15 points for the mathematical section over and above the average increases that would otherwise be expected. In other programs, results have ranged from no improvement in scores to average gains of 25-30 points for particular groups of students or particular programs. Recent studies of commercial coaching have shown a similar range of results. You should satisfy yourself that the results of a special program or course are likely to make a difference in relation to your college admissions plans.

- Generally, the soundest preparation for the SAT is to study widely with emphasis on academic courses and extensive outside reading. Since SAT score increases of 20-30 points result from about three additional questions answered correctly, your own independent study in addition to regular academic course work could result in some increase in your scores.

Test-Taking Tips

Think of the number of things you do easily every day that would seem mysterious or difficult if you didn't know how to approach them. For example, when you go to school or work each morning, you know that you have to turn left at one corner or right at another. And you have a good idea of how far away your school or your work is and how long it will take you to get there. But if you hadn't learned these things at one time or another and received tips from others on shortcuts and new routes, your trip would be much more difficult.

Taking the SAT and the TSWE does not have to be a mysterious experience. You already have read about how to prepare for the tests in general. Here are some specific test-taking tips that will help when you actually take the tests.

- ✓Within each group of questions of the same type, the easier questions usually are at the beginning of the group and the more difficult ones are at the end. (An exception to this is the reading comprehension questions. The reading passages usually are ordered easiest to hardest, but the questions that follow each passage are ordered according to the logic and organization of the passage.)
- ✓If you're working on a group of questions of a particular type and find that the questions are getting too difficult for you, quickly read through the rest of the questions in that group and answer only those you think you know. Then go on to the next group of questions in that section. (Again, this is not necessarily true of the questions about a reading passage. A difficult reading comprehension question might be followed by an easier one.)
- ✓You get just as much credit for correctly answering easy questions as you do for correctly answering difficult ones. So make sure you answer all the questions that seem easy to you before you spend time thinking about the questions that seem difficult.
- ✓You *can* guess. If you know that some of the choices for a question are definitely wrong, then it's to your advantage to guess from the remaining choices. But because of the way the test is scored, random guessing is unlikely to increase your score.
- ✓You *can* omit questions. Many students who do well on the SAT omit some questions. You can always return to questions you've omitted if you have time left to work on that section.
- ✓You don't have to answer every question correctly to score well. In fact, many students who receive average or slightly above-average scores answer only 40-60 percent of the questions correctly.
- ✓You get credit for each question you answer correctly. You lose a *fraction* for each question you answer incorrectly. You neither gain nor lose credit for questions you omit. (See page 62 for more detailed information on scoring.)
- ✓Use the test book for scratchwork and to mark questions you omitted, so you can go back to them if you have time. Do *not* make extra marks on the answer sheet. They may be misread as answers by the scoring machine.
- ✓If the scoring machine reads what looks like two answers for one question, that will be considered an omitted question. So it's in your best interest to keep your answer sheet free of any stray marks.
- ✓Do not omit an entire section of the test. If you do not respond to at least three SAT-verbal, SAT-math, or TSWE questions, you will receive the minimum score for that part.

Sample Questions and Explanations

Following are sample questions and explanations for each type of question that appears on the SAT. Pay special attention to the sample directions. You'll see them again on the actual test.

Verbal Sections of the SAT

The verbal sections of the SAT contain four types of questions:

- 25 antonyms,
- 20 analogies,
- 15 sentence completions, and
- 25 questions based on reading passages.

The antonyms usually take the least time per question, followed by analogies, sentence completion questions, and, finally, the reading comprehension questions. Individual students spend varying amounts of time working on the different types of questions. Some students can answer two or three antonyms a minute, but the same students may take more than seven minutes to read a 400-word passage and answer five questions on it.

Your answers to the 85 questions in the verbal sections make up your total verbal score. (See page 62.) The score report you receive will also show two subscores: (1) a vocabulary subscore, based on the antonym and analogy questions, and (2) a reading subscore, based on the sentence completions and the questions on the reading passages.

A careful balance of reading materials and words drawn from a variety of subject-matter fields helps ensure that the test is fair to students with different interests. However, no specialized knowledge in science, social studies, literature, or other fields is needed.

Antonyms (opposites)

Antonym questions primarily test the extent of your vocabulary. The vocabulary used in the antonym questions includes words that you are likely to come across in your general reading, although some words may not be the kind you use in everyday speech.

Directions: Each question below consists of a word in capital letters, followed by five lettered words or phrases. Choose the word or phrase that is most nearly opposite in meaning to the word in capital letters. Since some of the questions require you to distinguish fine shades of meaning, consider all the choices before deciding which is best.

EXAMPLE:
GOOD: (A) sour (B) bad (C) red (D) hot (E) ugly

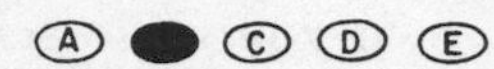

You can probably answer this example without thinking very much about the choices. However, most of the antonyms in the verbal section require more careful analysis. When you work on antonym questions, remember that:

1. Among the five choices offered, you are looking for the word that means the *opposite* of the given word. Words that have exactly the same meaning as the given word are not included among the five choices.

2. You are looking for the *best* answer. Read all of the choices before deciding which one is best, even if you feel sure you know the answer. For example:

   SUBSEQUENT: (A) primary (B) recent (C) contemporary (D) prior (E) simultaneous

   Subsequent means "following in time or order; succeeding." Someone working quickly might choose (B) *recent* because it refers to a past action and *subsequent* refers to an action in the future. However, choice (D) *prior* is the best answer. It is more nearly the opposite of *subsequent* than is *recent*.

3. Few words have exact opposites, that is, words that are opposite in all of their meanings. You should find the word that is *most nearly* opposite. For example:

   FERMENTING: (A) improvising (B) stagnating (C) wavering (D) plunging (E) dissolving

   Even though *fermenting* is normally associated with chemical reactions, whereas *stagnating* is normally associated with water, *fermenting* means being agitated and *stagnating* means being motionless. Therefore, choice (B) *stagnating* is the best of the five choices.

4. You need to be flexible. A word can have several meanings. For example:

   DEPRESS: (A) force (B) allow (C) clarify (D) elate (E) loosen

The word *depress* can mean "to push down." However, no word meaning "to lift up" is included among the choices. Therefore, you must consider another meaning of *depress*, "to sadden or discourage." Option (D) *elate* means to fill with joy or pride. The best answer is (D) *elate*.

5. You'll often recognize a word you have encountered in your reading but have never looked up in the dictionary. If you don't know the dictionary meaning of a word but have a feeling for how the word should be used, try to make up a short phrase or sentence using the word. This may give you a clue as to which choice is an opposite, even though you may not be able to define the word precisely.

   INCUMBENT: (A) conscious (B) effortless (C) optional (D) improper (E) irrelevant

   You may remember *incumbent* used in a sentence such as, "It is incumbent upon me to finish this." If you can think of such a phrase, you may be able to recognize that *incumbent* means "imposed as a duty" or "obligatory." Of the five choices, (A), (B), and (D) are in no way opposites of *incumbent* and you can easily eliminate them. Choice (E) means "not pertinent" and choice (C) means "not compulsory." Although choice (E) may look attractive, choice (C) *optional* is more nearly an exact opposite to *incumbent*. Choice (C), therefore, is the answer.

Some General Tips for Answering Antonym Questions

Answering antonyms depends on knowing the uses as well as the meanings of words, so just memorizing word lists is probably of little use. You're more likely to improve your performance on antonyms and other kinds of verbal questions by doing things that help you to think about words and the way they are used. So, it would be a good idea to:

- ✓ Read some good books or magazines on subjects with which you're not already familiar. This will give you a better idea of how even familiar words can have different meanings in different contexts.
- ✓ Use a dictionary when you come across words that you don't understand in your reading. This will help to broaden your vocabulary and consequently could improve your performance on the tests.

Analogies

Analogy questions test your ability to see a relationship in a pair of words, to understand the ideas expressed in the relationship, and to recognize a similar or parallel relationship.

Directions: Each question below consists of a related pair of words or phrases, followed by five lettered pairs of words or phrases. Select the lettered pair that best expresses a relationship similar to that expressed in the original pair.

EXAMPLE:
YAWN : BOREDOM : : (A) dream : sleep (B) anger : madness (C) smile : amusement (D) face : expression (E) impatience : rebellion

Ⓐ Ⓑ ● Ⓓ Ⓔ

The first step in answering an analogy question is to establish a precise relationship between the original pair of words (the two capitalized words) before you examine the five answer choices. In the example above, the relationship between *yawn* and *boredom* can best be stated as "(first word) is a physical sign of (second word)," or "(first word) is a facial expression of (second word)." The pair of words that best expresses a similar relationship is found in choice (C): a (smile) is a physical sign of (amusement), or a (smile) is a facial expression of (amusement). None of the other choices shares a precise relationship with the capitalized pair of words: a *dream* is something that occurs when you are asleep, but it is not usually thought of as being a sign of *sleep* as, for example, closed eyes or a snore might be; *anger* denotes strong displeasure and madness can refer to rage or insanity, but neither word is a physical sign of the other; an *expression* is something that appears on a *face*, but a *face* is not a sign of an *expression*; impatience may lead to rebellion or be characteristic of a rebellious person, but *impatience* is not a physical sign of *rebellion*.

Each analogy question contains a relationship between two pairs of words (the capitalized pair and the correct answer). Try to establish a relationship between each pair of words. For example:

SUBMISSIVE : LED : : (A) wealthy : employed (B) intolerant : indulged (C) humble : humiliated (D) incorrigible : taught (E) inconspicuous : overlooked

The relationship between *submissive* and *led* can be expressed as "to be submissive is to be easily led." Only choice (E) has the same relationship: "to be inconspicuous is to be easily overlooked."

To be *intolerant* is not to be easily *indulged*, to be *humble* is not to be easily *humiliated*, and to be *incorrigible* (or incapable of being reformed) is not to be easily *taught*. With regard to choice (A), although the wealthy may find it easier to get employment than do the poor, the statement "to be wealthy is to be easily employed" is an expression of opinion and not an expression of the relationship between the words according to their dictionary meanings.

Practice describing verbal relationships. Below are some examples of the kinds of relationships that could be used.

SONG : REPERTOIRE : : (A) score : melody (B) instrument : artist (C) solo : chorus (D) benediction : church (E) suit : wardrobe

The best answer is choice (E). The relationship between the words can be expressed as "several (first word) make up a (second word)." Several (songs) make up a (repertoire) as several (suits) make up a (wardrobe).

REQUEST : ENTREAT : : (A) control : explode (B) admire : idolize (C) borrow : steal (D) repeat : plead (E) cancel : invalidate

The best answer is choice (B). Although both of the capitalized words have similar meanings, they express different degrees of feeling; to (entreat) is to (request) with strong feeling as to (idolize) is to (admire) with strong feeling.

To answer analogy questions, you must think carefully about the precise meanings of words. For instance, if you thought the word "entreat" meant only "to ask" instead of "to ask urgently," you would have trouble establishing the correct relationship between *request* and *entreat*.

FAMINE : STARVATION : : (A) deluge : flood (B) drought : vegetation (C) war : treaty (D) success : achievement (E) seed : mutation

The best answer is choice (A). The relationship can be stated as (famine) results in (starvation) as a (deluge) results in a (flood). None of the other pairs of words expresses a causal relationship. Choice (C) is close, since a *treaty* often follows after a *war*, but we do not think of a war "causing" a treaty in the same way that a famine "causes" starvation.

AMPLIFIER : HEAR : : (A) turntable : listen (B) typewriter : spell (C) platter : eat (D) camera : feel (E) microscope : see

The best answer is choice (E). An (amplifier) magnifies in order to help a person (hear) in the same way that a (microscope) magnifies in order to help a person (see). Note that, in (A), while a *turntable* is part of a larger mechanism that allows a person to *listen*, the choice is not as good an answer as (E) because a *turntable* does not magnify anything. Choice (D) is also wrong for a similar reason: a *camera* produces pictures that may make a person *feel* something, but a *camera* does not magnify in order to help a person to *feel*.

Some choices may have relationships that are close but not parallel to the relationship in the original pair. Most of the pairs of words listed in the choices have relationships that can be stated; however, the correct answer has *most nearly* the same relationship as the original pair. Look at the following example.

KNIFE : INCISION : : (A) bulldozer : excavation (B) tool : operation (C) pencil : calculation (D) hose : irrigation (E) plow : agriculture

On the most general level, the relationship between *knife* and *incision* is that the object indicated by the first word is used to perform the action indicated by the second word. Since "a (knife) is used to make an (incision)," "a (bulldozer) is used to make an (excavation)," and "a (hose) is used for (irrigation)," there appear to be two correct answers. You need to go back and state the relationship more precisely. Some aspect of the relationship between the original pair exists in only one of the choices. A more precise relationship between *knife* and *incision* could be expressed as: "a knife cuts into something to make an incision" and "a bulldozer cuts into something to make an excavation." This relationship eliminates *hose : irrigation* as a possible answer. The best answer is choice (A).

Remember that a pair of words can have more than one relationship. For example:

PRIDE : LION : : (A) snake : python (B) pack : wolf (C) rat : mouse (D) bird : starling (E) dog : canine

A possible relationship between *pride* and *lion* might be that "the first word describes a characteristic of the second (especially in mythology)." Using this reasoning, you might look for an answer such as *wisdom : owl*, but none of the given choices has that kind of relationship. Another relationship between *pride* and *lion* is "a group of lions is called a pride"; therefore, the answer is (B) *pack : wolf*, since "a group of wolves is called a pack."

Some General Tips for Answering Analogy Questions

- State the relationship between the two capitalized words in a sentence or phrase as clearly in your mind as you can. Next, find the pair of words that has the most similar or parallel relationship.
- Always compare the relationship between the pair of capitalized words to the relationships between the pairs of words in each of the choices. Don't try to set up a relationship between the first word in the original pair and the first word in each of the five choices.

- Think carefully about the meanings of words. The words in analogy questions are used according to their dictionary definitions or meanings closely related to their dictionary definitions. The better you know the precise meanings of words, the less trouble you'll have establishing the correct relationships between them.

- Don't be misled by relationships that are close but not parallel to the relationship in the original pair. The correct answer has a relationship that is most nearly parallel to the relationship between the capitalized words.

Sentence Completion Questions

Sentence completion questions test your ability to recognize relationships among parts of a sentence. Each question has a sentence with one or two words missing. Below the sentence, five words or pairs of words are given. You must choose the word or set of words that best fits with the other parts of the sentence. In sentence completion questions, you have to know the meanings of the words offered as choices and you also have to know how to use those words properly in the context of a sentence. The sentences are taken from published material and cover a wide variety of topics. You'll find that even if you're not familiar with the topic of a sentence, there's enough information in the sentence for you to find the correct answer from the context of the sentence itself.

Directions: Each sentence below has one or two blanks, each blank indicating that something has been omitted. Beneath the sentence are five lettered words or sets of words. Choose the word or set of words that best fits the meaning of the sentence as a whole.

EXAMPLE:
Although its publicity has been ····, the film itself is intelligent, well-acted, handsomely produced, and altogether ····.
(A) tasteless . . respectable (B) extensive . . moderate
(C) sophisticated . . amateur (D) risqué . . crude
(E) perfect . . spectacular

● Ⓑ Ⓒ Ⓓ Ⓔ

The word *although* suggests that the publicity gave the wrong impression of the movie, so look for two words that are more or less opposite in meaning. Also, the second word has to fit in with "intelligent, well-acted, handsomely produced." Choices (D) and (E) are not opposites. The words in Choice (B) are somewhat opposite in meaning, but do not logically fulfill the expectation set up by the word *although*. Choice (C) can't be the correct answer, even though *sophisticated* and *amateur* are nearly opposites, because an "intelligent, well-acted, handsomely produced" film isn't amateurish. Only choice (A), when inserted in the sentence, makes a logical statement.

For a better understanding of sentence completion questions, read the following sample questions and explanations.

Nearly all the cultivated plants utilized by the Chinese have been of ···· origin; even rice, though known in China since Neolithic times, came from India.
(A) foreign (B) ancient (C) wild (D) obscure
(E) common

To answer this question, you need to consider the entire sentence — the part that comes after the semicolon as well as the part that comes before it. If you only consider the first part of the question, all five choices seem plausible. The second part of the sentence adds a specific example — that rice came to China from India. This idea of origin supports and clarifies the "origin" mentioned in the first part of the sentence and eliminates (C), (D), and (E) as possible answers. The mention of Neolithic times makes (B) harder to eliminate, but the sentence is not logical when (B) is used to fill in the blank because the emphasis in the second part of the sentence — country of origin — is inconsistent with that in the first — age. Only choice (A) produces a sentence that is logical and consistent.

The excitement does not ···· but ···· his senses, giving him a keener perception of a thousand details.
(A) slow . . diverts (B) blur . . sharpens
(C) overrule . . constricts (D) heighten . . aggravates
(E) forewarn . . quickens

Since the sentence has two blanks to be filled, you must make sure that both words make sense in the sentence. If you look for grammatical clues within the sentence, you will see that the word *but* implies that the answer will involve two words that are more or less opposite in meaning. If you keep this in mind, you can eliminate all of the choices except for (B) *blur . . sharpens*. Only the words in choice (B) imply opposition. Also, "sharpens his senses" is consistent with the notion that he has a "keener perception of a thousand details."

They argue that the author was determined to ···· his own conclusion, so he ···· any information that did not support it.
(A) uphold . . ignored (B) revise . . destroyed
(C) advance . . devised (D) disprove . . distorted
(E) reverse . . confiscated

The logic of the sentence makes it fairly easy to eliminate choices (B), (D), and (E). The first word in choice (A), *uphold*, and the first word in (C), *ad-*

vance, seem all right. However, the second word in choice (C), *devised*, does not make sense in the sentence. Why would an author who wished to advance his theory devise information that did not support it? Only choice (A) makes a logically consistent sentence.

She is a skeptic, ... to believe that the accepted opinion of the majority is generally ....

(A) prone . . infallible (B) afraid . . misleading
(C) inclined . . justifiable (D) quick . . significant
(E) disposed . . erroneous

The words to be inserted in the blank spaces in the question above must result in a statement that is consistent with the definition of a skeptic. Since a skeptic would hardly consider the accepted opinion of the majority as *infallible*, *justifiable*, or *significant*, you can eliminate choices (A), (C), and (D). A skeptic would not be afraid that the accepted opinion of the majority is misleading; a skeptic would believe that it was. Therefore, choice (B) is not correct. Only choice (E) *disposed. . erroneous* makes a logical sentence.

Some General Tips for Answering Sentence Completion Questions

- Read the entire sentence carefully; make sure you understand the ideas being expressed.
- Don't select an answer simply because it is a popular cliché or "sounds good."
- In a question with two blanks, the right answer must correctly fill both blanks. A wrong answer choice often includes one correct and one incorrect word.
- After choosing an answer, read the entire sentence to yourself and make sure that it makes sense.
- Consider all the choices; be sure you haven't overlooked a choice that makes a better and more accurate sentence than your choice does.

Reading Comprehension Questions

The reading comprehension questions on the SAT test your ability to read and understand a passage. The test will have one or more passages taken from any of the following categories:

Narrative:	(novels, short stories, biographies, essays)
Biological Science:	(medicine, botany, zoology)
Physical Science:	(chemistry, physics, astronomy)
Humanities:	(art, literature, music, philosophy, folklore)
Social Studies:	(history, economics, sociology, government)
Argumentative:	(the presentation of a definite point of view on some subject)

Each passage contains all the information you'll need to answer the questions that follow it.

Several types of questions are asked about the passage. Some ask about the main idea of a passage. Some questions ask about those ideas that are stated directly in the passage. Some ask you to recognize applications of the author's principles or opinions. In some questions you must make an inference from what you have read. And in others you must evaluate the way the author develops and presents the passage.

Following are a sample passage, sample questions, and explanations of each of the questions.

Directions: The passage below is followed by questions based on its content. Answer all questions following the passage on the basis of what is stated or implied in that passage.

Any survey of medieval town life delights in the color of guild organizations: the broiders and glovers, the shipwrights and upholsters, each with its guild hall, its distinctive livery, and its elaborate set of rules. But if life in the guilds and at the fairs provides a sharp contrast with the stodgy life on the manor, we must not be misled by surface resemblances into thinking that guild life represented a foretaste of modern life in medieval dress. It is a long distance from guilds to modern business firms, and it is well to fix in mind some of the differences.

In the first place, the guild was much more than just an institution for organizing production. Whereas most of its regulations concerned wages and conditions of work and specifications of output, they also dwelt at length on noneconomic matters: on a member's civic role, on his appropriate dress, and even on his daily deportment. Guilds were the regulators not only of production but of social conduct.

Between guilds and modern business firms there is a profound gulf. Unlike modern firms, the purpose of guilds was not first and foremost to make money. Rather, it was to preserve a certain orderly way of life — a way which envisaged a decent income for the master craftsmen but which was certainly not intended to allow any of them to become "big" businessmen. On the contrary, guilds were specifically designed to ward off any such outcome of an uninhibited struggle among their members. The terms of service and wages were fixed by custom. So, too, were the terms of sale: a guild member who cornered the supply of an item or bought wholesale to sell at retail was severely punished. Competition was strictly limited and profits were held to prescribed

levels. Advertising was forbidden, and even technical progress in advance of one's fellow guildsmen was considered disloyal.

Surely the guilds represent a more "modern" aspect of feudal life than the manor, but the whole temper of guild life was still far removed from the goals and ideals of modern business enterprise. There was no free competition and no restless probing for advantage. Existing on the margin of a relatively moneyless society, the guilds were organizations that sought to take the risks out of their slender enterprises. As such, they were as drenched in the medieval atmosphere as the manors.

Following are sample questions about this passage. You may be asked to identify the main idea or primary focus of the passage. For example:

1. The author is primarily concerned with

(A) analyzing the origins of the guild system
(B) explaining the relationships between manors, fairs, and modern business firms
(C) depicting the weaknesses of the guilds' business practices
(D) stressing the historical evolution of guilds to modern business firms
(E) discussing some differences between medieval and modern business practices

The answer to the question is (E). The passage compares medieval business practices, as represented by the guilds, with modern business practices. The author describes the guilds and suggests some ways in which they differ from contemporary business organizations. The most concise statement of what the author intends to discuss in the passage is made at the end of the first paragraph, in lines 8-10. Choice (A) is incorrect because the passage does not mention the origins of the guild system. Choice (B) is unacceptable because the author's main comparison is not between manors, fairs, and modern business firms, even though all are mentioned in the passage. Choices (C) and (D) are slightly harder to eliminate. Readers who think that the author is criticizing the guilds by pointing out the ways in which they differ from modern business enterprise are mistaken; there is no evidence in the passage to suggest that the author wants either to praise or to criticize the guilds. Choice (D) mentions the author's main concerns — guilds and modern business firms — but is incorrect because the passage does not deal with the evolution from medieval to modern practices.

Another type of question asks about details stated in the passage. Sometimes this type of question asks about a particular phrase or line; at other times, the part or parts of the passage referred to are not as precisely identified. For example:

2. According to the passage, modern business enterprises, compared to the medieval guilds, are

(A) more concerned with increasing profits
(B) influenced more by craftsmen than by tradesmen
(C) more subordinate to the demands of consumers
(D) less progressive in financial dealings
(E) less interested in quantity than quality

To answer this question, locate the parts of the passage that compare guilds and modern business — the beginnings of the third and fourth paragraphs. Lines 19-20 suggest that the foremost purpose of modern firms is to make money. Lines 35-38 indicate that "free competition" and "restless probing for advantage" are central to modern business enterprise. Choice (A) is the most appropriate answer among the choices given. There is no justification in the passage for any of the other choices. Some people might argue from their own experience or opinion that (C) is a possible answer. However, since the question says, "According to the passage ...," the answer must be based on what is stated in the passage.

Some questions ask you to make inferences based on the passage. For example:

3. It can be inferred that the guilds were organized as they were because

(A) life on the manors was boring and drab
(B) technical improvements were still improbable
(C) they stressed preservation and stability, not progress
(D) people in medieval times were interested in advancing individual liberty
(E) social status was determined by income

This question is not answered simply and directly in the passage itself, but the passage gives you information to draw on. In the third paragraph, the author notes that the purpose of guilds "was to preserve a certain orderly way of life" and that guilds were specifically designed "to ward off...uninhibited struggle among their members." In the fourth paragraph, the author states that the guilds "were organizations that sought to take the risks out of their slender enterprises." From these statements and the comparisons between guilds and modern business firms that the author makes elsewhere in the passage, choice (C) is the most reasonable conclusion to draw. Choice (A) is stated in the passage, but is not related to the purpose of the organization of the guilds. The statement about technical progress made in lines 31-33 weakens the plausibility of the inference in (B). The passage doesn't provide enough information to justify the inferences made in (D) and (E). This is a fairly easy and straightforward inference question. You may be asked others that will require somewhat more sophisticated reasoning processes.

Other types of questions ask you to apply information in the passage to situations that are not specifically mentioned in the passage or to evaluate the author's logic, organization, attitude, tone, or language. Following is an example of one type of question that asks you to apply information given in the passage.

4. According to the passage, which of the following would LEAST likely be found in a guild handbook?

(A) The fees a master guildsman should charge
(B) The bonus a member would receive for record sales
(C) The maximum number of hours a guildsman would be expected to work
(D) The steps a new shipwright would follow to become a master craftsman
(E) The organizations to which a member should contribute as an upstanding citizen

To answer this question, you must decide which of the five choices is least likely to have been included in a guild handbook. The passage does not mention a handbook, but it does provide enough information about the areas of business and personal life that the guilds attempted to regulate to enable you to make reasoned judgments. The passage suggests that (A), (C), and (E) would definitely be included in such a handbook and that (D) would be a logical area of concern and regulation for a guild. Choice (B) seems to be the least likely area of regulation and is, therefore, the correct answer. In fact, the statements made in the passage about the purpose of the guilds — to enable all master craftsmen to earn a decent income and to discourage ruthless competition among members — suggest that offering a bonus for record sales would indeed be an unlikely activity for a guild to engage in.

The question below is another type of evaluation question.

5. With which of the following statements concerning modern business firms would the author be most likely to agree?

(A) They make rules concerning appropriate business practices for employees.
(B) They permit the free play of price in terms of service and sales.
(C) Their main concern is the stability of profit levels.
(D) Their aim is to discourage competition among independent manufacturers.
(E) They are organized in such a way that cooperating monopolies will develop.

Paragraphs three and four provide information about the author's characterization of modern business practices and support choice (B) as the correct response. Choices (A), (C), and (D) are more true of guilds than of modern business firms. There is little or nothing in the passage to support (E) as the answer; the author stresses the competition rather than cooperation of modern businesses. When answering such questions, remember to read the question carefully and to look for evidence in the passage to support your choice. In this question, for example, you are not asked which of the statements about modern business is true or which of the statements you agree with, but which one the author is most likely to agree with based on what he or she has written in the passage. Sometimes questions that ask for the most likely or least likely answer require you to make careful distinctions between choices that are partly correct and those that are more complete or more accurate.

Some General Tips for Answering Reading Comprehension Questions

- Read each passage closely and attentively. Follow the author's reasoning; notice how each piece of information relates to the ideas being presented. Notice attitude, tone, and general style.
- You may want to mark an important fact or idea, but don't waste too much time underlining or making notes in the margin of the test book. Try to get a sense of the principal ideas, facts, and organization of the passage.
- A passage with a subject that is familiar to you or in which you are interested may be easier for you. If you find a passage that seems too difficult for you, you might want to skip it and go on. You would be omitting only a few questions and saving yourself time. You can always return to that passage if you finish before time is up for that section of the test.
- You might want to read the questions before you read the passage so that you have a sense of what to look for. But if the content of the passage is familiar to you, looking at the questions before you read the passage might be a waste of time. Try both methods when taking the practice test in this book and see if one approach is more helpful to you than the other.
- Answer questions on the basis of what is stated or implied in the passage. Don't answer questions on the basis of your personal opinion or knowledge.
- Read all of the choices before you choose your answer.
- Answer the question that is asked. Don't pick one of the choices simply because you know it's a true statement.

- Make sure the answer you choose is the best among the choices given. Don't be misled by choices that are partially true.
- In answering main idea questions, don't be distracted by statements that are true according to the passage but that are secondary to the central point.

Mathematical Sections of the SAT

Some questions in the mathematical sections of the SAT are like the questions in your math textbooks. Other questions ask you to do original thinking and may not be as familiar to you. The questions are designed for students who have had a year of algebra and some geometry. Many of the geometric ideas involved are usually taught in the elementary and junior high years, but a few of the questions involve topics that are first taught in high school geometry. Most of the questions are classified as arithmetic, algebra, or geometry, and there is approximately an equal number of each type.

When you take the SAT, remember to use the available space in the test book for scratchwork. You are not expected to do all the reasoning and figuring in your head.

Following is a review of some specific words, phrases, and concepts you should know. Sample questions and explanations follow the review. The two types of questions that appear in the mathematical sections are explained separately.

Mathematics Review

Some Mathematical Concepts with Which You Should Be Familiar

Arithmetic — simple addition, subtraction, multiplication, and division; percent; average; odd and even numbers; prime numbers; divisibility (for example, 24 is divisible by 8)

Algebra — negative numbers; simplifying algebraic expressions; factoring; linear equations; inequalities; simple quadratic equations; positive integer exponents; roots

Geometry — area (square, rectangle, triangle, and circle); perimeter of a polygon; circumference of a circle; volume of a box and cube; special properties of isosceles, equilateral, and right triangles; 30°-60°-90° and 45°-45°-90° triangles; properties of parallel and perpendicular lines; locating points on a coordinate grid

Words and Phrases You Should Know

When You See:	Think:
Positive Integers	1, 2, 3, 4, . . .
Negative Integers	$-1, -2, -3, -4, \ldots$
Integers	$\ldots, -4, -3, -2, -1, 0, 1, 2, 3, 4, \ldots$
Odd Numbers	$\pm1, \pm3, \pm5, \pm7, \pm9, \ldots$
Even Numbers	$0, \pm2, \pm4, \pm6, \pm8, \ldots$
Consecutive Integers	$n, n+1, n+2, \ldots$ (n = an integer)
Prime Numbers	2, 3, 5, 7, 11, 13, 17, 19, . . .

Arithmetic and Algebraic Concepts You Should Know

Odd and Even Numbers

Addition:

even + even = even
odd + odd = even
even + odd = odd

Multiplication:

even × even = even
even × odd = even
odd × odd = odd

Percent

Percent means hundredths or number out of 100, so that $\frac{40}{100}$ = 40 percent and 3 is 75 percent of 4 (because $\frac{3}{4} = \frac{75}{100}$ = 75 percent).

Some Percent Equivalents

$\frac{1}{10} = 0.1 = 10\%$

$\frac{1}{5} = 0.2 = 20\%$

$\frac{1}{2} = 0.5 = 50\%$

$\frac{1}{1} = 1.0 = 100\%$

$\frac{2}{1} = 2.0 = 200\%$

Note: To convert a fraction or decimal to percent, multiply by 100.

General Method of Converting a Fraction $\frac{a}{b}$ to a Percent:

$\frac{a}{b} = \frac{x}{100}$

$x = 100\left(\frac{a}{b}\right)$

Example: $\frac{3}{4} = \frac{x}{100}$

Therefore, $x = 100\left(\frac{3}{4}\right) = 75$

$\frac{3}{4} = \frac{75}{100} = 75\%$

Percents Greater Than 100

Problem: 5 is what percent of 2?

Solution 1: $\frac{5}{2} = \frac{x}{100}$

$$x = \frac{500}{2} = 250$$

Therefore, 5 is 250 percent of 2.

Solution 2: "5 is what percent of 2?" is equivalent to

$$5 = \frac{x}{100} \cdot 2 = \frac{2x}{100}$$

$$500 = 2x$$

$$x = 250$$

This solution is a fairly direct translation of the question into an algebraic statement as follows:

$$\underset{\downarrow}{5} \text{ is } \underbrace{\text{what percent}}_{\frac{x}{100}} \text{ of } \underset{\downarrow}{2}?$$

$$5 = \frac{x}{100} \cdot 2$$

Note that saying 5 is 250 percent of 2 is equivalent to saying that 5 is $2\frac{1}{2}$ times 2.

Problem: Sue earned \$10 on Monday and \$12 on Tuesday. The amount earned on Tuesday was what percent of the amount earned on Monday?

An equivalent question is "\$12 is what percent of \$10?"

Solution: $\frac{12}{10} = \frac{x}{100}$

$$x = \frac{1{,}200}{10} = 120$$

$$\text{So, } \frac{12}{10} = \frac{120}{100} = 120\%$$

Percents Less Than 1

Problem: 3 is what percent of 1,000?

Solution: $\frac{3}{1{,}000} = 0.003 = 0.3\%$ **or** $\frac{3}{10}$ **of 1 percent**

Problem: Socks are \$1.00 a pair or 2 pairs for \$1.99. The savings in buying 2 pairs is what percent of the total cost at the single pair rate?

Solution: At the single pair rate, 2 pairs would cost \$2.00, so the savings is only \$0.01. Therefore, you must answer the question "\$0.01 is what percent of \$2.00?" Because $\frac{0.01}{2.00} = \frac{0.5}{100}$**, the savings is 0.5% or** $\frac{1}{2}$ **of 1 percent.**

Average

The most common mathematical meaning of the word *average* is the arithmetic mean. The average (arithmetic mean) of a set of *n* numbers is the sum of the numbers divided by *n*. For example, the average of 10, 20, and 27 is

$$\frac{10 + 20 + 27}{3} = \frac{57}{3} = 19$$

Unless otherwise indicated, the term *average* will be used on the mathematical portion of the SAT to denote the arithmetic mean. Questions involving the average can take several forms. Some of these are illustrated below.

Finding the Average of Algebraic Expressions

Problem: Find the average of $(3x + 1)$ and $(x - 3)$.

Solution: $\frac{(3x + 1) + (x - 3)}{2} = \frac{4x - 2}{2} = 2x - 1$

Finding a Missing Number if Certain Averages Are Known

Problem: The average of a set of 10 numbers is 15. If one of these numbers is removed from the set, the average of the remaining numbers is 14. What is the value of the number removed?

Solution: The sum of the original 10 numbers is $10 \cdot 15 = 150$. The sum of the remaining 9 numbers is $9 \cdot 14 = 126$. Therefore, the value of the number removed must be $150 - 126 = 24$.

Finding a Weighted Average

Problem: In a group of 10 students, 7 are 13 years old and 3 are 17 years old. What is the average of the ages of these 10 students?

Solution: The solution is *not* the average of 13 and 17, which is 15. In this case the average is

$$\frac{7\,(13) + 3\,(17)}{10} = \frac{91 + 51}{10} = 14.2 \text{ years}$$

The expression "weighted average" comes from the fact that 13 gets a weight factor of 7 whereas 17 gets a weight factor of 3.

Finding the Average Speed in Distance-Rate-Time Problems

Problem: Jane traveled for 2 hours at a rate of 70 kilometers per hour and for 5 hours at a rate of 60 kilometers per hour. What was her average speed for the 7-hour period?

Solution: In this situation, the average speed is:

$$\frac{\text{Total Distance}}{\text{Total Time}}$$

The total distance is 2 (70) + 5 (60) = 400 km. The total time is 7 hours. Thus, the average speed was $\frac{440}{7} = 62\frac{6}{7}$ kilometers per hour. Note that in this example the average speed, $62\frac{6}{7}$, is not the average of the two separate speeds, which would be 65.

Squares of Integers

n	1	2	3	4	5	6	7	8	9	10	11	12
n^2	1	4	9	16	25	36	49	64	81	100	121	144

n	−1	−2	−3	−4	−5	−6	−7	−8	−9	−10	−11	−12
n^2	1	4	9	16	25	36	49	64	81	100	121	144

Signed Number Properties

positive × positive = positive
negative × negative = positive
negative × positive = negative
$-(a - b) = b - a$
$(-x)^2 = x^2$
If $x < 0$, $x^2 > 0$

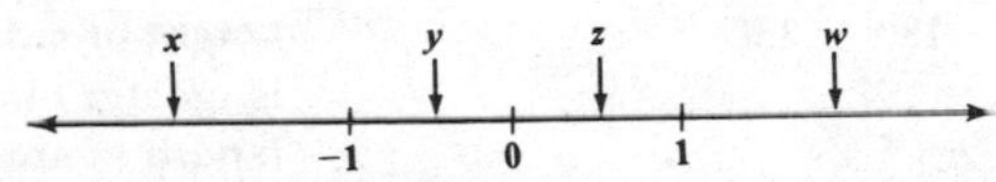

On the number line above: $x < y$ — For example, $-2 < -\frac{1}{2}$

$y^2 > 0$

$z^2 < z$ — For example, $(\frac{1}{2})^2 < \frac{1}{2}$

$x^2 > z$ — For example, $(-2)^2 > \frac{1}{2}$

$z^2 < w$
$x + z < 0$
$y - x > 0$

Factoring

$x^2 + 2x = x(x + 2)$
$x^2 - 1 = (x + 1)(x - 1)$
$x^2 + 2x + 1 = (x + 1)(x + 1) = (x + 1)^2$
$x^2 - 3x - 4 = (x - 4)(x + 1)$

Geometric Figures

Figures that accompany problems on the test are intended to provide information useful in solving the problems. They are drawn as accurately as possible EXCEPT when it is stated in a particular problem that the figure is not drawn to scale. Lines that appear to be straight may be assumed to be straight. Several examples to illustrate the way figures can be interpreted are given below.

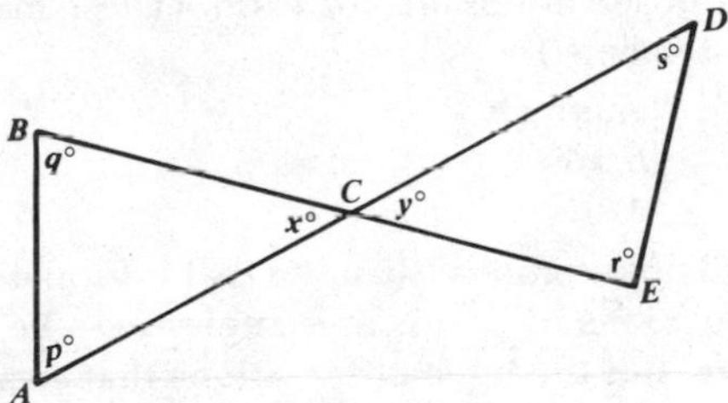

In this figure, you may assume that AD and BE are line segments that intersect at C. You should not assume that $AC = CD$, $p = 60$, or $r = 90$, even though they might look that way. Since $\angle ACB$ and $\angle DCE$ are vertical angles, you can conclude that $x = y$.

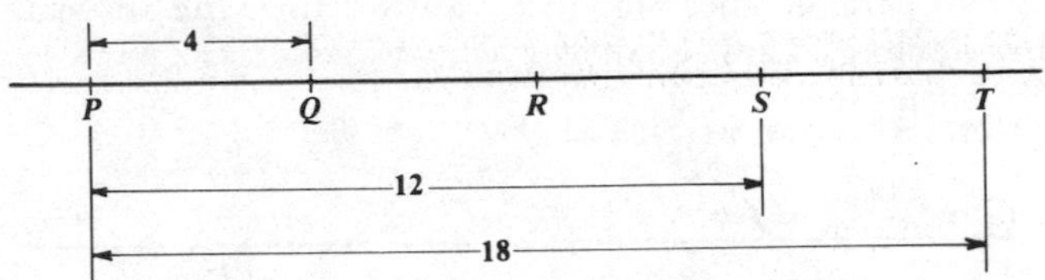

Note: Figure not drawn to scale.

Although the note indicates the figure is not drawn to scale, you may assume that points P, Q, R, S, and T are on line PT. You may also assume that Q is between P and R, that R is between Q and S, and that S is between R and T. You may *not* assume PQ, QR, RS, and ST are of equal length. In fact, since the lengths of PT and PS are shown to be 18 and 12, respectively, the length of ST is 6 while PQ has length 4. In general, even when a figure is not drawn to scale, points on lines may be assumed to be in the order shown, but specific lengths (for example, PQ and ST) might not be accurately represented. In such cases, your answer should be based on other information given about the figure such as the specific lengths shown.

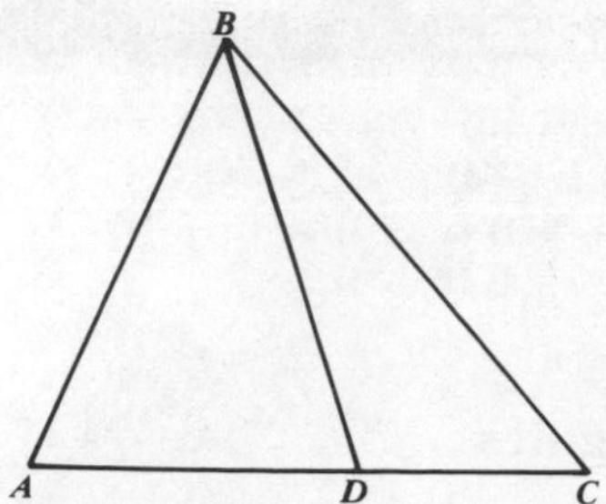

<u>Note</u>: Figure not drawn to scale.

This figure is also not drawn to scale. However, you may assume that *ABC*, *ABD*, and *DBC* are triangles, and that *D* is between *A* and *C*. The following are *valid* observations:

(1) length $AD <$ length AC
(2) $\angle ABD < \angle ABC$
(3) Area $\triangle ABD <$ Area $\triangle ABC$

The following observations are *not* valid. (These may or may not be true statements.):

(1) length $AD >$ length DC
(2) $\angle BAD = \angle BDA$
(3) $\angle DBC < \angle ABD$

The three valid observations illustrate that information about the relative positions of points and angles may be assumed from the figure, but the three observations that are *not* valid illustrate that specific lengths and degree measures might not be accurately shown.

Geometric Skills and Concepts

Properties of Parallel Lines

1. If two parallel lines are cut by a third line, the alternate interior angles are equal.
   For example:

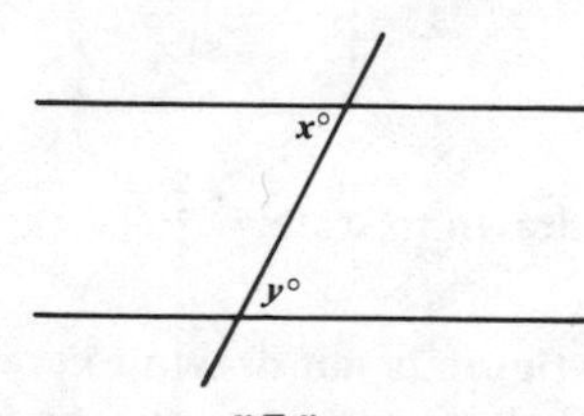

or

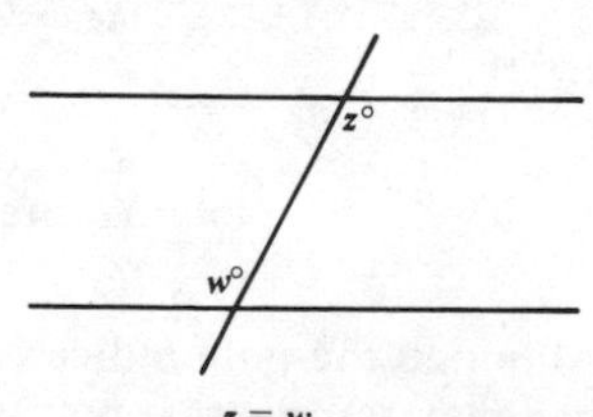

2. If two parallel lines are cut by a third line, the corresponding angles are equal.
   For example:

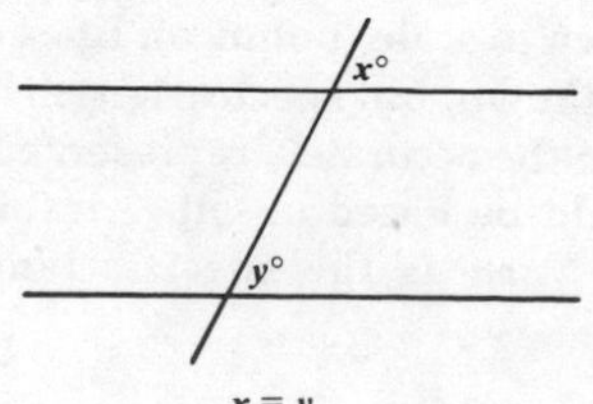

or

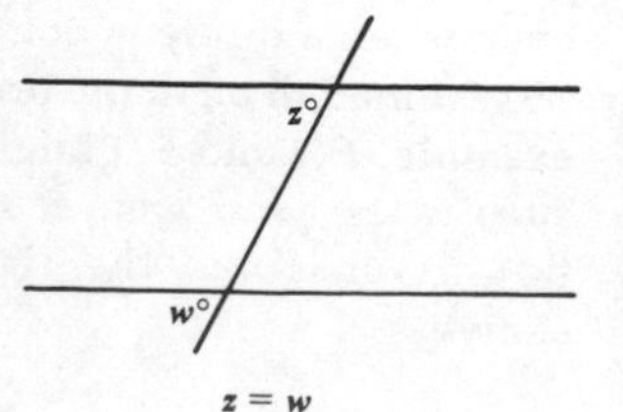

<u>Note</u>: Words like "alternate interior" or "corresponding" are generally <u>not</u> used on the test, but you do need to know which angles are equal.

Angle Relationships

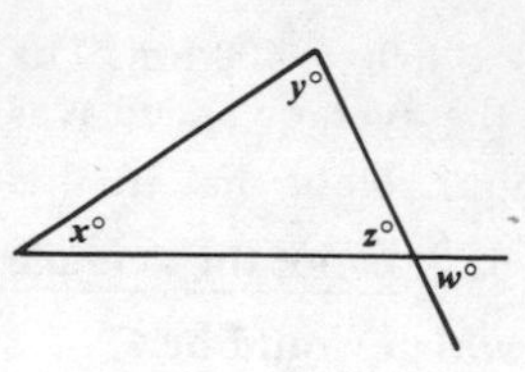

$x + y + z = 180$
(Because the sum of the interior angles of a triangle is 180°)

$z = w$
(When two straight lines intersect, vertical angles are equal.)

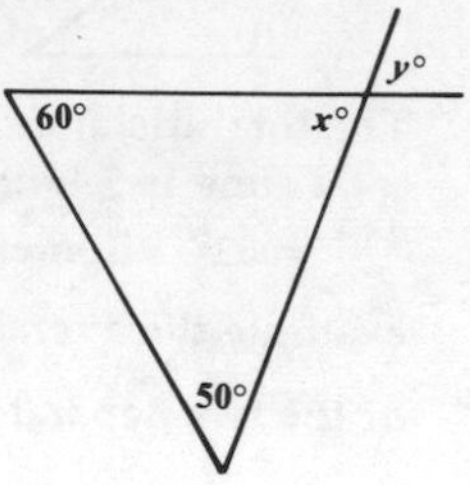

$y = 70$
(Because x is equal to y and $60 + 50 + x = 180$)

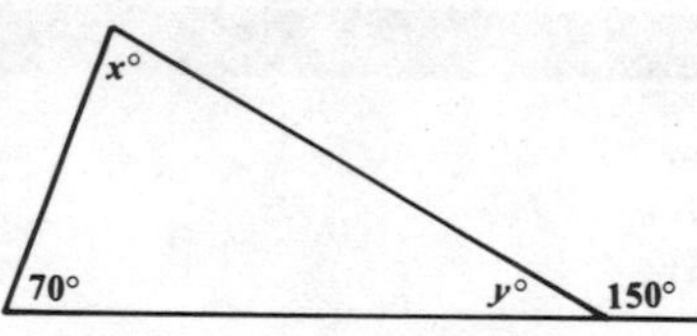

$y = 30$
(Because a straight angle is 180°, $y = 180 - 150$)

$x = 80$
(Because $70 + 30 + x = 180$)

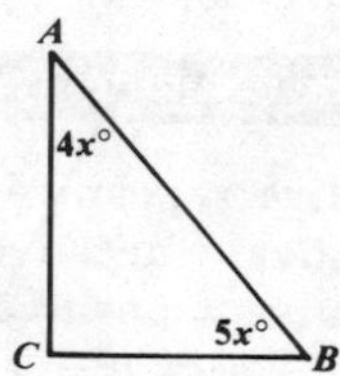

$x = 10$
(Because $4x + 5x = 90°$) Also, the length of side *AC* is greater than the length of side *BC* (Because $\angle B$ is greater than $\angle A$)

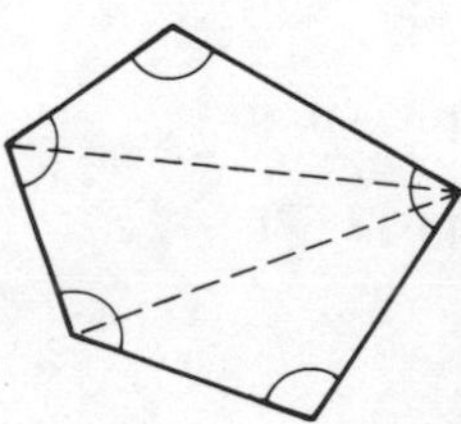

The sum of all angles of the polygon above is 3 (180°) = 540° because it can be divided into 3 triangles, each containing 180°.

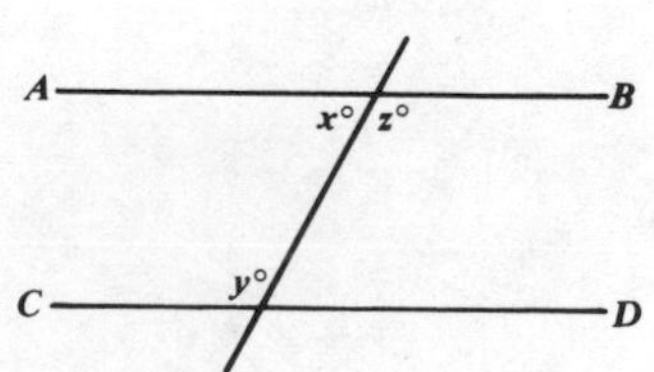

If *AB* is parallel to *CD*, then $x + y = 180$
(Because $x + z = 180$ and $y = z$)

Side Relationships

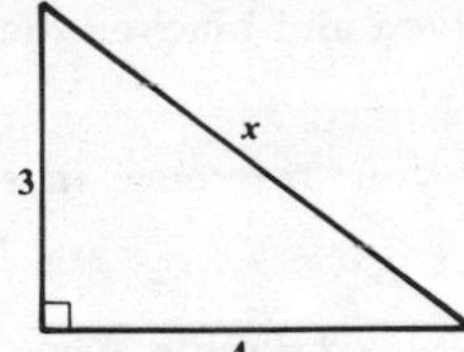

$x = 5$
(By the Pythagorean Theorem,
$x^2 = 3^2 + 4^2$
$x^2 = 9 + 16$
$x^2 = 25$
$x = \sqrt{25} = 5$)

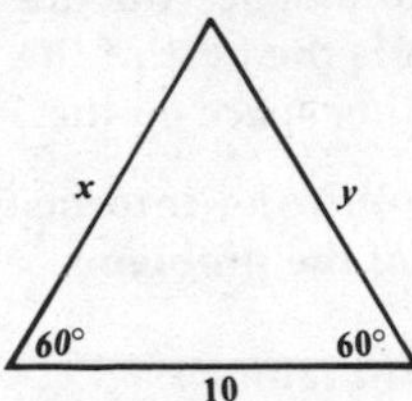

$x = y = 10$
(Because the unmarked angle is 60°, all angles of the triangle are equal, and, therefore, all sides of the triangle are equal)

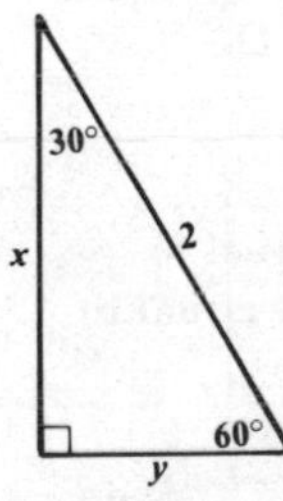

$y = 1$
(Because the length of the side opposite the 30° angle in a right triangle is half the length of the hypotenuse)

$x = \sqrt{3}$
(By the Pythagorean Theorem,
$x^2 + 1^2 = 2^2$
$x^2 = 3$
$x = \sqrt{3}$)

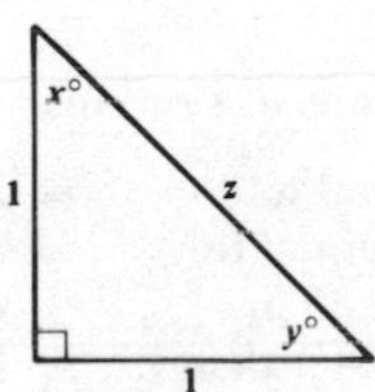

$x = y = 45°$
(Because two sides are equal, the right triangle is isosceles and angles x and y are equal. Also, $x + y = 90$ which makes both angles 45°)

$z = \sqrt{2}$
(Because $1^2 + 1^2 = z^2$)

Area and Perimeter Formulas

Area of a rectangle = length × width = $L \times W$
Perimeter of a rectangle = $2(L + W)$
Examples:

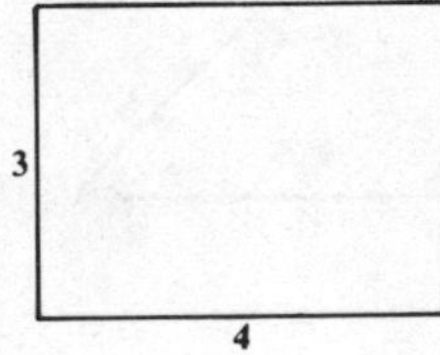

Area = 12

Perimeter = 14

Area = $(x - 3)(x + 3) = x^2 - 9$

Perimeter = $2[(x + 3) + (x - 3)] = 2(2x) = 4x$

Area of a circle = πr^2 (where r is the radius)
Circumference of a circle = $2\pi r = \pi d$ (where d is the diameter)
Examples:

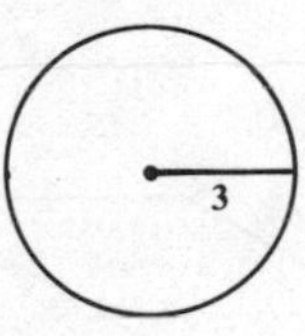

Area = $\pi(3^2) = 9\pi$
Circumference = $2\pi(3) = 6\pi$

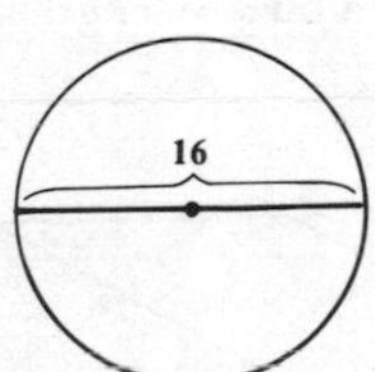

Area = $\pi(8^2) = 64\pi$
Circumference = $\pi(16) = 16\pi$

Area of a triangle = $\frac{1}{2}$ (base × altitude)

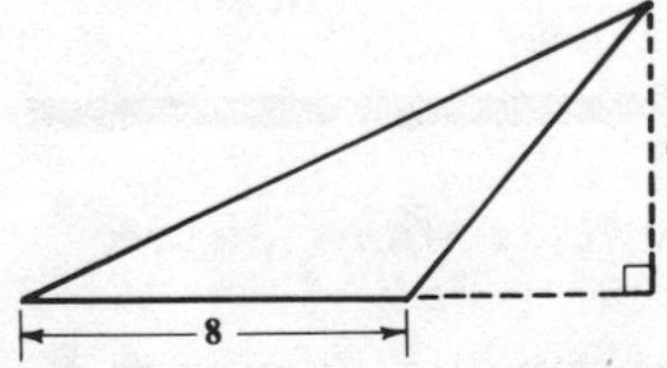

Area = $\frac{1}{2} \cdot 8 \cdot 6 = 24$

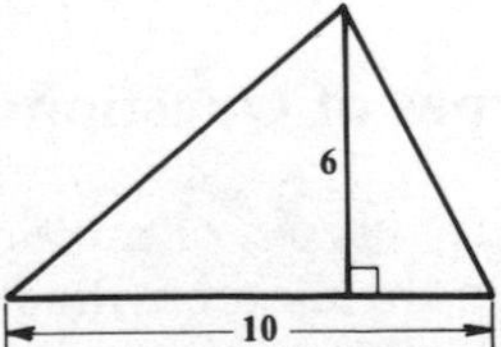

Area = $\frac{1}{2} \cdot 10 \cdot 6 = 30$

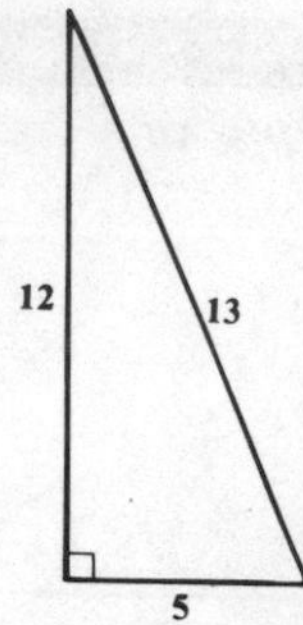

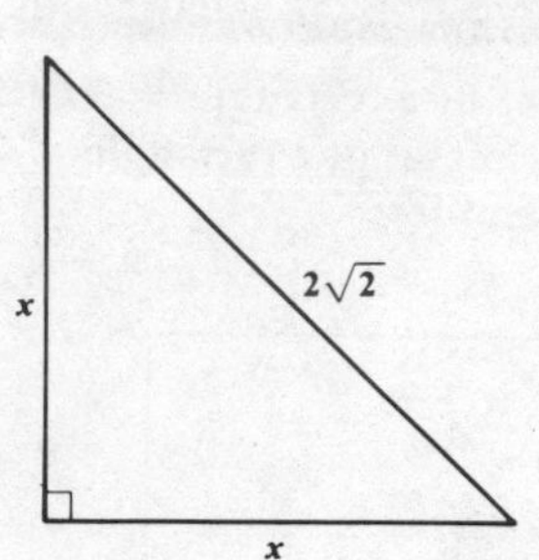

Area $= \frac{1}{2} \cdot 5 \cdot 12 = 30$

Perimeter $= 12 + 5 + 13 = 30$

$x = 2$

(Because $x^2 + x^2 = (2\sqrt{2})^2$

$2x^2 = 4 \cdot 2$

$x^2 = 4$

$x = 2$)

Area $= \frac{1}{2} \cdot 2 \cdot 2 = 2$

Perimeter $= 2 + 2 + 2\sqrt{2}$
$= 4 + 2\sqrt{2}$

Volume of a Rectangular Solid (box)

Volume of a box = length × width × height = L • W • H
Examples:

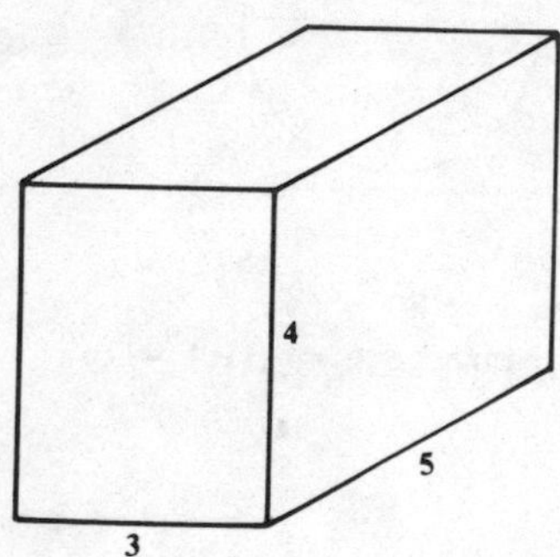

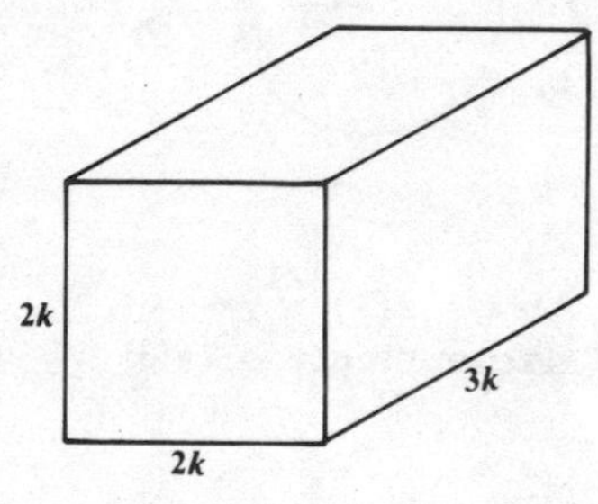

Volume $= 5 \cdot 3 \cdot 4 = 60$

Volume $= (3k)(2k)(2k) = 12k^3$

Types of Questions

Two types of multiple-choice questions are used in the mathematical sections of the SAT:

1. Standard multiple-choice questions (approximately two-thirds of the math questions)
2. Quantitative comparison questions (approximately one-third of the math questions)

The formulas and symbols given in the directions that follow appear in the test book. Learning them now will help you when you take the actual test.

Standard Multiple-Choice Questions

Directions: In this section solve each problem, using any available space on the page for scratchwork. Then decide which is the best of the choices given and blacken the corresponding space on the answer sheet.

The following information is for your reference in solving some of the problems.

Circle of radius r:
Area = πr^2;
Circumference = $2\pi r$
The number of degrees of arc in a circle is 360.
The measure in degrees of a straight angle is 180.

Triangle: The sum of the measures in degrees of the angles of a triangle is 180.

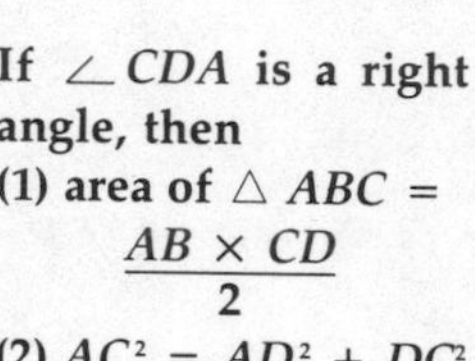

If $\angle CDA$ is a right angle, then
(1) area of $\triangle ABC = \frac{AB \times CD}{2}$
(2) $AC^2 = AD^2 + DC^2$

Definitions of symbols:

= is equal to	**≦ is less than or equal to**
≠ is unequal to	**≧ is greater than or equal to**
< is less than	**‖ is parallel to**
> is greater than	**⊥ is perpendicular to**

Note: Figures which accompany problems in this test are intended to provide information useful in solving the problems. They are drawn as accurately as possible EXCEPT when it is stated in a specific problem that its figure is not drawn to scale. All figures lie in a plane unless otherwise indicated. All numbers used are real numbers.

The problems that follow will give you an idea of the type of mathematical thinking required. First, try to answer each question yourself. Then read the explanation, which may give you new insights into solving the problem or point out techniques you'll be able to use again. Note that the directions indicate that you are to select the *best* of the choices given.

1. If $2a + b = 5$, then $4a + 2b =$

(A) $\frac{5}{4}$ (B) $\frac{5}{2}$ (C) 10 (D) 20 (E) 25

This is an example of a problem that requires realizing that $4a + 2b = 2(2a + b)$. Therefore, $4a + 2b = 2(2a + b) = 2(5) = 10$. The correct answer is (C).

2. If $16 \cdot 16 \cdot 16 = 8 \cdot 8 \cdot P$, then $P =$

(A) 4 (B) 8 (C) 32 (D) 48 (E) 64

This question can be solved by several methods. A time-consuming method would be to multiply the three 16s and then divide the result by the product of 8 and 8. A quicker approach would be to find what additional factors are needed on the right side of the equation to match those on the left side. These additional factors are two 2s and a 16, the product of which is 64. Yet another method involves solving for P as follows:

$$P = \frac{\overset{2}{\cancel{16}} \cdot \overset{2}{\cancel{16}} \cdot 16}{\cancel{8} \cdot \cancel{8}} = 2 \cdot 2 \cdot 16 = 64$$

The correct answer is (E).

3. The town of Mason is located on Eagle Lake. The town of Canton is west of Mason. Sinclair is east of Canton, but west of Mason. Dexter is east of Richmond, but west of Sinclair and Canton. Assuming all these towns are in the United States, which town is farthest west?

(A) Mason (B) Dexter (C) Canton (D) Sinclair (E) Richmond

For this kind of problem, drawing a diagram may help. In this case, a line can be effectively used to locate the relative position of each town. Start with the statement "The town of Canton is west of Mason" and, using abbreviations, draw the following:

W —+———————+— E
C M

From the remaining information, place the other towns in their correct order:

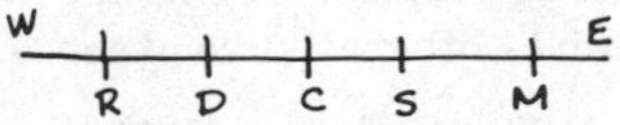

W —+—+—+—+—+— E
R D C S M

The final sketch shows that the town farthest west is Richmond (R) and the correct answer is (E).

4. If the average of seven x's is 7, what is the average of fourteen x's?

(A) $\frac{1}{7}$ (B) $\frac{1}{2}$ (C) 1 (D) 7 (E) 14

Don't get caught up in the wording of this problem, which might lead you to choose (E) 14. The average of any number of equal numbers such as x is always x. Since you are given that the average of seven x's is 7, it follows that $x = 7$ and that the average of fourteen x's is also 7. The correct answer is (D).

5. If the symbol ∇ between two expressions indicates that the expression on the right exceeds the expression on the left by 1, which of the following is (are) true for all real numbers x?

I. $x(x + 2) \nabla (x + 1)^2$
II. $x^2 \nabla (x + 1)^2$
III. $\frac{x}{y} \nabla \frac{x+1}{y+1}$

(A) None (B) I only (C) II only (D) III only (E) I and III

This kind of problem involves working with a newly defined symbol. One approach is to check the statements one at a time. Statement I reduces to $x^2 + 2x \nabla x^2 + 2x + 1$, so the expression on the right does exceed the expression on the left by 1. Therefore, statement I is true. Statement II reduces to $x^2 \nabla x^2 + 2x + 1$, so the right expression exceeds the left expression by $2x + 1$, which is not equal to 1 except when $x = 0$. This makes statement II false. Statement III is more difficult to check, but you can verify by subtraction or by substituting numbers (for example, $x = 3$, $y = 5$), that the expression on the right does not exceed the expression on the left by 1. Therefore, statement III is false. The only true statement is I, so the correct answer is (B).

In a problem of this kind, if you are able to decide about only one or two statements, you can still eliminate some choices and guess among those remaining. For example, if you can conclude that I is true, then the correct answer is either (B) or (E) because these choices contain statement I.

6. If a car travels X kilometers of a trip in H hours, in how many hours can it travel the next Y kilometers at this rate?

(A) $\frac{XY}{H}$ (B) $\frac{HY}{X}$ (C) $\frac{HX}{Y}$ (D) $\frac{H+Y}{X}$ (E) $\frac{X+Y}{H}$

You can solve this problem by using ratios or by using the distance formula.

Using the ratio method, X kilometers is to H hours as Y kilometers is to $\square$ hours, where $\square$ represents the amount of time required to travel Y kilometers:

$$\frac{X}{H} = \frac{Y}{\square}$$

$$X\square = HY$$

$$\square = \frac{HY}{X}$$

The correct answer is (B).

7. If 90 percent of P is 30 percent of Q, then Q is what percent of P?

(A) 3% (B) 27% (C) 30% (D) 270% (E) 300%

Writing an algebraic equation for this percent problem not only simplifies the work, it also helps you organize your thoughts. "90 percent of P is 30 percent of Q" can be written as $0.90P = 0.30Q$ (or $\frac{9}{10}P = \frac{3}{10}Q$).

"Q is what percent of P" tells you to find $\frac{Q}{P}$ and express it as a percent. $\frac{Q}{P} = 3$ and, therefore, Q is 300 percent of P and the correct answer is (E). (See pages 19-20 for a review of percent.)

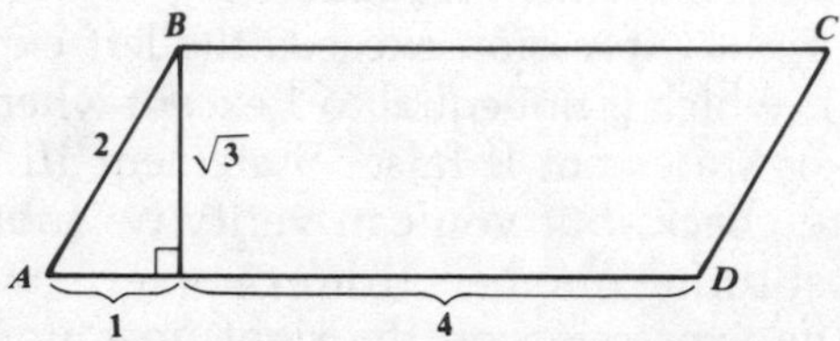

8. The figure above shows a piece of paper in the shape of a parallelogram with measurements as indicated. If the paper is tacked at its center to a flat surface and then rotated about its center, the points covered by the paper will be a circular region of diameter

(A) $\sqrt{3}$ (B) 2 (C) 5 (D) $\sqrt{28}$ (E) $\sqrt{39}$

The first step in solving the problem is to realize that the center of the parallelogram is the point of intersection of the two diagonals; thus, the diameter you are looking for is the length of the longer diagonal AC. One way to find AC is to think of the additional lines drawn as shown below.

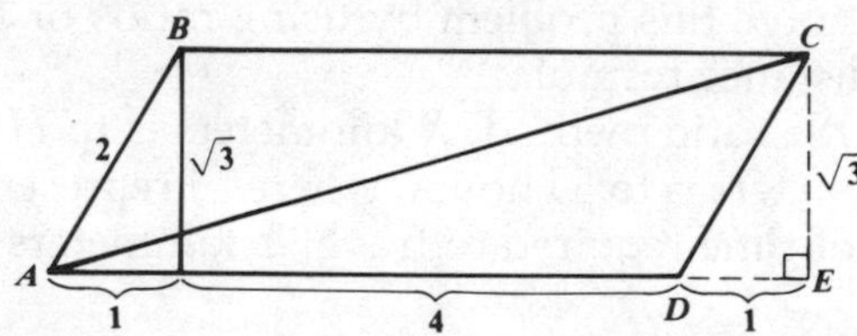

The triangles at each end are congruent (equal in size and shape), so the length of DE and CE are 1 and $\sqrt{3}$, respectively. AEC is a right triangle; therefore, the Pythagorean Theorem can be used in solving the problem:

$AC^2 = CE^2 + AE^2$

$AC^2 = (\sqrt{3})^2 + (6)^2 = 3 + 36 = 39$

The diameter AC is $\sqrt{39}$ and the correct answer is (E).

9. A number is divisible by 9 if the sum of its digits is divisible by 9. Which of the following numbers is divisible by 45?

(A) 63,345
(B) 72,365
(C) 99,999
(D) 72,144
(E) 98,145

It would be very time-consuming to divide each choice by 45. In order for a number to be divisible by 45 it must be divisible by both 9 and 5. Choices A, B, and E are divisible by 5, but choices C and D are not. So you can eliminate choices C and D immediately. You are given that a number is divisible by 9 if the sum of its digits is divisible by 9. The sum of the digits in choices A, B, and E are 21, 23, and 27, respectively.

Of these choices only 27 is divisible by 9. The correct answer is (E). Your scratchwork for this problem might appear as follows:

(A) 63,345 ~~21~~
(B) 72,365 ~~23~~
(C) ~~99,999~~
(D) ~~72,144~~
(E) 98,145 (27)

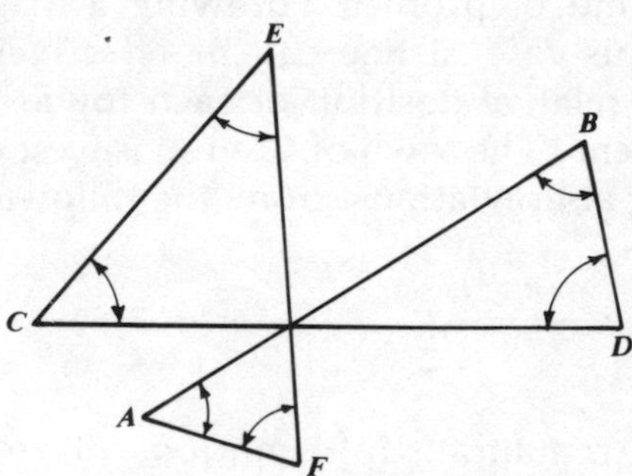

10. In the triangles above, if AB, CD, and EF are line segments, what is the sum of the measures of the six marked angles?

(A) 180° (B) 360° (C) 540° (D) 720°
(E) It cannot be determined from the information given.

This problem requires a creative problem-solving approach. One solution involves recognizing that the sum of the three unmarked angles in the triangles is 180°.

This can be seen from the figure at the top of page 27:

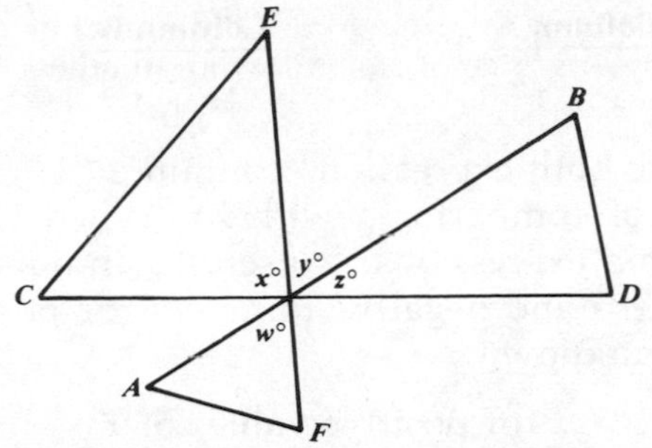

Because CD is a line segment, the sum of angles x, y, and z is 180°. Also, $y = w$ because they are vertical angles. Therefore, $x + w + z = 180$. Since the sum of the measures of all angles in the three triangles is 540° (3 • 180°) and the sum of the unmarked angles of the triangles in the original figure equals 180°, it follows that the sum of the marked angles is 540° − 180° = 360°. The correct answer is (B). With this type of problem, if you don't reach a solution in a minute or so, go on to the next problem and go back to it if you have time.

Quantitative Comparison Questions

Quantitative comparison questions emphasize the concepts of equalities, inequalities, and estimation. They generally involve less reading, take less time to answer, and require less computation than regular multiple-choice questions. Quantitative comparison questions may not be as familiar to you as other types of questions. Therefore, give special attention to the directions ahead of time.

Directions: Each of the following questions consists of two quantities, one in Column A and one in Column B. You are to compare the two quantities and on the answer sheet blacken space

A if the quantity in Column A is greater;
B if the quantity in Column B is greater;
C if the two quantities are equal;
D if the relationship cannot be determined from the information given.

Notes: 1. In certain questions, information concerning one or both of the quantities to be compared is centered above the two columns.
2. In a given question, a symbol that appears in both columns represents the same thing in Column A as it does in Column B.
3. Letters such as x, n, and k stand for real numbers.

EXAMPLES

	Column A	Column B	Answers	Explanations:
E1.	2×6	$2 + 6$	●ⒷⒸⒹ	(The answer is A because 12 is greater than 8.)
E2.	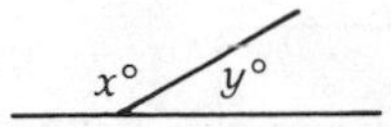 $180 - x$	y	ⒶⒷ●Ⓓ	(The answer is C because $x + y = 180$, thereby making $180 - x$ equal to y.)
E3.	$p - q$	$q - p$	ⒶⒷⒸ●	(The answer is D because nothing is known about either p or q.)

To solve a quantitative comparison problem, you compare the quantities in the two columns and decide whether one quantity is greater than the other, whether the two quantities are equal, or whether the relationship cannot be determined from the information given. Remember that your answer should be:

A if the quantity in Column A is greater;
B if the quantity in Column B is greater;
C if the two quantities are equal;
D if the relationship cannot be determined from the information given.

Problems are clearly separated and the *quantities to be compared are always on the same line as the number of the problem*. (See example 2 on page 25.) Figures and additional information provided for some problems appear *above* the quantities to be compared. The following are some practice problems with explanations to help you understand this type of question.

	Column A	Column B
1.	$(37)\left(\frac{1}{43}\right)(58)$	$(59)\left(\frac{1}{43}\right)(37)$

Because the numbers in this problem are fairly large, it may save time to study the multipliers first before attempting the calculations. Note that (37) and $\left(\frac{1}{43}\right)$ appear in both quantities; thus, the only numbers left for you to compare are 58 and 59. Since 59 > 58, the quantity on the right is greater and the correct answer is (B).

Figures are also included in some questions that appear in the quantitative comparison format.

Column A | **Column B**

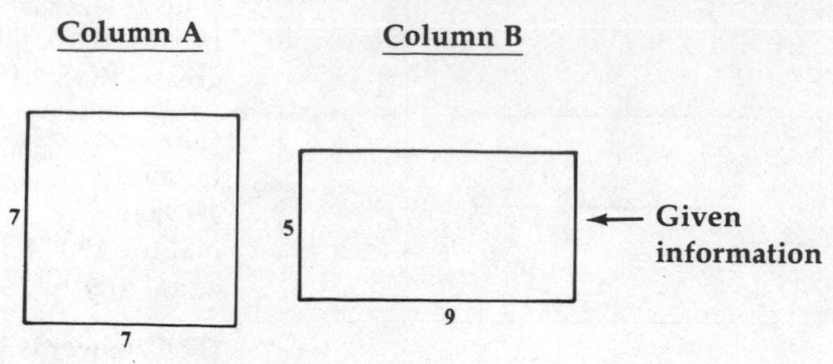

2. **The perimeter of the square** | **The perimeter of the rectangle** ← **Quantities to be compared**

It can be assumed that the units used to indicate measures in a given problem are the same in all figures in that problem unless otherwise stated. The correct answer is (C) because the perimeter of the square is 4 • 7 = 28 units and the perimeter of the rectangle is (2 • 5) + (2 • 9) = 28 units.

Column A | **Column B**

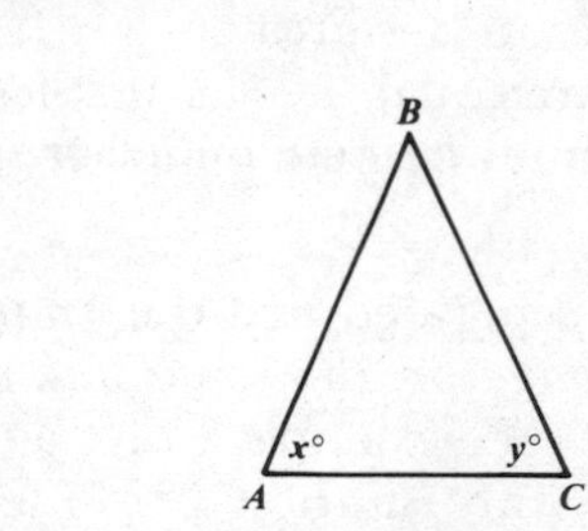

3. x | y

Since $AB = BC$, the angles opposite AB and BC are equal and, therefore, $x = y$. The correct answer is (C).

Column A | **Column B**

4. $\sqrt{2} - 1$ | $\sqrt{3} - 1$

For any positive number x, the symbol $\sqrt{x}$ denotes the positive square root of x. The fact that $\sqrt{3} > \sqrt{2}$ leads to the conclusion that $\sqrt{3} - 1 > \sqrt{2} - 1$. The correct answer is (B). Note that $x^2 = 9$ has two solutions, $x = 3$ or $x = -3$. However, $\sqrt{9} = 3$, not ± 3.

Column A | **Column B**

5. $x + 1$ | $2x + 1$

Because both expressions contain a "1," the problem is one of comparing x with $2x$. When you compare algebraic expressions, a useful technique is to consider zero and negative numbers for possible values of the unknown.

$2x > x$ for positive values of x
$2x = x$ for $x = 0$
$2x < x$ for negative values of x

The correct answer is (D), as the relationship cannot be determined from the information given. If you had been given that x was positive (that is, $x > 0$), the correct answer would have been (B) because $2x$ would be greater than x.

Column A | **Column B**

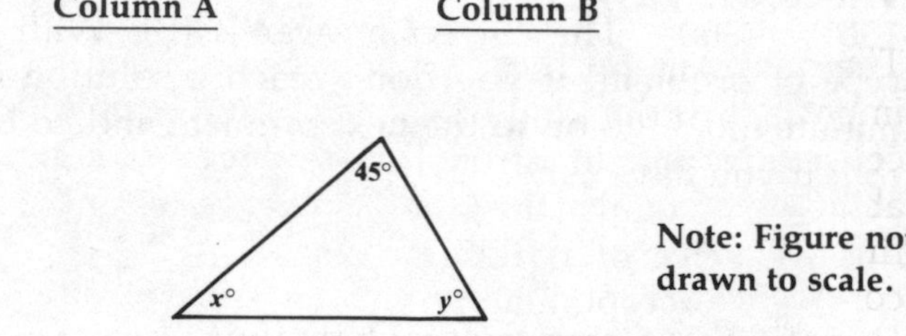

Note: Figure not drawn to scale.

6. y | 90

Because the sum of the angles of a triangle is 180, $x + y + 45 = 180$ or $x + y = 135$. Since $x < 45$, it follows that $y > 90$. The answer is (A). In this problem you should not try to determine the answer from the appearance of the figure because the note indicates that the figure is not drawn to scale.

Column A | **Column B**

$x \neq 1$

7. $\dfrac{x^2 - 1}{x - 1}$ | x

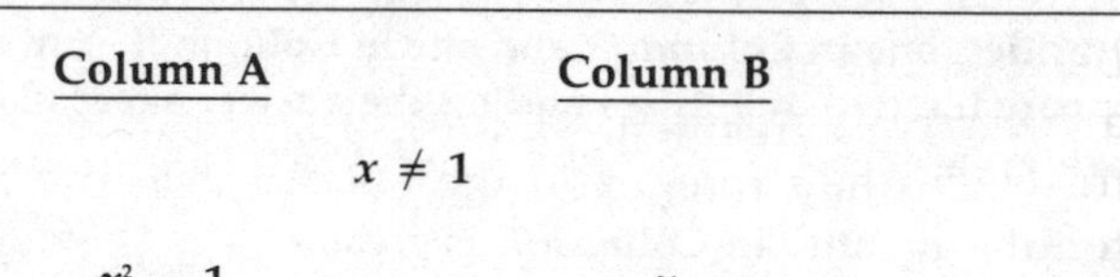

The condition $x \neq 1$ (read x is not equal to 1) is given because the algebraic fraction in Column A is not defined for $x = 1$ (the denominator becomes zero). The solution of this problem involves simplifying the fraction in Column A as follows:

$$\frac{x^2 - 1}{x - 1} = \frac{(x + 1)(x - 1)}{x - 1} = x + 1$$

Therefore, the quantity in Column A is equal to $x + 1$. Since $x + 1$ is always greater than x, the answer is (A).

	Column A	Column B
8.	**Area of a triangle with altitude 4**	**Area of a triangle with base 5**

To answer this question, you need to know how to find the area of a triangle. To find the area of a triangle, you need to know the length of a base and the altitude to that base. You can't find the "area of a triangle with altitude 4" without knowing the base, so the area of such a triangle could be any number depending on the length of the base. Likewise, you can't find the "area of a triangle with base 5" without knowing the length of the altitude. Since you can't tell anything about the two areas, the correct answer is (D).

The Test of Standard Written English

The questions on the TSWE measure skills that are important to the kind of writing you will do in most college courses. In particular, the questions test your ability to recognize the kind of language essential to a finished piece of writing — writing that would be considered acceptable by most educated readers and writers of American English.

The TSWE is made up of 50 questions of two types: usage questions and sentence correction questions. The test is arranged in the following way:

- 25 usage questions,
- 15 sentence correction questions, and
- 10 more usage questions.

The questions in the TSWE ask you to recognize several different types of language problems.

- *Use of basic grammar* — for example, subject-verb agreement, agreement of pronouns with the nouns to which they refer, and the correct use of a verb tense
- *Sentence structure* — for example, distinguishing between complete and incomplete sentences and recognizing when the connections between parts of a sentence are clear and when they are not
- *Choice of words* — for example, recognizing when words or phrases should be revised to make the meaning of a sentence clear or to make the language consistent with that normally expected of educated writers.

You will not be asked to define grammatical terms. No questions test spelling or capitalization. In a few questions, punctuation marks such as the semicolon or apostrophe are important in arriving at the correct answer, but these questions primarily test the structure in which the punctuation appears.

A good way to prepare for the TSWE is to practice writing and rewriting; pay particular attention to clarity and effectiveness of expression. You might try writing for a teacher, parent, friend, or fellow student who can respond directly to your writing. As with the SAT, reading the sample questions and explanations and taking the sample tests provided in this book will help you prepare for the TSWE. After you've taken and scored a sample test, look carefully at the questions you missed. Talk over those questions with your teachers and other students and look up the portions of your textbooks that discuss writing and problems in wording and sentence structure.

Usage Questions

The questions in this section measure skills that are important to writing well. In particular, they test your ability to recognize and use language that is clear, effective, and correct according to the requirements of standard written English, the kind of English found in most college textbooks.

Directions: The following sentences contain problems in grammar, usage, diction (choice of words), and idiom.

Some sentences are correct.

No sentence contains more than one error.

You will find that the error, if there is one, is underlined and lettered. Assume that elements of the sentence that are not underlined are correct and cannot be changed. In choosing answers, follow the requirements of standard written English.

If there is an error, select the one underlined part that must be changed to make the sentence correct and blacken the corresponding space on your answer sheet.

If there is no error, blacken answer space Ⓔ.

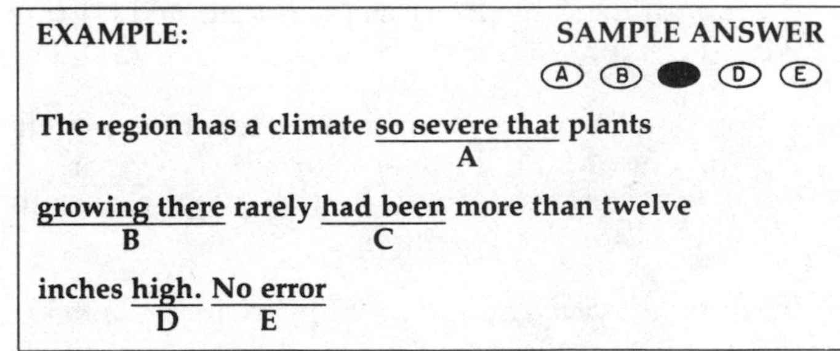

EXAMPLE: **SAMPLE ANSWER**

Ⓐ Ⓑ ● Ⓓ Ⓔ

The region has a climate so severe that (A) plants growing there (B) rarely had been (C) more than twelve inches high. (D) No error (E)

As you can see from the example, a usage question consists of a sentence in which four short portions of the sentence are underlined and lettered, and a fifth underline, "No error," follows. Sometimes the underlined portion of the sentence is only a single word, as in (D) above. In other cases it is a group of words or a phrase, as in (A), (B), and (C).

For each question, you must decide whether one of the underlined portions must be changed to make the sentence acceptable in standard written English. In the example above, the underlined portion lettered (C) must be changed because the verb *has* earlier in the sentence leads the reader to expect *are* or possibly *have been*. The tense of the verb at (C) must be changed to be consistent with the tense of *has*. Therefore, the correct answer to the example is (C).

It is true that changes could be made in the other underlined portions of the sentence in the example, but none of those changes is necessary to make the sentence acceptable. It is also true that the sentence could be corrected by changing *has* in the first part of the sentence to *had*, but in this type of question the change must be made in a portion of the sentence that is underlined. Notice that if none of the underlined portions needed to be changed, the correct answer would be (E). By choosing (E) as the answer, you would be indicating that the sentence was correct as written.

Most usage questions test your ability to recognize problems in basic grammatical structure or in choice of words. Some usage questions also test problems in sentence structure. To give you a better sense of the variety of problems tested by usage questions, a few more sample questions follow. Keep in mind the following suggestions as you work through the sample questions.

- ✓ For each question, read the entire sentence carefully but quickly.
- ✓ Go back over the sentence, looking at each underlined portion to see whether or not anything needs to be changed to make the sentence correct.
- ✓ If you find an error, mark the space on your answer sheet with the same letter as the underlined portion with the error.
- ✓ If you don't find an error, don't waste time searching for one. Mark the space for (E), No error, on your answer sheet to indicate that you believe the sentence is correct as written.
- ✓ In general, you should be able to move quickly through the usage questions on the test, since they do not involve much reading. If you mark the usage questions you want to return to, you will be more likely to allow enough time for the sentence correction questions, which probably will take more time per question.

The four sample questions that follow originally appeared in the TSWE. They are arranged in order of increasing difficulty. Together, the example question and the four samples should give you a sense of the difficulty level of the questions you will be asked.

1. One of the goals of (A) women's organizations is to encourage (B) projects that will make (C) life easier for (D) working mothers. No error (E)

Probably the first impression you get from reading the sentence is that nothing is really wrong with it. But before you make a final decision, you should look at the sentence again, especially at the underlined portions. The (A) portion, *goals of*, seems correct; *of* is the appropriate preposition for the context. The (B) portion, *is to encourage*, is a little more complicated but also seems correct; *is* is the appropriate verb to use with *one* and *to encourage* is alright following *is*, even though *encouraging* might be nearly as good. In (C), *make* is appropriate with the subject *projects* and is idiomatic in the expression *make life easier*. In (D), *easier* is a comparative form of *easy* and is used correctly, and *for* is the preposition that should follow it for the meaning intended.

Even though your analysis probably would not be as extensive as this, you should do something fairly similar, quickly checking each underlined portion of the sentence to make sure that each is acceptable as written. For some portions, you might have been able to think of another way of writing the sentence, even a way of improving it a little, but you probably decided that no changes were necessary in the underlined portions. At this point, you should have been able to decide on (E), No error, as the correct answer. Keep in mind that some usage questions are correctly answered with (E).

2. Probably (A) the best-known baseball player of all time, (B) Babe Ruth established a record for lifetime home runs that has only recently (C) been broke. (D) No error (E)

You may have noticed when you read the question for the first time that *broke* in (D) should be changed to *broken*. But if you didn't see the error immediately, or if you were not sure of it, you should look at the sentence again, especially at the underlined portions. In (A), *probably* is the appropriate adverb, in (B) *of all time* is an acceptable idiom and is used correctly, and in (C) the adverbs *only* and *recently* are acceptable together, with *only* modifying *recently*. But at (D), *broke* is clearly incorrect and needs to be changed to make the sentence acceptable in standard written English. The complete and correct verb for this part of the sentence is *has been broken*. With *has been*, the only possible form of the verb *break* that can be used is *broken*. The correct answer is (D).

3. Many travelers claim having seen (A) the Abominable Snowman, but (B) no one has proved that such a creature (C) actually (D) exists. No error (E)

The answer is (A). In the context of this sentence, the verb *claim* requires the expression *to have seen*; *claim having seen* is not idiomatic in American English and is therefore not acceptable. The word *but* at (B) provides a link between the two major parts of the sentence and appropriately suggests a contrast between the ideas they present. The expression at (C), *such a creature*, and the adverb *actually* at (D) are correct, although other expressions and adverbs could be substituted.

4. The administration's statements on (A) economic policy indicates (B) that the elimination of (C) hunger will be given (D) first priority. No error (E)

This question is more difficult than any of the others, so you may not immediately see the error in it. For a question as difficult as this one, you should be sure to look carefully at the underlined portions when you reread the sentence. In (A), *on* is correct and idiomatic, though the word *about* could possibly be substituted. Similarly, the preposition *of* is idiomatic with *elimination* in (C), and *elimination* is itself the right word for the meaning implied by the rest of the sentence. In (D), *will be given* is correct in tense and uses the correct form of the verb *give*. But *indicates* at (B) is incorrect; it is a singular verb and should not be used with the plural subject *statements*. The singular noun *policy* before (B) may appear at first to be the subject of the sentence, but a good writer would eventually see that the real subject *statements* is plural and therefore requires the plural verb *indicate*. The correct answer is (B).

Sentence Correction Questions

Directions: In each of the following sentences, some part or all of the sentence is underlined. Below each sentence you will find five ways of phrasing the underlined part. Select the answer that produces the most effective sentence, one that is clear and exact, without awkwardness or ambiguity, and blacken the corresponding space on your anwer sheet. In choosing answers, follow the requirements of standard written English. Choose the answer that best expresses the meaning of the original sentence.

Answer (A) is always the same as the underlined part. Choose answer (A) if you think the original sentence needs no revision.

EXAMPLE: **SAMPLE ANSWER**

Ⓐ ● Ⓒ Ⓓ Ⓔ

Laura Ingalls Wilder published her first book and she was sixty-five years old then.

(A) and she was sixty-five years old then
(B) when she was sixty-five years old
(C) at age sixty-five years old
(D) upon reaching sixty-five years
(E) at the time when she was sixty-five

Sentence correction questions present you with a sentence and four possible revisions of it — (B), (C), (D), or (E). The (A) version is always a repetition of the underlined portion of the original sentence. The underline in the original sentence tells you how much of the sentence will be revised in the other versions that are presented to you.

The example question above is a sentence in which the connection between the two major ideas is weak. The use of *and* to join the two clauses suggests that the ideas are of equal importance in the sentence, but the wording and the ideas in the clauses themselves suggest that the first idea should actually be the major point of the sentence and that the second should be secondary to it. Versions (B), (C), (D), and (E) all begin with more appropriate connecting words, but (B) is the only one in which the second idea of the sentence is clearly, concisely, and idiomatically expressed. Therefore, (B) is the correct answer.

The directions for the sentence correction questions tell you to look for the most effective sentence. In some questions you may find a version of the original sentence that has no grammatical errors, but that does not express the ideas of the sentence as effectively as another version. For other questions you may be able to think of a version you consider better than any of the choices, but you should select the version that is the *best* of those presented.

Sentence correction questions are primarily concerned with problems of sentence structure. But you'll also need to consider basic principles of grammar and word choice to decide which of the versions makes the clearest and most effective sentence. For example, some versions will be grammatically incorrect or the ideas in the sentence will be presented so awkwardly or imprecisely that they cannot be considered acceptable. You'll get a sense of the problems tested in the sentence correction questions from the discussion of the sample questions provided here. You'll also have an idea of the range of difficulty found in the questions, since the sample questions given here are arranged in order of increasing difficulty. To learn as much as possible from the sample questions, you should read carefully the directions that appear before the example question above and approach the questions with the following suggestions in mind.

- In each question, read the original sentence carefully but quickly. Note the underlined portion of the sentence because that is the portion that may have to be revised. Remember that the portion with no underline stays the same.
- Keep in mind the portion of the original sentence that stays the same when you read through each of the versions presented.
- Decide which version seems best. If you can't decide between two choices, go back and read each version you have chosen in the context of the entire sentence.
- If you still feel uncertain about your answer, put a mark next to that question in your test book and note which versions you thought might be correct. You can return to the question later if you have time.

1. Althea Gibson was the first Black American to win major tennis championships and played in the 1950s.

(A) Althea Gibson was the first Black American to win major tennis championships and played in the 1950s.
(B) Althea Gibson, being the first Black American to win major tennis championships, and playing in the 1950s.
(C) Althea Gibson, playing in the 1950s, being the first Black American to win major tennis championships.
(D) Althea Gibson, who played in the 1950s, was the first Black American to win major tennis championships.
(E) Althea Gibson played in the 1950s, she was the first Black American to win major tennis championships.

Here the original sentence is entirely underlined, so you can expect the versions that follow to be revisions of the whole sentence.

This question is fairly easy. You may have been able to decide which version of the sentence was best simply by reading through all of the choices. However, to help you feel more certain of your choice and to help you understand more fully how the decision can be made, it's worth looking separately at each version. The (A) version, the same as the original sentence, has a problem similar to the one in the previous example: *and* does not adequately convey the relationship between the two clauses in the sentence. The (B) version has the same problem and an additional one: the use of *being* and *playing* makes it an incomplete sentence. In the (C) version, *playing* seems at first to have corrected the original problem, but the use of *being* gives the second idea no more importance than the first and also makes this version an incomplete sentence. In (E), you can see that a comma is used improperly as a means of connecting two independent clauses. Thus, (D) is the only acceptable version. In (D), the major point appears in the main part of the sentence and receives most emphasis, while the less important point appears in the *who* clause and so is emphasized less.

You won't need to analyze most of the sentence correction questions in this much detail. You'll be able to make your decisions by reading through each version and looking closely at one or two of them. But you should use this approach for the questions that are most difficult for you, especially the ones you miss on the sample TSWE.

2. After placing the meatballs in a pan, the cook sautéed them until they were brown and then let them simmer in the sauce.

(A) and then let them simmer
(B) then they were simmered
(C) and then simmering it
(D) then letting them simmer
(E) and then the simmering was done

You should have read the original sentence quickly, noting that the entire portion preceding the underline as well as the short phrase after the underline will be the same in all versions of the sentence. The original sentence and choice (A) seem plausible, but you should go on to the other versions before making a final decision. In the (B) version, the unexpected shift from the *cook* as subject to *they* (the meatballs) is awkward and somewhat confusing. The (C) version uses *simmering* where *simmered* is needed to parallel *sautéed*. Furthermore, the pronoun *it* does not seem to refer back to anything named earlier in the sentence. In the (D) version, the use of *letting* rather than *let* again neglects the parallel with *sautéed*. The (E) version is wordy and, like the (B) version, involves a shift in which a passive construction replaces a more appropriate active one and in which the action is described without reference to the person responsible for it. Therefore, the best version of the sentence in this case is the original one, so the correct answer is (A).

3. Being as it was a full moon, the tides were exceptionally high when the storm struck.

(A) Being as it was a full moon
(B) With the moon as full
(C) Due to there being a full moon
(D) The moon was full
(E) Because the moon was full

The problems most immediately apparent in this question are problems in wording. The (A) version, like the underlined portion in the original sentence, uses *Being as,* an expression that is not considered acceptable in standard written English. In addition, the indirect *it was* construction introduces unnecessary wordiness. The (B) version seems acceptable in itself, but leads the reader to expect a construction (as it was) different from the one that follows in the rest of the sentence. In the (C) version, *due to* is used in a manner that is generally considered unacceptable usage, and *there being* introduces unnecessary wordiness. The (D) version is acceptable in its wording but, when combined with the rest of the sentence, results in the unacceptable joining of two independent clauses with a comma. What is needed in this sentence is an expression that is acceptable in good written English and that accurately reflects the relationship between the first and second parts of the sentence. Version (E) solves the problem—the word *because* indicates that the fullness of the moon was causally related to the high tides described in the second part of the sentence. Therefore, (E) is the correct answer.

4. The Dutch had been trading with the Orient since the sixteenth century, their ships have visited Persia and Japan.

(A) century, their ships have visited
(B) century while their ships had visited
(C) century, but their ships had been visiting
(D) century, when their ships visited
(E) century, where their ships were visiting

The original sentence and the (A) version present two problems. First, two independent statements are joined by a comma, with no indication of the relationship between them. Second, the tense of the verb *have visited* is not consistent with the tense of *had been trading* earlier in the sentence. The (B) version may appear to be acceptable, but the relationship between the ideas in the sentence is not the one implied by *while* and the use of *while* makes the sentence illogical. Similarly, the (C) version appears plausible, but the contrast implied by *but* is not appropriate to the relationship between the two parts of the sentence. The (D) version corrects both of the problems presented in the original sentence and is more logical than either (B) or (C). Notice that the tense of *visited* is consistent with the earlier verb *had been trading*. It suggests that Dutch ships had traveled to Persia and Japan in the sixteenth century, and that such travel was part of a process of Dutch trade with the Orient that continued until some later, unspecified time. Version (E) resembles (D), except that *where* is substituted for *when* and *were visiting* for *visited*. Since the connection with *century* is clearly one of time rather than place, the use of *where* is not appropriate. Futhermore, the use of *were visiting* would imply emphasis on visits occurring over a period of time. Such emphasis is not called for, because the purpose in this part of the sentence is to describe the point at which the Dutch began trading with the Orient. Therefore, (D) expresses most effectively the ideas in the two parts of the sentence as well as the relationship between them. The correct answer is (D).

The Sample Tests

The first SAT in this book (pages 37 - 61) is the actual test that was given on November 6, 1982. A complete TSWE also is included as part of this first test. (The experimental sections have been omitted because they contain questions that may be used in future editions of the test.) So that you will have an idea of what the actual test administration will be like, try to take this test under conditions as close as possible to those of the actual test. It probably will help if you:

- Set aside two and one-half hours when you will not be interrupted so that you can complete all of the test in one sitting. (The first sample test contains a TSWE in addition to the two verbal and two mathematical SAT sections, so two and one-half hours should be allowed for this test. The other sample tests include only the SAT sections, so only two hours should be allowed for these tests.)
- Sit at a desk with no other papers or books. You can't take a calculator, a dictionary, other books, or notes into the test room.
- Have a kitchen timer or clock in front of you for timing yourself on the sections.
- Allow yourself only 30 minutes for each section of the test.
- Tear out the practice answer sheet on page 35 and fill it in just as you will on the day of the test.
- Read the instructions on page 37. They are reprinted from the back cover of the test book. When you take a test, you will be asked to read them before you begin answering questions.
- After you finish the practice test, read "How To Score the Practice Test," on page 62.

Reviewing Your Performance

Although you're probably most interested in your scores, you should spend some time after you take this practice test reviewing your mistakes on actual questions and also your overall approach to the test. When you complete the test, ask yourself these questions:

- Did you finish most of the questions in each section? Although the last few questions in each section usually are very difficult and are omitted by many students, you might want to adjust your pacing if you didn't get to a large number of questions at the end of each section.
- Did you make a lot of careless mistakes? Perhaps you were rushing too fast and should slow down your pace.
- Did you spend too much time on particular questions? Perhaps you should have moved on after marking them in your text book (not the answer sheet) and gone back to them if you had extra time at the end of the section.
- Did you guess when you had eliminated some of the choices but weren't sure of the answer? (Remember, although wild guessing probably won't affect your scores, you shouldn't be too cautious either.)
- Were there particular types of questions that gave you more difficulty than others? If so, you might want to review the descriptions of those questions in the beginning of this book and then practice again on one of the other sample tests in this book.
- Did you spend so much time reading directions that you took time away from answering questions? If you become thoroughly familiar with the test directions printed in this book, you won't have to spend as much time reading them during the test.
- Look at the specific questions you missed. Did you get caught by a choice that was only partly correct? Figure out what step you overlooked in your reasoning.

For most students, practice on one or two sample tests is enough. If, however, you still feel uneasy about a particular type of question (or if you happen to enjoy taking tests), you can work on some of the other tests in this book. Whatever you do, don't memorize answers. It's highly unlikely that any of these actual questions will be on a test you will take. But whenever you run across a word or an idea that's new to you, be sure you learn what it means and how to use it.

COLLEGE BOARD—SCHOLASTIC APTITUDE TEST and Test of Standard Written English — Side 1

Use a No. 2 pencil only for completing this answer sheet. Be sure each mark is dark and completely fills the intended space. Completely erase any errors or stray marks.

1. YOUR NAME: (Print) ______ Last ______ First ______ M.I.

SIGNATURE: ______ DATE: ___/___/___

HOME ADDRESS: (Print) ______ Number and Street

______ City ______ State ______ Zip Code

CENTER: (Print) ______ City ______ State ______ Center Number

IMPORTANT: Please fill in these boxes exactly as shown on the back cover of your test book.

FOR ETS USE ONLY

2. TEST FORM

3. FORM CODE

4. REGISTRATION NUMBER (Copy from your Admission Ticket.)

5. YOUR NAME — First 4 letters of last name | First Init. | Mid. Init.

A B C D E F G H I J K L M N O P Q R S T U V W X Y Z

6. DATE OF BIRTH

Month: Jan. Feb. Mar. Apr. May June July Aug. Sept. Oct. Nov. Dec.

Day: 0 1 2 3 / 0 1 2 3 4 5 6 7 8 9

Year: 0 1 2 3 4 5 6 7 / 0 1 2 3 4 5 6 7 8 9

Form code: 0 1 2 3 4 5 6 7 8 9; A B C D E F G H I; J K L M N O P Q R; S T U V W X Y Z

7. SEX

Male

Female

8. TEST BOOK SERIAL NUMBER

Start with number 1 for each new section. If a section has fewer than 50 questions, leave the extra answer spaces blank.

SECTION 1

1–50: Ⓐ Ⓑ Ⓒ Ⓓ Ⓔ

SECTION 2

1–50: Ⓐ Ⓑ Ⓒ Ⓓ Ⓔ

(Cut here to detach.)

Q1205

I.N. 574001—110VV33P2723

COLLEGE BOARD — SCHOLASTIC APTITUDE TEST and Test of Standard Written English Side 2

Use a No. 2 pencil only for completing this answer sheet. Be sure each mark is dark and completely fills the intended space. Completely erase any errors or stray marks.

Start with number 1 for each new section. If a section has fewer than 50 questions, leave the extra answer spaces blank.

	SECTION 3	SECTION 4	SECTION 5	SECTION 6
1	A B C D E	A B C D E	A B C D E	A B C D E
2	A B C D E	A B C D E	A B C D E	A B C D E
3	A B C D E	A B C D E	A B C D E	A B C D E
4	A B C D E	A B C D E	A B C D E	A B C D E
5	A B C D E	A B C D E	A B C D E	A B C D E
6	A B C D E	A B C D E	A B C D E	A B C D E
7	A B C D E	A B C D E	A B C D E	A B C D E
8	A B C D E	A B C D E	A B C D	A B C D E
9	A B C D E	A B C D E	A B C D	A B C D E
10	A B C D E	A B C D E	A B C D	A B C D E
11	A B C D E	A B C D E	A B C D	A B C D E
12	A B C D E	A B C D E	A B C D	A B C D E
13	A B C D E	A B C D E	A B C D	A B C D E
14	A B C D E	A B C D E	A B C D	A B C D E
15	A B C D E	A B C D E	A B C D	A B C D E
16	A B C D E	A B C D E	A B C D	A B C D E
17	A B C D E	A B C D E	A B C D	A B C D E
18	A B C D E	A B C D E	A B C D	A B C D E
19	A B C D E	A B C D E	A B C D	A B C D E
20	A B C D E	A B C D E	A B C D	A B C D E
21	A B C D E	A B C D E	A B C D	A B C D E
22	A B C D E	A B C D E	A B C D	A B C D E
23	A B C D E	A B C D E	A B C D	A B C D E
24	A B C D E	A B C D E	A B C D	A B C D E
25	A B C D E	A B C D E	A B C D	A B C D E
26	A B C D E	A B C D E	A B C D	A B C D E
27	A B C D E	A B C D E	A B C D	A B C D E
28	A B C D E	A B C D E	A B C D E	A B C D E
29	A B C D E	A B C D E	A B C D E	A B C D E
30	A B C D E	A B C D E	A B C D E	A B C D E
31	A B C D E	A B C D E	A B C D E	A B C D E
32	A B C D E	A B C D E	A B C D E	A B C D E
33	A B C D E	A B C D E	A B C D E	A B C D E
34	A B C D E	A B C D E	A B C D E	A B C D E
35	A B C D E	A B C D E	A B C D E	A B C D E
36	A B C D E	A B C D E	A B C D E	A B C D E
37	A B C D E	A B C D E	A B C D E	A B C D E
38	A B C D E	A B C D E	A B C D E	A B C D E
39	A B C D E	A B C D E	A B C D E	A B C D E
40	A B C D E	A B C D E	A B C D E	A B C D E
41	A B C D E	A B C D E	A B C D E	A B C D E
42	A B C D E	A B C D E	A B C D E	A B C D E
43	A B C D E	A B C D E	A B C D E	A B C D E
44	A B C D E	A B C D E	A B C D E	A B C D E
45	A B C D E	A B C D E	A B C D E	A B C D E
46	A B C D E	A B C D E	A B C D E	A B C D E
47	A B C D E	A B C D E	A B C D E	A B C D E
48	A B C D E	A B C D E	A B C D E	A B C D E
49	A B C D E	A B C D E	A B C D E	A B C D E
50	A B C D E	A B C D E	A B C D E	A B C D E

9. SIGNATURE:

FOR ETS USE ONLY	VTR	VTFS	VRR	VRFS	VVR	VVFS	WER	WEFS	M4R	M4FS	M5R	M5FS	MTFS	
	VTW	VTCS	VRW	VRCS	VVW	VVCS	WEW	WECS	M4W		M5W		MTCS	

YOUR NAME (PRINT) ______________________________
LAST FIRST MI

TEST CENTER ______________________________
NUMBER NAME OF TEST CENTER ROOM NUMBER

IMPORTANT: The following codes are unique to your testbook. Copy them on your answer sheet exactly as shown.

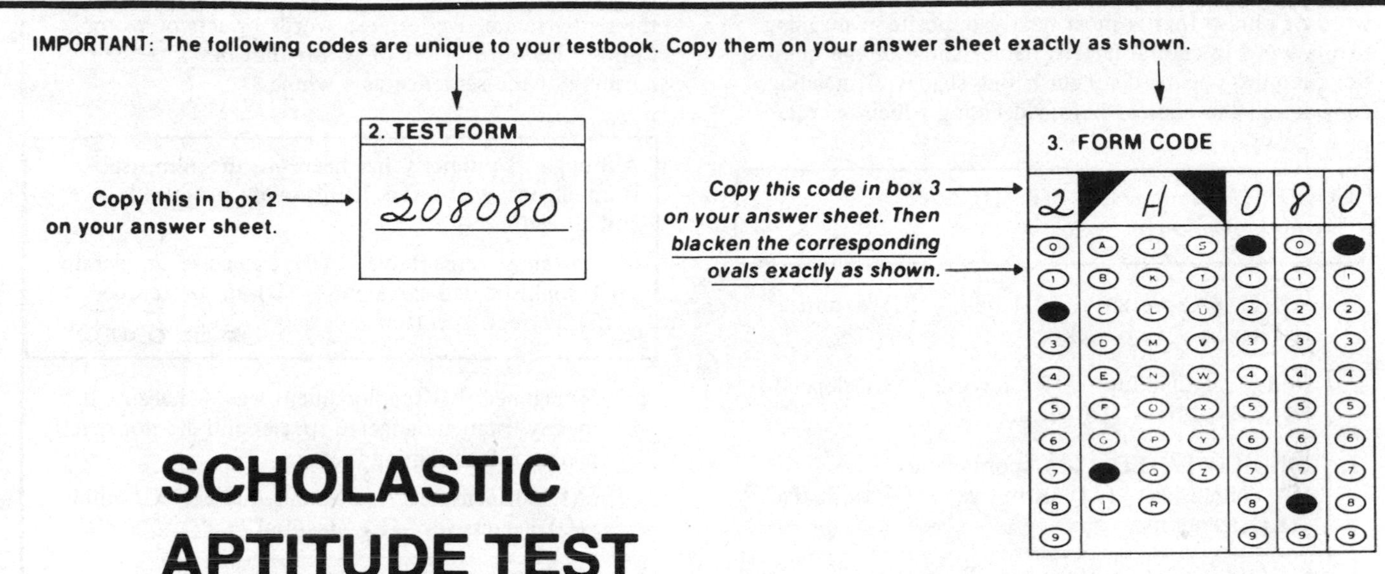

SCHOLASTIC APTITUDE TEST

and Test of Standard Written English

You will have three hours to work on the questions in this test book, which is divided into six 30-minute sections. The supervisor will tell you when to begin and end each section. If you finish before time is called, you may check your work on that section, but you are not to work on any other section.

Do not worry if you are unable to finish a section or if there are some questions you cannot answer. Do not waste time puzzling over a question that seems too difficult for you. You should work as rapidly as you can without sacrificing accuracy.

Students often ask whether they should guess when they are uncertain about the answer to a question. Your test scores will be based on the number of questions you answer correctly minus a fraction of the number you answer incorrectly. Therefore, it is improbable that random or haphazard guessing will change your scores significantly. If you have some knowledge of a question, you may be able to eliminate one or more of the answer choices as wrong. It is generally to your advantage to guess which of the remaining choices is correct. Remember, however, not to spend too much time on any one question.

Mark all your answers on the separate answer sheet. Mark only one answer for each question. Since the answer sheet will be machine scored, be sure that each mark is dark and that it completely fills the answer space. In each section of the answer sheet, there are spaces to answer 50 questions. When there are fewer than 50 questions in a section of your test, mark only the spaces that correspond to the question numbers. Do not make stray marks on the answer sheet. If you erase, do so completely, because an incomplete erasure may be scored as an intended response.

You may use the test book for scratchwork, but you will not receive credit for information written there.

(The passages for this test have been adapted from published material. The ideas contained in them do not necessarily represent the opinions of the College Board or Educational Testing Service.)

DO NOT OPEN THIS BOOK UNTIL THE SUPERVISOR TELLS YOU TO DO SO.

SECTION 1

Time—30 minutes

45 QUESTIONS

For each question in this section, choose the best answer and blacken the corresponding space on the answer sheet.

Each question below consists of a word in capital letters, followed by five lettered words or phrases. Choose the word or phrase that is most nearly opposite in meaning to the word in capital letters. Since some of the questions require you to distinguish fine shades of meaning, consider all the choices before deciding which is best.

Example:

GOOD: (A) sour (B) bad (C) red (D) hot (E) ugly

Ⓐ ● Ⓒ Ⓓ Ⓔ

1. WILT: (A) prevent (B) drain (C) expose (D) revive (E) stick
2. ISSUE: (A) dilute (B) revolve (C) depend (D) substitute (E) retract
3. PREMEDITATED: (A) spontaneous (B) conclusive (C) disruptive (D) vindictive (E) strenuous
4. SUMMARY: (A) bracing (B) accented (C) detailed (D) animated (E) disconcerting
5. WOE: (A) honesty (B) obedience (C) generosity (D) happiness (E) cleverness
6. RABID: (A) poignant (B) circular (C) skillful (D) dense (E) calm
7. AIR: (A) conceal (B) conform (C) detain (D) mislead (E) satisfy
8. CIRCUMSCRIBED: (A) unbounded (B) imperfect (C) injurious (D) readily evaded (E) barely legible
9. RANCOR: (A) carelessness (B) restlessness (C) inexperience (D) kindness (E) self-consciousness
10. PERIPHERAL: (A) colossal (B) central (C) condensed (D) subsequent (E) adjacent
11. PROFUSION: (A) activity (B) cleanliness (C) separation (D) adversity (E) scantiness
12. TURGID: (A) strong (B) glossy (C) deflated (D) easily described (E) haphazardly distributed
13. DISINTERESTED: (A) attractive (B) scholarly (C) biased (D) abandoned (E) profitable
14. DISPARITY: (A) fearfulness (B) punctuality (C) prejudice (D) similarity (E) notoriety
15. GARNER: (A) disfigure (B) hedge (C) connect (D) forget (E) disperse

Each sentence below has one or two blanks, each blank indicating that something has been omitted. Beneath the sentence are five lettered words or sets of words. Choose the word or set of words that best fits the meaning of the sentence as a whole.

Example:

Although its publicity has been ----, the film itself is intelligent, well-acted, handsomely produced, and altogether ----.

(A) tasteless..respectable (B) extensive..moderate (C) sophisticated..amateur (D) risqué..crude (E) perfect..spectacular

● Ⓑ Ⓒ Ⓓ Ⓔ

16. He claimed that the document was ---- because it merely listed endangered species and did not specify penalties for harming them.

    (A) indispensable (B) inadequate (C) punitive (D) aggressive (E) essential

17. The author makes no attempt at ---- order; a scene from 1960 is followed by one from 1968, which, in turn, is followed by one from 1964.

    (A) an impartial (B) an innovative (C) a motley (D) a chronological (E) an extemporaneous

18. Traditionally, countries with ---- frontiers requiring ---- must maintain a large army and support it by imposing taxes.

    (A) historic..markers
    (B) vulnerable..defense
    (C) vague..exploration
    (D) unwanted..elimination
    (E) contested..estimation

19. The ability to estimate distance comes only with ----; a baby reaches with equal confidence for its bottle or the moon.

    (A) tranquility (B) talent (C) experience (D) assurance (E) distress

20. She undertook a population census of the island with the ----, if not always the enthusiastic support, of the authorities.

    (A) objection (B) elation (C) suspicion (D) acquiescence (E) disdain

GO ON TO THE NEXT PAGE

Each passage below is followed by questions based on its content. Answer all questions following a passage on the basis of what is stated or implied in that passage.

One of the most significant political advances for the Black community in New York was the election of Harlemites to legislative offices. In 1920, for the first time, a Black man, E. A. Johnson, was nominated by a district organization for the state assembly. In electing Johnson, Harlem Republicans chose a well-qualified politician whose career symbolized a major transition in American history: the transfer of Black political power from the South to northern metropolitan centers.

Harlem was, until the early 1920's, solidly residential, but the Black vote was split between assembly districts which included substantial numbers of Jews in the Nineteenth District and Irish in the Twenty-First, as well as other ethnic groups. This unintentional gerrymander forced Blacks to share power with White politicians. By 1920, after a decade of mass migration, Blacks composed seventy percent of the population of each district. Blacks were aided by an active two-party system in Harlem. Although most Blacks voted for Republicans, the United Colored Democracy was a special organization within the Democratic Party. Its leader, Ferdinand Q. Morton, worked sympathetically with White Democratic bosses until 1935 when Mayor La Guardia, perhaps fortunately for the growing spirit of independence among Harlem Blacks, deliberately broke Morton's control of Black patronage.

Although Republican presidential candidates received Harlem's Black vote until 1932, Democratic mayoralty candidate John Hylan polled an amazing seventy-five percent of that vote in 1921. Black Democrats had represented Harlem on the Board of Aldermen before the twenties, but in 1922, with a landslide vote for Al Smith for governor of New York, Harlem became the first Black community in the nation to significantly support the Democratic Party. No longer could politicians boast that the Black vote could never be driven from the party of Lincoln.

After his victory in 1921, Hylan appointed Morton chairman of the Civil Service Commission, the first time a Black had held that important municipal post. Hylan's successor, James J. Walker, reappointed Morton to the post. In 1925, five Black physicians became, for the first time, regular staff members of the Harlem Hospital. This was the result of prodding from Morton, Republican aldermen, the NAACP, and the North Harlem Medical Society. And, after a decade of pressure, Black Republicans in the state assembly forced the creation of a new administrative entity by subdividing the old Seventh District. This intentional gerrymander guaranteed the election of two Black judges–another city first–to the municipal bench in 1929.

21. Which of the following titles best summarizes the content of the passage?
(A) The Black Migration to New York
(B) Harlem Politics in Transition
(C) The Black Vote in Presidential Elections
(D) Prominent Black Politicians
(E) The Black Vote and the Democratic Party

22. The career of E. A. Johnson is important to the main idea of the passage because it
(A) illustrates a precedent in the acquisition of political power by Harlem Blacks
(B) exemplifies the new aggressive politics of Blacks in the rural South
(C) symbolizes the thwarted political ambitions of American Blacks
(D) heralds the end of political subjugation of Blacks in the South
(E) reflects the desire of Harlem Blacks for separation from the White community

23. According to the passage, Black representation in the New York State Assembly before 1920 was hampered by the
(A) solidly residential nature of the Black community
(B) indifference of other ethnic groups
(C) division of the Black vote between two districts
(D) inability of Black voters to agree on candidates
(E) failure of Harlem voters to sponsor candidates

24. It can be inferred that, beginning with 1932, Harlem's Black vote was
(A) delivered by Ferdinand Q. Morton to the local Democrats
(B) split between two state assembly districts
(C) a point of controversy in all presidential primaries
(D) the controlling factor in the mayoral elections in New York
(E) frequently accorded to Democratic presidential candidates

25. The author cites Harlem's landslide vote for Al Smith in 1922 as an illustration of the
(A) desire of Harlemites to be free of political bosses
(B) Blacks' ability to vote as a unit in spite of gerrymandering
(C) need for a two-party system in Harlem
(D) changing party alignment of Black voters in Harlem
(E) fact that political analysts are often wrong in their predictions

GO ON TO THE NEXT PAGE

The reading passages in this test are brief excerpts or adaptations of excerpts from published material. The ideas contained in them do not necessarily represent the opinions of the College Board or Educational Testing Service. To make the text suitable for testing purposes, we may in some cases have altered the style, contents, or point of view of the original.

Studies of children's acquisition of language suggest that the faculty of language includes an inborn knowledge of the formal principles of language structure, a knowledge that depends on genetically determined portions of (usually) the left cerebral hemisphere. Although it is well established that the left hemisphere is specialized for language, one cannot say that language is "located" in this or that part of the hemisphere. What is known is that language disorders are the result of lesions in the left hemisphere. Disorders of language resulting from damage to the brain are called aphasias.

The anterior portion of the "language area" is termed Broca's area. Lesions in this area interfere with the motor and articulatory aspects of language. Speech is slow, labored, grammatically incorrect, and telegraphic; in extreme cases, it may be impossible to carry out. Writing is likewise severely impaired. Comprehension of the spoken or written word, however, may be unimpaired or nearly so. (It is interesting to note that under emotional stress, a patient with Broca's aphasia may be temporarily fluent.) Because Broca's area is close to the motor cortex, if the former is damaged, the latter is often damaged simultaneously. Hence, such patients often suffer from weakness or paralysis of the right side of the body. Similar lesions in the right hemisphere will cause a left-sided weakness or paralysis but will have no effect on language.

Damage to the posterior portion of the "language area," especially to Wernicke's area, results in a loss of comprehension of the spoken word and often of the written word. The patient's native language is now like a foreign language. In addition, the patient's speech is rapid and well-articulated, but without meaning. Writing is defective, and words that are heard cannot be repeated, although hearing itself is completely normal. Similar lesions in the right hemisphere usually have no effect on language.

Injuries to the "language area" in children result in severe aphasias, but the development of language mechanisms in the right hemisphere can often compensate for them to an extraordinary degree. This potential function of the right hemisphere is probably normally suppressed by the left hemisphere. In adults, aphasias from similar lesions are often permanent.

26. The author is primarily concerned with

(A) describing the process of language acquisition
(B) explaining potential treatments of language defects
(C) showing the importance of the left hemisphere of the brain to language mechanisms
(D) depicting various means of diagnosing language defects
(E) explaining why the left hemisphere of the brain dominates the right hemisphere

27. Unlike a patient with Wernicke's aphasia, a patient with Broca's aphasia can do which of the following?

(A) Comprehend written but not spoken language.
(B) Hear and read with comprehension.
(C) Speak articulately and also comprehend spoken language.
(D) Write and speak readily and coherently.
(E) Neither write nor understand his or her native language.

28. According to the passage, which of the following statements about the right hemisphere of the brain is (are) accurate?

I. It has the potential to serve as a "language area."
II. It controls the ability to comprehend but not the ability to speak a language.
III. If it is damaged, gross motor control of the left side of the body may be affected.

(A) I only
(B) I and II only
(C) I and III only
(D) II and III only
(E) I, II, and III

29. It can be inferred that aphasias in adults often result in permanent damage because

(A) much memory is lost
(B) adults have more trouble learning a foreign language
(C) the right hemisphere is no longer as adaptable as it once was
(D) brain cells in adults are especially vulnerable to infection
(E) adults can readily become adept at nonverbal communication

30. It can be inferred that the author uses which of the following as evidence for the specialization of the left hemisphere?

(A) Clinical studies of instances of damage in the left hemisphere
(B) Studies of language development in children without brain damage
(C) Microscopic examination of the left hemisphere
(D) Examples of the integration of functions of the left and right hemispheres
(E) Theoretical explanations of brain specialization

GO ON TO THE NEXT PAGE

Select the word or set of words that best completes each of the following sentences.

31. Edward was rather ---- about what paintings were hung in his study, but, in contrast, was quite ---- about what furniture was in the room.

(A) fastidious..indifferent
(B) inflexible..obstinate
(C) undecided..tentative
(D) demanding..definite
(E) submissive..timid

32. A curious self-interest, and not the concern for others which might have been expected, motivated his ----.

(A) ambition (B) malevolence (C) apathy (D) eccentricity (E) philanthropy

33. The dinner was a culinary -----, confirming to all its partakers the reputed ---- of the host.

(A) orgy..extravagance
(B) escapade..conventionality
(C) tragicomedy..expertise
(D) classic..ineptitude
(E) nightmare..infallibility

34. One of the paradoxes of life is the friction between our hunger for ---- and our grudging ---- that there is indeed nothing new under the sun.

(A) variety..denial
(B) infamy..acceptance
(C) novelty..awareness
(D) security..insistence
(E) conformity..admission

35. If improved technology enables researchers to perform more refined experiments, startling evidence may be uncovered that will lead to the ---- of even the most sacrosanct of scientific theories.

(A) tempering (B) diagnosing (C) utilization (D) supposition (E) formulation

Each question below consists of a related pair of words or phrases, followed by five lettered pairs of words or phrases. Select the lettered pair that best expresses a relationship similar to that expressed in the original pair.

Example:

YAWN : BOREDOM :: (A) dream : sleep
(B) anger : madness (C) smile : amusement
(D) face : expression (E) impatience : rebellion

Ⓐ Ⓑ ● Ⓓ Ⓔ

36. COW : BARN :: (A) pig : mud (B) chicken : coop (C) camel : water (D) cat : tree (E) horse : racetrack

37. LEAVE : LINGER :: (A) manipulate : manage (B) warrant : employ (C) surprise : astonish (D) cease : prolong (E) flout : violate

38. NOTES : SCALE :: (A) solos : harmony (B) sentences : punctuation (C) attitudes : fact (D) fractions : numerator (E) letters : alphabet

39. APPAREL : PERSON :: (A) plumage : bird (B) prey : animal (C) water : fish (D) insignia : officer (E) scenery : theater

40. SONG : RECITAL :: (A) author : bibliography (B) episode : series (C) coach : team (D) intermission : play (E) poetry : prose

41. ANALGESIC : PAIN ::
(A) vaccination : injection
(B) anesthetic : sleep
(C) antidote : poisoning
(D) prescription : medication
(E) liniment : ointment

42. FEINT : ILLUSION ::
(A) insanity : hallucination
(B) decoy : enticement
(C) ambush : cache
(D) impasse : exit
(E) ploy : vengeance

43. BURNISH : LUSTER :: (A) resist : aggression (B) preserve : area (C) accelerate : rapidity (D) pivot : reflex (E) plunge : distance

44. HEIRLOOM : INHERITANCE ::
(A) payment : currency (B) belongings : receipt (C) land : construction (D) legacy : bill (E) booty : plunder

45. PHILISTINE : CULTIVATED ::
(A) regionalist : authoritarian
(B) anarchist : disorderly
(C) capitalist : greedy
(D) visionary : practical
(E) eccentric : artistic

S T O P

IF YOU FINISH BEFORE TIME IS CALLED, YOU MAY CHECK YOUR WORK ON THIS SECTION ONLY. DO NOT WORK ON ANY OTHER SECTION IN THE TEST.

SECTION 2

Time—30 minutes

25 QUESTIONS

In this section solve each problem, using any available space on the page for scratchwork. Then decide which is the best of the choices given and blacken the corresponding space on the answer sheet.

The following information is for your reference in solving some of the problems.

Circle of radius r: Area $= \pi r^2$; Circumference $= 2\pi r$
The number of degrees of arc in a circle is 360.
The measure in degrees of a straight angle is 180.

Definitions of symbols:

$=$	is equal to	$\leq$	is less than or equal to
$\neq$	is unequal to	$\geq$	is greater than or equal to
$<$	is less than	$\parallel$	is parallel to
$>$	is greater than	$\perp$	is perpendicular to

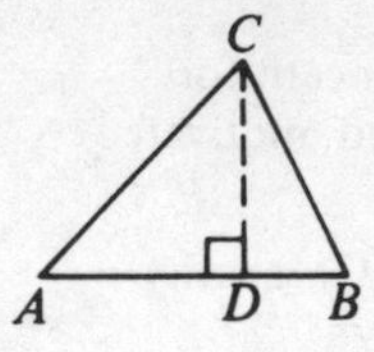

Triangle: The sum of the measures in degrees of the angles of a triangle is 180.
If $\angle CDA$ is a right angle, then

(1) area of $\triangle ABC = \dfrac{AB \times CD}{2}$

(2) $AC^2 = AD^2 + DC^2$

Note: Figures which accompany problems in this test are intended to provide information useful in solving the problems. They are drawn as accurately as possible EXCEPT when it is stated in a specific problem that its figure is not drawn to scale. All figures lie in a plane unless otherwise indicated. All numbers used are real numbers.

1. If $x^3 + y = x^3 + 5$, then $y =$

(A) -5 (B) $-\sqrt[3]{5}$ (C) $\sqrt[3]{5}$ (D) 5 (E) 5^3

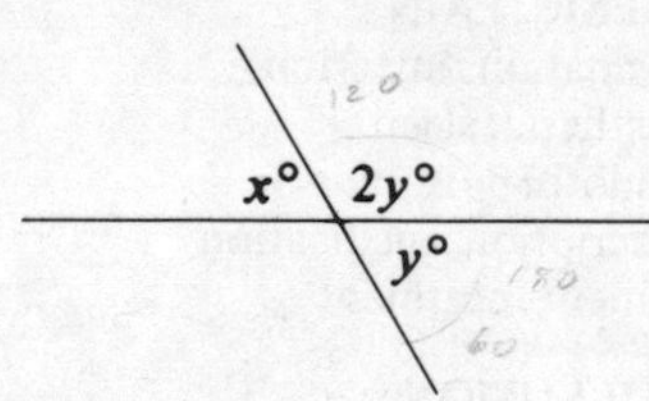

2. In the figure above, two lines intersect as shown. What is the value of x ?

(A) 30 (B) 60 (C) 90 (D) 120 (E) 180

3. If $x = -3$ and $y = 0$, then $x^2y + \dfrac{y}{x} =$

(A) 9
(B) 6
(C) 3
(D) 0
(E) -3

4. The number 99,999,999 is NOT divisible by

(A) 9 (B) 11 (C) 99
(D) 111 (E) 9,999

GO ON TO THE NEXT PAGE

Sun.	Mon.	Tue.	Wed.	Thu.	Fri.	Sat.
						30
29	28	27	26	25	24	23
22	21	20	19	18	17	16

5. If the days of a month are numbered consecutively backward as shown on the partial calendar above, on what day of the week will the day numbered 1 occur?

(A) Sunday (B) Monday (C) Tuesday
(D) Friday (E) Saturday

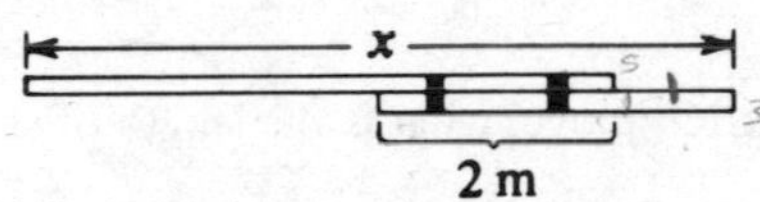

6. In the figure above, a 5-meter pole and a 3-meter pole are tied together so that the length of the overlapping portion is 2 meters. What is the length x of the two poles combined in this way?

(A) 4 m
(B) 5 m
(C) 6 m
(D) 7 m
(E) 8 m

Questions 7-8 refer to the following price list.

PLACE SETTING OF TABLEWARE

Item	Price
Dinner plate	\$2.95
Salad plate	\$2.45
Bowl	\$2.20
Cup	\$1.95
Saucer	\$1.90

7. Charles bought one of each of the 5 items listed. What was the average (arithmetic mean) price per item for the 5 items?

(A) \$2.00 (B) \$2.21 (C) \$2.29
(D) \$2.32 (E) \$2.39

8. If the price of each item in the list above is reduced by 10 percent during a sales promotion, which of the following is the amount of money saved by purchasing 8 saucers at the sale price?

(A) \$1.52 (B) \$1.73 (C) \$13.68
(D) \$15.20 (E) \$17.00

GO ON TO THE NEXT PAGE

9. Of the following numbers, which is the LEAST?

(A) 0.102
(B) 0.11
(C) 0.1201
(D) 0.101
(E) 0.1001

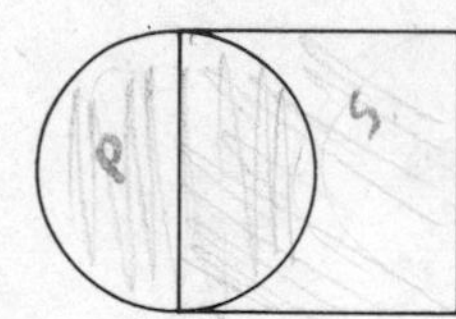

10. In the figure above, one side of the square is a diameter of the circle. If the area of the circle is p and the area of the square is s, which of the following must be true?

I. $s > p$
II. $s \geqq 2p$
III. $s < p$

(A) None (B) I only (C) II only
(D) III only (E) I and II

List I: 1, 3, 5, 7
List II: 2, 4, 6, 8

11. For how many different ordered pairs, (x, y), where x is a number from List I and y is a number from List II, is $x + y > 11$?

(A) Nine (B) Seven (C) Six
(D) Four (E) Three

12. If a and b are even integers, which of the following must be true?

I. $\frac{a+b}{2}$ is odd.
II. $a - b$ is even.
III. $a + b$ is divisible by 2.

(A) III only
(B) I and II only
(C) I and III only
(D) II and III only
(E) I, II, and III

13. If $x^2 - y^2 = 27$, then $3(x + y)(x - y) =$

(A) 9 (B) 24 (C) 27 (D) 36 (E) 81

14. Points A, B, X, and Y lie on the same line but not necessarily in that order. Given the lengths $AB = 12$, $BX = 2$, and $XY = 8$, what is length AY?

(A) 2
(B) 6
(C) 18
(D) 22
(E) It cannot be determined from the information given.

15. When x is divided by 7, the remainder is 4. What is the remainder when $2x$ is divided by 7?

(A) 1 (B) 2 (C) 3 (D) 4 (E) 5

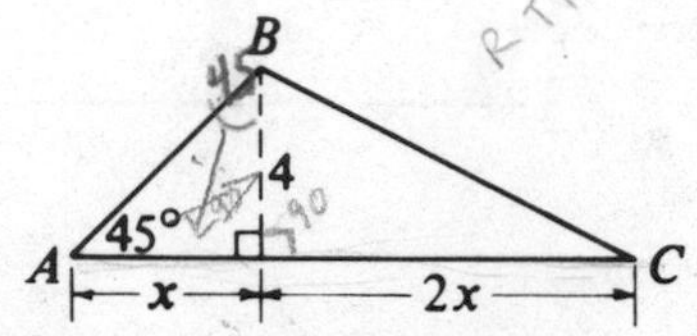

16. In $\triangle ABC$ above, what is the length of side AC?

(A) 24 (B) 18 (C) 12 (D) 8
(E) It cannot be determined from the information given.

17. If one hundred equally priced tickets cost a total of d dollars, then, in terms of d, five of these tickets cost how many dollars?

(A) $\frac{d}{20}$

(B) $\frac{d}{5}$

(C) $5d$

(D) $\frac{5}{d}$

(E) $\frac{20}{d}$

GO ON TO THE NEXT PAGE

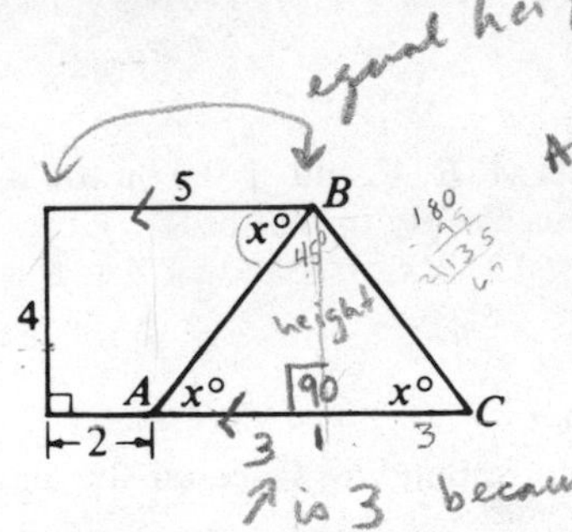

18. In the figure above, what is the area of $\triangle ABC$?

(A) 12
(B) 14
(C) 16
(D) 24
(E) 28

19. In a certain period, an agency's editors read 4 out of every 20 scripts submitted. What was the ratio of unread scripts to scripts read during that time?

(A) 3:4
(B) 4:5
(C) 5:4
(D) 4:1
(E) 5:1

20. In the figure above, what is y in terms of x?

(A) $90 + x$
(B) $90 + 2x$
(C) $180 - x$
(D) $180 - 2x$
(E) $2x$

21. Ten people meet and everybody shakes hands exactly once with everybody else. What is the total number of handshakes?

(A) 9 (B) 10 (C) 45 (D) 50 (E) 90

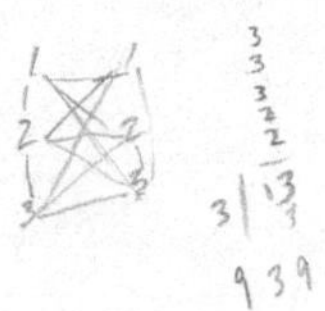

22. If $\frac{x}{y} = \frac{2}{3}$ and $\frac{y}{z} = \frac{-3}{2}$, which of the following must be true?

I. $\frac{x}{z} = -1$

II. $xy = 6$

III. $(x + z)^2 = 0$

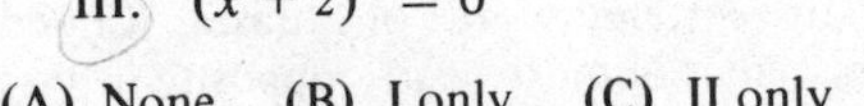

(A) None (B) I only (C) II only
(D) III only (E) I and III

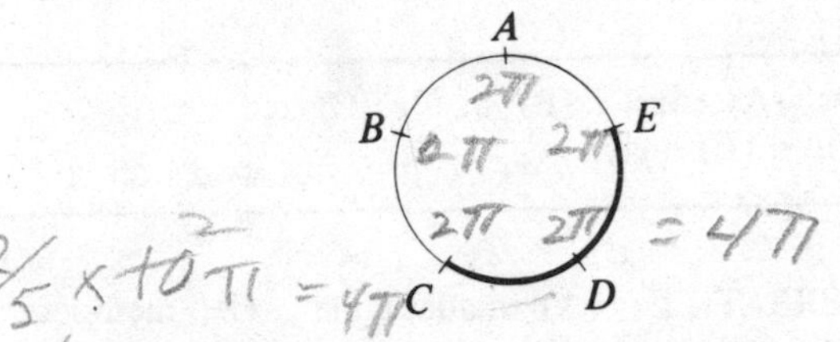

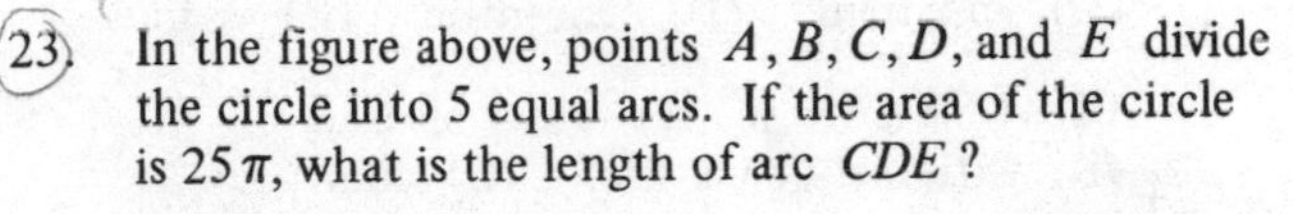

23. In the figure above, points $A, B, C, D,$ and E divide the circle into 5 equal arcs. If the area of the circle is 25π, what is the length of arc CDE?

(A) 2π
(B) 4π
(C) 5π
(D) 8π
(E) 10π

24. If x is an odd number, what is the sum of the next two odd numbers greater than $3x + 1$?

(A) $6x + 8$
(B) $6x + 6$
(C) $6x + 5$
(D) $6x + 4$
(E) $6x + 3$

25. In a race, if Bob's running speed was $\frac{4}{5}$ Alice's, and Chris's speed was $\frac{3}{4}$ Bob's, then Alice's speed was how many times the average (arithmetic mean) of the other two runners' speeds?

(A) $\frac{3}{5}$ (B) $\frac{7}{10}$ (C) $\frac{40}{31}$ (D) $\frac{10}{7}$ (E) $\frac{5}{3}$

S T O P

IF YOU FINISH BEFORE TIME IS CALLED, YOU MAY CHECK YOUR WORK ON THIS SECTION ONLY. DO NOT WORK ON ANY OTHER SECTION IN THE TEST.

SECTION 4

Time—30 minutes

40 QUESTIONS

For each question in this section, choose the best answer and blacken the corresponding space on the answer sheet.

Each question below consists of a word in capital letters, followed by five lettered words or phrases. Choose the word or phrase that is most nearly opposite in meaning to the word in capital letters. Since some of the questions require you to distinguish fine shades of meaning, consider all the choices before deciding which is best.

Example:

GOOD: (A) sour (B) bad (C) red (D) hot (E) ugly

Ⓐ ● Ⓒ Ⓓ Ⓔ

1. VERSATILE: (A) unadaptable (B) mediocre (C) impatient (D) egocentric (E) vicious

2. FRAUDULENT: (A) rather pleasing (B) extremely beneficial (C) courteous (D) authentic (E) simplified

3. PROTRUSION: (A) mirage (B) indentation (C) deceleration (D) disorder (E) fruitlessness

4. BOLT: (A) cleanse (B) slide (C) look upon (D) move sluggishly (E) exhibit proudly

5. ANTIQUATED: (A) fake (B) flat (C) modern (D) secret (E) applied

6. SNIPPET: (A) vague response (B) bargain (C) sudden plunge (D) fantasy (E) large amount

7. IMPUGN: (A) speak well of (B) describe in detail (C) forget to complete (D) disassociate (E) stimulate

8. RECANT:
(A) reduce
(B) ridicule
(C) prevent delivery of
(D) reaffirm belief in
(E) accept remuneration for

9. DEPRAVITY: (A) talent (B) certainty (C) noble behavior (D) successful venture (E) elaborate decoration

10. EPHEMERAL: (A) lasting (B) inhumane (C) contemporary (D) destructive (E) appropriate

Each sentence below has one or two blanks, each blank indicating that something has been omitted. Beneath the sentence are five lettered words or sets of words. Choose the word or set of words that best fits the meaning of the sentence as a whole.

Example:

Although its publicity has been ----, the film itself is intelligent, well-acted, handsomely produced, and altogether ----.

(A) tasteless. .respectable (B) extensive. .moderate (C) sophisticated. .amateur (D) risqué. .crude (E) perfect. .spectacular

● Ⓑ Ⓒ Ⓓ Ⓔ

11. In the North Pacific, the number of whales has been so drastically reduced that the sighting of even one is ---- event.

(A) a newsworthy (B) a treacherous (C) an everyday (D) an elaborate (E) an expected

12. Musicians' salaries have risen so much faster than concert admission prices and donations that some famous ---- are threatened with ----.

(A) composers. .silence
(B) orchestras. .bankruptcy
(C) works. .oblivion
(D) conductors. .strikes
(E) soloists. .taxation

13. In view of the ---- value of the new treatment for this complicated case, ---- with another physician is advisable.

(A) questionable. .a consultation
(B) necessary. .an interlude
(C) accepted. .an exploration
(D) impossible. .a confrontation
(E) presumed. .an argument

14. Parental devotion, especially if overly solicitous, has its ----, one of which is ---- a child's progress toward maturity.

(A) delusions. .envisioning
(B) excesses. .abetting
(C) targets. .ensuring
(D) rewards. .ameliorating
(E) pitfalls. .protracting

15. Chesnutt enables the reader to witness the people's conscious ---- of history, to observe how one group in society could ---- turn its back on the truth.

(A) manipulation. .inadvertently
(B) suppression. .accidentally
(C) investigation. .blithely
(D) distortion. .willfully
(E) tabulation. .involuntarily

Each question below consists of a related pair of words or phrases, followed by five lettered pairs of words or phrases. Select the lettered pair that best expresses a relationship similar to that expressed in the original pair.

Example:

YAWN : BOREDOM :: (A) dream : sleep (B) anger : madness (C) smile : amusement (D) face : expression (E) impatience : rebellion

Ⓐ Ⓑ ● Ⓓ Ⓔ

16. PAINTING : CANVAS :: (A) drawing : lottery (B) fishing : pond (C) writing : paper (D) shading : crayon (E) sculpting : design

17. VOLUME : SPHERE :: (A) altitude : triangle (B) diagonal : square (C) area : circle (D) angle : rectangle (E) length : cube

18. RAMSHACKLE : COLLAPSE ::
(A) intact : explode (B) threadbare : hem (C) waterlogged : sink (D) dilapidated : repair (E) flammable : quench

19. TRICK : ROGUE :: (A) stratagem : friend (B) sentence : criminal (C) accident : witness (D) conspiracy : traitor (E) novel : reader

20. CALIPERS : MEASURING :: (A) nails : hammering (B) crops : harvesting (C) glasses : polishing (D) decisions : weighing (E) scissors : cutting

21. WHEEDLE : FLATTERY ::
(A) inspire : creations (B) intimidate : threats (C) scrutinize : clues (D) accuse : denials (E) appreciate : offers

22. CACOPHONY : SOUND ::
(A) beauty : vision
(B) stench : smell
(C) decadence : age
(D) radiance : illumination
(E) ignorance : knowledge

23. LECHER : LUSTFUL ::
(A) glutton : surly (B) fanatic : ungodly (C) skinflint : miserly (D) disciplinarian : unruly (E) spendthrift : homely

24. INSOLVENCY : FUNDS :: (A) economy : inflation (B) coinage : money (C) exhaustion : energy (D) addiction : cure (E) liquidity : cash

25. SCOFF : DERISION ::
(A) soothe : mollification
(B) slander : repression
(C) swear : precision
(D) stimulate : appearance
(E) startle : speediness

GO ON TO THE NEXT PAGE

Each passage below is followed by questions based on its content. Answer all questions following a passage on the basis of what is stated or implied in that passage.

My grandmother's notorious pugnacity did not confine itself to the exercise of authority over the neighborhood. There was also the defense of her house and her furniture against the imagined encroachments of visitors. With my grandmother, this was not the gentle and tremulous protectiveness of certain frail people who infer the fragility of all things from the brittleness of their own bones and hear the crash of mortality in the perilous tinkling of a teacup. No, my grandmother's sentiment was more autocratic: she hated having her chairs sat in or her lawns stepped on or the water turned on in her sinks, for no reason but pure administrative efficiency; she even grudged the mailman his daily promenade up her sidewalk. Her home was a center of power, and she would not allow it to be insulted by easy or democratic usage. Under her jealous eye, its social properties had withered and it functioned in the family structure simply as a political headquarters. Family conferences were held there, consultations with the doctor and the clergy; unruly grandchildren were brought there for a lecture or an interval of thought-taking; wills were read and loans negotiated. The family had no friends, and entertaining was held to be a foolish and unnecessary courtesy required only by the bonds of a blood relationship. Holiday dinners fell, as a duty, on the lesser members of the organization: sons and daughters and cousins respectfully offered up baked alaska on a platter, while my grandparents sat enthroned at the table, and only their digestive processes acknowledged the festal nature of the day.

26. The author's main purpose in this passage is to

(A) review childhood impressions and fears
(B) mourn the vanishing unity of the nuclear family
(C) create a vivid portrait of a strong personality
(D) revive the memory of a dimly recalled ancestor
(E) commend some of a grandmother's firmly held principles

27. It can be inferred from the passage that all of the following are characteristic of the author's grandmother EXCEPT

(A) desire for order
(B) pride in authority
(C) disdain for sentiment
(D) reluctance to compromise
(E) jealousy of youth

28. The tone of the passage is best described as

(A) sympathetic and sentimental
(B) restrained and cautious
(C) apathetic and aloof
(D) satirical and candid
(E) bitter and loathing

Mars revolves around the Sun in 687 Earth days, which is equivalent to 23 Earth months. The axis of Mars's rotation is tipped at a 25° angle from the plane of its orbit, nearly the same as the Earth's tilt of about 23° Because the tilt causes the seasons, we know that Mars goes through a year with four seasons just as the Earth does.

From the Earth, we have long watched the effect of the seasons on Mars. In the Martian winter, in a given hemisphere, there is a polar ice cap. As the Martian spring comes to the Northern Hemisphere, for example, the north polar cap shrinks and material in the planet's more temperate zones darkens. The surface of Mars is always mainly reddish, with darker gray areas that, from the Earth, appear blue green. In the spring, the darker regions spread. Half a Martian year later, the same process happens in the Southern Hemisphere.

One possible explanation for these changes is biological: Martian vegetation could be blooming or spreading in the spring. There are other explanations, however. The theory that presently seems most reasonable is that each year during the Northern Hemisphere springtime, a dust storm starts, with winds that reach velocities as high as hundreds of kilometers per hour. Fine, light-colored dust is blown from slopes, exposing dark areas underneath. If the dust were composed of certain kinds of materials, such as limonite, the reddish color would be explained.

29. It can be inferred that one characteristic of limonite is its

(A) reddish color
(B) blue green color
(C) ability to change colors
(D) ability to support rich vegetation
(E) tendency to concentrate into a hard surface

30. According to the author, seasonal variations on Mars are a direct result of the

(A) proximity of the planet to the Sun
(B) proximity of the planet to the Earth
(C) presence of ice caps at the poles of the planet
(D) tilt of the planet's rotational axis
(E) length of time required by the planet to revolve around the Sun

31. It can be inferred that, as spring arrives in the Southern Hemisphere of Mars, which of the following is also occurring?

(A) The northern polar cap is increasing in size.
(B) The axis of rotation is tipping at a greater angle.
(C) A dust storm is ending in the Southern Hemisphere.
(D) The material in the northern temperate zones is darkening.
(E) Vegetation in the southern temperate zones is decaying.

GO ON TO THE NEXT PAGE

Heresy was a profoundly troublesome problem for Christians in twelfth- and thirteenth-century Europe. Heretics were those who deliberately dissented from accepted Christian belief and repudiated ecclesiastical authority in matters of faith. Differences in belief had disturbed the unity of the Christian Church from its beginning and had contributed to the split between Constantinople and Rome. But Western Christendom had never confronted a large-scale attack on its unity before the twelfth century. Essentially, the threat was a revival in a new form of Manichaeanism, an old heresy condemned by Church leaders in early medieval centuries. There had always been Christians who, from an orthodox point of view, had put too great an emphasis on the problem of evil. The Catharists, as the late-medieval Manichaeans were called, went even further and deified the principle of evil as an actual god of darkness. For them God was spirit and Satan was matter, and the two were engaged in a cosmic struggle in which humanity must take part. The body, particularly its sexual aspect, was to be denied. The *perfecti*, or leaders, were expected to live entirely without sin. For the mass of believers the chief duty was reverence toward the *perfecti*. Catharists rejected the Christian doctrine of the incarnation, believing that Christ could not have appeared in the corrupt human body. They also rejected the sacraments. In their religion there was one sacrament only, the *consolamentum*, a last absolution for sin usually administered just before death.

32. The passage is primarily concerned with presenting the
    (A) conflicts that led to the decline of the Middle Ages
    (B) difficulty Christianity has had with heresy throughout its history
    (C) origins of the belief in the split between mind and body
    (D) beliefs of the Catharists in relation to those of the established Western church
    (E) development of the Catharists from their predecessors, the Manichaeans

33. The author refers to Manichaeanism (line 12) chiefly in order to
    (A) contrast Manichaeans with the Catharists of the Middle Ages
    (B) define what is meant by heresy in the context of this discussion
    (C) emphasize that heresy has always been a problem for the Christian church
    (D) show that the beliefs of the Catharists had a precedent
    (E) demonstrate the consistency of the established Christian doctrine

34. It can be inferred that each of the following applies to the *perfecti* EXCEPT that they
    (A) received the veneration of their followers
    (B) enjoyed luxuries denied to their followers
    (C) rejected the sacrament of marriage
    (D) should not have had need of the *consolamentum*
    (E) were deeply concerned with spiritual matters

35. According to the passage, one way in which Catharist doctrine differed from accepted Christian belief was the Catharist notion that Christ
    (A) was not free from sin
    (B) demanded that humans live without pleasure
    (C) did not assume human form
    (D) rejected the performance of sacrements
    (E) overemphasized the problem of evil

GO ON TO THE NEXT PAGE

Certain economists have criticized advertising as economically wasteful. Most of these attacks usually concentrate on competition in advertising. Other attacks focus on the relative cost of advertising as a percentage of sales. Sometimes an arbitrary percentage, such as 5 percent of total sales, is selected as the dividing line between "high" and more "reasonable" levels of expenditure. Such cutoff points are meaningless, however, since the proper relative expenditure for advertising is a function of the product's characteristics. It is not an accident that relative advertising costs are highest for low-priced items that are available from many retail outlets and are subject to frequent repeat purchases (for example, soaps, soft drinks, cigarettes, etc.).

Particularly criticized as wasteful are emotional appeals, persuasion, and "tug-of-war" advertising when it appears that their main effect is to shift sales among firms rather than to increase the total sales volume of the industry. In such cases, it has been charged that advertising departs from its main function, which is to inform consumers. However we must bear in mind that in a competitive economy such as ours, a company must try to persuade consumers to buy its goods rather than someone else's and that unsold goods are not being put to use.

Sometimes critics claim that if advertising succeeds in expanding the total demand for a product, the result is a shift of demand from other products, the producers of which will then be forced to advertise to attempt to recover their position. The net result of such "counter-advertising" is to add to costs and to prices. But all increases in demand do not necessarily represent a diversion from other products. Thus, an expanded demand for new products can be accompanied by an increase in income and in purchasing power flowing from their production.

Another claim is that advertising is wasteful because it is said to create useless or undesirable wants at the expense of things for which there is greater social need. When advertising makes consumers want and buy such products as powerful automobiles with fancy racing stripes and large, ostentatious swimming pools, critics argue, there is less money available to improve public hospitals, build better schools, or combat juvenile delinquency.

These criticisms of socially undesirable wants are value judgments reached by some economists on the basis of their own subjective standards. The real question is who is to decide what is good for consumers and what they should purchase? In a free economy, there is a wide diversity in opinion as to what combinations of goods and services should be made available. Each one of us must decide what purchases will yield the greatest satisfactions. We may be misled on occasion by popular fads, advertising, or even advice from friends. But these decisions, in the final analysis, are made by the buyers and not by the advertisers, as the latter have so often discovered to their regret.

36. The primary purpose of the passage is to

(A) criticize advertising as economically wasteful
(B) describe and discuss effective advertising strategies
(C) find fault with various arguments that have been made against advertising
(D) persuade consumers to pay more attention to advertising
(E) define and describe counteradvertising and the range of effects it has had

37. According to the fourth paragraph, some economists feel that certain products detract from the general well-being because they

(A) decrease the demand for public services
(B) cost the consumer more than they are worth
(C) are attractive to only a small segment of the public
(D) increase the necessity for businesses to employ expensive counteradvertising
(E) divert money that might have been spent on social improvements

GO ON TO THE NEXT PAGE

38. Which of the following best expresses the author's reaction to those who argue that advertising contributes to the formation of socially undesirable consumer demands?

(A) The critics do not independently formulate the criteria they employ.
(B) The arguments used by the critics are not based on appropriate standards.
(C) Too few economists have input in determining what the ideal components of a desirable market should be.
(D) The theories of these critics cannot predict trends in the popularity of a product.
(E) Businesses are not likely to spend too much money on ineffective advertising.

39. The author apparently feels that which of the following is most important for our economy?

(A) Laws that regulate advertising
(B) A better understanding of advertising strategies
(C) Freedom for advertisers and consumers
(D) A better evaluation of consumer needs
(E) Objective standards for rating the quality of goods

40. With which of the following statements about marketing would the author most probably agree?

I. Emotional appeal does not necessarily constitute an unfair advertising practice.
II. Buyers should be allowed to choose the kinds of products they want to purchase.
III. The consumer needs to be legally protected against certain forms of advertising.

(A) I only
(B) II only
(C) III only
(D) I and II only
(E) II and III only

S T O P

IF YOU FINISH BEFORE TIME IS CALLED, YOU MAY CHECK YOUR WORK ON THIS SECTION ONLY. DO NOT WORK ON ANY OTHER SECTION IN THE TEST.

5

SECTION 5

Time—30 minutes

35 QUESTIONS

In this section solve each problem, using any available space on the page for scratchwork. Then decide which is the best of the choices given and blacken the corresponding space on the answer sheet.

The following information is for your reference in solving some of the problems.

Circle of radius r: Area $= \pi r^2$; Circumference $= 2\pi r$
The number of degrees of arc in a circle is 360.
The measure in degrees of a straight angle is 180.

Definitions of symbols:

$=$	is equal to	$\leq$	is less than or equal to
$\neq$	is unequal to	$\geq$	is greater than or equal to
$<$	is less than	$\parallel$	is parallel to
$>$	is greater than	$\perp$	is perpendicular to

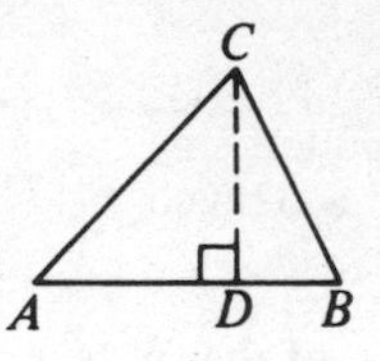

Triangle: The sum of the measures in degrees of the angles of a triangle is 180.
If $\angle CDA$ is a right angle, then

(1) area of $\triangle ABC = \frac{AB \times CD}{2}$

(2) $AC^2 = AD^2 + DC^2$

Note: Figures which accompany problems in this test are intended to provide information useful in solving the problems. They are drawn as accurately as possible EXCEPT when it is stated in a specific problem that its figure is not drawn to scale. All figures lie in a plane unless otherwise indicated. All numbers used are real numbers.

---

1. If $\frac{9}{5} + \frac{x}{5} = 2$, then $x =$

   (A) 0 (B) 1 (C) 2 (D) 3 (E) 4

2. A triangle with sides of lengths 4, 8, and 9 has the same perimeter as an equilateral triangle with side of length

   (A) $5\frac{1}{2}$ (B) 6 (C) $6\frac{1}{2}$ (D) 7 (E) $7\frac{1}{2}$

3. If $x = \frac{y}{5}$ and $10x = 14$, then $y =$

   (A) 28
   (B) 14
   (C) 7
   (D) 5
   (E) 2

4. If 14 is 5 more than x and 12 is 3 less than y, then $x - y =$

   (A) 24 (B) 6 (C) 0 (D) −2 (E) −6

5. The memory capacity of one microcomputer is 4K bytes, whereas a larger computer has a memory capacity of 32K bytes (K = 1,024). The memory capacity of the larger computer is how many times that of the smaller?

   (A) 6
   (B) 6K
   (C) 8
   (D) 8K
   (E) 28

6. A set of numbers P is called "heavier" than a set of numbers Q if every number in P is exactly twice some number in Q. If $P = \{2, 6, 10, 14\}$, then P is "heavier" than which of the following?

   (A) $\left\{\frac{1}{2}, \frac{3}{2}, \frac{5}{2}, \frac{7}{2}\right\}$

   (B) $\{1, 2, 3, 4\}$

   (C) $\{1, 3, 4, 7\}$

   (D) $\{1, 3, 5, 7\}$

   (E) $\{4, 12, 20, 28\}$

7. In a certain city, the average (arithmetic mean) of the high temperature readings for four days was 63°F. If the high temperature readings on the first three days were 62°F, 56°F, and 68°F, respectively, what was the high reading on the fourth day in degrees Fahrenheit?

   (A) 70 (B) 66 (C) 63 (D) 62 (E) 58

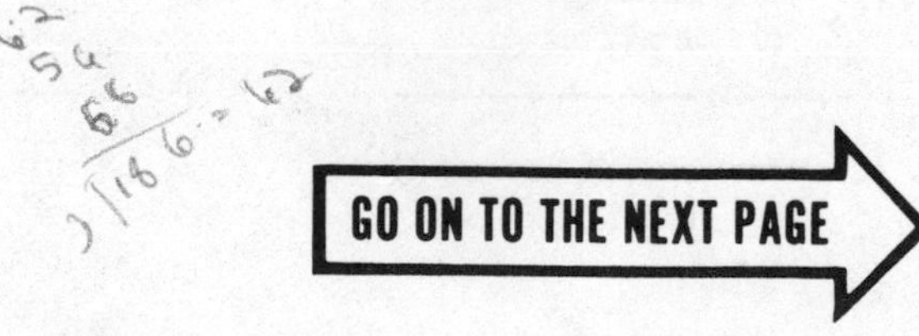

Questions 8-27 each consist of two quantities, one in Column A and one in Column B. You are to compare the two quantities and on the answer sheet blacken space

A if the quantity in Column A is greater;
B if the quantity in Column B is greater;
C if the two quantities are equal;
D if the relationship cannot be determined from the information given.

Notes:
1. In certain questions, information concerning one or both of the quantities to be compared is centered above the two columns.
2. In a given question, a symbol that appears in both columns represents the same thing in Column A as it does in Column B.
3. Letters such as x, n, and k stand for real numbers.

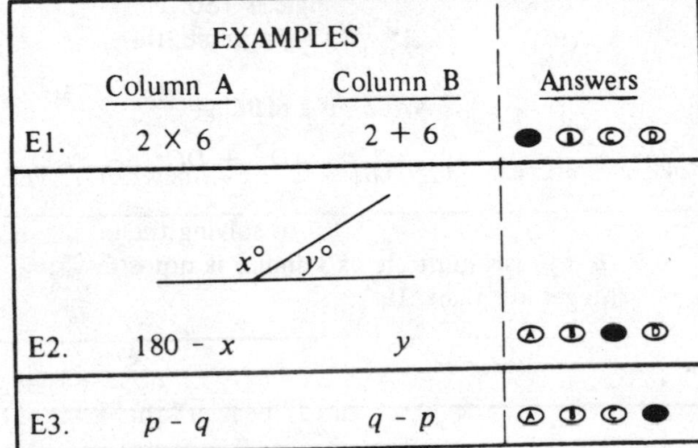

EXAMPLES

	Column A	Column B	Answers
E1.	2×6	$2 + 6$	● Ⓑ Ⓒ Ⓓ
E2.	$180 - x$	y	Ⓐ Ⓑ ● Ⓓ
E3.	$p - q$	$q - p$	Ⓐ Ⓑ Ⓒ ●

	Column A	Column B
8.	0	0×2
9.	$a + 25$	$a - 5$

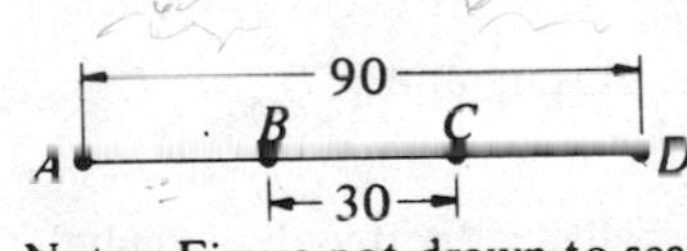

Note: Figure not drawn to scale.

On segment AD, length AB is not equal to length CD.

	Column A	Column B
10.	Length AC	Length BD

When a certain pitcher contains 3 cups of water, the pitcher contains half its capacity.

	Column A	Column B
11.	The capacity, in cups, of the pitcher	6 cups
12.	The cost of a stereo that is marked "15% off"	The cost of a television set that is marked "20% off"

	Column A	Column B

$x = -2$
$y = 1$

13.	The value of $3y^2 - 2x$	0

A triangle has angles with measures $x°$, $100°$, and $z°$.

14.	90	x
15.	$a(b + c)$	$b + c$

$y = 2x + 3$
$x \geq 0$

16.	x	y

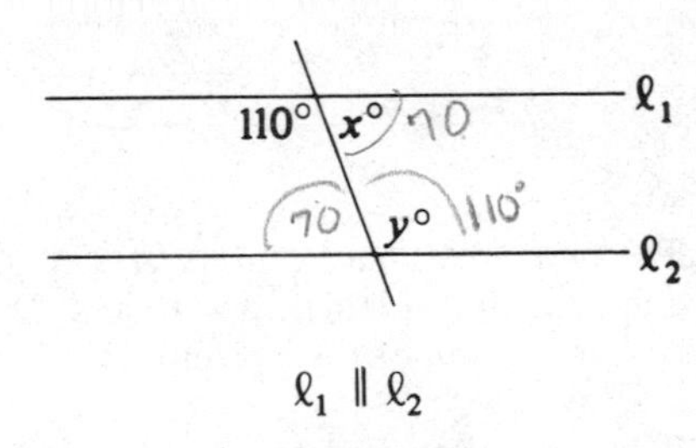

$\ell_1 \parallel \ell_2$

17.	$x + 40$	y

$-1, 0, 1, -1, 0, 1, \ldots$

The numbers $-1, 0, 1$ repeat in a sequence as shown.

18.	The 34th number in the sequence	0

GO ON TO THE NEXT PAGE

SUMMARY DIRECTIONS FOR COMPARISON QUESTIONS

Answer: A if the quantity in Column A is greater;
B if the quantity in Column B is greater;
C if the two quantities are equal;
D if the relationship cannot be determined from the information given.

	Column A	Column B
19.	A speed of one meter per second	A speed of 60 meters per hour

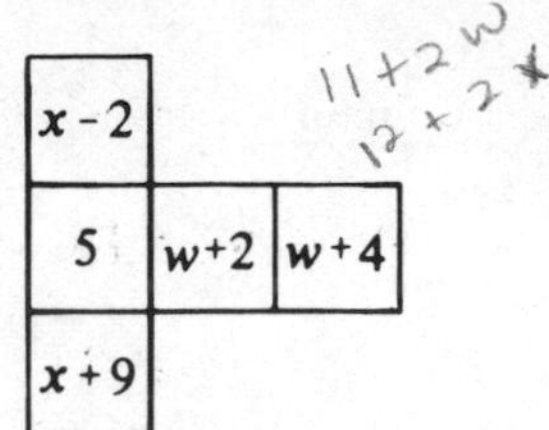

The sum of the three numbers in the column is equal to the sum of the three numbers in the row.

	Column A	Column B
20.	x	w

The ratio of Tina's weight to Rita's weight is 3 : 2.
The ratio of Rita's weight to Maria's weight is 1 : 2.

	Column A	Column B
21.	Tina's weight	Maria's weight

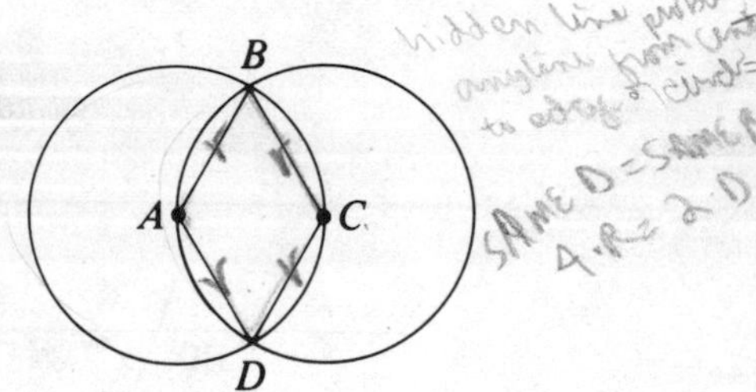

The two circles have centers A and C, respectively, and diameter of length x. B and D are the points of intersection of the two circles.

	Column A	Column B
22.	Perimeter of quadrilateral $ABCD$	$2x$

$y > 2x - 1$
$x > y$

	Column A	Column B
23.	x	1

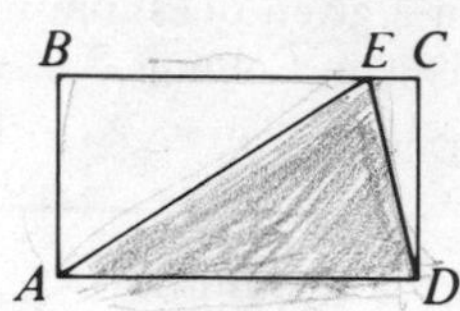

$ABCD$ is a rectangle.

	Column A	Column B
24.	Perimeter of ΔABE	Perimeter of ΔAED

$2n + 1$ is a multiple of 3 and n is a positive integer less than 10.

	Column A	Column B
25.	n	5

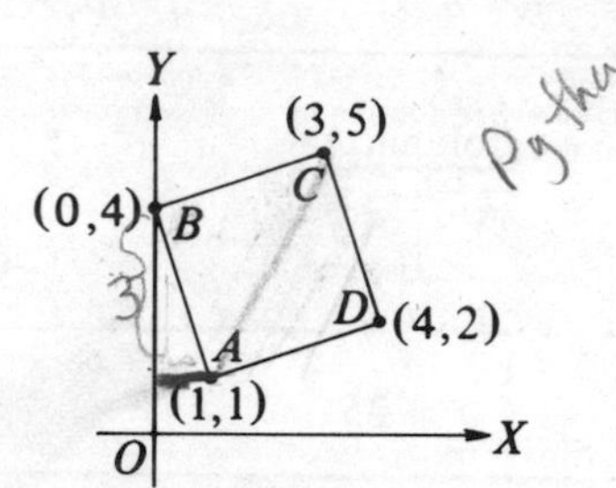

	Column A	Column B
26.	Area of square $ABCD$	10

x is called a "perfect hypercube" if $x = y^4$ and y is a positive integer.

	Column A	Column B
27.	The number of perfect hypercubes less than 1,000	5

GO ON TO THE NEXT PAGE

Solve each of the remaining problems in this section using any available space for scratchwork. Then decide which is the best of the choices given and blacken the corresponding space on the answer sheet.

28. The number of seniors at East High School is $\frac{2}{3}$ the number of juniors and the number of juniors is $\frac{3}{4}$ the number of sophomores. What is the number of seniors if the total enrollment for the three classes is 360 ?

(A) 160 (B) 120 (C) 100
(D) 80 (E) 60

Questions 29-30 refer to the operation defined by the equation $a \oplus b = ab + a$.

29. $3 \oplus 4 =$

(A) 7
(B) 12
(C) 15
(D) 16
(E) 21

30. If $4 \oplus 6 = x \oplus 5$, then $x =$

(A) 3 (B) $\frac{14}{3}$ (C) $\frac{24}{5}$ (D) 5 (E) 6

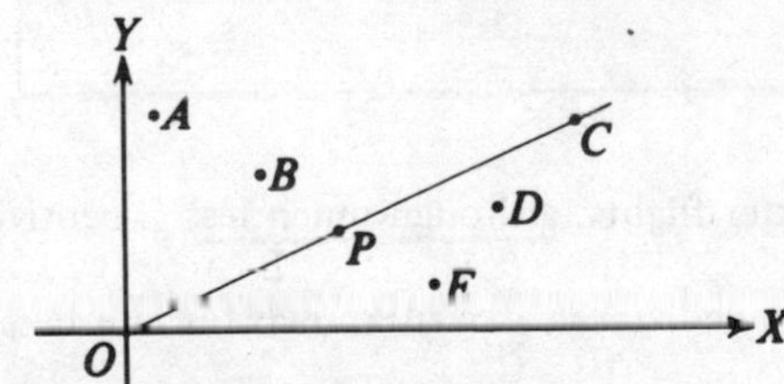

31. In the graph above, point P has coordinates (x, y). If $r > x > y > s$, which of the following points could have coordinates (r, s)?

(A) A (B) B (C) C (D) D (E) E

32. If $3 = b^x$, then $3b$ must equal

(A) b^{x+1}
(B) b^{x+2}
(C) b^{x+3}
(D) b^{2x}
(E) b^{3x}

$\sqrt{68}$ cm, 3 cm, 8 cm, 3 cm, 2 cm, $\sqrt{68}$ cm, 2 cm, 8 cm, 3 cm

33. If the wedge above is half of a rectangular solid, what is the total surface area of this wedge in square centimeters?

(A) $\sqrt{68} + 14$
(B) $\sqrt{68} + 46$
(C) $6\sqrt{68} + 14$
(D) $3\sqrt{68} + 46$
(E) $6\sqrt{68} + 46$

34. Jim is now twice as old as Polly. In 2 years Jim will be n years old. In terms of n, how old will Polly be then?

(A) $\frac{n}{2}$

(B) $\frac{n}{2} + 1$

(C) $\frac{n}{2} + 2$

(D) $n + 2$

(E) $2n$

35. The price of a shirt, after it was reduced 20 percent, was P dollars. What was the price of the shirt before the reduction?

(A) \$1.80P (B) \$1.25P (C) \$1.20P
(D) \$0.80P (E) \$0.75P

S T O P

IF YOU FINISH BEFORE TIME IS CALLED, YOU MAY CHECK YOUR WORK ON THIS SECTION ONLY. DO NOT WORK ON ANY OTHER SECTION IN THE TEST.

SECTION 6

Time—30 minutes

50 QUESTIONS

The questions in this section measure skills that are important to writing well. In particular, they test your ability to recognize and use language that is clear, effective, and correct according to the requirements of standard written English, the kind of English found in most college textbooks.

Directions: The following sentences contain problems in grammar, usage, diction (choice of words), and idiom.

Some sentences are correct.
No sentence contains more than one error.

You will find that the error, if there is one, is underlined and lettered. Assume that elements of the sentence that are not underlined are correct and cannot be changed. In choosing answers, follow the requirements of standard written English.

If there is an error, select the one underlined part that must be changed to make the sentence correct and blacken the corresponding space on your answer sheet.

If there is no error, blacken answer space Ⓔ .

EXAMPLE:

The region has a climate so severe that (A) plants growing there (B) rarely had been (C) more than twelve inches high. (D) No error (E)

SAMPLE ANSWER

Ⓐ Ⓑ ● Ⓓ Ⓔ

1. Most people listen to the weather forecast every day, but (A) they know hardly nothing (B) about (C) the forces that influence (D) the weather. No error (E)

2. Him (A) and the other (B) delegates immediately (C) accepted the resolution drafted by (D) the neutral states. No error (E)

3. The foundations of (A) psychoanalysis were established by Sigmund Freud, who begun (B) to develop (C) his theories in (D) the 1880's. No error (E)

4. Charter flights, although (A) much less (B) expensive than scheduled travel, is (C) well known for late takeoffs and other (D) inconveniences. No error (E)

5. Many women reenter the job market when (A) their (B) youngest (C) children started (D) kindergarten. No error (E)

6. After facing (A) so many groups of angry people, Martin Luther King, Jr. became accustomed to (B) confrontations that were (C) unpredictable and even (D) potentially explosive. No error (E)

GO ON TO THE NEXT PAGE

7. During (A) the early Middle Ages, before the development of the printing press, virtually (B) the only books were those (C) that are laboriously (D) copied by monks. No error (E)

8. The decision that has just been (A) agreed with (B) by the committee members should serve as a basis for their (C) work in the years to come (D). No error (E)

9. In her novels, Nella Larson focused on (A) the problems of young black women which (B) lived in (C) Europe and America during (D) the 1920's. No error (E)

10. As general supervisor, Ms. Rodríguez expects (A) her staff to work (B) as carefully and as hard (C) the way (D) she herself does. No error (E)

11. People who dislike cats sometimes (A) criticize them for being (B) aloof and independent; people who are fond of (C) cats often admire them for (D) the same qualities. No error (E)

12. Only a few feet (A) beyond (B) those abandoned and crumbling (C) buildings stand (D) a beautiful cluster of weeping willow trees. No error (E)

13. In contrasting to (A) the popular view, the characteristic way of life of many (B) Native American peoples was (C) neither nomadic nor (D) warlike. No error (E)

14. Until recently (A), Americans drank (B) five cups of coffee for every (C) cup of tea, but now they are drinking more of it (D). No error (E)

15. All our neighbors are wondering what (A) the government will do (B) about the raising (C) gasoline prices and the shortage of (D) oil. No error (E)

16. There are (A) certain areas of (B) the southern United States where (C) snow has never fallen (D). No error (E)

17. When (A) Pelé was playing (B) soccer, he was as talented as, or more talented than (C), baseball or basketball (D). No error (E)

18. The needs of children often (A) are not taken (B) into account (C) in the design of public buildings nor (D) residential areas. No error (E)

GO ON TO THE NEXT PAGE

19. In a recent created wildlife refuge, the birds
A
are now building their nests, thereby
B C
greatly changing the ecology of the area.
D
No error
E

20. Because flashes of light distract them, entertainers
A
often request that people with a camera refrain from
B C D
taking pictures during performances. No error
E

21. Color blindness may handicap one in some
A
respects, but you can still function normally
B C
in almost all situations you encounter. No error
D E

22. Rising at a rate of ten inches per hour, the Red River
A B
soon posed a serious threat to the residents of the
C D
valley. No error
E

23. Astronomy and astrology are both concerned in
A B
the heavenly bodies, but their purposes and
C
methods are quite different. No error
D E

24. As the discussion between the two candidates
A
continued, they spoke more and more loudly
B C
and with less and less dignity. No error
D E

25. The doctor lived in the tropics for three years
A B
before he was inflicted by malaria. No error
C D E

GO ON TO THE NEXT PAGE

Directions: In each of the following sentences, some part or all of the sentence is underlined. Below each sentence you will find five ways of phrasing the underlined part. Select the answer that produces the most effective sentence, one that is clear and exact, without awkwardness or ambiguity, and blacken the corresponding space on your answer sheet. In choosing answers, follow the requirements of standard written English. Choose the answer that best expresses the meaning of the original sentence.

Answer (A) is always the same as the underlined part. Choose answer (A) if you think the original sentence needs no revision.

EXAMPLE:

Laura Ingalls Wilder published her first book and she was sixty-five years old then.

(A) and she was sixty-five years old then
(B) when she was sixty-five years old
(C) at age sixty-five years old
(D) upon reaching sixty-five years
(E) at the time when she was sixty-five

SAMPLE ANSWER

26. Because dodo birds could not fly, so they were killed by the hogs and monkeys brought to the islands by the explorers.

(A) fly, so they were killed
(B) fly, they were killed
(C) fly and they were killed
(D) fly, and this allowed them to be killed
(E) fly, killing them

27. Performing before an audience for the first time, fear suddenly overcame the child and she could not remember her lines.

(A) fear suddenly overcame the child and she could not remember her lines
(B) the lines could not be remembered by the child because she was overcome by fear
(C) the child was suddenly overcome by fear and could not remember her lines
(D) the child was suddenly overcome by fear, she could not remember her lines
(E) suddenly the child was overcome by fear, and consequently not remembering her lines

28. Young people are not rejecting marriage, but some postponing it.

(A) some postponing it
(B) some are postponing it
(C) it is postponed by some of them
(D) it is being postponed
(E) some having postponed it

29. Violin makers know that the better the wood is seasoned, the better the results for the tone of the instrument.

(A) better the results for the tone of the instrument
(B) better the tone of the instrument
(C) better the result is for the instrument's tone
(D) resulting tone will be better
(E) result will be a better instrument tone

30. Although today many fabrics are made from synthetic fibers, at one time all natural fibers were used in their manufacture.

(A) all natural fibers were used in their manufacture
(B) all fabrics were made of natural fibers
(C) they were making them all of natural fibers
(D) they made fabrics all of natural fibers
(E) their manufacture was of all natural fibers

31. Between three and four per cent of all children born with hearing defects serious enough to require medical treatment.

(A) born with hearing defects
(B) being born with hearing defects that are
(C) are born with hearing defects
(D) are born with hearing defects, these are
(E) born with hearing defects which are

GO ON TO THE NEXT PAGE

6

32. Issued in Great Britain in 1840, the first gummed postage stamp in history was known as the "Penny Black."

(A) the first gummed postage stamp in history was known as
(B) they called the first gummed postage stamp in history
(C) history refers to the first gummed postage stamp as
(D) was the first gummed postage stamp in history,
(E) the first gummed postage stamp in history being known as

33. A number of parents are concerned about the protection of high school athletes and the many injuries being reported.

(A) athletes and the many injuries being reported
(B) athletes and numerous reports of injuries
(C) athletes because of reports of numerous injuries
(D) athletes, but many injuries are being reported
(E) athletes, numerous injuries have been reported

34. Many inferior films earn a great deal of money for their producers, some extremely good ones do not.

(A) Many inferior films earn
(B) Many an inferior film earns
(C) With many inferior films which earn
(D) However, many inferior films earn
(E) Although many inferior films earn

35. Gas rationing would force consumers to use their cars less, use public transportation more, while conserving gasoline.

(A) while conserving
(B) as well as conserving
(C) conserving
(D) and thereby conserve
(E) to conserve

36. Dolphins have a basic social organization, a system of communication, and their brains are highly developed.

(A) and their brains are highly developed
(B) and highly developed brains
(C) with highly developed brains
(D) while their brains are developed highly
(E) but their brains are developed highly

37. The Romans built many magnificent aqueducts and roads, they were truly the great engineers of the ancient world.

(A) roads, they were truly the great
(B) roads, consequently they were truly the great
(C) roads and as a consequence, they were truly the greatest
(D) roads; truly the great
(E) roads; they were truly the great

38. The Japanese began their remarkable postwar recovery, but they were able to recover from the psychological effects of the war.

(A) recovery, but they were
(B) recovery, where they were
(C) recovery only when they were
(D) recovery only when being
(E) recovery because it was

39. For success in sports, it is important not only to be in good physical condition but also to know the rules of the game.

(A) to be in good physical condition but also to know
(B) being in good physical condition but also to know
(C) to be in good physical condition but also knowing
(D) being in good physical condition but also knowing
(E) that one be in good physical condition but also that you know

40. Founded in 1910, the Urban League was established and has continuously had for its purpose the aim of assisting blacks who live in large cities.

(A) was established and has continuously had for its purpose the aim of
(B) was established to aim in the purpose of
(C) has continuously had for its purpose the aim of
(D) has always aimed at
(E) was with the purpose of

GO ON TO THE NEXT PAGE

Note: The remaining questions are like those at the beginning of the section.

Directions: For each sentence in which you find an error, select the one underlined part that must be changed to make the sentence correct and blacken the corresponding space on your answer sheet.

If there is no error, blacken answer space Ⓔ .

EXAMPLE:

The region has a climate so severe that plants
A
growing there rarely had been more than twelve
B C
inches high. No error
D E

SAMPLE ANSWER

Ⓐ Ⓑ ● Ⓓ Ⓔ

41. Idealists are not always as ignorant of realities as his
A B C
critics would like to believe. No error
D E

42. Once an Italian colony, Eritrea was captured by
A B
the British in 1941 and was united with Ethiopia
C
in the early 1950's. No error
D E

43. More women are competing in athletics as new
A B C
opportunities for training develop and as sports
programs will expand. No error
D E

44. Mayor Jameson was eager to demonstrate that she
A B
was not prejudiced in favor of any particular political
groups and residents of specific areas of the city.
C D
No error
E

45. In any lively debate, there is at least two sides to
A B C
an issue and five arguments for every point of
D
view presented. No error
E

46. After she had spoke for fifteen minutes, the
A
senator answered candidly the questions asked by
B
the reporters, whose skepticism was obvious.
C D
No error
E

47. Demonstrating new products is a more expensive
A
but more effective sales technique than
B
merely talking about them. No error
C D E

48. Moscow's city officials plan doubling the size of
A
the city's subway system, which already includes
B
more than one hundred miles of track. No error
C D E

49. The speaker argued that neither industry nor
A
government have taken full responsibility
B
for reducing the spiral of inflation. No error
C D E

50. The average taxpayer waits until April to file a
A
tax return unless they expect to receive a refund
B C
of considerable size. No error
D E

S T O P

IF YOU FINISH BEFORE TIME IS CALLED, YOU MAY CHECK YOUR WORK ON THIS SECTION ONLY. DO NOT WORK ON ANY OTHER SECTION IN THE TEST.

How to Score the Practice Test

Before you can find out what your scores are on the College Board 200 to 800 scale, you need to determine your SAT verbal and mathematical, and TSWE raw scores. The steps for doing so for each section of the test and a scoring worksheet are provided below. Use the table on page 64 to check your correct and incorrect answers for each section.

Determining Your Raw Scores

SAT-Verbal Sections 1 and 4

Step A: Count the number of correct answers for section 1 and record this number in the space provided on the worksheet. Then do the same for the incorrect answers. (Do not count omitted answers.) To determine subtotal A, use the formula:

$$\text{number correct} - \frac{\text{number incorrect}}{4} = \text{subtotal A}$$

Step B: Count the number of correct answers and the number of incorrect answers for section 4 and record the numbers in the spaces provided on the worksheet. To determine subtotal B, use the formula:

$$\text{number correct} - \frac{\text{number incorrect}}{4} = \text{subtotal B}$$

Step C: To obtain C, add subtotal A to subtotal B, keeping any decimals. Enter the resulting figure on the worksheet.

Step D: To obtain D, your raw verbal score, round C to the nearest whole number. (For example, any number from 44.50 to 45.49 rounds to 45.) Enter the resulting figure on the worksheet.

SAT-Mathematical Sections 2 and 5

Step A: Count the number of correct answers and the number of incorrect answers for section 2 and record the numbers in the spaces provided on the worksheet. To determine subtotal A, use the formula:

$$\text{number correct} - \frac{\text{number incorrect}}{4} = \text{subtotal A}$$

Step B: Count the number of correct answers and the number of incorrect answers for the *five-choice questions (questions 1 through 7 and 28 through 35)* in section 5 and record the numbers in the spaces provided on the worksheet. To determine subtotal B, use the formula:

$$\text{number correct} - \frac{\text{number incorrect}}{4} = \text{subtotal B}$$

Step C: Count the number of correct answers and the number of incorrect answers for the *four-choice questions (questions 8 through 27)* in section 5 and record the numbers in the spaces provided on the worksheet. To determine subtotal C, use the formula:

$$\text{number correct} - \frac{\text{number incorrect}}{3} = \text{subtotal C}$$

Step D: To obtain D, add subtotal A, subtotal B, and subtotal C, keeping any decimals. Enter the resulting figure on the worksheet.

Step E: To obtain E, your raw mathematical score, round D to the nearest whole number. (For example, any number from 44.50 to 45.49 rounds to 45.) Enter the resulting figure on the worksheet.

TSWE: Section 6

Step A: Count the number of correct answers for section 6 and record the number in the space provided on the worksheet. Then do the same for the incorrect answers. (Do not count omitted answers.) To determine your unrounded raw score, use the formula:

$$\text{number correct} - \frac{\text{number incorrect}}{4} = \text{total unrounded raw score}$$

Step B: To obtain B, your raw TSWE score, round A to the nearest whole number. (For example, any number from 34.50 to 35.49 rounds to 35.) Enter the resulting figure on the worksheet.

SCORING WORKSHEET FOR THE PRACTICE TEST

SAT-Verbal Sections

A. Section 1: ________ − 1/4 (________) = ________
no. correct — no. incorrect — subtotal A

B. Section 4: ________ − 1/4 (________) = ________
no. correct — no. incorrect — subtotal B

C. Total unrounded raw score (Total A + B) ________
C

D. Total rounded raw verbal score (Rounded to nearest whole number) ________
D

SAT-Mathematical Sections

A. Section 2: ________ − 1/4 (________) = ________
no. correct — no. incorrect — subtotal A

B. Section 5: Questions 1 through 7 and 28 through 35 (5-choice) ________ − 1/4 (________) = ________
no. correct — no. incorrect — subtotal B

C. Section 5: Questions 8 through 27 (4-choice) ________ − 1/3 (________) = ________
no. correct — no. incorrect — subtotal C

D. Total unrounded raw score (Total A + B + C) ________
D

E. Total rounded raw math score (Rounded to nearest whole number) ________
E

TSWE

A. Section 6: Total unrounded raw score ________ − 1/4 (________) = ________
no. correct — no. incorrect — A

B. Total rounded raw TSWE score (Rounded to nearest whole number) ________
B

ANSWERS TO PRACTICE TEST QUESTIONS AND PERCENTAGE OF STUDENTS ANSWERING EACH QUESTION CORRECTLY

Section 1—Verbal			Section 2—Mathematical			Section 4—Verbal			Section 5—Mathematical			Section 6—TSWE		
Question number	Correct answer	Percentage of students answering the question correctly	Question number	Correct answer	Percentage of students answering the question correctly	Question number	Correct answer	Percentage of students answering the question correctly	Question number	Correct answer	Percentage of students answering the question correctly	Question number	Correct answer	Percentage of students answering the question correctly
1	D	93%	1	D	93%	1	A	85%	1	B	89%	1	B	90%
2	E	88	2	B	76	2	D	68	2	D	80	2	A	94
3	A	82	3	D	82	3	B	63	3	C	70	3	B	90
4	C	82	4	D	70	4	D	74	4	E	72	4	C	78
5	D	77	5	A	88	5	C	63	5	C	60	5	D	86
6	E	61	6	C	81	6	E	43	6	D	71	6	E	88
7	A	67	7	C	84	7	A	35	7	B	63	7	D	74
8	A	55	8	A	63	8	D	29	8	C	98	8	B	64
9	D	36	9	E	65	9	C	25	9	A	79	9	B	80
10	B	47	10	B	45	10	A	29	10	D	76	10	D	74
11	E	26	11	E	66	11	A	86	11	C	82	11	E	88
12	C	29	12	D	61	12	B	70	12	D	85	12	D	64
13	C	28	13	E	62	13	A	89	13	A	82	13	A	52
14	D	31	14	E	58	14	E	54	14	A	72	14	D	72
15	E	26	15	A	48	15	D	53	15	D	68	15	C	70
16	B	94	16	C	58	16	C	92	16	B	72	16	E	76
17	D	93	17	A	43	17	C	81	17	C	65	17	D	66
18	B	88	18	A	41	18	C	72	18	B	71	18	D	65
19	C	74	19	D	31	19	D	50	19	A	48	19	A	52
20	D	37	20	A	24	20	E	61	20	B	40	20	C	43
21	B	70	21	C	29	21	B	49	21	B	42	21	A	50
22	A	56	22	E	17	22	B	41	22	C	41	22	E	63
23	C	56	23	B	15	23	C	23	23	B	23	23	B	57
24	E	38	24	B	19	24	C	30	24	B	37	24	E	47
25	D	55	25	D	10	25	A	21	25	D	26	25	D	44
26	C	52				26	C	59	26	C	18	26	B	92
27	B	50				27	E	71	27	C	13	27	C	68
28	C	36				28	D	37	28	D	28	28	B	88
29	C	65				29	A	87	29	C	71	29	B	50
30	A	38				30	D	78	30	B	35	30	B	60
31	A	52				31	A	43	31	E	38	31	C	74
32	E	17				32	D	24	32	A	19	32	A	67
33	A	39				33	D	24	33	D	23	33	C	59
34	C	22				34	B	49	34	B	13	34	E	70
35	A	09				35	C	68	35	B	08	35	D	56
36	B	87				36	C	25				36	B	66
37	D	70				37	E	71				37	E	53
38	E	74				38	B	22				38	C	60
39	A	45				39	C	21				39	A	62
40	B	58				40	D	29				40	D	29
41	C	41										41	C	67
42	B	18										42	E	72
43	C	21										43	D	75
44	E	20										44*	C	
45	D	16										45	B	48
												46	A	68
												47	E	61
												48	A	55
												49	B	42
												50	C	44

Notes: The percentages for the SAT-verbal and SAT-mathematical sections are based on the analysis of the answer sheets for a random sample of juniors and seniors who took this test in November 1982 and whose mean scores were 434 on the SAT-verbal sections and 473 on the SAT-mathematical sections.

The percentages for TSWE are based on the analysis of the answer sheets for a random sample of all students who took this test in April 1981 and whose mean score was 43.

*Question 44 in Section 6 in the edition of the TSWE administered on April 4, 1981, was not counted in computing scores. In the practice test in this book, this question is printed as it appears in a later edition.

SCORE CONVERSION TABLE
Practice SAT and TSWE

Raw Score	College Board Scaled Score		Raw Score	College Board Scaled Score		Raw Score	College Board Scaled Score
	SAT-Verbal	SAT-Math		SAT-Verbal	SAT-Math		TSWE
85	800		40	460	600		
84	780		39	450	590		
83	760		38	440	580		
82	750		37	440	570		
81	740		36	430	560	50	60 +
80	730		35	420	550	49	60 +
79	720		34	420	540	48	60 +
78	710		33	410	530	47	60 +
77	700		32	410	530	46	60 +
76	690		31	400	520	45	60 +
75	680		30	390	510	44	59
74	670		29	390	500	43	58
73	660		28	380	490	42	57
72	650		27	370	480	41	56
71	650		26	370	470	40	55
70	640		25	360	460	39	54
69	630		24	350	450	38	53
68	630		23	350	440	37	52
67	620		22	340	430	36	51
66	610		21	330	420	35	50
65	610		20	320	420	34	49
64	600		19	320	410	33	47
63	600		18	310	400	32	46
62	590		17	300	390	31	45
61	580		16	300	380	30	44
60	580	800	15	290	370	29	43
59	570	780	14	280	360	28	42
58	570	770	13	270	350	27	41
57	560	760	12	270	350	26	40
56	550	750	11	260	340	25	39
55	550	740	10	250	330	24	38
54	540	730	9	240	320	23	37
53	530	720	8	240	310	22	35
52	530	710	7	230	300	21	34
51	520	700	6	220	300	20	33
50	520	690	5	210	290	19	32
49	510	680	4	200	280	18	31
48	500	670	3	200	270	17	30
47	500	660	2	200	260	16	29
46	490	650	1	200	250	15	28
45	490	640	0	200	250	14	27
44	480	640	− 1	200	240	13	26
43	470	630	− 2	200	230	12	25
42	470	620	− 3	200	220	11	23
41	460	610	− 4	200	210	10	22
			− 5	200	210	9	21
			− 6 or below	200	200	8 or below	20

Finding Your College Board Scores

Use the table on page 65 to find the College Board scores that correspond to your raw scores on this edition of the SAT. For example, if you received a raw verbal score of 32 on this edition of the test, your College Board score would be 410. If your raw mathematical score were 22, your College Board score would be 430 for this edition. If your raw TSWE score were 31, your College Board score would be 45 for this edition.

Because some editions of the SAT may be slightly easier or more difficult than others, statistical adjustments are made in the scores to ensure that each College Board score indicates the same level of performance, regardless of the edition of the SAT you take. A given raw score will correspond to different College Board scores, depending on the edition of the test taken. A raw score of 40, for example, may convert to a College Board score of 460 on one edition of the SAT, but might convert to a College Board score of 480 on another edition of the test.

When you take the SAT, your score is likely to differ somewhat from the score you obtained on a sample test. People perform at different levels at different times, for reasons unrelated to the test itself. The precision of any test also is limited because it represents only a sample of all the possible questions that could be asked.

How Difficult Were the Questions?

The table on page 64 gives the percentages of a sample of students who chose the correct answer for each question. (These students obtained a mean SAT-verbal score of 434, mean SAT-mathematical score of 473, and mean TSWE score of 43.) These percentages will give you an idea of how difficult each question was.

For example, 77 percent of this group of students answered question 5 in verbal section 1 correctly. However, only 36 percent selected the correct answer for question 9 in section 1. In other words, question 5 was easier than question 9 for the students who took this edition of the SAT.

After the Test

Receiving Your Score Report

About six weeks after you take the SAT and TSWE, you will receive a report that includes your scores and percentile ranks. With the report, you'll receive a booklet, *Your Score Report*, which will help you interpret and understand the scores, percentile ranks, and other information on your report.

SAT Question-and-Answer Service

If you take the SAT on one of the dates for which the SAT Question-and-Answer Service is available, you may order the service anytime up to five months after the test date. You will receive a copy of your test questions and answer sheet, a list of the correct answers, and scoring instructions. See the *Student Bulletin* for additional information and an order form.

A Sample Score Report

A sample score report for a fictional student is provided on page 67. The report has five major parts:

1. Identification Information
   This is the information that will be used to identify your record, which is stored at Educational Testing Service. If you have any questions about your report, call or write to the College Board's Admissions Testing Program at the address given on page 8.

2. High School Information
   This information comes from the Student Descriptive Questionnaire (SDQ), which you fill out when you register to take the test. It describes your high school and summarizes your grades.

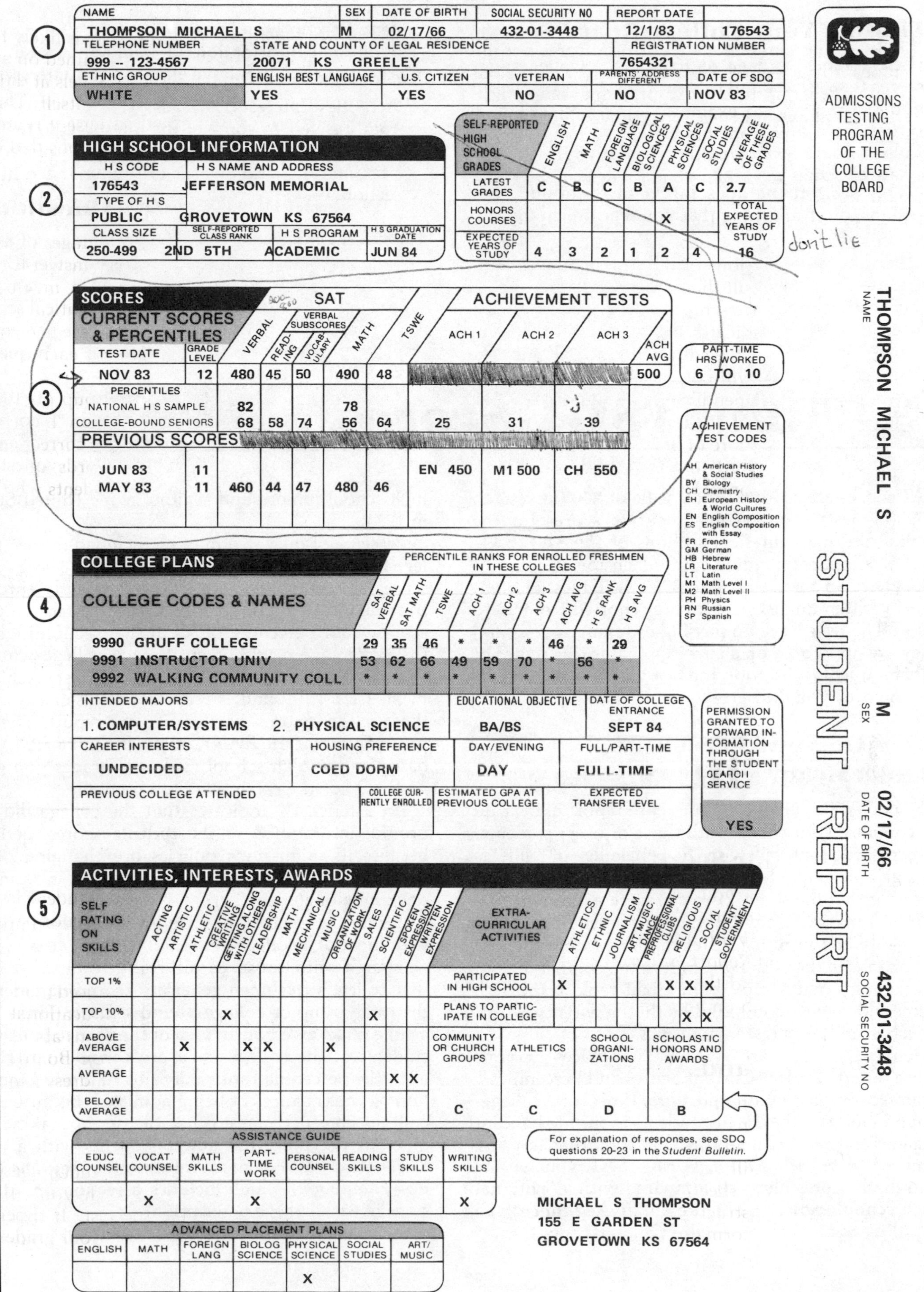

NAME	SEX	DATE OF BIRTH	SOCIAL SECURITY NO	REPORT DATE	
THOMPSON MICHAEL S	M	02/17/66	432-01-3448	12/1/83	176543

TELEPHONE NUMBER	STATE AND COUNTY OF LEGAL RESIDENCE	REGISTRATION NUMBER
999 -- 123-4567	20071 KS GREELEY	7654321

ETHNIC GROUP	ENGLISH BEST LANGUAGE	U.S. CITIZEN	VETERAN	PARENTS' ADDRESS DIFFERENT	DATE OF SDQ
WHITE	YES	YES	NO	NO	NOV 83

ADMISSIONS TESTING PROGRAM OF THE COLLEGE BOARD

HIGH SCHOOL INFORMATION

H S CODE	H S NAME AND ADDRESS		
176543	JEFFERSON MEMORIAL		
TYPE OF H S			
PUBLIC	GROVETOWN KS 67564		
CLASS SIZE	SELF-REPORTED CLASS RANK	H S PROGRAM	H S GRADUATION DATE
250-499	2ND 5TH	ACADEMIC	JUN 84

SELF-REPORTED HIGH SCHOOL GRADES	ENGLISH	MATH	FOREIGN LANGUAGE	BIOLOGICAL SCIENCES	PHYSICAL SCIENCES	SOCIAL STUDIES	AVERAGE OF THESE GRADES
LATEST GRADES	C	B	C	B	A	C	2.7
HONORS COURSES					X		TOTAL EXPECTED YEARS OF STUDY
EXPECTED YEARS OF STUDY	4	3	2	1	2	4	16

SCORES

CURRENT SCORES & PERCENTILES — TEST DATE	GRADE LEVEL	SAT VERBAL	VERBAL SUBSCORES: READING	VERBAL SUBSCORES: VOCABULARY	SAT MATH	TSWE	ACHIEVEMENT TESTS: ACH 1	ACH 2	ACH 3	ACH AVG
NOV 83	12	480	45	50	490	48				500
PERCENTILES — NATIONAL H S SAMPLE		82			78					
COLLEGE-BOUND SENIORS		68	58	74	56	64	25	31	39	
PREVIOUS SCORES										
JUN 83	11						EN 450	M1 500	CH 550	
MAY 83	11	460	44	47	480	46				

PART-TIME HRS WORKED
6 TO 10

ACHIEVEMENT TEST CODES

AH American History & Social Studies
BY Biology
CH Chemistry
EH European History & World Cultures
EN English Composition
ES English Composition with Essay
FR French
GM German
HB Hebrew
LR Literature
LT Latin
M1 Math Level I
M2 Math Level II
PH Physics
RN Russian
SP Spanish

COLLEGE PLANS

PERCENTILE RANKS FOR ENROLLED FRESHMEN IN THESE COLLEGES

COLLEGE CODES & NAMES	SAT VERBAL	SAT MATH	TSWE	ACH 1	ACH 2	ACH 3	ACH AVG	H S RANK	H S AVG
9990 GRUFF COLLEGE	29	35	46	*	*	*	46	*	29
9991 INSTRUCTOR UNIV	53	62	66	49	59	70	*	56	*
9992 WALKING COMMUNITY COLL	*	*	*	*	*	*	*	*	*

INTENDED MAJORS	EDUCATIONAL OBJECTIVE	DATE OF COLLEGE ENTRANCE
1. COMPUTER/SYSTEMS 2. PHYSICAL SCIENCE	BA/BS	SEPT 84

CAREER INTERESTS	HOUSING PREFERENCE	DAY/EVENING	FULL/PART-TIME
UNDECIDED	COED DORM	DAY	FULL-TIME

PREVIOUS COLLEGE ATTENDED	COLLEGE CURRENTLY ENROLLED	ESTIMATED GPA AT PREVIOUS COLLEGE	EXPECTED TRANSFER LEVEL

PERMISSION GRANTED TO FORWARD INFORMATION THROUGH THE STUDENT SEARCH SERVICE
YES

ACTIVITIES, INTERESTS, AWARDS

SELF RATING ON SKILLS	ACTING	ARTISTIC	ATHLETIC	CREATIVE WRITING	GETTING ALONG WITH OTHERS	LEADERSHIP	MATH	MECHANICAL	MUSIC	ORGANIZATION OF WORK	SALES	SCIENTIFIC	SPOKEN EXPRESSION	WRITTEN EXPRESSION
TOP 1%														
TOP 10%					X							X		
ABOVE AVERAGE			X			X	X			X				
AVERAGE													X	X
BELOW AVERAGE														

EXTRACURRICULAR ACTIVITIES	ATHLETICS	ETHNIC	JOURNALISM	ART, MUSIC, DANCE	PREPROFESSIONAL CLUBS	RELIGIOUS	SOCIAL	STUDENT GOVERNMENT
PARTICIPATED IN HIGH SCHOOL	X					X	X	X
PLANS TO PARTICIPATE IN COLLEGE							X	X

COMMUNITY OR CHURCH GROUPS	ATHLETICS	SCHOOL ORGANIZATIONS	SCHOLASTIC HONORS AND AWARDS
C	C	D	B

For explanation of responses, see SDQ questions 20-23 in the *Student Bulletin*.

ASSISTANCE GUIDE							
EDUC COUNSEL	VOCAT COUNSEL	MATH SKILLS	PART-TIME WORK	PERSONAL COUNSEL	READING SKILLS	STUDY SKILLS	WRITING SKILLS
	X		X				X

ADVANCED PLACEMENT PLANS						
ENGLISH	MATH	FOREIGN LANG	BIOLOG SCIENCE	PHYSICAL SCIENCE	SOCIAL STUDIES	ART/MUSIC
				X		

MICHAEL S THOMPSON
155 E GARDEN ST
GROVETOWN KS 67564

THOMPSON MICHAEL S
NAME

STUDENT REPORT

M
SEX

02/17/66
DATE OF BIRTH

432-01-3448
SOCIAL SECURITY NO

3. Scores
   This section summarizes your test scores and includes all of your scores from any Admissions Testing Program tests (SAT or Achievement Test) that you have taken at any time while in high school.
4. College Plans
   This section includes information about your plans for future study that you reported in the Student Descriptive Questionnaire. It also provides additional information, if available, about colleges in which you have expressed an interest.
5. Activities, Interests, Awards
   Your answers to some of the questions in the Student Descriptive Questionnaire about your activities, interests, and awards are summarized in this section.

SAT and TSWE Scores

SAT scores are reported on a scale of 200 (lowest) to 800 (highest). You receive separate scores for the verbal and mathematical sections of the SAT. SAT-verbal subscores (reading comprehension and vocabulary) are on a scale of 20 to 80. TSWE (Test of Standard Written English) scores are reported from 20 to 60+. The tests have no passing or failing scores, and they are not scored on a curve — that is, the scores of other students who took the test with you had no effect on how you did.

What Do Your Percentile Ranks Mean?

The percentile ranks on your score report allow you to compare your scores with those of other students. A percentile rank tells you the percentage of students in a given group whose scores were below yours. Remember that the same score can have a different percentile rank for different groups, depending on the ability of the group. (For example, a runner whose time ranks in the 80th percentile when compared with the junior varsity track team might rank in the 50th percentile when compared with the varsity team, which usually has faster runners.)

Percentile ranks are given in two places on your score report. Under "Current Scores and Percentiles," your scores are compared with those of "college-bound seniors," that is, all students in the most recent high school graduating class who took that test any time while in high school. For the SAT, your verbal and math scores also are compared with a "national high school sample," a representative sample of all high school juniors and seniors in the United States in 1974.

Percentile ranks also may be included in the "College Plans" section of your score report. There, your scores are compared with those of recently enrolled freshmen in each college you named to receive your scores. Your percentile ranks in that section indicate the percentage of freshmen in each college who received lower scores than you on each test. Achievement Tests 1, 2, and 3 represent the same tests as those in the "Scores" section of your report. The last two columns (HS RANK and HS AVERAGE) are based on the high school rank and grades you gave on the Student Descriptive Questionnaire.

An asterisk (*) indicates that the college did not provide information on its students' scores, perhaps because its admissions policies are changing or its programs are too varied to be described in terms of one group of students.

If your percentile ranks are lower when compared with those of a college's enrolled freshmen than when compared with those of all college-bound seniors, that college's freshmen generally scored higher than the total group of college-bound seniors. These percentile ranks give you an idea of the academic level of students at the colleges you are considering. However, the percentile ranks may not be a good indication of your chances of being admitted, because most colleges consider many other factors in making admissions decisions and admit students with a wide range of scores. For more information, see *The College Handbook,* which includes a section on admissions in each college description.

How Precise Are Your Scores?

When you consider your scores, keep in mind that no test can measure anyone's abilities with perfect accuracy. If you took a different edition of a test or the same edition on different days, your score probably would be different each time. If you were to take a test an infinite number of times, your scores would tend to cluster about an average value. Testing specialists call this average your "true score," the score you would get if a test could measure your ability with perfect accuracy. To measure the extent to which students' obtained scores vary from their true scores, an index called the standard error of measurement (SEM) is used.

For the SAT, the SEM is about 30 points. About two-thirds of those taking the test score within 30 points (or one SEM) of their true score. If your true score is 430, for example, the chances are about 2 out of 3 that you will score between 400 and 460 (430 plus or minus 30).

You should think of your scores in terms of score bands rather than precise measurements — a 400 SAT score, for example, should be thought of as probably being anywhere between 370 and 430. This will help you realize that a small difference between your score and another student's on the same test may not indicate any real difference in ability. College admissions officers also are advised to look at scores this way.

Will Your Scores Go Up if You Take the Test Again?

As indicated earlier, you are not likely to get exactly the same score on a test twice. Improving your score a great deal also is unlikely. Some students who repeat tests do improve their scores, but, on the average, these increases are small.

The *average* increase for a junior who takes the SAT again when a senior is about 15 points for the verbal score and 15 points for the math score. About two out of three students who retake the test improve their scores, but the scores of about one student in three go down. About one student in 20 gains 100 or more points, and about one in 100 loses 100 or more points. Students whose first SAT scores are low are more likely to achieve score gains. Students whose initial scores are high are less likely to achieve score gains.

If you repeat a test, all your scores appear on your score report. Colleges evaluate multiple scores on the same test in different ways. Some look at all the scores on your report; others use just the highest, most recent, or an average.

Who Receives Your Scores?

A copy of your report will be sent to your high school if you give your high school code number when you register for the test. Reports also will be sent to any colleges and scholarship programs whose code numbers you give. These are listed in the "College Plans" section of the report sent to you and to your high school.

The College Board may use your scores and descriptive information for research, but no information that can be identified with you is ever released without your consent.

How Do Colleges Use Your Score Report?

Your SAT scores give college admissions officers an idea of how far you have developed some of the abilities you will need to do well in college courses. The scores also help them compare you more easily with students from schools with various grading standards. Admissions people know that although your high school grades are the best *single* indicator of your readiness to do college work, a combination of your high school grades and your SAT scores together provides a better indicator than either one alone.

Some colleges also use Achievement Tests in making admissions decisions, for course placement, or both. The TSWE is a placement test designed to identify students who may need help in developing their writing skills. Your college may use it to help place you in the freshman English course that is right for you.

Colleges vary in the way they use test scores, but few, if any, make admissions decisions based on scores alone. Therefore, low or high scores should neither discourage you nor make you overconfident. Admissions officers often consider the descriptive information on your score report as well as other information sent by you and your school.

Different colleges value different qualities in applicants: One college may be looking for leadership potential, while another may place more weight on various extracurricular activities. Some colleges have open admissions policies and admit almost all applicants. Some will admit students with particular qualities they want, even if the students' grades and scores indicate they will have to make an extra effort. Whatever your scores, remember that probably there are many colleges that could meet your needs and where you would be happy.

SAT
Form Code 2I

FORM CODE 2I

1

SECTION 1

Time—30 minutes

45 QUESTIONS

For each question in this section, choose the best answer and blacken the corresponding space on the answer sheet.

Each question below consists of a word in capital letters, followed by five lettered words or phrases. Choose the word or phrase that is most nearly opposite in meaning to the word in capital letters. Since some of the questions require you to distinguish fine shades of meaning, consider all the choices before deciding which is best.

Example:

GOOD: (A) sour (B) bad (C) red (D) hot (E) ugly

Ⓐ ● Ⓒ Ⓓ Ⓔ

1. HUMANE: (A) mutinous (B) brutal (C) misty (D) lavish (E) proud

2. SERVICEABLE: (A) informal (B) useless (C) impure (D) unfamiliar (E) temporary

3. SCOFF AT: (A) impose on (B) follow up (C) quarrel with (D) get away with (E) speak highly of

4. DILUTE: (A) concentrate (B) infiltrate (C) extricate (D) excavate (E) accelerate

5. CONVERGE: (A) avoid (B) stop (C) wind down (D) move apart (E) fall behind

6. JEOPARDIZE: (A) hasten (B) exaggerate (C) shelter (D) turn aside (E) melt away

7. ABHOR: (A) confuse (B) shout (C) advise (D) unite (E) admire

8. DISSUADE: (A) explain (B) argue (C) address (D) detail (E) induce

9. AUGMENT: (A) immobilize (B) reduce (C) parody (D) irritate (E) hide

10. VERDANT: (A) false (B) unlikely (C) moist (D) unclear (E) barren

11. AMASS: (A) err (B) squander (C) prolong (D) conceal (E) beautify

12. EPHEMERAL: (A) numerical (B) timeless (C) methodical (D) peerless (E) fearful

13. EXTRANEOUS: (A) intermediate (B) inaccessible (C) relevant (D) intermittent (E) effective

Mar 85 gun

14. FURTIVE: (A) flagrant (B) refined (C) confused (D) creative (E) inquisitive

15. INNOCUOUS: (A) indigent (B) restrained (C) ambitious (D) injurious (E) understandable

Each sentence below has one or two blanks, each blank indicating that something has been omitted. Beneath the sentence are five lettered words or sets of words. Choose the word or set of words that best fits the meaning of the sentence as a whole.

Example:

Although its publicity has been ----, the film itself is intelligent, well-acted, handsomely produced, and altogether ----.

(A) tasteless. .respectable (B) extensive. .moderate (C) sophisticated. .amateur (D) risqué. .crude (E) perfect. .spectacular

● Ⓑ Ⓒ Ⓓ Ⓔ

16. Although few in number, women in Congress have had ---- impact on a variety of issues.

(A) an arbitrary
(B) a negligible
(C) a substantial
(D) a minor
(E) an inadvertent

17. As a scientist, Leonardo da Vinci was capable of ----, but his mistakes are remarkably few in light of his ----.

(A) error. .accomplishments
(B) artistry. .failures
(C) genius. .works
(D) trivia. .lapses
(E) innovation. .achievements

18. In a recent biography of this renowned millionaire, the subject emerges as a ---- and gentle man, proving that money does not necessarily ----.

(A) lonely. .alienate
(B) perceptive. .enlighten
(C) generous. .corrupt
(D) dignified. .ennoble
(E) headstrong. .liberate

19. Goodrich's summary of the aims of modern science is so ---- as to be useless; he seems to consider everything and its opposite to be aims.

(A) unobtrusive (B) discriminatory (C) generalized (D) skeptical (E) practical

20. Drake hungered for riches, and with this ---- came a ruthless capacity for action.

(A) indolence (B) avarice (C) aversion (D) irresolution (E) fantasy

GO ON TO THE NEXT PAGE

1

Each passage below is followed by questions based on its content. Answer all questions following a passage on the basis of what is stated or implied in that passage.

Beowulf, the greatest extant work composed in Old English, is thought to have been written in England during the first half of the eighth century A.D. It is a historical poem about the pagan past, or an attempt at one–literal historical fidelity founded on modern research was, of course, unknown at the time. It is a poem by a learned Christian writing of earlier times, who, looking back on the heroism and sorrow, feels in them something permanent and something symbolical.

Nearly all the censure, and most of the praise, that has been bestowed on *Beowulf* has been due either to the belief that it was something that it was not–for example, primitive, pagan, an allegory (political or mythical), or most often, an epic; or to disappointment at the discovery that it was itself and not something that the scholar would have liked better–for example, a heathen heroic ballad, a history of Sweden, a manual of Germanic antiquities, or a statement of Nordic theology.

The pitfalls of such an approach to *Beowulf* are best expressed in an allegory. A man inherited a field in which there was an accumulation of old stone, part of an old hall. Of the old stone, some had already been used in building the house in which the man actually lived, not far from the old house of his ancestors. Of the rest, the man took some and built a tower. But when his friends came, they perceived at once (without troubling to climb the steps) that these stones had formerly belonged to a more ancient building. So they pushed the tower over, with no little labor, in order to look for hidden carvings and inscriptions, or to discover when the man's distant ancestors had obtained their building material. Some, suspecting a deposit of coal under the soil, began to dig for it and forgot even the stones. They all said: "This tower is most interesting." But they also said (after pushing it over): "What a muddle it is in!" And even the man's own descendants, who might have been expected to consider what he had been about, were heard to murmur: "He is such an odd fellow! Imagine his using these old stones just to build a nonsensical tower! Why did he not restore the old house? He had no sense of proportion." But from the top of that tower the man had been able to look out upon the sea.

21. Which of the following would be the most appropriate title for the passage?
    (A) *Beowulf*: An Anglo-Saxon Masterpiece
    (B) *Beowulf* As Allegory
    (C) How Not to Read *Beowulf*
    (D) The Historical Accuracy of *Beowulf*
    (E) The Tower in *Beowulf*

22. According to the passage, the author of *Beowulf* saw the past as
    (A) needing to be preserved in the most minute detail possible
    (B) leading naturally to Christian beliefs of the eighth century
    (C) possessing something valuable for people of all times
    (D) demonstrating a violence that has since vanished
    (E) containing a complex and fascinating literature

23. In the allegory, it can be inferred that the man who built the tower represents
    (A) the author of the passage
    (B) one of the scholars who criticize *Beowulf*
    (C) the poet who wrote *Beowulf*
    (D) the main character of *Beowulf*
    (E) the poem *Beowulf* itself

24. Which of the following statements best expresses the message of the allegory?
    (A) Scholarly research always does more harm than good.
    (B) The best way to understand a work of art is to take it apart and examine the pieces.
    (C) Art should be practical and not merely enjoyable.
    (D) Those who focus on their own interests often miss the point of a work of art.
    (E) Only works of art that are entirely original will last.

25. The author's attitude toward the *Beowulf* critics described in the passage is one of
    (A) tolerant acceptance
    (B) grudging admiration
    (C) unallayed suspicion
    (D) gentle mockery
    (E) lofty indifference

GO ON TO THE NEXT PAGE

Tuberculosis, measles, chicken pox, mumps, and influenza constitute a roster of infectious diseases with which people of traditional urban societies remain well acquainted. For all these diseases except tuberculosis and influenza, a single case of illness forms antibodies in the bloodstream that give the individual prolonged, often lifelong, immunity. As a result, these diseases have most commonly afflicted children, and continue to do so where vaccinations and other artificial methods have not altered the natural patterns of disease propagation. In traditional urban societies, such childhood diseases need not be very serious, in the sense that nursing care can usually assure recovery. When a given population has adapted sufficiently to survive the childhood diseases that can only persist among large, concentrated human populations, it has acquired a very potent biological weapon. For these same infections, when invading a human population without any previous exposure to them, are likely to kill a high proportion of those who fall sick. Infections in all populations usually manifest their greatest virulence among young adults, owing, some doctors believe, to excessive vigor in this age-group's antibody reactions to the invading disease organism. Epidemic population losses within the twenty-to-forty age bracket are obviously far more damaging to society at large than comparably numerous destruction of either the very young or the very old. If an initial exposure of a society to one unfamiliar infection is swiftly followed by similarly destructive exposure to others, the structural cohesion of the community is almost certain to collapse.

Historians studying political and social changes brought about by invasions and military campaigns have found that epidemiologists can shed considerable light on their work. The disruptive effect of an epidemic on a population without immunities is likely to be even greater than the actual loss of life, severe as that may be. Often survivors are demoralized and lose all faith in age-old customs and beliefs that had not prepared them for such a disaster. For example, there were significant psychological and social consequences of the medical fact that a smallpox epidemic arrived in Mexico with the Spaniards and decimated the Aztec population during the conquest. An unknown disease that killed only Aztecs and left the invaders unharmed seemed to show a partiality that could only be explained by both parties as supernatural, and that circumstance left little room for doubt about which side of the struggle enjoyed divine favor. The religions, priesthoods, and ways of life built around the traditional Aztec gods were unable to compete with such a demonstration of the impressive power of the god worshipped by the Spanish.

26. Which of the following is the most suitable title for this passage?

(A) New Forms of Old Diseases
(B) Childhood Diseases in the New World
(C) Effects of Infection on Ancient Civilizations
(D) The Epidemic as a Force in Social Change
(E) Invasions, Conquests, and Mortality

27. The author focuses on the interaction between infectious diseases and human populations in order to show that the relationship

(A) has been overemphasized by public health agencies
(B) is responsible for the development of traditional urban societies
(C) can have political and social repercussions
(D) reveals novel aspects of human physiology
(E) must be appreciated before civilization can advance

28. According to the passage, which of the following is true when an infectious disease has been present in a population for a long time?

(A) A large portion of the population has developed long-term immunity.
(B) The population has had little or no contact with the diseases of neighboring populations.
(C) The percentage of 20 to 40 year olds in the population becomes disproportionately small.
(D) Standards of nursing care are not very high.
(E) The social structure has recently been drastically altered.

29. Which of the following is implied by the statement about the Aztec religious institutions being "unable to compete" (line 54) with the Spanish god?

(A) The Spanish missionaries were extraordinarily persuasive.
(B) The Aztec society enthusiastically adopted Spanish values.
(C) The epidemic did not appear to affect the strength of the Aztecs.
(D) Neither the Aztecs nor the Spanish had elaborate religious rituals.
(E) The Aztecs and the Spanish thought immunity to a disease might indicate divine favor.

30. How is the second paragraph related to the first paragraph?

(A) It demonstrates the need for mass immunization against the diseases described in the first paragraph.
(B) It illustrates the historical significance of the medical principles described in the first paragraph.
(C) It challenges the assumption in the first paragraph that infections are not a major health hazard.
(D) It repeats the description given in the first paragraph of infectious disease among an affected population.
(E) It points out the need for more medical information about the contagious diseases described in the first paragraph.

GO ON TO THE NEXT PAGE

Select the word or set of words that best completes each of the following sentences.

31. We were less offended by the irate professor's ---- than we were curious about how he had gained this familiarity with a stevedore's vocabulary.

(A) profanity (B) apathy (C) sophistry (D) pretentiousness (E) punctiliousness

32. The indigenous inhabitants of America have been called "Indians" thanks to one of the greatest ---- ever to be ---- by history: when Columbus discovered the New World, he thought he had reached India.

(A) enigmas. .foreshadowed
(B) misnomers. .obliterated
(C) predictions. .immortalized
(D) misapprehensions. .hallowed
(E) truths. .contradicted

33. Although aware of the hazards of extrapolating a life-style from a bone fragment or the reconstruction of a skull, most anthropologists by the nature of their work are inclined to indulge in ----.

(A) indecision (B) pessimism (C) reticence (D) skepticism (E) speculation

34. Considering the ---- of Juan Rulfo's published works and their enduring influence, we can conclude that few other writers have ---- so much in so few pages.

(A) abstruseness. .divulged
(B) paucity. .contributed
(C) immaturity. .developed
(D) vituperation. .experienced
(E) realism. .printed

35. Such a solemn, almost ---- tone is not really appropriate for this biography because, although its subject experienced many misfortunes, she strongly believed in the value of ----.

(A) reverent. .accuracy
(B) pompous. .catharsis
(C) lugubrious. .levity
(D) supercilious. .fatalism
(E) incongruous. .candor

Each question below consists of a related pair of words or phrases, followed by five lettered pairs of words or phrases. Select the lettered pair that best expresses a relationship similar to that expressed in the original pair.

Example:

YAWN : BOREDOM :: (A) dream : sleep (B) anger : madness (C) smile : amusement (D) face : expression (E) impatience : rebellion

Ⓐ Ⓑ ● Ⓓ Ⓔ

36. STANZA : POEM :: (A) prose : story (B) rhyme : proverb (C) climax : play (D) comedy : tragedy (E) chapter : novel

37. ISOLATE : APART :: (A) agitate : lengthy (B) refrigerate : cool (C) duplicate : alone (D) concentrate : active (E) regulate : large

38. PATENT : INVENTOR ::
(A) advertisement : merchant
(B) money : customer
(C) copyright : author
(D) monopoly : consumer
(E) novelty : journalist

39. SUGARCOATING : TASTE :: (A) analysis : thought (B) eyelid : sight (C) static : sound (D) perfume : smell (E) regret : pleasure

40. LETTER : CORRESPONDENCE :: (A) hunger : nutrition (B) invitation : loneliness (C) bell : silence (D) lock : entry (E) comment : dialogue

41. STRUT : VANITY :: (A) flaunt : humility (B) swagger : pride (C) amble : determination (D) cringe : dignity (E) simper : greed

42. QUIP : CLEVER :: (A) insult : derogatory (B) hint : tactless (C) plea : superficial (D) pledge : truthful (E) complaint : valid

43. STALEMATE : VICTORY :: (A) strategy : diplomacy (B) bias : impartiality (C) majority : election (D) satisfaction : peace (E) leadership : battle

44. SEQUESTER : JURY :: (A) eradicate : problem (B) quarantine : patient (C) elect : politician (D) liquidate : opponent (E) evacuate : city

45. DESPOT : RULER :: (A) counselor : potentate (B) teller : banker (C) peasant : duchess (D) magnate : businessman (E) anarchist : authority

S T O P

IF YOU FINISH BEFORE TIME IS CALLED, YOU MAY CHECK YOUR WORK ON THIS SECTION ONLY. DO NOT WORK ON ANY OTHER SECTION IN THE TEST.

SECTION 2

Time—30 minutes

25 QUESTIONS

In this section solve each problem, using any available space on the page for scratchwork. Then decide which is the best of the choices given and blacken the corresponding space on the answer sheet.

The following information is for your reference in solving some of the problems.

Circle of radius r: Area $= \pi r^2$; Circumference $= 2\pi r$
The number of degrees of arc in a circle is 360.
The measure in degrees of a straight angle is 180.

Definitions of symbols:

$=$	is equal to	$\leqq$	is less than or equal to
$\neq$	is unequal to	$\geqq$	is greater than or equal to
$<$	is less than	$\parallel$	is parallel to
$>$	is greater than	$\perp$	is perpendicular to

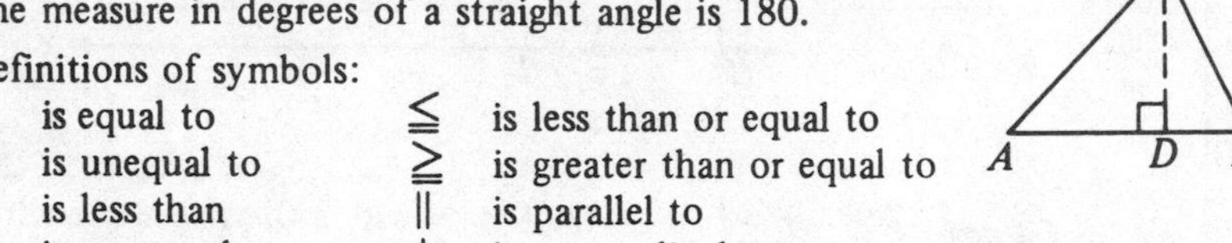

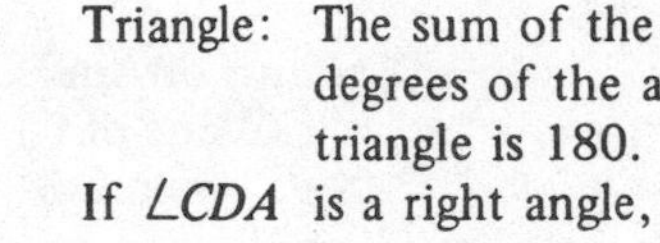

Triangle: The sum of the measures in degrees of the angles of a triangle is 180.

If $\angle CDA$ is a right angle, then

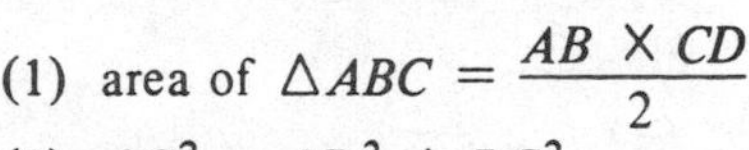

(1) area of $\triangle ABC = \dfrac{AB \times CD}{2}$

(2) $AC^2 = AD^2 + DC^2$

Note: Figures which accompany problems in this test are intended to provide information useful in solving the problems. They are drawn as accurately as possible EXCEPT when it is stated in a specific problem that its figure is not drawn to scale. All figures lie in a plane unless otherwise indicated. All numbers used are real numbers.

---

1. If $6 - x = 0$, then $10 - x =$

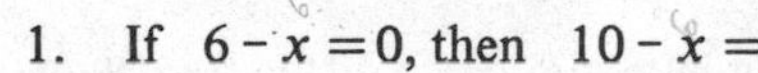

(A) 16 (B) 10 (C) 6 (D) 4 (E) 0

2. Joe buys a tennis racket and one can of tennis balls for \$38. Mary buys the same-priced racket and two cans of the same-priced tennis balls for \$41. How much does one of these rackets cost?

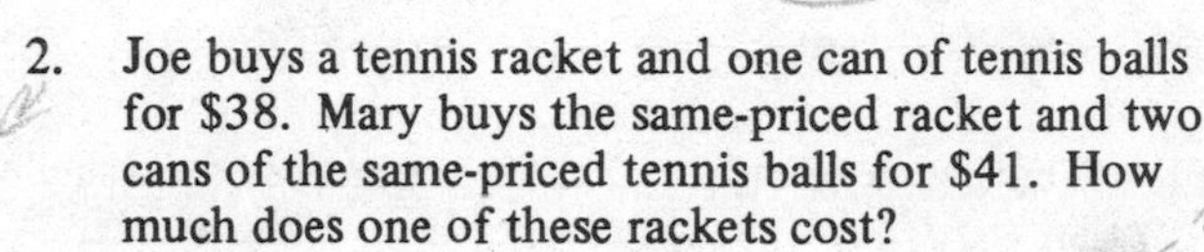

(A) \$33
(B) \$34
(C) \$35
(D) \$36
(E) \$37

3. Kim was k years of age 2 years ago. In terms of k, how old will Kim be 2 years from now?

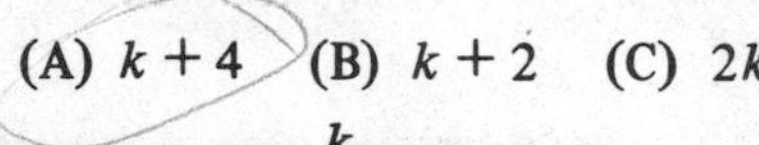

(A) $k + 4$ (B) $k + 2$ (C) $2k$

(D) k (E) $\dfrac{k}{2}$

4. Club A has 10 members and Club B has 15. If a total of 21 people belong to the two clubs, how many people belong to both clubs?

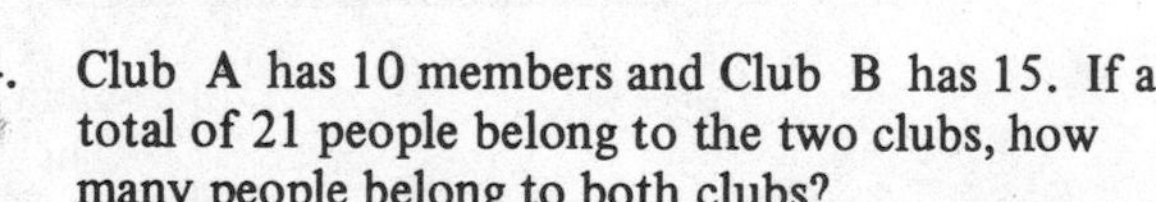

(A) 3
(B) 4
(C) 5
(D) 6
(E) 7

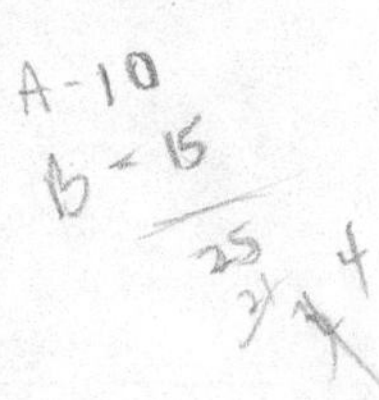

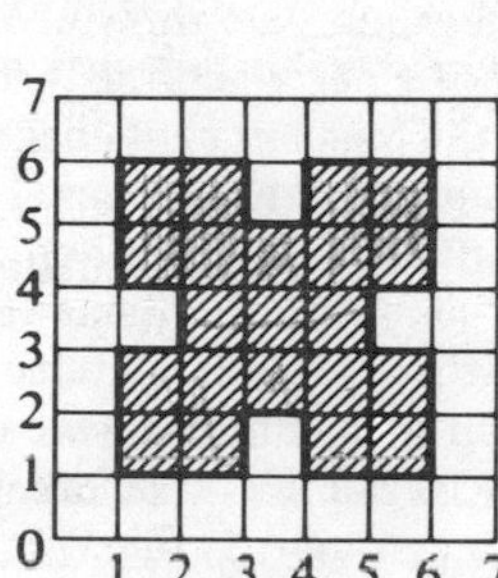

5. In the figure above, what is the area of the shaded region?

(A) 21 (B) 24 (C) 25 (D) 28 (E) 32

GO ON TO THE NEXT PAGE

6. If $x - y = 7$, what is the value of $x^2 - y^2$?

(A) 0
(B) 14
(C) 49
(D) 98
(E) It cannot be determined from the information given.

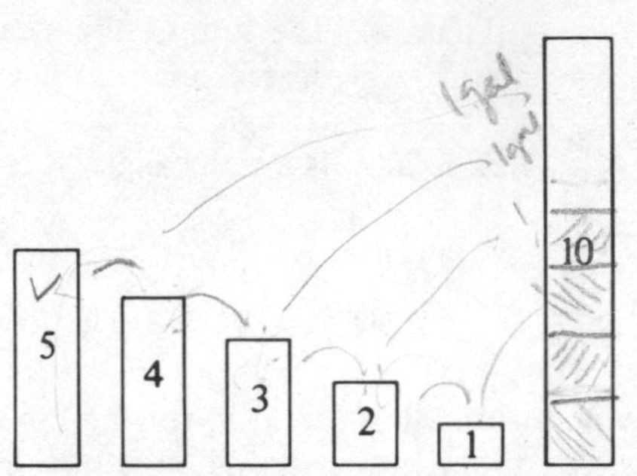

7. The figure above represents six containers whose capacities, in gallons, are shown. The 5-gallon container is full of vinegar and the rest are empty. The contents of the 5-gallon container are used to fill the 4-gallon container and the excess is poured into the 10-gallon container. The 4-gallon container is then used to fill the 3-gallon container and the excess is poured into the 10-gallon container. The process is repeated until all containers are empty except the 1-gallon and 10-gallon containers. What percent of the 10-gallon container is filled?

(A) 4% (B) 6% (C) 40%
(D) 60% (E) 140%

8. If the product of the digits of a two-digit number is odd, then the sum of those digits must be

(A) even
(B) odd
(C) less than or equal to 5
(D) greater than 5 and less than 10
(E) 18

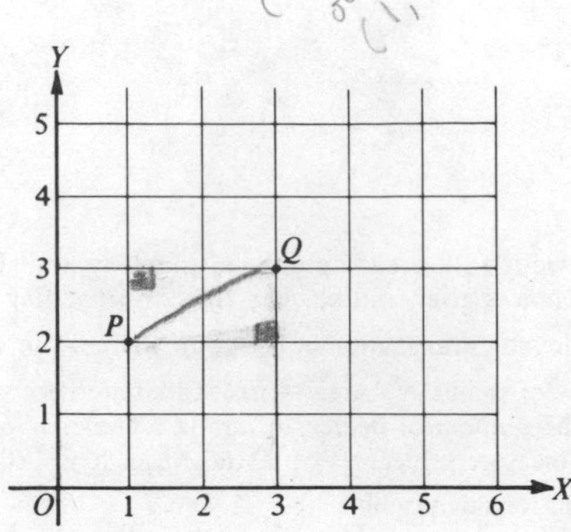

9. If a right triangle is drawn on the grid above with PQ as the hypotenuse, which of the following could be the coordinates of the vertex of the right angle?

(A) (1,4) (B) (2,1) (C) (2,4)
(D) (3,1) (E) (3,2)

10. If $\sqrt{x}$ is a whole number, which of the following is NOT necessarily a whole number?

(A) $\frac{\sqrt{x}}{2}$ (B) x (C) x^2 (D) $2\sqrt{x}$ (E) x^3

11. The degree measures of the three angles of a triangle are p, q, and r, respectively. If p is the average (arithmetic mean) of q and r, then $p =$

(A) 30°
(B) 45°
(C) 60°
(D) 90°
(E) 120°

GO ON TO THE NEXT PAGE

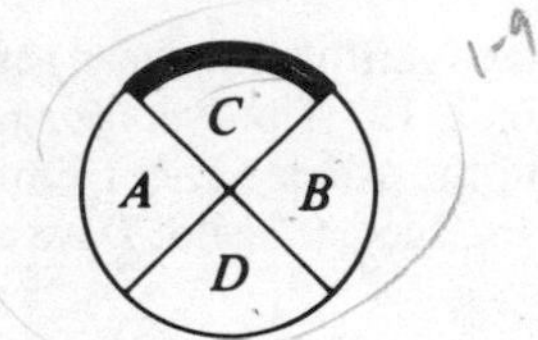

Questions 12-13 refer to the figure above in which A, B, C, and D represent four of the digits from 1 to 9, inclusive, and $A + B = 10C + D$.

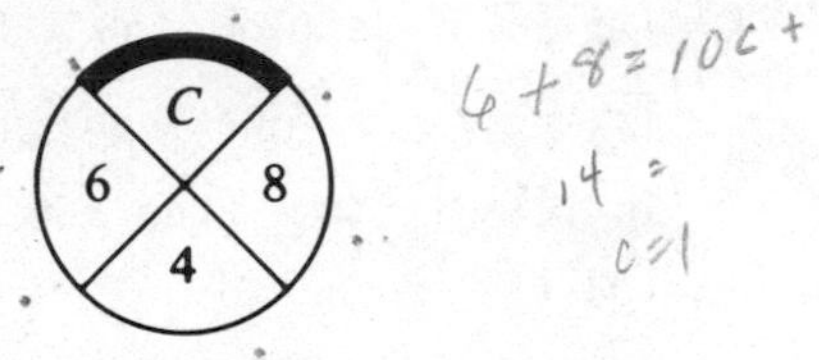

12. In the figure above, what does C represent?

(A) 1 (B) 4 (C) 6 (D) 8 (E) 10

---

13. Under the stated conditions, all of the following could be values of $A + B$ EXCEPT

(A) 12 (B) 14 (C) 16 (D) 17 (E) 22

---

14. If j, k, m, and n are positive integers and if $j > k$ and $m > n$, which of the following must be greater than zero?

I. $j - k$
II. $k - m$
III. $m \div n$

(A) I only (B) II only (C) I and III only
(D) II and III only (E) I, II, and III

15. A tank contains 33.6 liters of gasoline. The tank is emptied in 3 days. If $\frac{1}{7}$ of the gasoline is used the 1st day, twice that quantity is used on the 2nd day, and the rest is used on the 3rd day, how many liters were used on the 3rd day?

(A) 9.6
(B) 11.2
(C) 19.2
(D) 24.0
(E) 28.8

16. If N is a prime number greater than 9, then the sum of N, $2N$, and $4N$ is divisible by 1, N, and

(A) 2
(B) 4
(C) 6
(D) 7
(E) 8

17. If $x = a - 4$ and $y = a + 5$, then $x - y$ is equal to which of the following?

(A) -9
(B) -1
(C) 1
(D) 9
(E) $2a + 1$

18. If 8 people are standing on the circumference of a circle, what is the LEAST number of people who must move so that all 8 will be standing in a straight line?

(A) 4
(B) 5
(C) 6
(D) 7
(E) 8

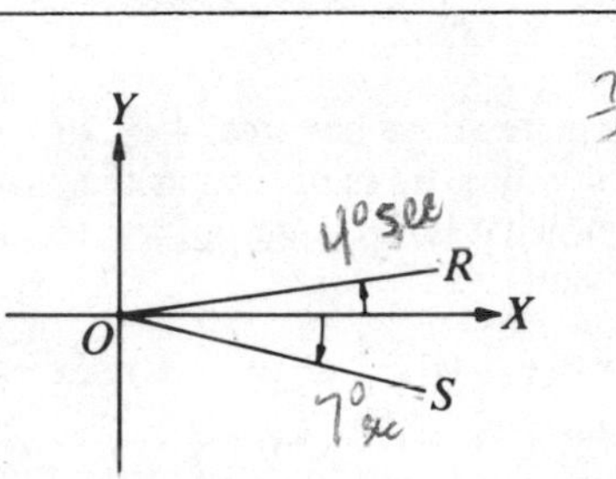

19. In the figure above, OR and OS start on OX and revolve simultaneously in the plane in opposite directions around point O. If OR revolves at $4°$ per second and OS at $7°$ per second, how many complete revolutions will OS have made when OR has made exactly 336 complete revolutions?

(A) 192
(B) 448
(C) 588
(D) 630
(E) It cannot be determined from the information given.

GO ON TO THE NEXT PAGE

20. P is the set of 8 consecutive integers whose sum is 4. Q is the set of 6 consecutive integers whose sum is 9. How many members of Q are members of P?

(A) None
(B) One
(C) Four
(D) Five
(E) Six

21. Of the 60 people in a room, $\frac{2}{3}$ are women and $\frac{2}{5}$ are smokers. What is the maximum number of women in the room who can be nonsmokers?

(A) 16
(B) 24
(C) 34
(D) 36
(E) 40

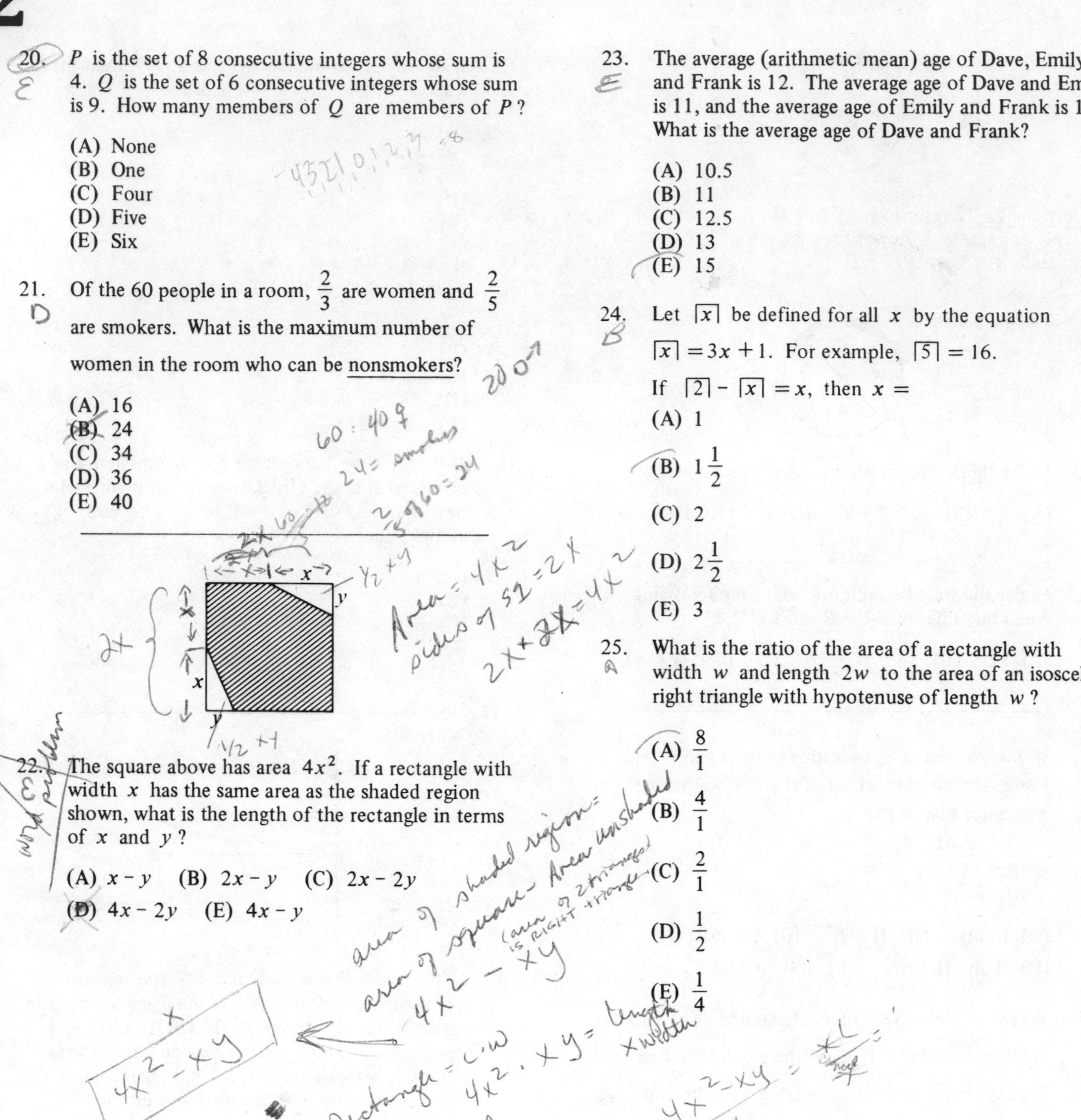

22. The square above has area $4x^2$. If a rectangle with width x has the same area as the shaded region shown, what is the length of the rectangle in terms of x and y?

(A) $x - y$ (B) $2x - y$ (C) $2x - 2y$
(D) $4x - 2y$ (E) $4x - y$

23. The average (arithmetic mean) age of Dave, Emily, and Frank is 12. The average age of Dave and Emily is 11, and the average age of Emily and Frank is 10. What is the average age of Dave and Frank?

(A) 10.5
(B) 11
(C) 12.5
(D) 13
(E) 15

24. Let $\lceil x \rceil$ be defined for all x by the equation $\lceil x \rceil = 3x + 1$. For example, $\lceil 5 \rceil = 16$. If $\lceil 2 \rceil - \lceil x \rceil = x$, then $x =$

(A) 1
(B) $1\frac{1}{2}$
(C) 2
(D) $2\frac{1}{2}$
(E) 3

25. What is the ratio of the area of a rectangle with width w and length $2w$ to the area of an isosceles right triangle with hypotenuse of length w?

(A) $\frac{8}{1}$
(B) $\frac{4}{1}$
(C) $\frac{2}{1}$
(D) $\frac{1}{2}$
(E) $\frac{1}{4}$

S T O P

IF YOU FINISH BEFORE TIME IS CALLED, YOU MAY CHECK YOUR WORK ON THIS SECTION ONLY. DO NOT WORK ON ANY OTHER SECTION IN THE TEST.

SECTION 4

Time—30 minutes

40 QUESTIONS

For each question in this section, choose the best answer and blacken the corresponding space on the answer sheet.

Each question below consists of a word in capital letters, followed by five lettered words or phrases. Choose the word or phrase that is most nearly opposite in meaning to the word in capital letters. Since some of the questions require you to distinguish fine shades of meaning, consider all the choices before deciding which is best.

Example:

GOOD: (A) sour (B) bad (C) red (D) hot (E) ugly

Ⓐ ● Ⓒ Ⓓ Ⓔ

1. MUTED: (A) done quickly (B) seen vaguely (C) turned under (D) made louder (E) kept clean

2. SHORTHANDED: (A) leisurely (B) lengthened (C) overstaffed (D) unrivaled (E) extraordinary

3. DISSECTION: (A) understanding (B) assembly (C) detection (D) preference (E) relationship

4. DEMENTED: (A) of doubtful origin (B) of sound mind (C) dangerous (D) fruitful (E) pliable

5. ACUITY: (A) sympathy (B) boldness (C) dullness (D) proper behavior (E) half-hearted decision

6. DISPUTATIOUS: (A) questionable (B) sincere (C) conciliatory (D) disappointing (E) inoperable

7. TRANSIENCE: (A) urgency (B) immaturity (C) unfamiliarity (D) everlastingness (E) falseheartedness

8. ANOMALOUS:
(A) showing no emotion
(B) holding as security
(C) voicing no opinion
(D) fitting a pattern
(E) relating an event

9. VILIFICATION:
(A) acclaim
(B) activity
(C) clear communication
(D) acquisition of possessions
(E) reduction in size

10. SURREPTITIOUS: (A) aboveboard (B) credible (C) vulnerable (D) highly successful (E) freely chosen

Each sentence below has one or two blanks, each blank indicating that something has been omitted. Beneath the sentence are five lettered words or sets of words. Choose the word or set of words that best fits the meaning of the sentence as a whole.

Example:

Although its publicity has been ----, the film itself is intelligent, well-acted, handsomely produced, and altogether ----.

(A) tasteless. .respectable (B) extensive. .moderate (C) sophisticated. .amateur (D) risqué. .crude (E) perfect. .spectacular

● Ⓑ Ⓒ Ⓓ Ⓔ

11. In the late nineteenth century, scientists were mystified by the schooling behavior of certain fish; today's marine biologists are still ---- by the behavior of these fish.

(A) baffled (B) inspired (C) bored (D) frightened (E) convinced

12. Perhaps because they feel ---- by the rules of school and society, many children long for an escape to another world.

(A) emancipated (B) nurtured (C) assuaged (D) intrigued (E) constricted

13. Many artists maintained that the arts commission was guilty of discrimination because it not only ---- to appoint more minorities to policy-making positions but also attempted to ---- three female program directors.

(A) refused. .recruit (B) agreed. .promote (C) tried. .fire (D) failed. .oust (E) hesitated. .retain

14. The fact that poverty often ---- in highly industrialized areas may indicate that the condition is ---- by industrial progress itself.

(A) thrives. .thwarted (B) occurs. .engendered (C) arrives. .threatened (D) recurs. .alleviated (E) languishes. .encouraged

15. He has several talents that ---- the possibility of genius; however, no one of them is quite transcendent enough to ---- that possibility.

(A) preclude. .surpass
(B) intimate. .realize
(C) proclaim. .condone
(D) vindicate. .challenge
(E) verify. .disprove

Each question below consists of a related pair of words or phrases, followed by five lettered pairs of words or phrases. Select the lettered pair that best expresses a relationship similar to that expressed in the original pair.

Example:

YAWN : BOREDOM :: (A) dream : sleep (B) anger : madness (C) smile : amusement (D) face : expression (E) impatience : rebellion

16. BYSTANDER : EVENT :: (A) juror : verdict (B) culprit : crime (C) tourist : journey (D) spectator : game (E) model : portrait

17. GLACIER : ICE :: (A) rain : snow (B) bay : ocean (C) cloud : storm (D) river : water (E) pond : fish

18. STAR : CONSTELLATION :: (A) crew : airplane (B) member : club (C) weather : forecast (D) partner : associate (E) hymn : church

19. FULL-BLOWN : ROSE :: (A) withered : vine (B) prolific : weed (C) fertile : field (D) edible : corn (E) ripe : tomato

20. ACTOR : PLAYWRIGHT :: (A) editor : novelist (B) competitor : mascot (C) collector : painter (D) attorney : witness (E) soloist : composer

21. PARALLEL : MEET :: (A) opaque : see (B) horizontal : span (C) eternal : end (D) philosophical : judge (E) conventional : grow

22. RESPITE : DRUDGERY ::
(A) rumor : information
(B) malady : hygiene
(C) lull : conversation
(D) embarkation : navigation
(E) divorce : marriage

23. WAIVE : RIGHT :: (A) exercise : authority (B) forgo : pleasure (C) inhibit : imagination (D) release : feeling (E) denounce : country

24. INSIPID : FLAVOR ::
(A) concise : brevity (B) meticulous : care (C) banal : triviality (D) inane : significance (E) fortuitous : chance

25. EMBROIL : ARGUMENT :: (A) enlarge : picture (B) fuel : resentment (C) raise : stake (D) snare : net (E) conspire : defeat

GO ON TO THE NEXT PAGE

Each passage below is followed by questions based on its content. Answer all questions following a passage on the basis of what is stated or implied in that passage.

Lately it has become customary to equate wisdom with knowledge and knowledge with science. Hence science equals wisdom, and as we all need the latter, we must therefore all have the former. Nonsense. Science, whose truths depend on the social beliefs of the time and the cultural atmosphere in which they are created, is but one special and actually rather small part of knowledge. If you learned by heart all the non-scientific articles in an encyclopedia, you would indeed be a very knowledgeable person, though an unscientific one. Wisdom is a quite special condition, and one which all people should strive to attain if conditions on this planet are ever to improve. It has extraordinarily little to do with science.

Another confusion is that between logical, rational thought and science. Now science does require logic and rationality. But it has no monopoly on either. Logic and rationality are far older than science, and in many circumstances more useful. And they are required, along with inventiveness and ingenuity and creativity, to improve current conditions. But to say that only science can bring progress is to deny humanity its very essence—its ability to create, to invent, and to think. Human beings have always displayed these qualities, and will continue to do so. In fact, it is these qualities that bring about progress.

26. According to the passage, all of the following can be said of science EXCEPT:

(A) Science can contribute to knowledge.
(B) Science and knowledge are essentially the same.
(C) Science is not an absolutely objective pursuit.
(D) Science alone will not bring about progress.
(E) Scientific doctrines are subject to change.

27. The author's attitude toward those who equate science with progress is best described as

(A) dispassionate (B) contemptuous
(C) threatening (D) sympathetic
(E) complimentary

28. The author's statements about logic, rational thought, and science in the second paragraph support a belief that

(A) scientific thinking is only one area in which logic and rationality are valuable
(B) other disciplines are less effective and less beneficial than science
(C) logical reasoning is more useful than science because it is older
(D) the qualities of logic and rationality are often lacking in science
(E) logic and rational thought at times invalidate the findings of science

GO ON TO THE NEXT PAGE

Elizabeth's father was fond of the country and of books; and from these tastes had risen his principal enjoyments. To his wife he was very little otherwise indebted, than as her ignorance and folly had contributed to his amusement. This is not the sort of happiness which a man would in general wish to owe to his wife; but where other powers of entertainment are wanting, the true philosopher will derive benefit from such as are given.

Elizabeth, however, had never been blind to the impropriety of her father's behavior as a husband. She had always seen it with pain; but respecting his abilities, and grateful for his affectionate treatment of herself, she endeavored to forget what she could not overlook, and to banish from her thoughts that continual breach of conjugal obligation and decorum which, in exposing his wife to the contempt of her own children, was so highly reprehensible. But she never felt so strongly as now the disadvantages which must attend the children of so unsuitable a marriage, nor ever been so fully aware of the evils arising from so ill-judged a direction of talents; talents which, rightly used, might at least have preserved the respectability of his daughters, even if incapable of enlarging the mind of his wife.

29. The passage suggests that the "powers of entertainment" that "are wanting" (lines 7-8) in the life of Elizabeth's father include

(A) amusement at the ignorance and folly of his wife
(B) the enjoyment he derives from books
(C) pleasure in his wife's company
(D) satisfaction from his social position
(E) pride in his children

30. The passage suggests that Elizabeth agrees with her father's opinion of

(A) the intellectual ability of his wife
(B) the disadvantages of marriage
(C) how a talented man should spend his time
(D) the example a father should set for his children
(E) how to preserve the reputation of children

31. The passage can best be described as

(A) a description of a disagreement between a woman and her parents
(B) an analysis of the reasons for the disintegration of a marriage
(C) an account of one woman's reflections on the problems in her parents' marriage
(D) a discussion of a young woman's attitude toward marriage
(E) a description of a foolish wife and mother

GO ON TO THE NEXT PAGE

According to a listing in the twenty-fifth anniversary issue of *La Prensa*, a Spanish-language newspaper published in San Antonio, Texas, a total of 451 different Spanish-language newspapers were published in the United States between 1876 and 1937. These newspapers served the Hispanic communities as necessary vehicles for the exchange of news, information, and opinions. Their relative success or failure often mirrored the special effects on the Hispanic communities of general economic, cultural, and political forces in the United States at the time they were published. The short-run newspapers were especially sensitive to the ups and downs of the economy, but almost all of the Spanish-language newspapers were equally vulnerable to the Great Depression of the thirties.

One of the longest-lasting survivors in this highly competitive market was *La Prensa*, which had a solid commercial basis and depended on advertising sales for financial support. *La Prensa's* editor, Ignacio Lozano, consistently steered a course that was perceived as politically nonpartisan. The newspaper first appeared in 1913, with a political posture designed to be neutral and pacifistic at a time when the Mexican Revolution of 1910-1911 had left Hispanic communities in the United States wearied of continuing political hostilities. The appeal of the newspaper, whether intended or not, was based on its ability to project an image of a mediator and an agent of peace. This public view, in addition to a well-organized business approach, helped *La Prensa* survive stiff competition and economic crises.

Lozano, according to his biographer, carefully planned the focus of *La Prensa's* coverage. Whereas many newspapers tended to be biased in their coverage of developments in Mexico, or to concentrate on American news, Lozano insisted on objective reporting of the politics of the homeland. Subscribers wanted to read about developments brought about by the Revolution; many of the political exiles and refugees wanted to know about postwar conditions so that they could determine when they should return to Mexico. Lozano also allocated a section of the newspaper for announcements of local events, devoted a small section to literature, and included an abundance of advertising. Within its first year, *La Prensa* increased its circulation from 1,500 to 10,000 copies per issue and became a daily. In the 1920's, the newspaper had correspondents in Mexico City, New York City, and Paris. By 1926, it had begun publishing another newspaper in Los Angeles, *La Opinión*, had become a member of El Congreso Panamericano de Periodistas, an international association of journalists, and had joined a New York news service. This type of success helped *La Prensa* survive the Great Depression while other newspapers, both Spanish- and English-language, were going out of business.

32. Which of the following is the most appropriate title for the passage?

(A) The Success of *La Prensa*
(B) The Political Career of Ignacio Lozano
(C) *La Prensa*'s Coverage of the Mexican Revolution of 1910-1911
(D) The Effects of the Great Depression on Spanish-Language Newspapers
(E) The Influence of Spanish-Language Newspapers in Hispanic Communities

33. According to the passage, which of the following most strongly affected the financial well-being of Spanish-language newspapers?

(A) Fluctuations in the size of Hispanic communities
(B) Changing economic trends
(C) The types of commercial advertisements published
(D) The high quality of news reporting
(E) The outcome of the Mexican Revolution of 1910

34. The author seems to consider which of the following as LEAST important to the success of *La Prensa*?

(A) Its nonpartisan political image
(B) Its large number of advertisements
(C) Its publication of poetry and fiction
(D) Ignacio Lozano's editorial policies
(E) Ignacio Lozano's business sense

35. Which of the following can be inferred from the passage about the first several issues of *La Prensa*?

(A) The coverage of Mexican affairs was not as objective as Lozano wished.
(B) The circulation per issue was nearly 10,000 copies.
(C) The issues included reports from the paper's news correspondents around the world.
(D) The issues were not published every day of the week.
(E) The issues were printed in both Spanish and English.

36. The passage suggests that *La Prensa* was probably useful to all of the following members of the Hispanic community EXCEPT those

(A) interested in reading Hispanic views about domestic and foreign affairs
(B) wanting to read literature written in Spanish
(C) interested in information about events in the San Antonio area of Texas
(D) seeking to expand business dealings within the Hispanic community
(E) wanting to read editorials supporting a particular side in the Mexican Revolution

GO ON TO THE NEXT PAGE

A fissionable atom is one that, after capturing a neutron, will split, releasing energy and more neutrons. The only naturally occurring fissionable material that can serve as a fuel for an atomic reactor is the very rare uranium, U-235. The more plentiful U-238, however, can be converted into fissionable plutonium, which may then function as a fuel. This phenomenon has made possible the so-called breeder reactor. All that is needed is a supply of neutrons sufficient to continue a chain reaction and also to manufacture more plutonium from U-238. Plutonium (which is first made when U-238 captures high-energy neutrons from an initial charge of fissioning U-235) is the source of these neutrons, for when a plutonium atom captures a neutron, it fissions, yielding an average of 2.9 neutrons. One of these can be captured by another plutonium atom, thus sustaining the chain reaction, and most of the remainder can be captured by atoms of U-238. Thus the amount of fuel in a breeder reactor gradually increases.

Thorium may also be used in a breeding cycle because, when thorium captures a neutron, an atom of fissionable U-233 is formed. This latter atom functions similarly to plutonium except that it produces an average of only 2.3 neutrons per fission.

37. The passage is primarily concerned with

(A) defining what is meant when it is said that an atom is fissionable
(B) revealing that atoms of U-235 can be transformed into atoms of plutonium
(C) debating the social desirability of the use of breeder reactors
(D) discussing fission and the breeding cycles of certain fissionable materials
(E) proposing the thorium cycle as a preferred alternative to the plutonium cycle

38. According to the passage, an atom of which of the following substances, "after capturing a neutron, will split, releasing energy and more neutrons" (lines 1-2) ?

I. U-235
II. Plutonium
III. U-233

(A) I only (B) II only (C) I and III only (D) II and III only (E) I, II, and III

39. The passage suggests that, when an atom of U-238 in a breeder reactor captures one of the neutrons released by fissioning plutonium atoms, which of the following happens to the atom of U-238 ?

(A) It fissions to become U-235.
(B) It fissions, releasing 2.9 neutrons.
(C) It is converted to plutonium.
(D) It is converted to a fissionable atom of U-233.
(E) It remains unchanged until more neutrons are captured.

40. The passage suggests that the elements in which of the following pairs operate analogously in their respective breeding cycles?

I. Thorium and plutonium
II. U-235 and thorium
III. Plutonium and U-233

(A) I only (B) II only (C) III only (D) II and III only (E) I, II, and III

S T O P

IF YOU FINISH BEFORE TIME IS CALLED, YOU MAY CHECK YOUR WORK ON THIS SECTION ONLY. DO NOT WORK ON ANY OTHER SECTION IN THE TEST.

SECTION 5

Time—30 minutes

35 QUESTIONS

In this section solve each problem, using any available space on the page for scratchwork. Then decide which is the best of the choices given and blacken the corresponding space on the answer sheet.

The following information is for your reference in solving some of the problems.

Circle of radius r: Area $= \pi r^2$; Circumference $= 2\pi r$

The number of degrees of arc in a circle is 360.

The measure in degrees of a straight angle is 180.

Definitions of symbols:

$=$	is equal to	$\leq$	is less than or equal to
$\neq$	is unequal to	$\geq$	is greater than or equal to
$<$	is less than	$\parallel$	is parallel to
$>$	is greater than	$\perp$	is perpendicular to

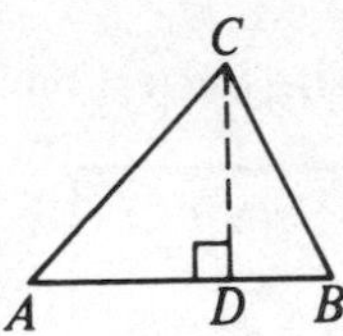

Triangle: The sum of the measures in degrees of the angles of a triangle is 180.

If $\angle CDA$ is a right angle, then

(1) area of $\triangle ABC = \dfrac{AB \times CD}{2}$

(2) $AC^2 = AD^2 + DC^2$

Note: Figures which accompany problems in this test are intended to provide information useful in solving the problems. They are drawn as accurately as possible EXCEPT when it is stated in a specific problem that its figure is not drawn to scale. All figures lie in a plane unless otherwise indicated. All numbers used are real numbers.

---

1. If $x + 1 + x + 2 + x + 3 = 1 + 2 + 3$, then $3x =$

   (A) -1
   (B) 0
   (C) $\frac{1}{3}$
   (D) 1
   (E) 3

2. If a penguin swims at an average rate of 4 meters per second, how many seconds will it take for the penguin to swim 50 meters?

   (A) 11 (B) 11.5 (C) 12 (D) 12.5 (E) 13

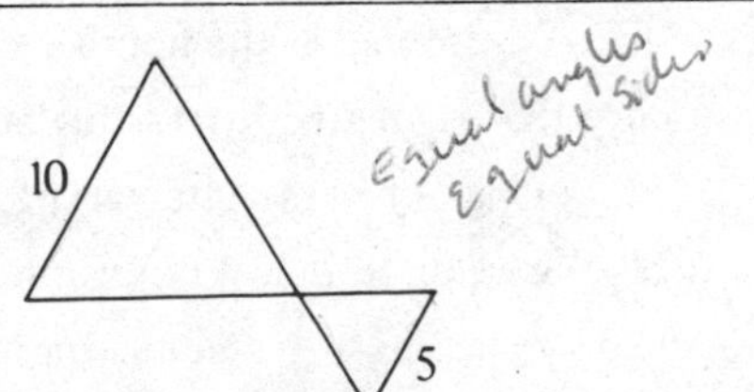

3. The two triangles above are equilateral with sides as shown. The ratio of the perimeter of the larger triangle to that of the smaller is

   (A) $\frac{50}{1}$ (B) $\frac{15}{1}$ (C) $\frac{4}{1}$ (D) $\frac{3}{1}$ (E) $\frac{2}{1}$

4. John had exactly \$7 before Bill paid him a \$26 debt. After the debt was paid, Bill had $\frac{1}{3}$ the amount that John then had. How much did Bill have before the debt was paid?

   (A) \$33 (B) \$35 (C) \$36
   (D) \$37 (E) \$47

5. Which of the following is an expression for 3 times the sum of c and the square of d?

   (A) $3(c + d^2)$
   (B) $3c + d^2$
   (C) $3(c + d)^2$
   (D) $3cd^2$
   (E) $3(c + \sqrt{d})$

6. $2(a)(-b)(-c)(-d) + 2abcd =$

   (A) $4abcd$
   (B) $-4abcd$
   (C) $-4a^2b^2c^2d^2$
   (D) $4a^2b^2c^2d^2$
   (E) 0

7. If $xy \neq 0$, then $\left(\dfrac{x^6y^5}{x^3y^2}\right)^2 =$

   (A) x^9y^9
   (B) x^9y^5
   (C) x^6y^6
   (D) x^5y^5
   (E) x^4y^6

5

Questions 8-27 each consist of two quantities, one in Column A and one in Column B. You are to compare the two quantities and on the answer sheet blacken space

- A if the quantity in Column A is greater;
- B if the quantity in Column B is greater;
- C if the two quantities are equal;
- D if the relationship cannot be determined from the information given.

Notes:
1. In certain questions, information concerning one or both of the quantities to be compared is centered above the two columns.
2. In a given question, a symbol that appears in both columns represents the same thing in Column A as it does in Column B.
3. Letters such as x, n, and k stand for real numbers.

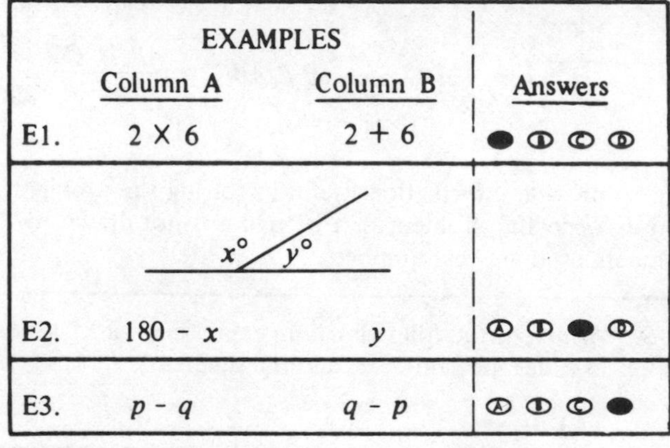

EXAMPLES

	Column A	Column B	Answers
E1.	2×6	$2 + 6$	● Ⓑ Ⓒ Ⓓ
E2.	$180 - x$	y	Ⓐ Ⓑ ● Ⓓ
E3.	$p - q$	$q - p$	Ⓐ Ⓑ Ⓒ ●

	Column A	Column B
8.	$1(2 + 3(4 + 5))$	$5(4 + 3(2 + 1))$

The monthly rainfall in City X for April was 5 inches.

9.	The amount of rainfall in City X from April 1st through April 4th	The amount of rainfall in City X from April 1st through April 8th
10.	$0.4 \times 10{,}000$	40×100

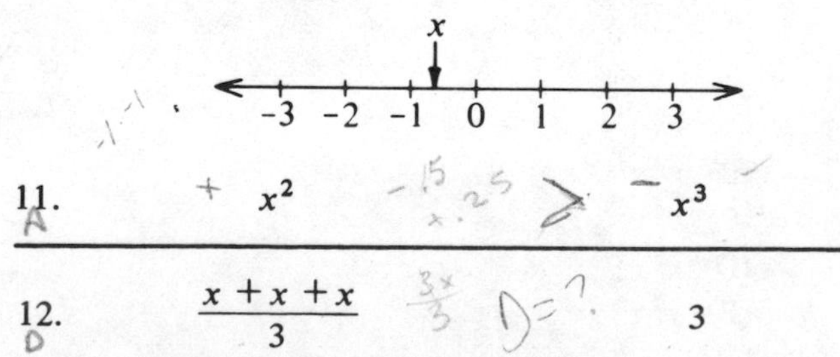

11.	x^2	x^3
12.	$\frac{x + x + x}{3}$	3
13.	The amount of sales tax on \$6.00 at a rate of 4%	The amount of sales tax on \$5.00 at a rate of 5%

	Column A	Column B

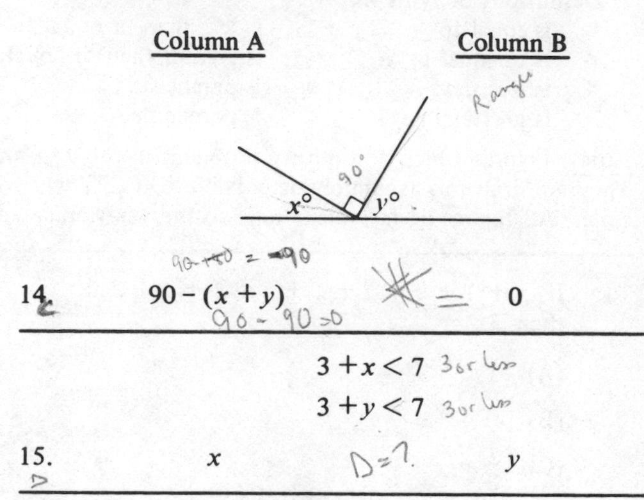

14.	$90 - (x + y)$	0

$3 + x < 7$

$3 + y < 7$

15.	x	y

0 1 2 3 4 5 6 7 8 9 10 11

If x and y are positive integers less than 12, $x \boxdot y$ is defined as the number in the figure above that is located by starting at the number x and moving $(y - 1)$ intervals of x units each in a clockwise direction. For example, $6 \boxdot 2 = 0$, since by starting at 6 and moving 1 interval of 6 units in a clockwise direction, the number located will be 0.

16.	$5 \boxdot 4$	10
17.	$10^6 - 10$	$10^5 + 10$

GO ON TO THE NEXT PAGE

SUMMARY DIRECTIONS FOR COMPARISON QUESTIONS

Answer:
A if the quantity in Column A is greater;
B if the quantity in Column B is greater;
C if the two quantities are equal;
D if the relationship cannot be determined from the information given.

Column A | **Column B**

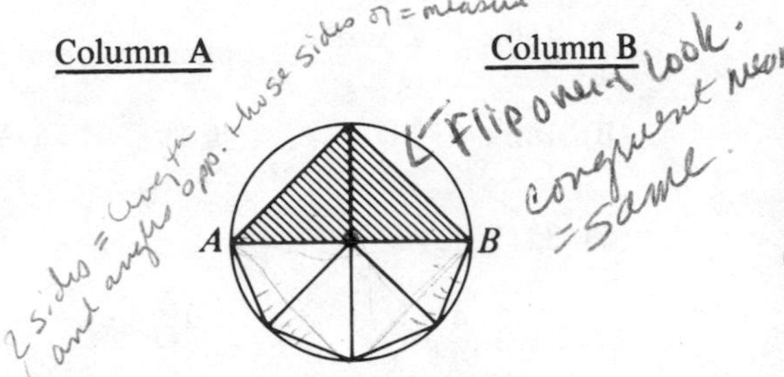

The shaded triangles with bases on diameter *AB* are isosceles and congruent. The unshaded triangles are isosceles and congruent.

18. Total area of shaded triangular regions | Total area of unshaded triangular regions

PURCHASES BY THREE BOYS ON JANUARY 7, 1982

	Al	Bob	Ed
Number of Shirts	1	1	2
Number of Pants	1	2	1
Total Cost	\$40	\$x	\$y

19. x | y

20. The average (arithmetic mean) of 13, 42, and 67 | The average (arithmetic mean) of 0, 13, 42, and 67

$1 - a,\ 2 - 2a,\ 3 - 3a, \ldots,\ n - na$ is a sequence of numbers in which $n > 15$.

21. The sum of the first 15 terms of the sequence above when $a = 1$ | 0

Column A | **Column B**

n is an odd positive integer greater than 1.

22. $(-1)^n\left(\frac{1}{2}\right)^{n-1}$ | $(-1)^{n-1}\left(\frac{1}{2}\right)^n$

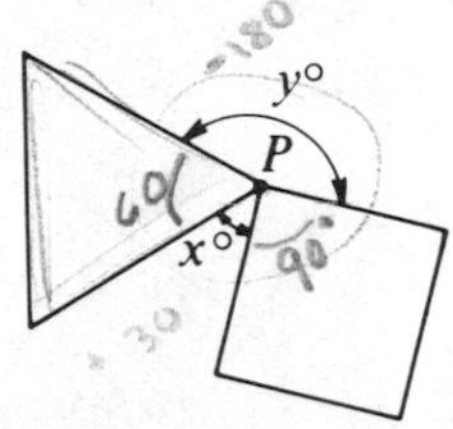

The square and the equilateral triangle have vertex *P* in common.

23. $x + y$ | 200

Along a certain highway, City R is 12 kilometers from City P and 25 kilometers from City Q.

24. The distance in kilometers from City P to City Q along this highway | 13 kilometers

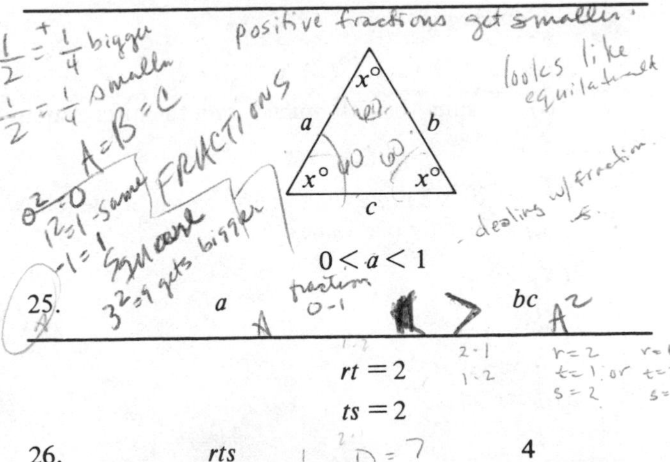

$0 < a < 1$

25. a | bc

$rt = 2$

$ts = 2$

26. rts | 4

$\boxed{x}$ denotes the greatest integer less than or equal to x. For example: $\boxed{4.2} = 4$ and $\boxed{3} = 3$

27. $\boxed{5.2} + \boxed{-5.2}$ | 0

GO ON TO THE NEXT PAGE

Solve each of the remaining problems in this section using any available space for scratchwork. Then decide which is the best of the choices given and blacken the corresponding space on the answer sheet.

28. Let $x = y \div z$, where $yz \neq 0$. If both y and z are multiplied by 6, then x is

(A) increased by 1

(B) decreased by 1

(C) multiplied by 6

(D) multiplied by $\frac{1}{6}$

(E) not changed

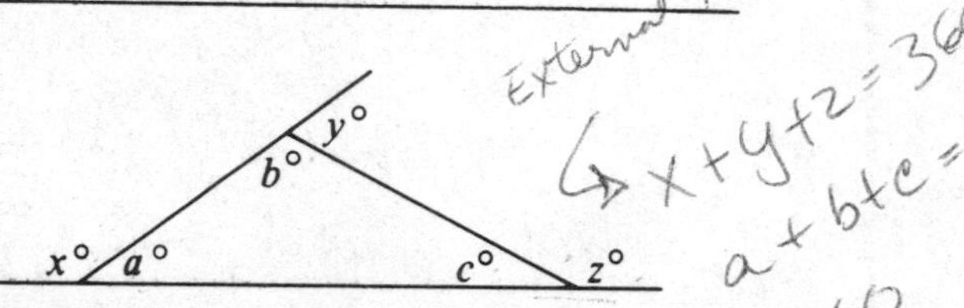

29. In the figure above, $x + y + z - (a + b + c) =$

(A) 360
(B) 180
(C) 90
(D) 0
(E) −90

30. If $1 + \frac{x}{y} = 0$, then $\frac{y}{x} + \frac{x}{y}$ is equal to which of the following?

(A) −2 (B) −1 (C) 0 (D) 2
(E) It cannot be determined from the information given.

31. If $x + y$ is 3 more than $x - y$, which of the following has exactly one value?

(A) x
(B) y
(C) $x + y$
(D) $x - y$
(E) xy

32. $\frac{3x}{60}$ hours and $\frac{4y}{300}$ minutes together equal how many seconds?

(A) $180x + 48y$

(B) $180x + \frac{4}{5}y$

(C) $3x + 48y$

(D) $3x + \frac{4}{5}y$

(E) $\frac{3x}{60^3} + \frac{4y}{18{,}000}$

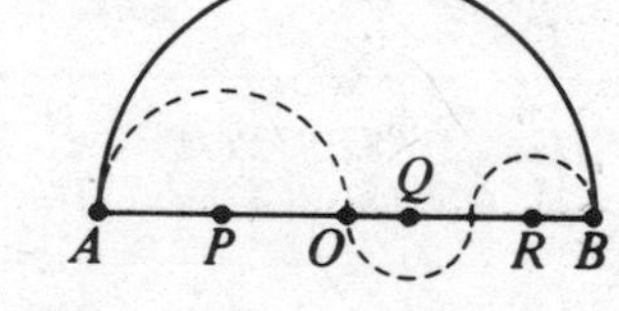

33. Points $P, O, Q,$ and R are the midpoints of the diameters of the 4 semicircles in the figure above. AB is a line segment containing the diameters of these semicircles. If $OB = 6$, what is the length of the dotted path from A to B?

(A) 3π (B) 6π (C) 9π (D) 12π (E) 36π

34. In a certain garden, $\frac{1}{5}$ of the flowering plants represents $\frac{1}{10}$ of all the plants. What is the ratio of flowering plants to nonflowering plants in that garden?

(A) 1:1 (B) 1:2 (C) 1:5
(D) 1:9 (E) 1:10

35. The lengths of the edges of a rectangular solid are whole numbers. If the volume of the solid is 11, what is the total area of its six faces?

(A) 26
(B) 44
(C) 46
(D) 52
(E) 66

S T O P

IF YOU FINISH BEFORE TIME IS CALLED, YOU MAY CHECK YOUR WORK ON THIS SECTION ONLY. DO NOT WORK ON ANY OTHER SECTION IN THE TEST.

Correct Answers for Scholastic Aptitude Test
Form Code 2I

VERBAL		MATHEMATICAL	
Section 1	Section 4	Section 2	Section 5
1. B	1. D	1. D	1. B
2. B	2. C	2. C	2. D
3. E	3. B	3. A	3. E
4. A	4. B	4. B	4. D
5. D	5. C	5. A	5. A
6. C	6. C	6. E	6. E
7. E	7. D	7. C	7. C
8. E	8. D	8. A	*8. B
9. B	9. A	9. E	*9. D
10. E	10. A	10. A	*10. C
11. B	11. A	11. C	*11. A
12. B	12. E	12. A	*12. D
13. C	13. D	13. E	*13. B
14. A	14. B	14. C	*14. C
15. D	15. B	15. C	*15. D
16. C	16. D	16. D	*16. B
17. A	17. D	17. A	*17. A
18. C	18. B	18. C	*18. B
19. C	19. E	19. C	*19. D
20. B	20. E	20. E	*20. A
21. C	21. C	21. D	*21. C
22. C	22. C	22. E	*22. B
23. C	23. B	23. E	*23. A
24. D	24. D	24. B	*24. D
25. D	25. D	25. A	*25. A
26. D	26. B		*26. D
27. C	27. B		*27. B
28. A	28. A		28. E
29. E	29. C		29. B
30. B	30. A		30. A
31. A	31. C		31. B
32. D	32. A		32. B
33. E	33. B		33. B
34. B	34. C		34. A
35. C	35. D		35. C
36. E	36. E		
37. B	37. D		
38. C	38. E		
39. D	39. C		
40. E	40. C		
41. B			
42. A			
43. B			
44. B			
45. D			

*Indicates four-choice questions. (All of the other questions are five-choice.)

The Scoring Process

Machine-scoring is done in three steps:

- *Scanning.* Your answer sheet is "read" by a scanning machine and the oval you filled in for each question is recorded on a computer tape.
- *Scoring.* The computer compares the oval filled in for each question with the correct response. Each correct answer receives one point; omitted questions do not count toward your score. For each wrong answer, a fraction of a point is subtracted to correct for random guessing. For questions with five answer choices, one-fourth of a point is subtracted for each wrong response; for questions with four answer choices, one-third of a point is subtracted for each wrong response. The SAT-verbal test has 85 questions with five answer choices each. If, for example, a student has 44 right, 32 wrong, and 9 omitted, the resulting raw score is determined as follows:

  $$44 \text{ right} - \frac{32 \text{ wrong}}{4} = 44 - 8 = 36 \text{ raw score points}$$

  Obtaining raw scores frequently involves the rounding of fractional numbers to the nearest whole number. For example, a raw score of 36.25 is rounded to 36, the nearest whole number. A raw score of 36.50 is rounded upward to 37.
- *Converting to reported scaled score.* Raw test scores are then placed on the College Board scale of 200 to 800 through a process that adjusts scores to account for minor differences in difficulty among different editions of the test. This process, known as equating, is performed so that a student's reported score is not affected by the edition of the test taken nor by the abilities of the group with whom the student takes the test. As a result of placing SAT scores on the College Board scale, scores earned by students at different times can be compared. For example, an SAT-verbal score of 400 on a test taken at one administration indicates the same level of developed verbal ability as a 400 score obtained on a different edition of the test taken at another time.

How to Score the Test

You can verify the College Board SAT scores reported to you recently by using the information in this booklet along with the copy of your answer sheet. *Before you begin, check that the first two characters (number and letter) of the form code you marked in item 3 on your answer sheet are the same as the form code printed on the front of this booklet.* Compare the responses shown on the copy of your answer sheet with the list of correct answers.

SAT-Verbal Sections 1 and 4

Step A: Count the number of correct answers for *section 1* and record the number in the space provided on the worksheet on the next page. Then do the same for the incorrect answers. (Do not count omitted answers.) To determine subtotal A, use the formula:

$$\text{number correct} - \frac{\text{number incorrect}}{4} = \text{subtotal A}$$

Step B: Count the number of correct answers and the number of incorrect answers for *section 4* and record the numbers in the spaces provided on the worksheet. To determine subtotal B, use the formula:

$$\text{number correct} - \frac{\text{number incorrect}}{4} = \text{subtotal B}$$

Step C: To obtain C, add subtotal A to subtotal B, keeping any decimals. Enter the resulting figure on the worksheet.

Step D: To obtain D, your raw verbal score, round C to the nearest whole number. (For example, any number from 44.50 to 45.49 rounds to 45.) Enter the resulting figure on the worksheet.

Step E: To find your reported SAT-verbal score, look up the total raw verbal score you obtained in step D in the conversion table on the back cover. Enter this figure on the worksheet. (The SAT-verbal score you just recorded and your reported SAT-verbal score should be identical. If not, see the paragraph at the bottom of the next page.)

SAT-Mathematical Sections 2 and 5

Step A: Count the number of correct answers and the number of incorrect answers for *section 2* and record the numbers in the spaces provided on the worksheet. To determine the subtotal A, use the formula:

$$\text{number correct} - \frac{\text{number incorrect}}{4} = \text{subtotal A}$$

Step B: Count the number of correct answers and the number of incorrect answers for the *five-choice questions (questions 1 through 7 and 28 through 35) in section 5* and record the numbers in the spaces provided on the worksheet. To determine the subtotal B, use the formula:

$$\text{number correct} - \frac{\text{number incorrect}}{4} = \text{subtotal B}$$

Step C: Count the number of correct answers and the number of incorrect answers for the *four-choice questions (questions 8 through 27) in section 5* and record the numbers in the spaces provided on the worksheet. To determine the subtotal C, use the formula:

$$\text{number correct} - \frac{\text{number incorrect}}{3} = \text{subtotal C}$$

Step D: To obtain D, add subtotal A, subtotal B, and subtotal C, keeping any decimals. Enter the resulting figure on the worksheet.

Step E: To obtain E, your raw mathematical score, round D to the nearest whole number. (For example, any number from 44.50 to 45.49 rounds to 45.) Enter the resulting figure on the worksheet.

Step F: To find your reported SAT-mathematical score, look up the total raw mathematical score you obtained in E in the conversion table on the back cover. Enter this figure on the worksheet. (The SAT-mathematical score you just recorded and your reported SAT-mathematical score should be identical. If not, see the paragraph at the bottom of the next page.)

SAT-SCORING WORKSHEET

FORM CODE 2I

SAT-Verbal Sections

	no. correct		no. incorrect		
A. Section 1:	33	– ¼ (	8	) =	~~25~~ 31 subtotal A
B. Section 4:	30	– ¼ (	~~10~~ 2½	) =	~~30~~ 27½ subtotal B

C. Total unrounded raw score (Total A + B) ~~45~~ 58.5 C

D. Total rounded raw score (Rounded to nearest whole number) 59 D

E. SAT-verbal reported scaled score (See the conversion table on the back cover.) [570] SAT-verbal score

SAT-Mathematical Sections

	no. correct		no. incorrect		
A. Section 2:	13	– ¼ (	6	) =	11.5 subtotal A
B. Section 5: Questions 1 through 7 and 28 through 35 (5-choice)	6	– ¼ (	0	) =	6 subtotal B
C. Section 5: Questions 8 through 27 (4-choice)	9	– ⅓ (	3	) =	8 subtotal C

D. Total unrounded raw score (Total A + B + C) 25.5 D

E. Total rounded raw score (Rounded to nearest whole number) 26 E

F. SAT-mathematical reported scaled score (See the conversion table on the back cover.) [470] SAT-math score

470
570
1040

Should you have any questions on these scoring instructions, you may call the phone number below. If, after following the above scoring directions and checking your work at least twice, your results disagree with the SAT-verbal or SAT-mathematical score reported on your ATP score report, you may request rescoring of your answer sheet. If rescoring confirms that an error had been made (resulting in either higher or lower scores than those originally reported), corrected reports will be sent to all recipients of your original scores. Please send your request to:

College Board ATP
Box 592
Princeton, NJ 08541
Attention: Rescore Request
Telephone: (609) 771-7600

Please indicate whether it is your SAT-verbal or SAT-mathematical score, or both, that you want to be rescored. When you write, please include a copy of this scoring worksheet on which you did your calculations.

Score Conversion Table
Scholastic Aptitude Test
Form Code 2I

Raw Score	College Board Reported Score		Raw Score	College Board Reported Score	
	SAT-Verbal	SAT-Math		SAT-Verbal	SAT-Math
85	800		40	450	600
84	780		39	450	590
83	770		38	440	580
82	760		37	430	570
81	750		36	430	560
80	740		35	420	550
79	730		34	410	540
78	720		33	410	530
77	710		32	400	520
76	700		31	390	510
75	690		30	380	500
74	680		29	380	490
73	670		28	370	480
72	660		27	360	480
71	650		26	360	470
70	650		25	350	460
69	640		24	340	450
68	630		23	340	440
67	630		22	330	430
66	620		21	330	420
65	610		20	320	410
64	610		19	310	410
63	600		18	310	400
62	590		17	300	390
61	590		16	290	380
60	580	800	15	290	380
59	570	780	14	280	370
58	570	770	13	270	360
57	560	760	12	270	350
56	560	750	11	260	350
55	550	740	10	260	340
54	540	730	9	250	330
53	540	720	8	240	330
52	530	710	7	240	320
51	520	700	6	230	320
50	520	690	5	220	310
49	510	680	4	210	300
48	510	680	3	210	300
47	500	670	2	200	290
46	490	660	1	200	280
45	490	650	0	200	280
44	480	640	−1	200	270
43	470	630	−2	200	260
42	470	620	−3	200	260
41	460	610	−4	200	250
			−5	200	240
			−6	200	230
			−7	200	220
			−8	200	210
			−9	200	210
			−10 or below	200	200

SAT
Form Code 3E

(Cut here to detach.)

COLLEGE BOARD—SCHOLASTIC APTITUDE TEST and Test of Standard Written English

Side 1

Use a No. 2 pencil only for completing this answer sheet. Be sure each mark is dark and completely fills the intended space. Completely erase any errors or stray marks.

1.

YOUR NAME: (Print) ______ Last ______ First ______ M.I.

SIGNATURE: ______ **DATE:** ___ / ___ / ___

HOME ADDRESS: (Print) ______ Number and Street

______ City ______ State ______ Zip Code

CENTER: (Print) ______ City ______ State ______ Center Number

IMPORTANT: Please fill in these boxes exactly as shown on the back cover of your test book.

FOR ETS USE ONLY

2. TEST FORM

3. FORM CODE

4. REGISTRATION NUMBER
(Copy from your Admission Ticket.)

5. YOUR NAME

First 4 letters of last name | First Init. | Mid. Init.

6. DATE OF BIRTH

Month | Day | Year

Jan. Feb. Mar. Apr. May June July Aug. Sept. Oct. Nov. Dec.

7. SEX

Male
Female

8. TEST BOOK SERIAL NUMBER

Start with number 1 for each new section. If a section has fewer than 50 questions, leave the extra answer spaces blank.

SECTION 1

Questions 1–50: (A) (B) (C) (D) (E)

SECTION 2

Questions 1–50: (A) (B) (C) (D) (E)

Q1205

I.N. 574001—110VV33P2723

COLLEGE BOARD — SCHOLASTIC APTITUDE TEST and Test of Standard Written English Side 2

Use a No. 2 pencil only for completing this answer sheet. Be sure each mark is dark and completely fills the intended space. Completely erase any errors or stray marks.

Start with number 1 for each new section. If a section has fewer than 50 questions, leave the extra answer spaces blank.

SECTION 3

SECTION 4

SECTION 5

SECTION 6

9. SIGNATURE: ______________________

FOR ETS USE ONLY	VTR	VTFS	VRR	VRFS	VVR	VVFS	WER	WEFS	M4R	M4FS	M5R	M5FS	MTFS	
	VTW	VTCS	VRW	VRCS	VVW	VVCS	WEW	WECS	M4W		M5W		MTCS	

SECTION 1

Time — 30 minutes

45 QUESTIONS

For each question in this section, choose the best answer and blacken the corresponding space on the answer sheet.

Each question below consists of a word in capital letters, followed by five lettered words or phrases. Choose the word or phrase that is most nearly opposite in meaning to the word in capital letters. Since some of the questions require you to distinguish fine shades of meaning, consider all the choices before deciding which is best.

Example:

GOOD: (A) sour (B) bad (C) red (D) hot (E) ugly Ⓐ ● Ⓒ Ⓓ Ⓔ

1. CHERISH: (A) despise (B) utilize (C) aspire (D) encourage (E) compete
2. VETO: (A) predict (B) discuss (C) approve (D) display (E) evaluate
3. EXTINGUISH: (A) graze (B) revive (C) correct (D) intrude (E) exceed
4. CEREMONIOUS: (A) active (B) enjoyable (C) permanent (D) informal (E) widespread
5. SYMMETRY: (A) exclusion (B) imbalance (C) isolation (D) immensity (E) validity
6. DOCUMENT: (A) edit (B) withhold (C) reproduce in full (D) write for pay (E) leave unsupported
7. HARBOR: (A) enlighten (B) burden (C) permit (D) prepare for (E) turn away
8. BREADTH: (A) rarity (B) mobility (C) complexity (D) narrowness (E) roughness
9. NOXIOUS: (A) diffuse (B) unique (C) beneficial (D) latent (E) static
10. REPREHENSIBLE: (A) matchless (B) praiseworthy (C) interesting (D) difficult to control (E) seldom recognized
11. SCANTY: (A) adept (B) copious (C) prosaic (D) candid (E) mellow
12. ADULATION: (A) initiation (B) vilification (C) injustice (D) purification (E) deliverance
13. PRODIGIOUS: (A) questionable (B) approximate (C) ultimate (D) adjacent (E) minuscule
14. TENSILE: (A) inelastic (B) genuine (C) tough (D) sympathetic (E) inharmonious
15. AMITY: (A) strife (B) irrelevance (C) realism (D) topicality (E) unseemliness

Each sentence below has one or two blanks, each blank indicating that something has been omitted. Beneath the sentence are five lettered words or sets of words. Choose the word or set of words that best fits the meaning of the sentence as a whole.

Example:

Although its publicity has been ----, the film itself is intelligent, well-acted, handsomely produced, and altogether ----.

(A) tasteless. .respectable (B) extensive. .moderate (C) sophisticated. .amateur (D) risqué. .crude (E) perfect. .spectacular ● Ⓑ Ⓒ Ⓓ Ⓔ

16. The ambassador's papers are not ---- reading, but one who reads slowly and attentively will be richly repaid.
    (A) petty (B) valuable (C) insightful (D) easy (E) plausible
17. It is inaccurate to describe Hopkins as a crusader for progressive reforms, for, although he debunks certain popular myths, he is not really ---- of change.
    (A) an advocate (B) a censor (C) an adversary (D) a caricature (E) a descendant
18. He was lonely and might have considered himself miserable were it not for a kind of hysterical ----, which he could neither account for nor ----.
    (A) depression. .enhance
    (B) apathy. .tolerate
    (C) contentment. .enjoy
    (D) merriment. .conquer
    (E) sorrow. .comprehend
19. Occasionally ---- strain of the bacteria appears, changed by some molecular misprint from what was once only ---- into a life-taking poison.
    (A) a new. .an epidemic
    (B) a deficient. .a derivative
    (C) an erratic. .a rudiment
    (D) a virulent. .a nuisance
    (E) an advanced. .a disease
20. The discussions were often ----, degenerating at times into name-calling contests.
    (A) lofty (B) auspicious (C) acrimonious (D) lethargic (E) pragmatic

Each passage below is followed by questions based on its content. Answer all questions following a passage on the basis of what is stated or implied in that passage.

I agree that children need to be—and usually want very much to be—taught right from wrong. But I believe that realistic fiction for children is one of the very hardest media in which it can be done. It is hard not to get entangled in simplistic moralism, and all you end up with are the "baddies" and the "goodies" you had hoped to avoid. Or you can trot out the cliché that "there's a little bit of bad in the best of us and a little bit of good in the worst of us," a dangerous trivialization of the fact that there is tremendous potential for good and for evil in every one of us. Or you can try the "problem books." The problem of drugs, of divorce, of prejudice, and so on—as if evil were merely a problem, something that can be solved, that has an answer, like a problem in fifth-grade arithmetic. That is escapism, that posing of evil as a "problem," instead of what it is: all the pain and suffering and injustice we will meet throughout our lives, and must admit, in order to live human lives at all.

But what, then, is the writer for children to do? Can one present the child with evil as an insoluble problem—something neither the child nor any adult can do anything about at all? To give the child a picture of a land haunted by famines or the cruelties of a brutal parent, and say, "Well, this is how it is. What are you going to make of it?"—that is surely unethical. If you suggest that there is a solution to these monstrous facts, you are lying to the child. If you insist that there is not, you are overwhelming the child with a burden that he or she is not strong enough yet to carry.

Children do need protection and shelter. But they also need the truth. And it seems to me that the way you can speak absolutely honestly and factually about both good and evil to children is to talk about themselves, their inner selves. That is something they can cope with; indeed, their job in growing up is to become themselves. They cannot do this if they feel the task is hopeless or if they are led to think there is no task.

Fantasy is the language of the inner self. I personally find it the appropriate language in which to tell stories to children—and others. I make that statement with some confidence, having behind me the authority of a very great poet, who put it much more boldly. "The great instrument of moral good," Shelley said, "is the imagination."

21. The author's primary goal in the passage is to do which of the following?

(A) Criticize children's literature for being unrealistic
(B) Demonstrate that morality is not a fit subject for children's literature
(C) Argue that imaginative fiction is more suitable than realistic fiction for teaching morality to children
(D) Propose a solution for the problem of evil in children's literature
(E) Describe the way in which fantasy puts children in touch with the inner selves that they must obey

22. The author's attitude toward children appears to be one of

(A) concern for the development of their moral integrity
(B) idealization of their inexperience and vulnerability
(C) contempt for their inability to accept unpleasant facts
(D) exaggerated sympathy for their problems in daily life
(E) envy of their willingness to learn about morality

23. According to the author, it is the duty of children's literature to

(A) protect children from learning about anything unpleasant or distressing
(B) simplify moral issues so that children can understand them
(C) force children to deal with the facts of pain and suffering
(D) reassure children that every problem has a solution
(E) present truth in a way that children can accept and understand

24. In the passage the author indicates that much of human experience is

(A) wretched and unbearable
(B) difficult and unfair
(C) routine and boring
(D) unpredictable and meaningless
(E) pleasant and secure

25. In presenting the argument, the author does all of the following EXCEPT

(A) define a term
(B) resolve a problem
(C) refer to an authority
(D) illustrate through an analogy
(E) cite a psychological study

GO ON TO THE NEXT PAGE

The reading passages in this test are brief excerpts or adaptations of excerpts from published material. The ideas contained in them do not necessarily represent the opinions of the College Board or Educational Testing Service. To make the text suitable for testing purposes, we may in some cases have altered the style, contents, or point of view of the original.

One important facet of colonial America's early development was the role played by slave artisans from Africa. Slave art was an art of anonymity—an art that rose from slavery in the form of skilled handicrafts—an art descended from African imagery and later rechanneled as a functional aesthetic, finding its way to the wrought iron balconies of New Orleans and to the magnificent ornamentation on the mansions of Charleston, South Carolina. Although they received little credit for their labor, slave artisans accomplished necessary work in preindustrial America and became one of the first classes of technical experts in the New World.

Afro-American arts and crafts originated on the west coast of Africa where they were important in all aspects of communal life. Unlike the Europeans, who tended to perceive art objects only as "curios," Africans viewed the arts as functional and art objects were created for specific use in ceremonies as well as in numerous domestic activities. Many Africans were master artisans, demonstrating various skills and great proficiency in the fashioning of wood, bone, and ivory, in weaving, in pottery-making, and in the making of clothes, tools, and other implements. There is also strong evidence that some African groups were skilled in the building trades, whereas others proved skillful in developing exquisite sculptured objects of bronze through new casting techniques.

The major factors surrounding the development of the slave-artisan class included the diversification of farming and industry and the scarcity of labor to meet the needs of colonial America. As a solution to this problem, slaves were employed in every conceivable fashion. The diversity of occupations held by slave artisans is a clear example of why skilled slaves became very important agents in the rise of manufacturing.

Although research concerning slave artisans is lacking, certain general conclusions are apparent. Black artisans constituted a specialized labor force in colonial America. Without their achievements it is difficult to imagine how the colonists would have survived and prospered. As producers of goods, contributors to the building trades, manufacturers of furniture, and designers of household objects and decor, slave artisans also aided America in its aesthetic development. Their creativity and cleverness laid the foundation for furthering the development of the Afro-American artist.

26. The author is primarily concerned with
(A) describing the slave artisans' response to the limited opportunities for creative expression in colonial America
(B) discussing the slaves' artistic heritage and the role their skills played in preindustrial America
(C) depicting the specific talents of slave artisans in the areas of decoration and design
(D) noting that contemporary Black art emerged from the work of slave artisans
(E) praising the long history of the artistic tradition of Africa

27. It can be inferred that one reason slave art was "an art of anonymity" (line 3) was that the slave artisans
(A) received inadequate fees for their work
(B) were believed to do stylized work
(C) did not receive individual credit for their work
(D) were required to work only on specifically assigned projects
(E) relied on the artistic techniques of their ancestors

28. With which of the following statements regarding artisans in Africa would the author most likely agree?
(A) They were the most respected members of their societies.
(B) They were rewarded for their contributions to the community.
(C) Their skills related primarily to manufacturing activities.
(D) All members of a society were considered artisans.
(E) They played a vital role in communal life.

29. According to the passage, slave artisans were important to colonial America because they
(A) helped meet the needs of its preindustrial society
(B) persuaded the colonists to diversify farming and industry
(C) recognized the need for new and more complex manufacturing procedures
(D) taught other slaves skills that led to greater freedom
(E) helped to develop plantations into self-sufficient communities

30. The author cites specific examples of the work of slave artisans primarily to
(A) show that they had mastered basic craft skills
(B) indicate the conventional and imitative nature of their work
(C) explain why they were considered technical experts rather than artists
(D) attest to the quality and variety of their work
(E) emphasize the limited opportunities granted to them

GO ON TO THE NEXT PAGE

Select the word or set of words that best completes each of the following sentences.

31. Many sportswriters have been caught up in the activities about which they write and have become advocates and ---- when they ought to have been ----.

(A) promoters. .colleagues
(B) participants. .collaborators
(C) apologists. .critics
(D) opponents. .antagonists
(E) disputants. .defenders

32. His inability to fathom the latest trends in art led him to fear that his critical faculties had ---- during his long absence.

(A) diversified (B) atrophied (C) converted (D) predominated (E) multiplied

33. Though her lecture contained ideas that were provocative and systematically presented, her style of delivery was so ---- that I actually dozed off.

(A) galling (B) pungent (C) desultory (D) soporific (E) theatrical

34. Fuentes' subtly persuasive arguments for continuity in Latino culture ---- readers to recognize that their future cannot be ---- from the way they treat their past.

(A) implore. .deciphered
(B) condition. .inferred
(C) invite. .divorced
(D) command. .projected
(E) inspire. .elicited

35. Like most ---- literature, this moving remembrance of the poet's parents primarily expresses lamentation for their deaths.

(A) dogmatic (B) elegiac (C) abstract (D) dramatic (E) striking

Each question below consists of a related pair of words or phrases, followed by five lettered pairs of words or phrases. Select the lettered pair that best expresses a relationship similar to that expressed in the original pair.

Example:

YAWN : BOREDOM :: (A) dream : sleep
(B) anger : madness (C) smile : amusement
(D) face : expression (E) impatience : rebellion

Ⓐ Ⓑ ● Ⓓ Ⓔ

36. JUDGE : COURTHOUSE :: (A) physician : hospital (B) clergyman : library (C) farmer : house (D) visitor : hotel (E) mathematician : computer

37. MUMBLE : INDISTINCT :: (A) relent : gentle (B) stumble : graceful (C) enunciate : clear (D) define : difficult (E) grunt : shrill

38. COLORS : SPECTRUM :: (A) experiments : laboratory (B) panes : glass (C) guests : party (D) letters : alphabet (E) leaves : tree

39. TADPOLE : FROG :: (A) stream : river (B) acorn : oak (C) politician : diplomat (D) negative : photograph (E) student : graduate

40. ABODE : VAGRANT :: (A) ship : pirate (B) fort : sentry (C) faith : prophet (D) costume : eccentric (E) community : outcast

41. CREDITS : MOVIE :: (A) selections : album (B) by-lines : newspaper (C) reviews : journal (D) reruns : television (E) cartoons : government

42. AMORPHOUS : SHAPE :: (A) amorous : trust (B) temporal : patience (C) enticing : guile (D) bland : zest (E) classical : harmony

43. EVIL:MALEFACTOR ::
(A) selfishness:hermit
(B) talent:virtuoso
(C) benevolence:miser
(D) mischief:benefactor
(E) friendliness:thief

44. DIGRESS : SPEECH :: (A) dissemble : truth (B) meander : travel (C) narrate : climax (D) deter : progress (E) circumnavigate : globe

45. PLAINTIVE : SORROW :: (A) systematic : brevity (B) elusive : eloquence (C) confident : defeat (D) distasteful : pessimism (E) contemptuous : disdain

STOP

IF YOU FINISH BEFORE TIME IS CALLED, YOU MAY CHECK YOUR WORK ON THIS SECTION ONLY. DO NOT WORK ON ANY OTHER SECTION IN THE TEST.

SECTION 2

Time—30 minutes

25 QUESTIONS

In this section solve each problem, using any available space on the page for scratchwork. Then decide which is the best of the choices given and blacken the corresponding space on the answer sheet.

The following information is for your reference in solving some of the problems.

Circle of radius r: Area $= \pi r^2$; Circumference $= 2\pi r$

The number of degrees of arc in a circle is 360.

The measure in degrees of a straight angle is 180.

Definitions of symbols:

$=$	is equal to	$\leq$	is less than or equal to
$\neq$	is unequal to	$\geq$	is greater than or equal to
$<$	is less than	$\parallel$	is parallel to
$>$	is greater than	$\perp$	is perpendicular to

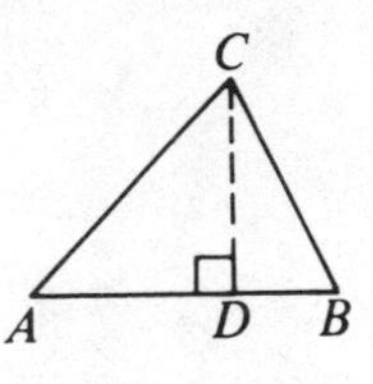

Triangle: The sum of the measures in degrees of the angles of a triangle is 180.

If $\angle CDA$ is a right angle, then

(1) area of $\triangle ABC = \dfrac{AB \times CD}{2}$

(2) $AC^2 = AD^2 + DC^2$

Note: Figures which accompany problems in this test are intended to provide information useful in solving the problems. They are drawn as accurately as possible EXCEPT when it is stated in a specific problem that its figure is not drawn to scale. All figures lie in a plane unless otherwise indicated. All numbers used are real numbers.

---

1. If $x - 7 = 5 - x$, then $x =$

   (A) -6 (B) -1 (C) 1 (D) 6 (E) 12

2. A gymnast competed in a meet and received the following scores for three events: 9.5 for bars, 8.7 for balance beam, and 8.8 for floor routine. What is the average (arithmetic mean) of these three scores?

   (A) 8.9
   (B) 9.0
   (C) 9.1
   (D) 9.2
   (E) 9.3

3. On a number line, if point P has coordinate -3 and point Q has coordinate 5, what is the length of segment PQ?

   (A) 2 (B) 4 (C) 5 (D) 8 (E) 64

4. If $\dfrac{(20+50)+(30+N)}{2} = 70$, then $N =$

   (A) 30
   (B) 40
   (C) 50
   (D) 60
   (E) 70

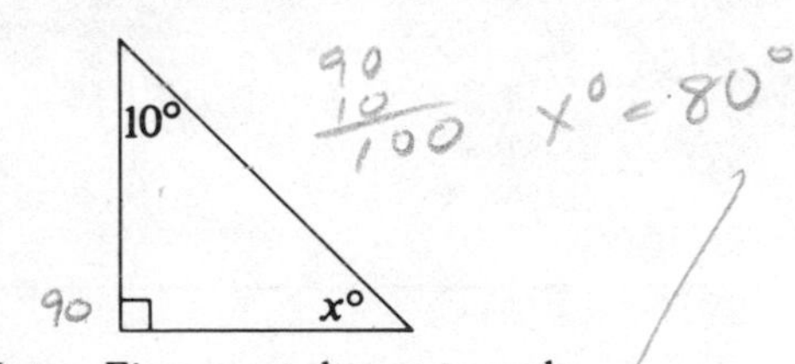

Note: Figure not drawn to scale.

5. In the right triangle above, $x - 10 =$

   (A) 60
   (B) 70
   (C) 80
   (D) 90
   (E) 100

---

6. If $(x+3)^2 = (x-3)^2$, then $x =$

   (A) 0 (B) 1 (C) 3 (D) 6 (E) 9

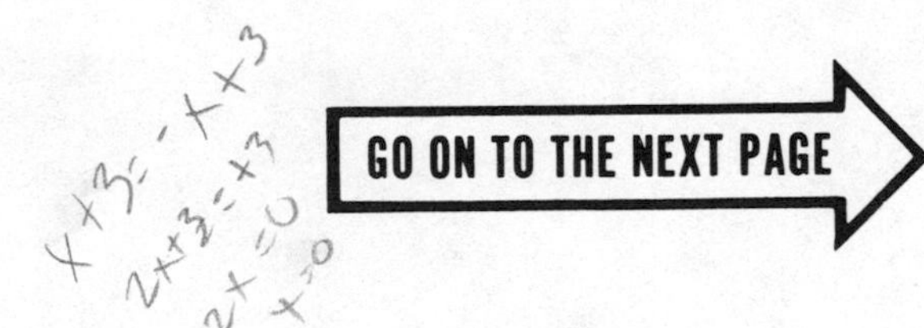

7. Ms. Jones borrowed \$1,000 for a year. The cost of the loan was 6 percent of the amount borrowed, to be paid back together with the loan at the end of the year. What was the total amount needed to pay off the loan?

(A) \$1,000.60
(B) \$1,006.00
(C) \$1,060.00
(D) \$1,600.00
(E) \$6,000.00

8. If $\frac{5}{x} = 1$ and $\frac{y}{2} = 3$, then $\frac{3+x}{y+3} =$

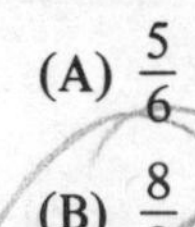

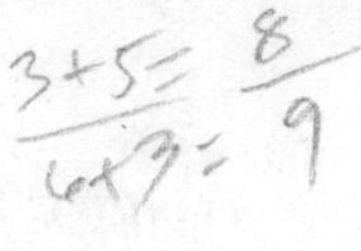

(A) $\frac{5}{6}$

(B) $\frac{8}{9}$

(C) 1

(D) $\frac{9}{8}$

(E) $\frac{6}{5}$

Candidate	Number of Votes Received
A	20
B	45
C	102
D	x
E	y

9. In a class of 300 students, 5 students were running for the position of student representative. If every student in the class voted for exactly one candidate and the distribution of votes is given in the table above, what is the maximum possible value of x ?

(A) 60 (B) 133 (C) 167
(D) 233 (E) 300

10. If $\rfloor x \lfloor$ is defined by the equation $\rfloor x \lfloor = \frac{\sqrt{x}}{2}$ for all whole numbers x, which of the following equals 5 ?

(A) $\rfloor 10 \lfloor$ (B) $\rfloor 20 \lfloor$ (C) $\rfloor 25 \lfloor$
(D) $\rfloor 50 \lfloor$ (E) $\rfloor 100 \lfloor$

11. To the nearest thousand, what is the number of seconds in a 24-hour day?

(A) 8,000
(B) 9,000
(C) 86,000
(D) 87,000
(E) 90,000

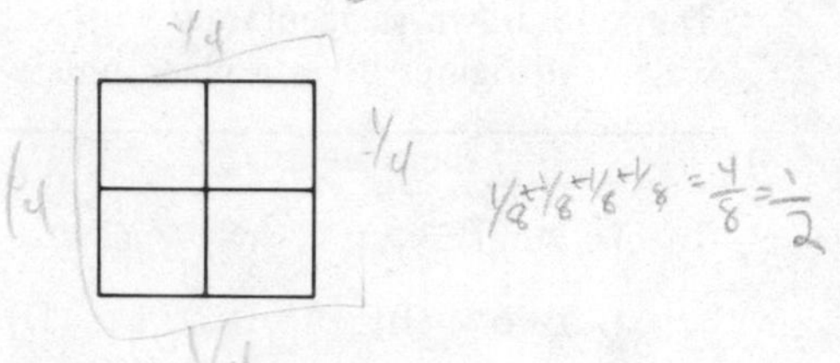

12. The figure above is a square divided into four equal smaller squares. If the perimeter of the large square is 1, then the perimeter of a small square is

(A) $\frac{1}{16}$ (B) $\frac{1}{8}$ (C) $\frac{1}{6}$ (D) $\frac{1}{4}$ (E) $\frac{1}{2}$

13. If $\frac{5}{6} = \frac{x}{5}$, then $x =$

(A) $\frac{6}{25}$ (B) $\frac{6}{5}$ (C) $\frac{25}{6}$ (D) 6 (E) 25

GO ON TO THE NEXT PAGE

14. A jar contains 10 pencils, some sharpened and some unsharpened. Each of the following could be the ratio of sharpened to unsharpened pencils EXCEPT

(A) 1 : 1
(B) 3 : 2
(C) 4 : 1
(D) 5 : 1
(E) 9 : 1

15. Cube X has a volume of 27. If point C is the center of one face of cube X and point D is the center of the opposite parallel face, what is the length of line segment CD ?

(A) 3
(B) $3\sqrt{2}$
(C) 6
(D) $6\sqrt{2}$
(E) 9

16. Initially, there are exactly 18 bananas on a tree. If one monkey eats $\frac{1}{3}$ of the bananas and another monkey eats $\frac{1}{3}$ of the bananas that are left, how many bananas are still on the tree?

(A) 4
(B) 6
(C) 8
(D) 10
(E) 16

17. If $\frac{a}{b} + \frac{c}{d} = 4$, what is the value of $\frac{b}{a} + \frac{d}{c}$?

(A) $\frac{1}{4}$ (B) 1 (C) $\frac{4}{3}$ (D) 4

(E) It cannot be determined from the information given.

18. Which of the following is the greater of two numbers whose product is 220 and whose sum is 10 more than the difference between the two?

(A) 5 (B) 10 (C) 22 (D) 44 (E) 55

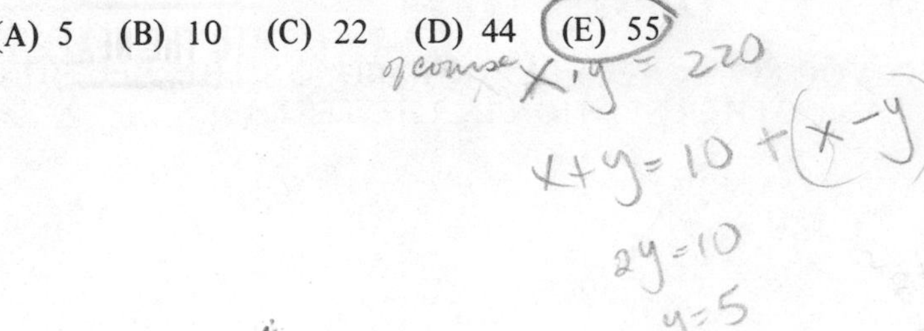

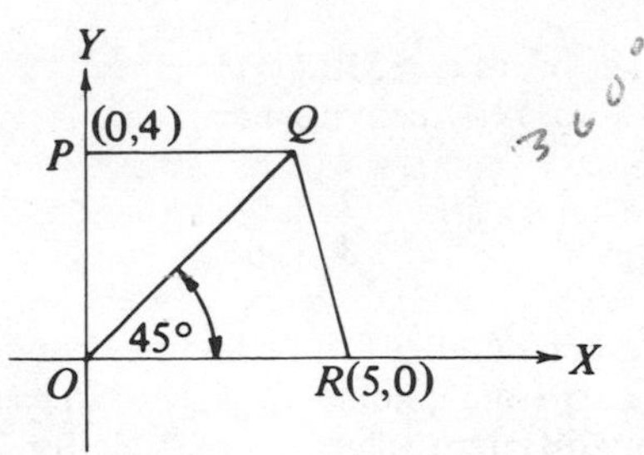

19. In the figure above, if $PQ \parallel OR$, what is the area of quadrilateral $PQRO$?

(A) 9 (B) 14 (C) 18 (D) 36

(E) It cannot be determined from the information given.

20. On the last day of a one-week sale, customers numbered 149 through 201 were waited on. How many customers were waited on that day?

(A) 51 (B) 52 (C) 53 (D) 152 (E) 153

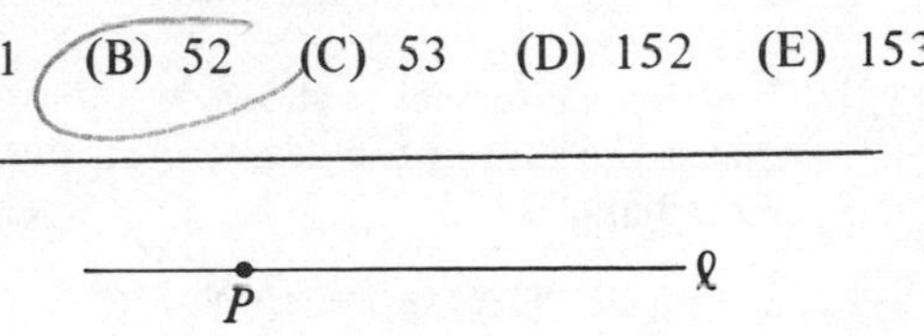

21. If two points, Q and R, are each placed to the right of point P on line ℓ above so that $2PQ = 3PR$, what will be the value of $\frac{RQ}{PR}$?

(A) $\frac{1}{2}$ (B) $\frac{2}{5}$ (C) $\frac{2}{3}$ (D) $\frac{3}{2}$

(E) It cannot be determined from the information given.

GO ON TO THE NEXT PAGE

X	Y
1	4
2	5
3	6

22. If x is a number from column X and y is a number from column Y in the table above, how many different values are possible for $x + y$?

(A) Nine (B) Eight (C) Seven (D) Six (E) Five

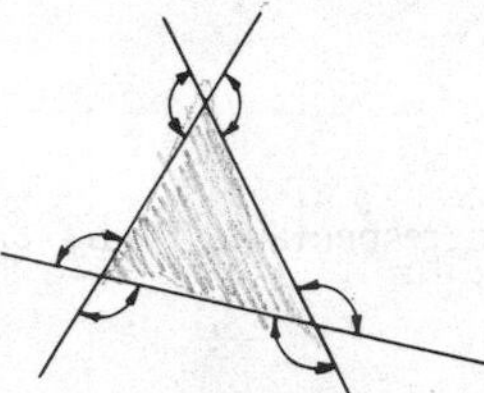

23. Three lines intersect as shown in the figure above. What is the sum of the degree measures of the marked angles?

(A) 360° (B) 540° (C) 720° (D) 900°
(E) It cannot be determined from the information given.

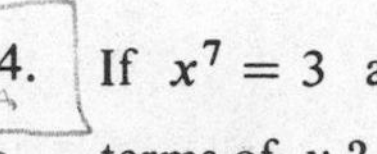

24. If $x^7 = 3$ and $x^6 = \frac{2}{y}$, what is the value of x in terms of y?

(A) $\frac{3}{2}y$

(B) $\frac{2}{3}y$

(C) $\frac{1}{3}y$

(D) $3y$

(E) $3 - \frac{2}{y}$

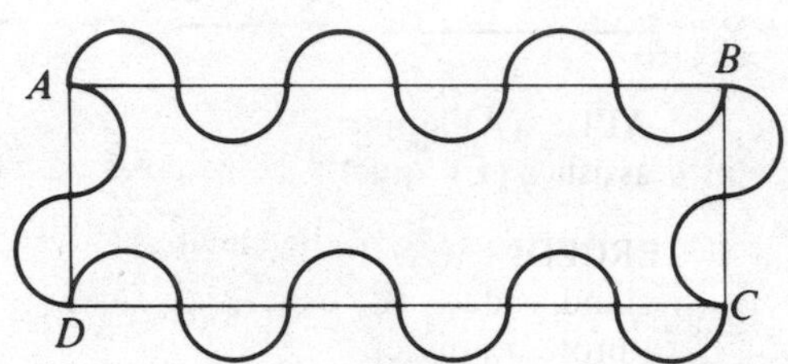

25. In the figure above, $ABCD$ is a rectangle and the curved path is made up of 16 semicircles of equal diameter. If the total length of this curved path is 32π, then the area of rectangle $ABCD$ is

(A) 24 (B) 32 (C) 48 (D) 64 (E) 192

S T O P

IF YOU FINISH BEFORE TIME IS CALLED, YOU MAY CHECK YOUR WORK ON THIS SECTION ONLY. DO NOT WORK ON ANY OTHER SECTION IN THE TEST.

SECTION 4

Time—30 minutes

40 QUESTIONS

For each question in this section, choose the best answer and blacken the corresponding space on the answer sheet.

Each question below consists of a word in capital letters, followed by five lettered words or phrases. Choose the word or phrase that is most nearly opposite in meaning to the word in capital letters. Since some of the questions require you to distinguish fine shades of meaning, consider all the choices before deciding which is best.

Example:

GOOD: (A) sour (B) bad (C) red (D) hot (E) ugly

Ⓐ ● Ⓒ Ⓓ Ⓔ

1. RECALL: (A) oppose (B) forget (C) injure (D) assist (E) quiet
2. INTERCEDE: (A) render harmless (B) stand aside (C) direct incompetently (D) protect publicly (E) convene hastily
3. GRANDIOSE: (A) attractive (B) unhealthy (C) bright and shiny (D) small and unimpressive (E) soft and manageable
4. UNNERVE: (A) warn (B) release (C) evaluate (D) strengthen (E) believe
5. RUFFIANISM: (A) gentle behavior (B) cold disdain (C) false piety (D) ignorant statement (E) wishful thinking
6. PALPABLE: (A) retroactive (B) decorative (C) imperturbable (D) not tangible (E) not trustworthy
7. MIRED: (A) dismissed (B) corrected (C) unsound (D) unhampered (E) unregulated
8. DISPARAGE: (A) praise profusely (B) surrender silently (C) fraternize (D) exorcise (E) reprieve
9. DISSONANCE: (A) practicality (B) agreement (C) probability (D) loyalty (E) cheerfulness
10. CAJOLE: (A) animate (B) browbeat (C) measure up to (D) work intensively (E) determine rapidly

Each sentence below has one or two blanks, each blank indicating that something has been omitted. Beneath the sentence are five lettered words or sets of words. Choose the word or set of words that best fits the meaning of the sentence as a whole.

Example:

Although its publicity has been ----, the film itself is intelligent, well-acted, handsomely produced, and altogether ----.

(A) tasteless. .respectable (B) extensive. .moderate (C) sophisticated. .amateur (D) risqué. .crude (E) perfect. .spectacular

● Ⓑ Ⓒ Ⓓ Ⓔ

11. Medieval kingdoms did not become constitutional republics overnight; on the contrary, the change was ----.

    (A) unpopular (B) unexpected (C) advantageous (D) sufficient (E) gradual

12. This carefully researched book is useful because it ---- the ---- concerns and influences that have connected women writers over three centuries.

    (A) omits. .essential
    (B) distorts. .ephemeral
    (C) charts. .underlying
    (D) dispels. .unimpeachable
    (E) foresees. .documented

13. The reef's fragile surface of living polyps is probably more ---- to wounds and infection than a child's skin; indeed, merely brushing against living coral ---- its delicate protoplasm.

    (A) resistant. .revives (B) susceptible. .enhances (C) immune. .imperils (D) vulnerable. .damages (E) attractive. .impairs

GO ON TO THE NEXT PAGE

14. Though discrepant popular belief makes the findings appear to be ----, recent behavioral studies suggest that most teen-agers are actually happy.

(A) discriminating (B) heretical (C) anticipated (D) obligatory (E) depressing

15. The validity of her experimental findings was so ---- that even the most ---- investigators could not refrain from extolling her.

(A) enigmatic. .officious
(B) fallacious. .credulous
(C) unassailable. .disputatious
(D) inevitable. .convivial
(E) dubious. .skeptical

Each question below consists of a related pair of words or phrases, followed by five lettered pairs of words or phrases. Select the lettered pair that best expresses a relationship similar to that expressed in the original pair.

Example:

YAWN : BOREDOM :: (A) dream : sleep (B) anger : madness (C) smile : amusement (D) face : expression (E) impatience : rebellion

Ⓐ Ⓑ ● Ⓓ Ⓔ

16. HEIGHT : MOUNTAIN :: (A) depth : trench (B) shade : tree (C) weight : age (D) speed : highway (E) mineral : mine

17. CENSUS : POPULATION :: (A) election : government (B) criterion : judgment (C) inventory : stock (D) drought : thirst (E) recipe : cake

18. POET : WORDS :: (A) sculptor : stone (B) painter : artistry (C) sailor : ocean (D) physician : care (E) philosopher : book

19. CONTEMPLATION : THINKER :: (A) corrosion : chemist (B) construction : builder (C) sullenness : fighter (D) hesitation : liar (E) pain : soldier

20. RIDDLED : HOLES :: (A) untangled : knots (B) wrinkled : materials (C) flawed : repairs (D) pitted : indentations (E) sharpened : injuries

21. MUSE : INSPIRATION :: (A) editor : personality (B) model : criticism (C) epic : superstition (D) plot : characterization (E) patron : support

22. VEHEMENT : ENERGY ::
(A) domineering : caution
(B) compassionate : sympathy
(C) dauntless : fear
(D) ruthless : suspicion
(E) amiable : apathy

23. FLAGRANT : OBSERVER ::
(A) blaring : listener
(B) monotonous : speaker
(C) mischievous : prankster
(D) temporary : visitor
(E) aggressive : attacker

24. ASTUTE : INSIGHT :: (A) dutiful : efficiency (B) affable : friendliness (C) gullible : dependence (D) zealous : nobility (E) proud : ambition

25. LABOR : RESPITE :: (A) opinion : dissent (B) commitment : betrayal (C) action : resentment (D) error : erasure (E) debate : lull

GO ON TO THE NEXT PAGE

Each passage below is followed by questions based on its content. Answer all questions following a passage on the basis of what is stated or implied in that passage.

However one chooses to define weather and climate, there is a simple practical distinction between them: weather is a matter of everyday experience, whereas climate is a statistical generalization of that experience. Weather is what usually interests us, but to interpret it correctly we must first determine what the underlying climate is in general; otherwise, we have no yardstick for comparison. In a sense, climate is like the carrier wave in radio broadcasting on which the irregular signals of programming—weather—are superimposed. We have to study the "normal" distribution of the meteorological elements before we can begin to understand the "variability around the norm" that constitutes weather.

Of all the climatic elements, solar radiation is the most basic. The intensity and duration of sunshine is a partial indication of this radiation, but there are also invisible parts of the radiation that have not by any means been as closely studied. Cloud cover is possibly the next most important because it determines both how much solar radiation reaches the ground and how much is radiated back into space from the Earth's surface. Temperature, which depends on radiation, influences cloud cover and controls humidity, and is obviously important in itself. Winds and pressure are interdependent, the latter representing the weight of the atmosphere, the former representing the air movement that ensues when adjacent vertical columns of the atmosphere have different weights. Humidity indicates the amount of water in vapor form in the atmosphere; precipitation measures the amount of water in its liquid or solid phase that falls to the Earth's surface.

26. Which of the following is the best title for the passage?

(A) Weather and Its Consequences
(B) Technology and Climate
(C) Can Weather Be Controlled?
(D) Climate: A Mixed Blessing
(E) The Components of Climate

27. Which of the following comparisons most closely parallels the relationship between weather and climate described in the first paragraph?

(A) A particular game to a team's season record
(B) A heat-seeking missile to a fighter plane
(C) A bacterium to its colony
(D) An element to a compound
(E) A waterfall to a lake

28. It can be inferred from the passage that the definition of precipitation includes which of the following?

I. Water vapor
II. Rain and snow
III. Hail and sleet

(A) II only (B) I and II only
(C) I and III only (D) II and III only
(E) I, II, and III

"It seems very odd, very sad," Margaret returned, "that you can never act unselfishly in society affairs. If I wished to go and see those girls just to do them a pleasure, and perhaps because they're new in town and lonely, I might do them good, even–but it would be impossible."

"Quite," said her aunt. "Such a thing would be quixotic. Society doesn't rest upon any such basis. It can't; it would go to pieces if people acted from unselfish motives."

"Then it isn't society at all!" said the girl. "All its favors are really bargains. Its gifts are for gifts back again."

"Yes, that is true," said Mrs. Horn, with no more sense of a judgment in the fact than the political economist has in the fact that wages are the measure of necessity and not of merit. "You get what you pay for. It's a matter of business." She satisfied herself with this formula, but she did not dislike her niece's revolt against it. That was part of Margaret's originality, which pleased her aunt in proportion to her own conventionality; she was really a timid person, and she liked the show of courage which Margaret's magnanimity often reflected upon her. She thought that she set bounds to the girl's originality because she recognized them. Margaret understood this better than her aunt and knew that she had consulted her about going to see the girls out of deference and with no expectation of luminous instruction.

29. Mrs. Horn would most likely consider which of the following a good example of the way society actually works?

(A) A celebrity lavishly supports a charity organization solely to obtain favorable publicity.
(B) A city government intervenes to halt construction of a shopping center in a residential district.
(C) A parent provides a child with high ideals but cannot translate theory into practice.
(D) A building contractor secretly replaces expensive materials with shabby and inadequate goods.
(E) A doctor receives a prestigious award for the discovery of a cure for a dangerous disease.

30. According to the passage, Margaret asked Mrs. Horn's opinion because she

(A) wished to emulate her aunt's behavior in society
(B) could not choose a suitable course of action
(C) thought she would receive good advice
(D) needed to bolster her aunt's self-confidence
(E) wanted to show respect for her aunt

31. According to the passage, Mrs. Horn sees her relationship with Margaret as one in which she

(A) protects Margaret from the natural evil of society
(B) consoles Margaret in her disillusionment and loss of innocence
(C) enlightens Margaret by pointing out limitations of her ideas
(D) humiliates Margaret through constant proof that she is wrong
(E) irritates Margaret by frequent intrusions into her personal life

Rodents are the largest order of mammals, both in number of species and in individuals, outnumbering all other warm-blooded quadrupeds and bipeds combined. There is considerable variation in this order, which includes beavers, porcupines, rats, lemmings, badgers, and the familiar cage pets, gerbils and hamsters. Rodents are ubiquitous, inhabiting almost every continent, either as natives or as immigrants. Most are hypertense and forever on the alert for predators, since rodents are the principal item on the menus of most furred and feathered carnivores. The common denominator among rodents is their teeth—oversize, chisel-like incisors that grow constantly throughout their lives and that are kept sharp and trimmed by constant chewing on wood, nuts, plaster walls, or other hard matter. Untrimmed, their teeth will grow into inward-curving tusks that can seriously injure or even kill them.

The most familiar rodents are rats and mice, whose usefulness as laboratory animals and as important links in the food chain is virtually unrivaled. In laboratories all over the world, domesticated rats and mice are the prime subjects of scientific experiments and research projects that aim to cure human diseases and determine the effects of myriad drugs on human beings. Because rodents are similar to humans in the adaptability of their eating habits, rats and mice are invaluable to scientists doing studies on diet and nutrition. Another asset is the rodents' life span; in the wild, rats and mice rarely live longer than one year because they are preyed on by a large number of animals, including snakes, dogs, cats, owls, and hawks, but in captivity they may live as long as three years. Such a period is just right for studies on aging, growth, and heredity. In addition, rats and mice are a perfect size to house and handle with ease in laboratories. In the United States alone, scientific studies use some 18 million rats each year. It is the rare person who has not reaped, directly or indirectly, the benefits of the medical and psychological research done with these adaptable rodents.

To most people, the destructiveness and havoc rats and mice wreak on the environment far outweigh any of their virtues. Yet the vast majority of rodents are actually beneficial and essential to the overall balance of nature; they furnish food for other animals and prey on insects, whose numbers they keep in check. These rodents should never be confused with the true villains of the order: the brown or Norway rat, the black rat, and the innocent-looking house mouse. As carriers of plague, typhus, and other epidemic diseases, this trio has inflicted death and misery on the world since prehistoric times. The Black Death, the most catastrophic plague in history, killed approximately one-quarter of the population of medieval Europe and was almost certainly spread by rats, which serve as hosts for plague-bearing fleas.

32. The author states that the laboratory rodents' life span is especially helpful to scientists studying

(A) the effect of captivity on laboratory animals
(B) means of controlling the rodent population
(C) population distribution and predatory patterns
(D) genetic characteristics and growth patterns
(E) the social habits of rodents

33. The passage mentions all of the following facts about rodents EXCEPT that they

(A) eat insects
(B) are amphibious
(C) are easy to handle
(D) chew constantly
(E) can eat a variety of foods

34. It can be inferred that the author thinks rodents are useful for all of the following reasons EXCEPT that they

(A) tend to be very alert
(B) can make excellent laboratory animals
(C) are similar to humans in some ways
(D) are a source of food for other animals
(E) are an important part of the balance of nature

35. According to the author, which of the following is (are) true of rodents?

I. They are a staple in the diets of many predators.
II. Many laboratory rodents live longer than wild rodents do.
III. Most species spread devastating diseases.

(A) I only
(B) II only
(C) III only
(D) I and II only
(E) II and III only

36. Which of the following best describes the development of this passage?

(A) Major points, minor points
(B) Statement of problem, examples, proposed solution
(C) Introduction, positive factors, negative factors
(D) Introduction, cause, results
(E) Thesis, analogy, antithesis

GO ON TO THE NEXT PAGE

"What if all scientists were to publish anonymously?" I was asked this question recently by Dr. Lester Green. "Don't you think," he continued, "that scientific literature would be far less cluttered with nearly useless and carelessly produced articles were the authors to receive no public credit for their contributions? We might, in fact, be able to achieve that great nirvana in which science would be practiced for its own sake, rather than for fame and fortune."

What lies at the heart of the notion pondered by Green is the idea that individual and community interests are necessarily separate entities. Does Green seriously believe that the best interests of society would be served by depersonalizing science? Would he suggest that artists not sign their paintings?

"The highest form of vanity is love of fame," wrote George Santayana. But is an ambition for fame the worst reason for practicing science? Dr. Samuel Johnson said, "None but a blockhead ever wrote except for money." We scientists might paraphrase him, "None but a blockhead ever published a scientific article except for recognition."

Furthermore, anonymity leads to secrecy and secrecy in science is deplorable. Even when countries are at war, recognition of individual performance is necessary. True, scientists have, during periods of crisis such as the Second World War, sacrificed public recognition. In time, however, most of the important breakthroughs were credited to their discoverers.

37. The author's purpose in the passage is apparently to

(A) trace the history of an idea
(B) merge two differing views of an issue
(C) discredit the majority of research scientists
(D) argue against a proposed change
(E) demand a new set of standards

38. It can be inferred that Dr. Green is dissatisfied with the

(A) desire for anonymity among noted scientists
(B) overall quality of articles appearing in scientific literature
(C) small number of articles published by scientists
(D) recent emphasis on secrecy in the scientific community
(E) lack of recognition given to scientists who publish articles

39. Which of the following best describes the author's attitude toward the "nirvana" (line 8) mentioned by Dr. Green?

(A) Excited enthusiasm
(B) Indulgent tolerance
(C) Fascinated curiosity
(D) Cautious skepticism
(E) Disapproving dismissal

40. The author implies that an artist who did not sign his or her painting should be regarded as

(A) a fool (B) a martyr (C) an egotist
(D) a conformist (E) a pioneer

S T O P

IF YOU FINISH BEFORE TIME IS CALLED, YOU MAY CHECK YOUR WORK ON THIS SECTION ONLY. DO NOT WORK ON ANY OTHER SECTION IN THE TEST.

SECTION 5

Time—30 minutes

35 QUESTIONS

In this section solve each problem, using any available space on the page for scratchwork. Then decide which is the best of the choices given and blacken the corresponding space on the answer sheet.

The following information is for your reference in solving some of the problems.

Circle of radius r: Area $= \pi r^2$; Circumference $= 2\pi r$
The number of degrees of arc in a circle is 360.
The measure in degrees of a straight angle is 180.

Definitions of symbols:

$=$	is equal to	$\leq$	is less than or equal to
$\neq$	is unequal to	$\geq$	is greater than or equal to
$<$	is less than	$\parallel$	is parallel to
$>$	is greater than	$\perp$	is perpendicular to

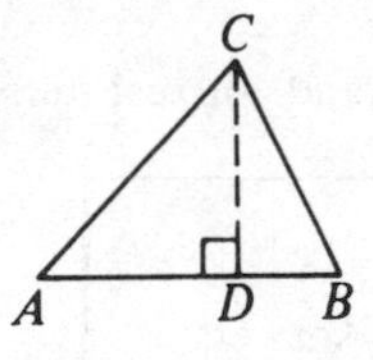

Triangle: The sum of the measures in degrees of the angles of a triangle is 180.

If $\angle CDA$ is a right angle, then

(1) area of $\triangle ABC = \frac{AB \times CD}{2}$

(2) $AC^2 = AD^2 + DC^2$

Note: Figures which accompany problems in this test are intended to provide information useful in solving the problems. They are drawn as accurately as possible EXCEPT when it is stated in a specific problem that its figure is not drawn to scale. All figures lie in a plane unless otherwise indicated. All numbers used are real numbers.

---

1. A man's grocery bill is \$8, but the store deducts \$1.50 from his bill for coupons. If the man gives the grocery clerk \$10, how much change should he get?

(A) \$8.50
(B) \$6.50
(C) \$5.50
(D) \$4.50
(E) \$3.50

2. Which of the following numbers is divisible by 3 and 5, but not by 2 ?

(A) 955
(B) 975
(C) 990
(D) 995
(E) 999

3. The members of a club decided to wash cars in order to earn money for the club. Each member of the club washed 3 cars and charged \$2 per car. When they had finished, their receipts totalled \$66, which included \$6 in tips. How many members were in the club?

(A) 9
(B) 10
(C) 11
(D) 20
(E) 22

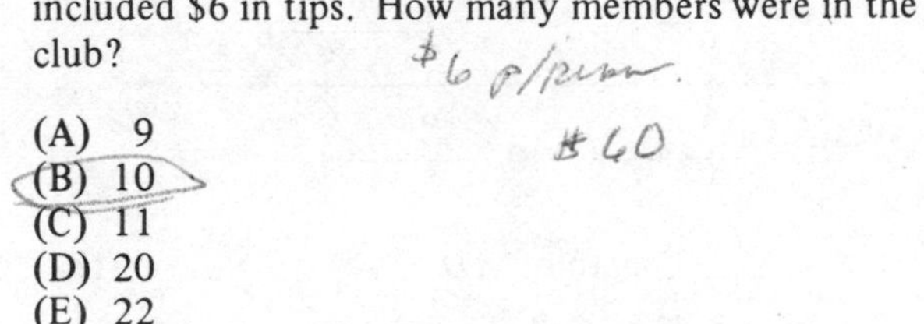

4. If x and y are positive integers such that $x^2 + y^2 = 13$ and $x > y$, then $x - y =$

(A) 1 (B) 2 (C) 3 (D) 4 (E) 5

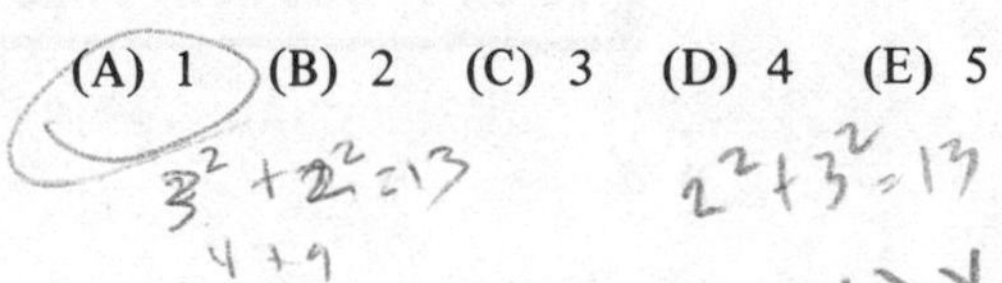

5. If the perimeter of a rectangular garden plot is 80 meters, which of the following could be the length of one of its sides?

I. 30 meters
II. 40 meters
III. 50 meters

(A) I only (B) II only (C) III only
(D) I and II (E) II and III

6. A wire of uniform diameter and composition that weighs 32 pounds is cut into two pieces. One piece is 90 yards long and weighs 24 pounds. What was the length, in yards, of the original wire?

(A) 60
(B) 120
(C) 135
(D) 270
(E) 360

7. If $\frac{1}{2}$ of a number is 2 more than $\frac{1}{3}$ of the number, what is the number?

(A) 2
(B) 6
(C) 12
(D) 20
(E) 24

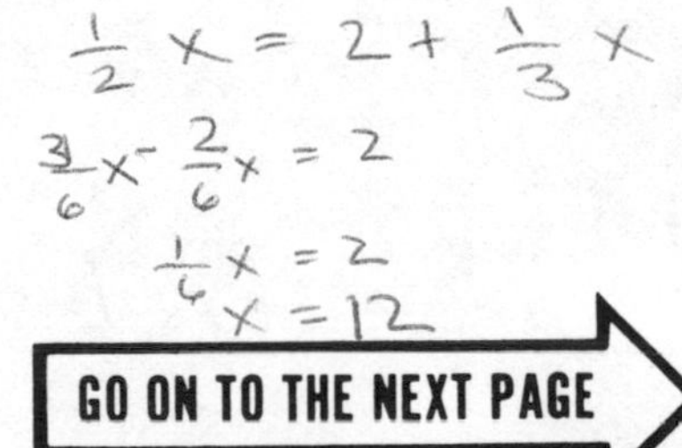

GO ON TO THE NEXT PAGE

5

Questions 8-27 each consist of two quantities, one in Column A and one in Column B. You are to compare the two quantities and on the answer sheet blacken space

A if the quantity in Column A is greater;
B if the quantity in Column B is greater;
C if the two quantities are equal;
D if the relationship cannot be determined from the information given.

Notes:
1. In certain questions, information concerning one or both of the quantities to be compared is centered above the two columns.
2. In a given question, a symbol that appears in both columns represents the same thing in Column A as it does in Column B.
3. Letters such as x, n, and k stand for real numbers.

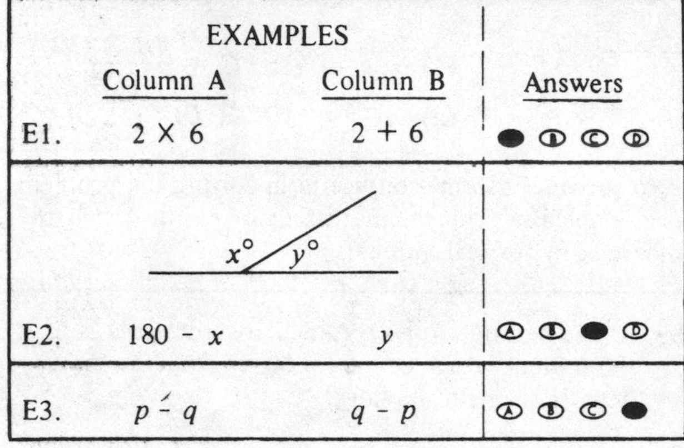

	EXAMPLES Column A	Column B	Answers
E1.	2×6	$2 + 6$	● Ⓑ Ⓒ Ⓓ
E2.	$180 - x$	y	Ⓐ Ⓑ ● Ⓓ
E3.	$p - q$	$q - p$	Ⓐ Ⓑ Ⓒ ●

Column A | Column B

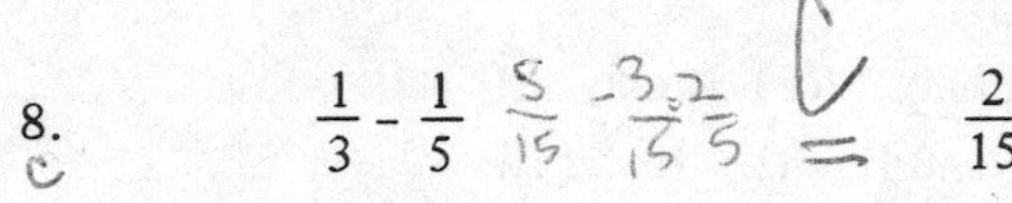

8. $\frac{1}{3} - \frac{1}{5}$ | $\frac{2}{15}$

n is a negative integer.

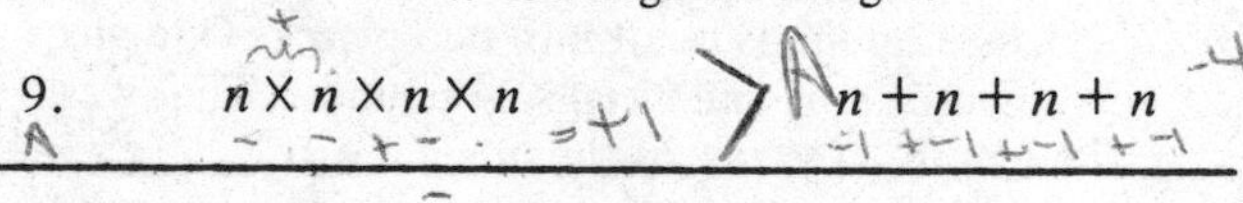

9. $n \times n \times n \times n$ | $n + n + n + n$

$P = \{1, 2, 3, 4\}$
$Q = \{1, 2, 3, 4, 5\}$

10. The number that is a member of set Q but not of set P. | A number that is a member of both sets P and Q

$x = \frac{1}{4}$

$y = \frac{1}{2}$

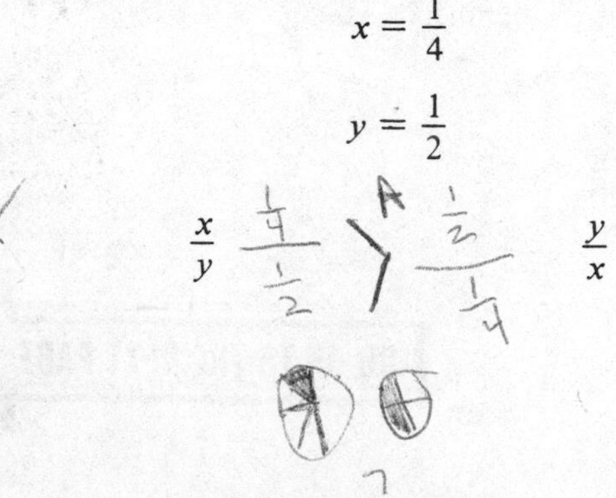

11. $\frac{x}{y}$ | $\frac{y}{x}$

Column A | Column B

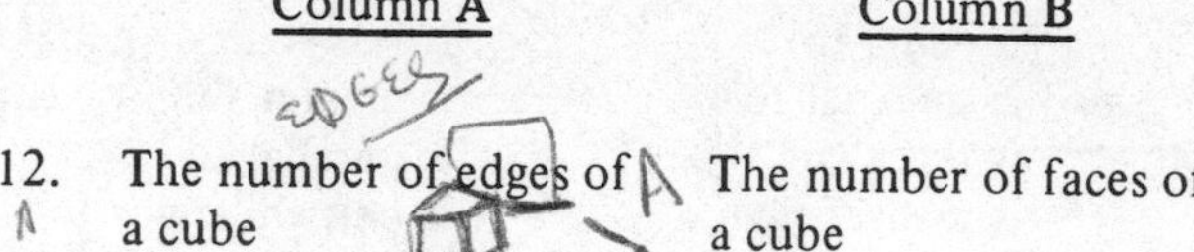

12. The number of edges of a cube | The number of faces of a cube

n is an integer.

13. The remainder when n is divided by 9 | The remainder when n is divided by 6

14. Average (arithmetic mean) of −9, −8, 8, and 9 | Average (arithmetic mean) of −7, −6, 0, 6, and 7

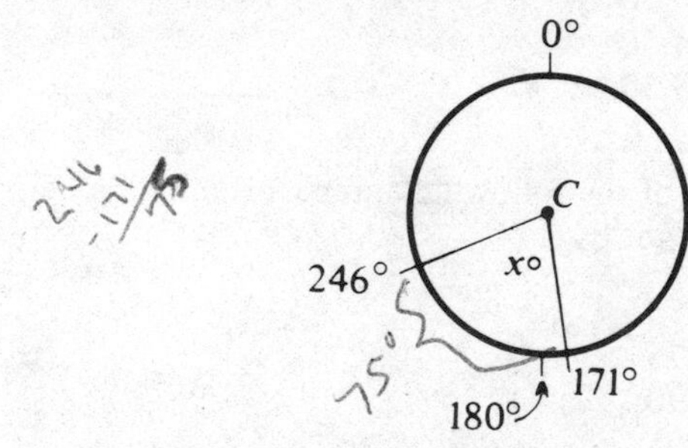

C is the center of the circle.
$x > 0$

15. x | 66

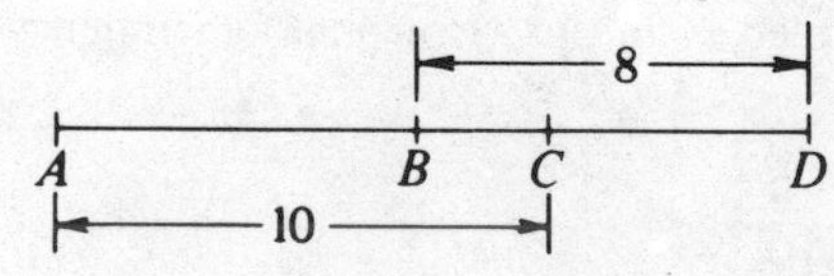

16. Length of AD | 18

GO ON TO THE NEXT PAGE

SUMMARY DIRECTIONS FOR COMPARISON QUESTIONS

Answer: A if the quantity in Column A is greater;
B if the quantity in Column B is greater;
C if the two quantities are equal;
D if the relationship cannot be determined from the information given.

Column A	Column B

$-5 < x < -3$

$-7 < y < -5$

x and y are even integers.

17. x | y

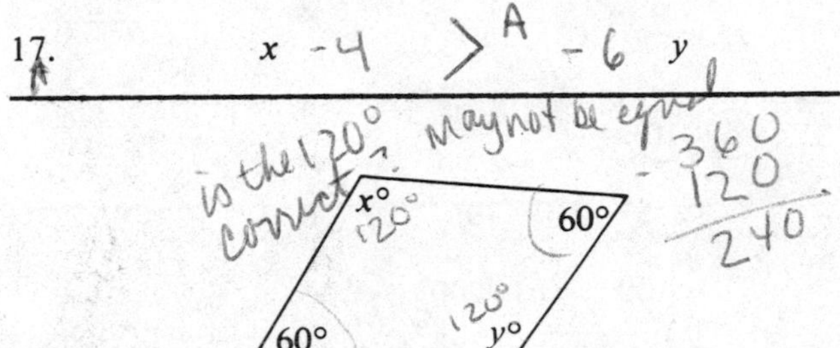

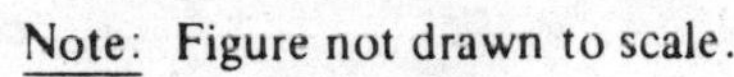

Note: Figure not drawn to scale.

18. x | y

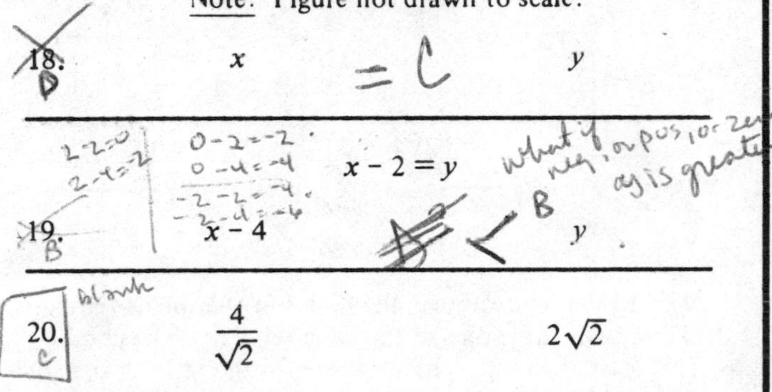

$x - 2 = y$

19. $x - 4$ | y

20. $\frac{4}{\sqrt{2}}$ | $2\sqrt{2}$

$x = 501$

$y = 500$

21. $(x + y)(x - y)$ | 1,000

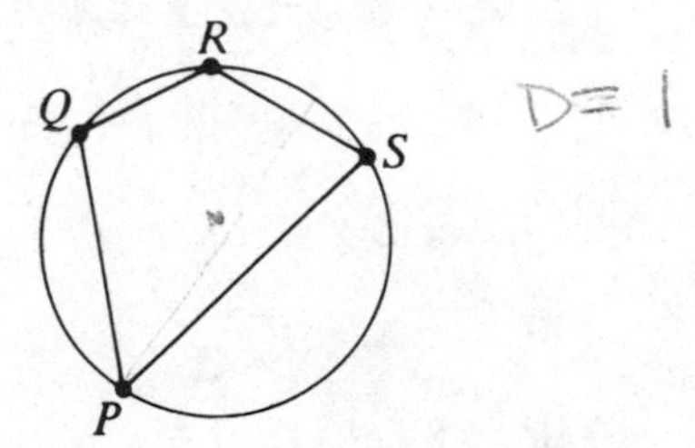

The diameter of the circle is 1.

P, Q, R, and S are on the circumference of the circle.

22. Perimeter of quadrilateral $PQRS$ | 4

Column A	Column B

A fair six-sided die with faces numbered 1 through 6 is to be rolled twice.

23. The probability of obtaining a 6 on the top face on the first roll and a 5 on the top face on the second roll | The probability of obtaining a 5 on the top face on both the first and second rolls

x and y are consecutive terms of a sequence whose terms alternate, 1, −2, 1, −2, 1, −2, etc.

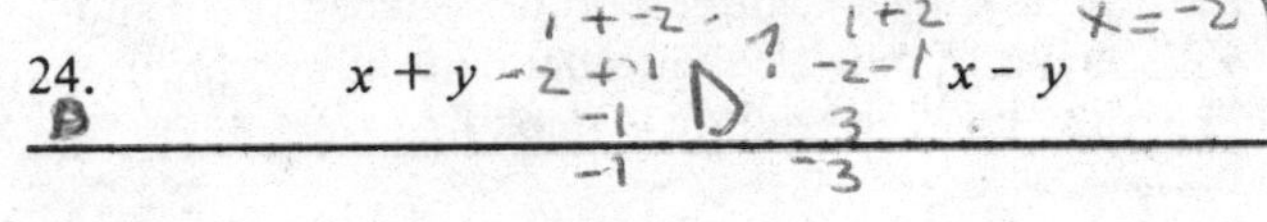

24. $x + y$ | $x - y$

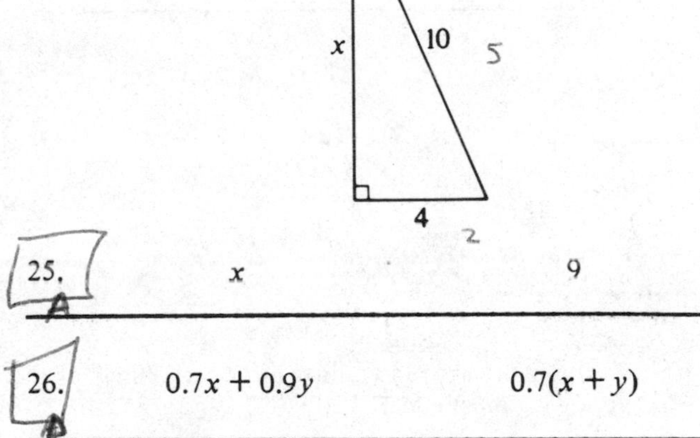

25. x | 9

26. $0.7x + 0.9y$ | $0.7(x + y)$

a, b, and c are positive.

27. Average (arithmetic mean) of a, b, and c | Average (arithmetic mean) of a^2, b^2, and c^2

GO ON TO THE NEXT PAGE

5

Solve each of the remaining problems in this section using any available space for scratchwork. Then decide which is the best of the choices given and blacken the corresponding space on the answer sheet.

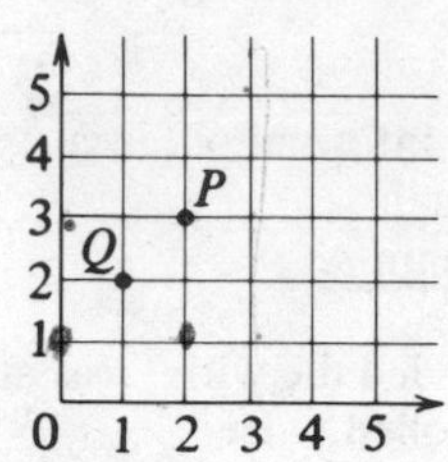

28. Which of the following points, when plotted on the grid above, will be twice as far from $P(2, 3)$ as from $Q(1, 2)$?

(A) (0, 1) (B) (0, 3) (C) (1, 3)
(D) (3, 4) (E) (3, 5)

29. If 15 kilograms of pure water is added to 10 kilograms of pure alcohol, what percent by weight of the resulting solution is alcohol?

(A) $66\frac{2}{3}\%$ (B) 40% (C) 25%
(D) 15% (E) 10%

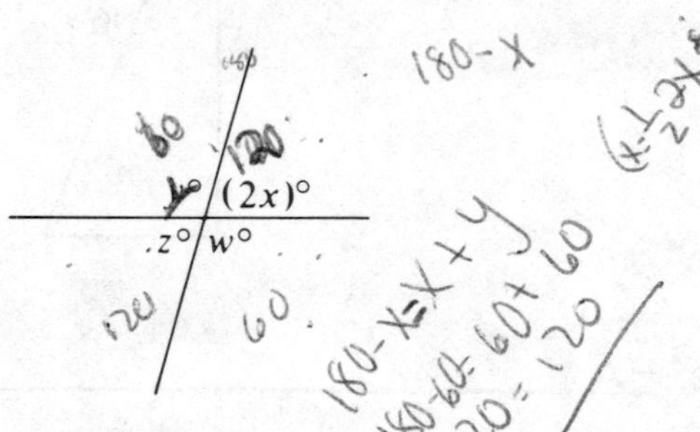

30. In the figure above two lines intersect. Which of the following must equal $180 - x$?

(A) $x + y$ (B) $x + z$ (C) $y + z$
(D) $y + w$ (E) $z + w$

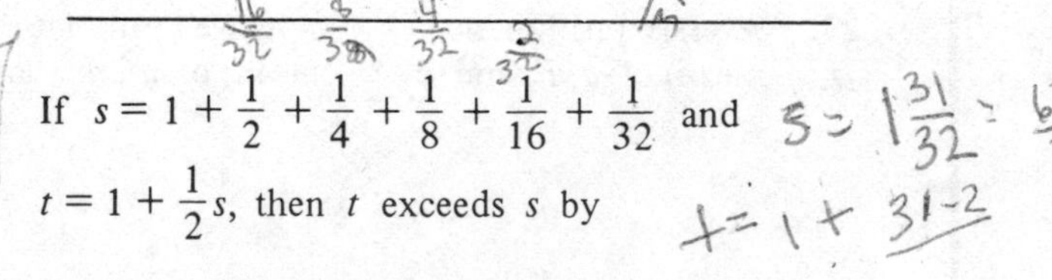

31. If $s = 1 + \frac{1}{2} + \frac{1}{4} + \frac{1}{8} + \frac{1}{16} + \frac{1}{32}$ and $t = 1 + \frac{1}{2}s$, then t exceeds s by

(A) $\frac{1}{4}$ (B) $\frac{1}{8}$ (C) $\frac{1}{16}$ (D) $\frac{1}{32}$ (E) $\frac{1}{64}$

Questions 32-33 refer to the following definition.

For all positive integers n,

let $\textcircled{n} = \frac{1}{2}n$ if n is even;

let $\textcircled{n} = 2n$ if n is odd.

32. If y is a prime number greater than 2, then $\textcircled{y} =$

(A) $\frac{1}{4}y$ (B) $\frac{1}{2}y$ (C) y (D) $2y$ (E) $4y$

33. $\textcircled{5} \cdot \textcircled{10} =$

(A) $\textcircled{15}$ (B) $\textcircled{30}$ (C) $\textcircled{50}$
(D) $\textcircled{100}$ (E) $\textcircled{200}$

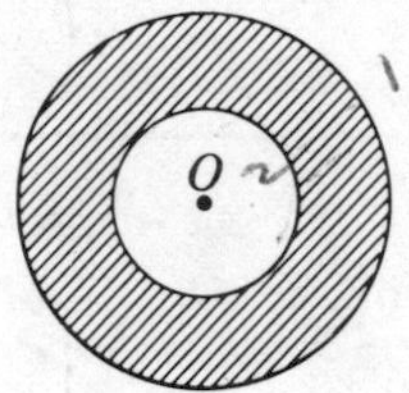

34. In the figure above, the radius of the smaller circle is half the radius of the larger circle. If the circles have the same center O, what is the ratio of the area of the shaded region to the area of the larger circle?

(A) 4:5 (B) 3:4 (C) 1:2
(D) 1:4 (E) 1:8

35. If the operation Δ is defined for all positive x and y by $x \Delta y = \frac{xy}{x + y}$, which of the following must be true for positive x, y, and z?

I. $x \Delta x = \frac{1}{2}x$

II. $x \Delta y = y \Delta x$

III. $x \Delta (y \Delta z) = (x \Delta y) \Delta z$

(A) I only (B) I and II only (C) I and III only
(D) II and III only (E) I, II, and III

S T O P

IF YOU FINISH BEFORE TIME IS CALLED, YOU MAY CHECK YOUR WORK ON THIS SECTION ONLY. DO NOT WORK ON ANY OTHER SECTION IN THE TEST.

Correct Answers for Scholastic Aptitude Test Form Code 3E

VERBAL		MATHEMATICAL	
Section 1	Section 4	Section 2	Section 5
1. A	1. B	1. D	1. E
2. C	2. B	2. B	2. B
3. B	3. D	3. D	3. B
4. D	4. D	4. B	4. A
5. B	5. A	5. B	5. A
6. E	6. D	6. A	6. B
7. E	7. D	7. C	7. C
8. D	8. A	8. B	*8. C
9. C	9. B	9. B	*9. A
10. B	10. B	10. E	*10. A
11. B	11. E	11. C	*11. B
12. B	12. C	12. E	*12. A
13. E	13. D	13. C	*13. D
14. A	14. B	14. D	*14. C
15. A	15. C	15. A	*15. A
16. D	16. A	16. C	*16. B
17. A	17. C	17. E	*17. A
18. D	18. A	18. D	*18. D
19. D	19. B	19. C	*19. B
20. C	20. D	20. C	*20. C
21. C	21. E	21. A	*21. A
22. A	22. B	22. E	*22. B
23. E	23. A	23. C	*23. C
24. B	24. B	24. A	*24. D
25. E	25. E	25. E	*25. A
26. B	26. E		*26. D
27. C	27. A		*27. D
28. E	28. D		28. A
29. A	29. A		29. B
30. D	30. E		30. A
31. C	31. C		31. E
32. B	32. D		32. D
33. D	33. B		33. D
34. C	34. A		34. B
35. B	35. D		35. E
36. A	36. C		
37. C	37. D		
38. D	38. B		
39. B	39. E		
40. E	40. A		
41. B			
42. D			
43. B			
44. B			
45. E			

*Indicates four-choice questions. (All of the other questions are five-choice.)

The Scoring Process

Machine-scoring is done in three steps:

- *Scanning.* Your answer sheet is "read" by a scanning machine and the oval you filled in for each question is recorded on a computer tape.
- *Scoring.* The computer compares the oval filled in for each question with the correct response. Each correct answer receives one point; omitted questions do not count toward your score. For each wrong answer, a fraction of a point is subtracted to correct for random guessing. For questions with five answer choices, one-fourth of a point is subtracted for each wrong response; for questions with four answer choices, one-third of a point is subtracted for each wrong response. The SAT-verbal test has 85 questions with five answer choices each. If, for example, a student has 44 right, 32 wrong, and 9 omitted, the resulting raw score is determined as follows:

$$44 \text{ right} - \frac{32 \text{ wrong}}{4} = 44 - 8 = 36 \text{ raw score points}$$

  Obtaining raw scores frequently involves the rounding of fractional numbers to the nearest whole number. For example, a raw score of 36.25 is rounded to 36, the nearest whole number. A raw score of 36.50 is rounded upward to 37.

- *Converting to reported scaled score.* Raw test scores are then placed on the College Board scale of 200 to 800 through a process that adjusts scores to account for minor differences in difficulty among different editions of the test. This process, known as equating, is performed so that a student's reported score is not affected by the edition of the test taken nor by the abilities of the group with whom the student takes the test. As a result of placing SAT scores on the College Board scale, scores earned by students at different times can be compared. For example, an SAT-verbal score of 400 on a test taken at one administration indicates the same level of developed verbal ability as a 400 score obtained on a different edition of the test taken at another time.

How to Score the Test

You can verify the College Board SAT scores reported to you recently by using the information in this booklet along with the copy of your answer sheet. *Before you begin, check that the first two characters (number and letter) of the form code you marked in item 3 on your answer sheet are the same as the form code printed on the front of this booklet.* Compare the responses shown on the copy of your answer sheet with the list of correct answers.

SAT-Verbal Sections 1 and 4

Step A: Count the number of correct answers for *section 1* and record the number in the space provided on the worksheet on the next page. Then do the same for the incorrect answers. (Do not count omitted answers.) To determine subtotal A, use the formula:

$$\text{number correct} - \frac{\text{number incorrect}}{4} = \text{subtotal A}$$

Step B: Count the number of correct answers and the number of incorrect answers for *section 4* and record the numbers in the spaces provided on the worksheet. To determine subtotal B, use the formula:

$$\text{number correct} - \frac{\text{number incorrect}}{4} = \text{subtotal B}$$

Step C: To obtain C, add subtotal A to subtotal B, keeping any decimals. Enter the resulting figure on the worksheet.

Step D: To obtain D, your raw verbal score, round C to the nearest whole number. (For example, any number from 44.50 to 45.49 rounds to 45.) Enter the resulting figure on the worksheet.

Step E: To find your reported SAT-verbal score, look up the total raw verbal score you obtained in step D in the conversion table on the back cover. Enter this figure on the worksheet. (The SAT-verbal score you just recorded and your reported SAT-verbal score should be identical. If not, see the paragraph at the bottom of the next page.)

SAT-Mathematical Sections 2 and 5

Step A: Count the number of correct answers and the number of incorrect answers for *section 2* and record the numbers in the spaces provided on the worksheet. To determine the subtotal A, use the formula:

$$\text{number correct} - \frac{\text{number incorrect}}{4} = \text{subtotal A}$$

Step B: Count the number of correct answers and the number of incorrect answers for the *five-choice questions (questions 1 through 7 and 28 through 35) in section 5* and record the numbers in the spaces provided on the worksheet. To determine the subtotal B, use the formula:

$$\text{number correct} - \frac{\text{number incorrect}}{4} = \text{subtotal B}$$

Step C: Count the number of correct answers and the number of incorrect answers for the *four-choice questions (questions 8 through 27) in section 5* and record the numbers in the spaces provided on the worksheet. To determine the subtotal C, use the formula:

$$\text{number correct} - \frac{\text{number incorrect}}{3} = \text{subtotal C}$$

Step D: To obtain D, add subtotal A, subtotal B, and subtotal C, keeping any decimals. Enter the resulting figure on the worksheet.

Step E: To obtain E, your raw mathematical score, round D to the nearest whole number. (For example, any number from 44.50 to 45.49 rounds to 45.) Enter the resulting figure on the worksheet.

Step F: To find your reported SAT-mathematical score, look up the total raw mathematical score you obtained in E in the conversion table on the back cover. Enter this figure on the worksheet. (The SAT-mathematical score you just recorded and your reported SAT-mathematical score should be identical. If not, see the paragraph at the bottom of the next page.)

FORM CODE 3E

SAT-SCORING WORKSHEET

SAT-Verbal Sections

A. Section 1: ______ no. correct − ¼ (______ no. incorrect) = ______ subtotal A

B. Section 4: ______ no. correct − ¼ (______ no. incorrect) = ______ subtotal B

C. Total unrounded raw score (Total A + B) ______ C

D. Total rounded raw score (Rounded to nearest whole number) ______ D

E. SAT-verbal reported scaled score (See the conversion table on the back cover.) ______ SAT-verbal score

SAT-Mathematical Sections

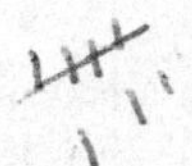

A. Section 2: ______ no. correct − ¼ (______ no. incorrect) = ______ subtotal A

B. Section 5: Questions 1 through 7 and 28 through 35 (5-choice) ______ no. correct − ¼ (______ no. incorrect) = ______ subtotal B

C. Section 5: Questions 8 through 27 (4-choice) ______ no. correct − ⅓ (______ no. incorrect) = ______ subtotal C

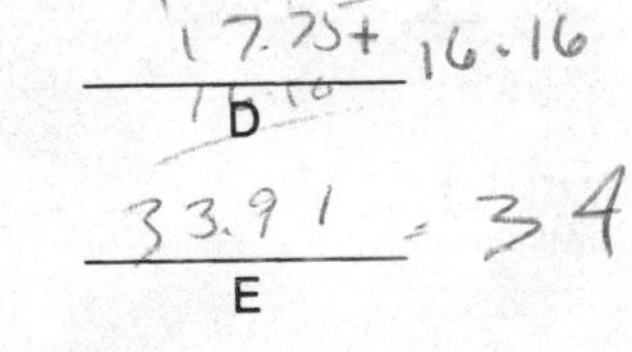

D. Total unrounded raw score (Total A + B + C) ______ D

E. Total rounded raw score (Rounded to nearest whole number) ______ E

F. SAT-mathematical reported scaled score (See the conversion table on the back cover.) ______ SAT-math score

Should you have any questions on these scoring instructions, you may call the phone number below. If, after following the above scoring directions and checking your work at least twice, your results disagree with the SAT-verbal or SAT-mathematical score reported on your ATP score report, you may request rescoring of your answer sheet. If rescoring confirms that an error had been made (resulting in either higher or lower scores than those originally reported), corrected reports will be sent to all recipients of your original scores. Please send your request to:

College Board ATP
Box 592
Princeton, NJ 08541
Attention: Rescore Request
Telephone: (609) 771-7600

Please indicate whether it is your SAT-verbal or SAT-mathematical score, or both, that you want to be rescored. When you write, please include a copy of this scoring worksheet on which you did your calculations.

Score Conversion Table
Scholastic Aptitude Test
Form Code 3E

Raw Score	College Board Reported Score		Raw Score	College Board Reported Score	
	SAT-Verbal	SAT-Math		SAT-Verbal	SAT-Math
85	800		40	460	610
84	780		39	450	600
83	770		38	450	590
82	760		37	440	580
81	750		36	430	570
80	740		35	430	560
79	730		34	420	550
78	720		33	420	540
77	710		32	410	530
76	700		31	400	520
75	690		30	400	510
74	680		29	390	500
73	670		28	380	490
72	660		27	380	480
71	660		26	370	470
70	650		25	360	460
69	640		24	360	450
68	630		23	350	450
67	630		22	340	440
66	620		21	340	430
65	610		20	330	420
64	600		19	320	410
63	600		18	320	400
62	590		17	310	390
61	580		16	300	380
60	580	800	15	290	380
59	570	780	14	290	370
58	570	770	13	280	360
57	560	760	12	270	350
56	550	750	11	270	340
55	550	740	10	260	340
54	540	740	9	250	330
53	530	730	8	240	320
52	530	720	7	240	310
51	520	710	6	230	310
50	520	700	5	220	300
49	510	690	4	220	290
48	510	680	3	210	280
47	500	670	2	200	280
46	490	660	1	200	270
45	490	660	0	200	260
44	480	650	−1	200	250
43	480	640	−2	200	250
42	470	630	−3	200	240
41	460	620	−4	200	230
			−5	200	220
			−6	200	210
			−7	200	210
			−8 or below	200	200

SAT
Form Code 3F

FORM CODE 3F

SECTION 1

Time—30 minutes

45 QUESTIONS

For each question in this section, choose the best answer and blacken the corresponding space on the answer sheet.

ch question below consists of a word in capital letters, lowed by five lettered words or phrases. Choose the d or phrase that is most nearly opposite in meaning he word in capital letters. Since some of the questions require you to distinguish fine shades of meaning, consider all the choices before deciding which is best.

Example:

GOOD: (A) sour (B) bad (C) red (D) hot (E) ugly

1. CONTAMINATE: (A) activate (B) exhibit (C) diagnose (D) cleanse (E) generate
2. EXPLICIT: (A) illegal (B) fulfilled (C) flat (D) unclear (E) fortunate
3. INDUSTRIOUS: (A) sensitive (B) lazy (C) cruel (D) imitative (E) unpaid
4. DEPLETE: (A) disclose (B) surround (C) add to (D) vary from (E) respond to
5. MARRED: (A) overheated (B) enjoyable (C) perfect (D) comfortable (E) tart
6. CLAMOR: (A) temporary setback (B) orderly discussion (C) disguised sympathy (D) plain demeanor (E) fair judgment
7. CONCUR: (A) laugh (B) disagree (C) compensate (D) release (E) exceed
8. PLASTIC: (A) unavailable (B) jagged (C) receding (D) indivisible (E) rigid
9. FLEDGLING: (A) impostor (B) veteran (C) opponent (D) reluctant supporter (E) accurate reporter
10. AMBULATORY: (A) bedridden (B) hostile (C) contagious (D) frail (E) glum
11. BUTTRESS: (A) straighten (B) forward (C) undermine (D) show off (E) observe secretly
12. SACCHARINE: (A) caustic (B) allergic (C) magnetic (D) reticent (E) polluted
13. EXPEDITE: (A) absolve (B) encompass (C) alter radically (D) speak in anger (E) make more difficult
14. VENERATION: (A) intrusion (B) collaboration (C) irreverence (D) continence (E) inversion
15. DESICCATE: (A) darken (B) sedate (C) migrate (D) soak (E) erase

Each sentence below has one or two blanks, each blank indicating that something has been omitted. Beneath the sentence are five lettered words or sets of words. Choose the word or set of words that best fits the meaning of the sentence as a whole.

Example:

Although its publicity has been ----, the film itself is intelligent, well-acted, handsomely produced, and altogether ----.

(A) tasteless. .respectable (B) extensive. .moderate (C) sophisticated. .amateur (D) risqué. .crude (E) perfect. .spectacular

16. With all its ----, the journey had nonetheless been an extremely eventful and successful one.
(A) discomfort (B) adventure (C) glory (D) diligence (E) accomplishment

17. The reactor is a tool of enormous ----: its energy is turned to the service of many disciplines, from metallurgy to archaeology.
(A) versatility (B) disparity (C) vagueness (D) fragility (E) fluctuation

18. The ---- of music these days provides the exposure that enables any person to discover that he or she has an ---- for some sort of music.
(A) polyphony. .esteem
(B) enrichment. .articulation
(C) classicism. .aptitude
(D) vibrance. .antipathy
(E) accessibility. .appreciation

19. There is little chance of ---- in a static society in which all people think and live alike.
(A) consensus (B) boredom (C) regularity (D) tranquility (E) innovation

20. By comparing the actual architectural ---- of the Aztec pyramids with those reported in ancient Aztec documents, it is possible to ---- the general descriptive accuracy of these records.
(A) designs. .falsify (B) details. .assess (C) blueprints. .delay (D) devices. .initiate (E) dimensions. .ignore

GO ON TO THE NEXT PAGE

Each passage below is followed by questions based on its content. Answer all questions following a passage on the basis of what is stated or implied in that passage.

Usually the designation "father of modern biology" is given to William Harvey. In the early 1600's, Harvey observed that the beating heart expelled the blood within it. He then reasoned: if the heart contains two ounces of blood and beats sixty-five times each minute, then it must eject into the body over ten pounds of blood per minute. It had previously been thought that blood was derived from the food that is eaten. But one cannot imagine ten pounds of blood being formed anew each minute from the amount of food a person consumes. Reflection on this observation and simple deduction led Harvey to postulate that blood expelled by the heart must circulate through the body and return to the heart. He then performed experiments to investigate the hypothesis. He showed that obstruction of a vein causes pooling of blood on the side of the obstruction away from the heart. He showed that the bleeding arises from the nearest end to the heart of a severed artery and the farthest end of a severed vein. And he demonstrated with elegant simplicity the function of the venous valves, concerning which he wrote that "so provident a cause as nature had not so plac'd many valves without design."

Harvey's discovery of the circulation of blood was a monumental and far-reaching contribution to science. In the first place, it discredited the beliefs of fourteen centuries that the heart was not a muscular organ and that the blood passed through the septum between the right and left ventricles. In addition, Harvey knowingly or unknowingly used the scientific method in almost astoundingly modern fashion. And, finally, he bolstered his already incontrovertible claim to immortality by conceiving the heart as a pump, for in this notion Harvey heralded a new view concerning living organisms—though he did not appreciate the meaning of his own work on this score. But to his successors his work gave proof to the concept that a living organism could be viewed as a material machine. Descartes was quick to praise Harvey for "having broken the ice in this matter," and in his own discourses he relied heavily on the work of Harvey to illustrate the mechanical nature of living objects. Their only difference from man-made machines, he insisted, was in the degree of complexity. With these assertions, sudden new excitement entered the realm of biological thought. For it now seemed reasonable that if the living organism were a material mechanism, then it, too, could be investigated by the new method of science.

21. It can be inferred that Harvey is considered the "father of modern biology" because

(A) he was the first to document his findings
(B) his experiments could be easily duplicated
(C) everyone before him had thought of the heart as a muscular organ
(D) he was the first to describe with precision the position of the heart
(E) he introduced the concept of mechanism into biology

22. The author seems to regard Harvey's work as which of the following?

(A) Revolutionary (B) Hypothetical
(C) Controversial (D) Rudimentary
(E) Prosaic

23. With which of the following is the passage primarily concerned?

(A) Explaining the workings of the human heart and the blood system
(B) Tracing the development of biology from Harvey to Descartes
(C) Discussing early misconceptions about the heart and blood
(D) Describing the significance to biology of William Harvey's work
(E) Criticizing investigations made prior to the adoption of the new scientific method

24. It can be inferred that Harvey's observation of pooling of blood on the side of a vein obstruction away from the heart led him to the conclusion that

(A) the blood was returning to the heart
(B) blood was manufactured as it circulated
(C) blood was expelled from the heart with each beat
(D) the heart had to pump harder when the blood was far away from it
(E) previous calculations as to the amount of blood contained by the body were incorrect

25. It can be inferred from the passage that the concept of mechanism was important to the scientific method because it supported the idea that

(A) living organisms were part of a universal design
(B) scientists could work together, each one performing part of an experiment
(C) hypotheses must be based on experimental evidence
(D) the somewhat complicated method could lead to a simplistic theory of life
(E) organisms could be expected to function in understandable and regular ways

The reading passages in this test are brief excerpts or adaptations of excerpts from published material. The ideas contained in them do not necessarily represent the opinions of the College Board or Educational Testing Service. To make the text suitable for testing purposes, we may in some cases have altered the style, contents, or point of view of the original.

FOIBLE

Is it wicked to take pleasure in spring, and other seasonal changes? Is it politically reprehensible, while we are living under an imperfect social order, to point out that life is frequently more worth living because of a bluebird's song, a maple tree in October, or some other natural phenomenon that does not cost money and does not have what newspaper editors call a political angle? There is no doubt that many people think so. A favorable reference to "Nature" in one of my articles is likely to bring me abusive letters, and though the key word in these letters is usually "sentimental," two ideas seem to be mixed up in them. One is that any pleasure in the actual process of life encourages a sort of political quietism. People, so the thought runs, ought to be discontented; we ought to multiply our wants and not simply increase our enjoyment of the things we already have. The other idea is that this is the age of machines and that to dislike the machine, or even to want to limit its domination, is reactionary and slightly ridiculous. Love of nature, the argument goes, is a foible of urbanized people who have no notion what nature is really like; those who have to deal with the soil do not love it, and take at most a utilitarian interest in birds and flowers. To love the country one must live in the town, merely taking an occasional weekend ramble at the warmer times of the year.

History disproves this last notion. The other idea seems to me wrong in a subtler way. Certainly we ought to be discontented, we ought not simply to make the best of a bad job, and yet if we kill all pleasure in the actual process of life, what sort of future are we preparing for ourselves? If we cannot enjoy the return of spring, what will we do with the leisure that the machine will give us? If our economic and political problems are solved, life may become simpler instead of more complex, and the sort of pleasure one gets from finding the first violet will loom larger than the sort one gets from watching the Sunday football game on television. By retaining one's childhood love of trees, butterflies, and even toads, one makes a peaceful and decent future a little more probable. But by preaching the doctrine that only steel and concrete are to be admired, one makes it a little surer that human beings will have no outlet for their surplus energy except in hatred and leader-worship.

26. Which of the following statements best represents the author's response to the opening question?

(A) Yes, spring never gave a person freedom.
(B) Yes, the seasons are unimportant in a machine age.
(C) Yes, pleasure has no place in an unjust society.
(D) No, nature makes us forget our discontent.
(E) No, appreciation of nature makes life more bearable.

27. According to the passage, many readers find references to nature in the author's articles to be

(A) politically offensive
(B) delightfully sentimental
(C) morally admirable
(D) inadequately documented
(E) carelessly irrelevant

28. In the last sentence, the author states that exclusive admiration of "steel and concrete" may have which of the following effects?

(A) Alienation from the ideals of society
(B) Disappearance of parks and wooded areas
(C) Loss of sympathy for the perceptions of a child's mind
(D) Replacement of human affections with mechanical efficiency
(E) Diversion of natural impulses to harmful ends

29. The author answers his opponents by doing all of the following EXCEPT

(A) providing an explanation of his own views
(B) asking rhetorical questions
(C) refuting each argument exhaustively
(D) taking a longer view than they do
(E) claiming to understand their point of view

30. The author would most likely agree with which of the following statements?

(A) Financial price determines value.
(B) Life will become increasingly complex.
(C) Farmers have no affection for nature.
(D) Machines can serve a beneficial purpose.
(E) Childhood values do not suit adults.

GO ON TO THE NEXT PAGE

Select the word or set of words that best completes each of the following sentences.

31. All these plans and programs are going to produce no ---- changes in our cities since they touch only the surface of the ugliness, the ---- ways in which the system manifests its disorders.

(A) exterior. .bizarre
(B) minimal. .obnoxious
(C) appreciable. .vital
(D) visible. .petty
(E) significant. .superficial

32. His ---- disposition, by turns sunny and sullen, was a reflection not of inner turmoil but of external stimuli.

(A) somber (B) contentious (C) stoic
(D) volatile (E) callous

33. While regent of Japan, Hideyoshi desired approval of his poetry, and since there was no dearth of sycophants at the court, his work was almost unanimously ----.

(A) amended (B) distilled (C) interred
(D) collated (E) extolled

34. So great was her desire to explain every nuance of her metaphysical theory that even the variety and copiousness of her native language seemed ---- the ---- of that desire.

(A) inadequate to. .fervor
(B) untapped by. .intensity
(C) untouched by. .rigor
(D) sufficient for. .fanaticism
(E) unmatched by. .torpor

35. The present court is ----, for never before has partisan politics played such a demonstrable role in judicial decisions or so ---- the quality of jurisprudence.

(A) unique. .colored
(B) effective. .interrupted
(C) impartial. .reflected
(D) perfect. .investigated
(E) didactic. .complicated

Each question below consists of a related pair of words or phrases, followed by five lettered pairs of words or phrases. Select the lettered pair that best expresses a relationship similar to that expressed in the original pair.

Example:

YAWN : BOREDOM :: (A) dream : sleep
(B) anger : madness (C) smile : amusement
(D) face : expression (E) impatience : rebellion

Ⓐ Ⓑ ● Ⓓ Ⓔ

36. FISH : OCEAN :: (A) snake : path (B) bird : cage
(C) bear : zoo (D) camel : desert
(E) elephant : river

37. PAINTER : SMOCK :: (A) mason : trowel
(B) lumberjack : ax (C) baby : bib
(D) umpire : baseball (E) prophet : beard

38. SOB : GRIEF :: (A) apology : punishment
(B) letter : acceptance (C) whisper : silence
(D) cheer : approval (E) voice : music

39. LOTTERY : DRAWING :: (A) gambling : dice
(B) election : tally (C) education : grades
(D) football : practice (E) hockey : penalties

40. AVIARY : FLY :: (A) aquarium : swim
(B) kennel : climb (C) solarium : observe
(D) satellite : launch (E) terrarium : glide

41. CRESCENDO : INTENSITY ::
(A) innocence : youth (B) acceleration : speed
(C) uproar : attention (D) adaptation : power
(E) abbreviation : length

42. CONFLUENCE : STREAMS ::
(A) greenhouse : plants (B) foundation : buildings
(C) resemblance : pictures (D) junction : roads
(E) ebb : tides

43. FLIPPANT : DEFERENTIAL ::
(A) vain : handsome (B) frivolous : serious
(C) devout : sincere (D) studious : intelligent
(E) indifferent : apathetic

44. CONJUGAL : MARRIAGE ::
(A) spiritual : sin (B) corrupt : politics
(C) fiscal : money (D) deteriorating : alliance
(E) blissful : retirement

45. PERFIDY : TRAITOR ::
(A) execution : criminal (B) loyalty : contributor
(C) veracity : patriot (D) generosity : benefactor
(E) pacifism : belligerent

S T O P

IF YOU FINISH BEFORE TIME IS CALLED, YOU MAY CHECK YOUR WORK ON THIS SECTION ONLY.
DO NOT WORK ON ANY OTHER SECTION IN THE TEST.

SECTION 2

Time—30 minutes

25 QUESTIONS

In this section solve each problem, using any available space on the page for scratchwork. Then decide which is the best of the choices given and blacken the corresponding space on the answer sheet.

The following information is for your reference in solving some of the problems.

Circle of radius r: Area $= \pi r^2$; Circumference $= 2\pi r$
The number of degrees of arc in a circle is 360.
The measure in degrees of a straight angle is 180.

Definitions of symbols:

$=$	is equal to	$\leq$	is less than or equal to
$\neq$	is unequal to	$\geq$	is greater than or equal to
$<$	is less than	$\parallel$	is parallel to
$>$	is greater than	$\perp$	is perpendicular to

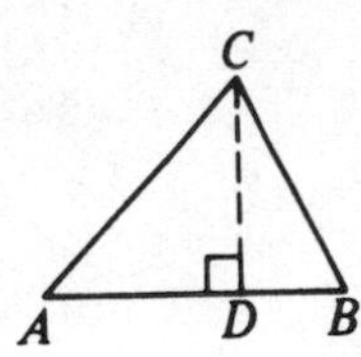

Triangle: The sum of the measures in degrees of the angles of a triangle is 180.

If $\angle CDA$ is a right angle, then

(1) area of $\triangle ABC = \frac{AB \times CD}{2}$

(2) $AC^2 = AD^2 + DC^2$

Note: Figures which accompany problems in this test are intended to provide information useful in solving the problems. They are drawn as accurately as possible EXCEPT when it is stated in a specific problem that its figure is not drawn to scale. All figures lie in a plane unless otherwise indicated. All numbers used are real numbers.

---

1. Jane had 4.25 meters of rope and used 3.5 meters. How many meters of rope does she have left?

   (A) 0.25 (B) 0.75 (C) 1.25
   (D) 1.75 (E) 7.75

2. Which of the following is NOT equal to a whole number?

   (A) $\frac{54+27}{3}$ (B) $\frac{54+27}{9}$ (C) $\frac{54+27}{18}$
   (D) $\frac{54+27}{27}$ (E) $\frac{54+27}{81}$

3. If the price of nails has been increased from 5 pounds for \$1 to 3 pounds for \$1, how many fewer pounds can now be bought for \$6 than could be bought before?

   (A) 2
   (B) 3
   (C) 8
   (D) 12
   (E) 15

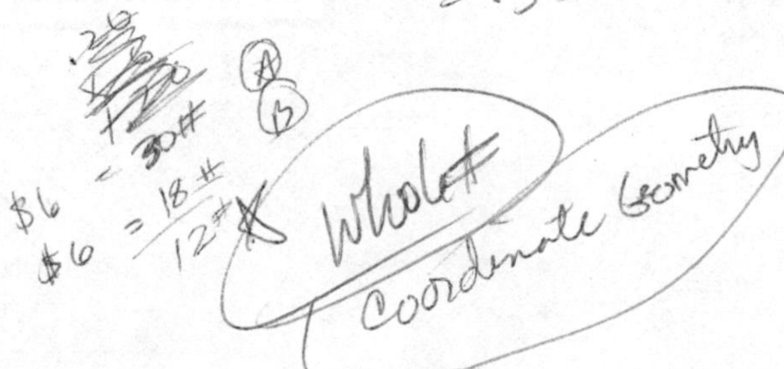

4. The expression "2 less than the product 3 times x" can be written as

   (A) $\frac{3x}{2}$
   (B) $2 - 3x$
   (C) $3x - 2$
   (D) $(3 - 2)x$
   (E) $2 + 3x$

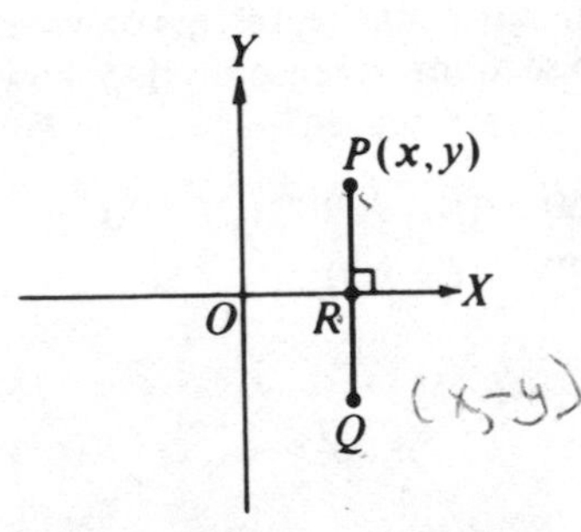

5. If $PR = RQ$ in the figure above, what are the coordinates of point Q?

   (A) $(x, -y)$ (B) (y, x) (C) $(y, -x)$
   (D) $(-x, y)$ (E) $(-x, -y)$

GO ON TO THE NEXT PAGE

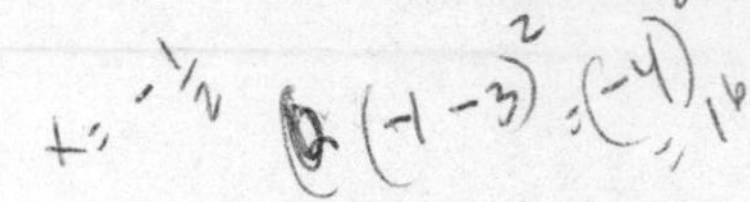

6. If $2x = -1$, then $(2x - 3)^2 =$

(A) 0 (B) 1 (C) 4 (D) 16 (E) 25

7. If $9 \times 9 \times 9 = \dfrac{27 \times 27}{r}$, then $r =$

(A) $\frac{1}{3}$

(B) 1

(C) 3

(D) 6

(E) 9

8. $0.84^2 - 0.83^2 =$

(A) 0.00167
(B) 0.0167
(C) 0.167
(D) 16.70
(E) 167.0

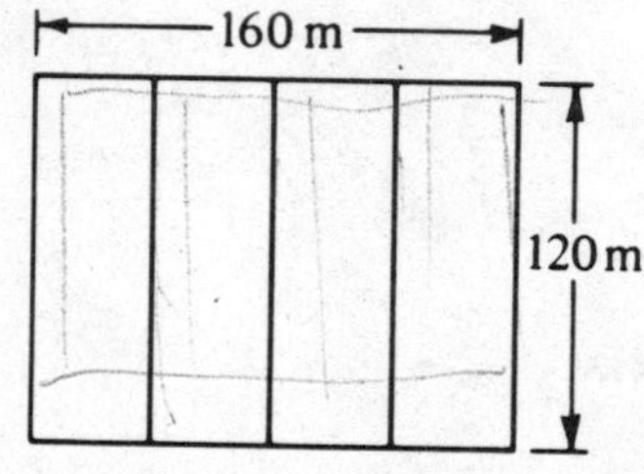

9. A gardener wants to enclose a rectangular lot and divide it into four equal parts, as shown above. If every line segment represents one section of fence and no sections of fence overlap, how many meters of fencing are needed?

(A) 560 (B) 760 (C) 800
(D) 920 (E) 980

10. The average (arithmetic mean) of a student's scores on four tests was 78. If she received a score of 70 on each of the first two tests and 84 on the third, what was her score on the fourth test?

(A) 58
(B) 69
(C) 77
(D) 80
(E) 88

11. If $x - y = 8$, what is the value of $x^2 - y^2$?

(A) −64 (B) −16 (C) 16 (D) 64
(E) It cannot be determined from the information given.

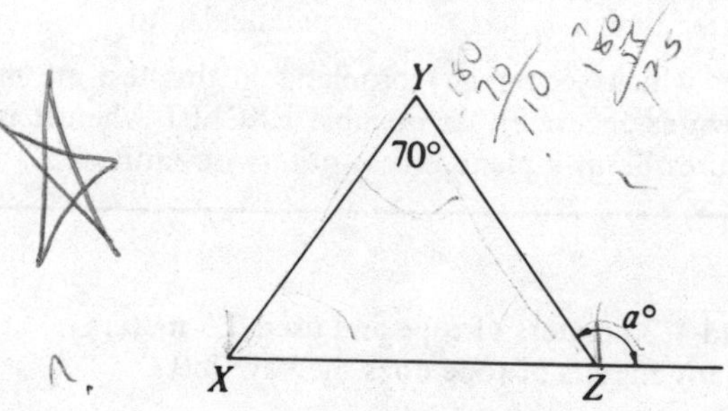

12. In $\triangle XYZ$ above, if $XY = YZ$, then $a =$

(A) 125 (B) 115 (C) 110 (D) 70 (E) 55

13. The fraction $\frac{45}{60}$ equals all of the following EXCEPT

(A) $\frac{3}{4}$ (B) $\frac{6}{8}$ (C) $\frac{9}{12}$ (D) $\frac{12}{15}$ (E) $\frac{15}{20}$

14. If $ax + y = x + 2y = 7$ and $x = 1$, then $a =$

(A) 2
(B) 3
(C) 4
(D) 5
(E) 6

GO ON TO THE NEXT PAGE

15. If the distances between points A, B, and C are equal, which of the following could be true?

I. A, B, and C are vertices of an equilateral triangle.
II. A, B, and C are vertices of a right triangle.
III. B and C lie on an arc of a circle with center A.

(A) I only (B) II only (C) III only
(D) I and III (E) II and III

16. Let k be any integer. If $\overrightarrow{k} = 2k$ and $\overleftarrow{k} = \frac{1}{2}k$, what does the product $\overrightarrow{k}$ times $\overleftarrow{k}$ equal?

(A) 1 (B) 4 (C) $\frac{k^2}{2}$ (D) k (E) k^2

17. What fraction of 15 hours is 15 seconds?

(A) $\frac{1}{60}$

(B) $\frac{1}{225}$

(C) $\frac{1}{360}$

(D) $\frac{1}{3,600}$

(E) $\frac{1}{54,000}$

Questions 18-19 refer to the following definition.

The d-distance of an integer M from an integer N is $M - N$.

18. What is the d-distance of 5 from -5 ?

(A) -10 (B) -5 (C) 0 (D) 5 (E) 10

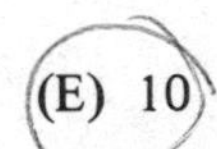

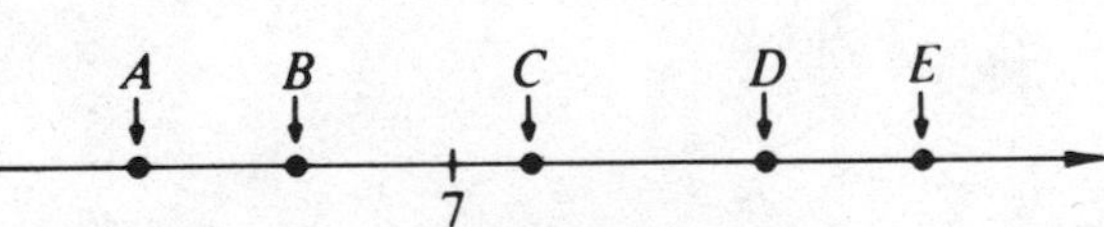

19. Of the integers indicated on the number line above, which has the least d-distance from 7 ?

(A) A (B) B (C) C (D) D (E) E

20. At a certain college, x liters of milk are needed per month for each student. At this rate, y liters of milk will supply z students for how many months?

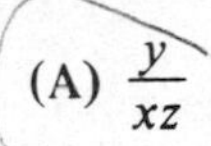

(A) $\frac{y}{xz}$

(B) $\frac{z}{xy}$

(C) $\frac{xy}{z}$

(D) $\frac{yz}{x}$

(E) xyz

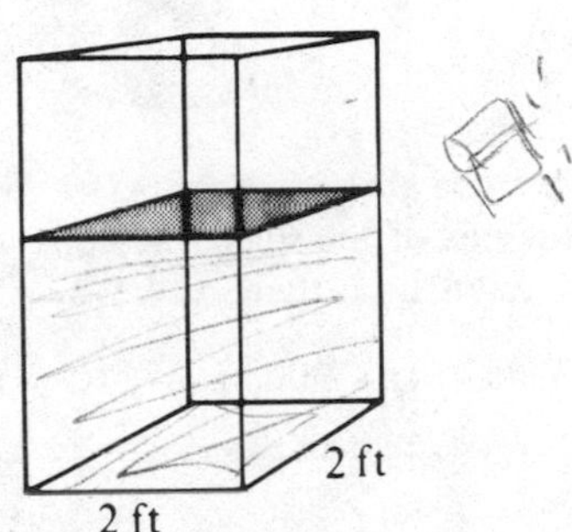

21. The figure above shows water in a tank whose base is 2 feet by 2 feet. When a solid cube 1 foot on an edge is completely immersed in the water, how many inches will the water rise in the tank?

(A) $\frac{1}{4}$ (B) 3 (C) 4 (D) 12 (E) 24

GO ON TO THE NEXT PAGE

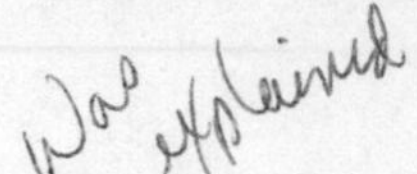

22. N years ago Sue was twice as old as Joe was. If Joe is now 25 years old, how old is Sue now in terms of N?

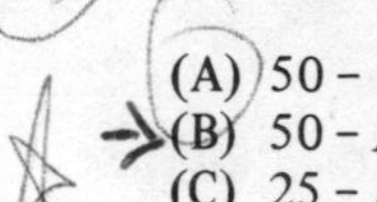

(A) $50 - 2N$
(B) $50 - N$
(C) $25 - N$
(D) $25 + N$
(E) $50 + N$

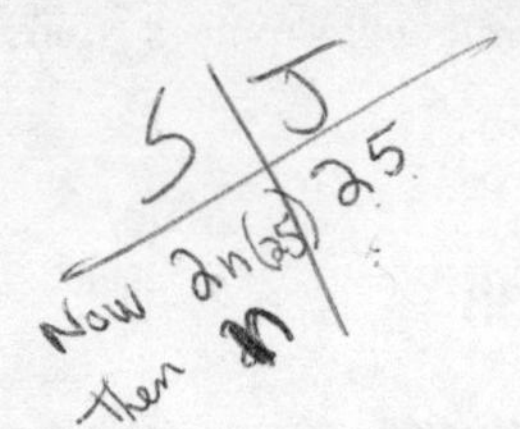

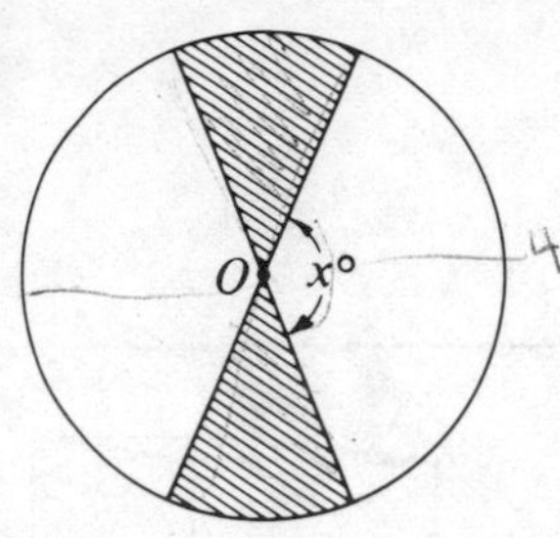

23. The circle above has center O and radius 2. If the total area of the shaded regions formed by the two diameters is π, then $x =$

(A) 45 (B) 90 (C) 120 (D) 135 (E) 270

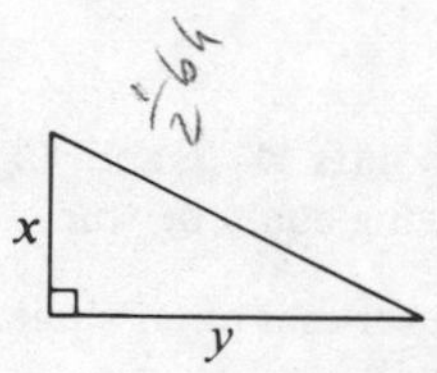

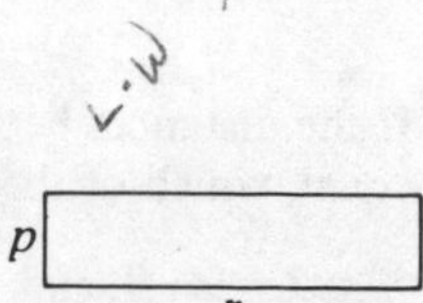

24. If the triangle and rectangle above have equal areas and if $\frac{pr}{2} = 60$, then $xy =$

(A) 240 (B) 120 (C) 60 (D) 30 (E) 15

25. If the sum of the first n positive integers is x, then, in terms of n and x, which of the following equals the sum of the next n integers?

(A) nx
(B) $n + x$
(C) $n^2 + x$
(D) $2n + x$
(E) $n + 2x$

S T O P

IF YOU FINISH BEFORE TIME IS CALLED, YOU MAY CHECK YOUR WORK ON THIS SECTION ONLY. DO NOT WORK ON ANY OTHER SECTION IN THE TEST.

SECTION 3

Time—30 minutes

40 QUESTIONS

For each question in this section, choose the best answer and blacken the corresponding space on the answer sheet.

Each question below consists of a word in capital letters, followed by five lettered words or phrases. Choose the word or phrase that is most nearly opposite in meaning to the word in capital letters. Since some of the questions require you to distinguish fine shades of meaning, consider all the choices before deciding which is best.

Example:

GOOD: (A) sour (B) bad (C) red (D) hot (E) ugly

Ⓐ ● Ⓒ Ⓓ Ⓔ

1. MINGLE: (A) revolve (B) despise (C) flow smoothly (D) remain apart (E) regulate well

2. VALID: (A) unjustified (B) impervious (C) unrepentant (D) inevitable (E) unclaimed

3. EGG ON: (A) remove (B) restrain (C) respect (D) conclude (E) immerse

4. CONVENTIONAL: (A) ornamental (B) unorthodox (C) misunderstood (D) widely dispersed (E) rapidly constructed

5. OPTIMUM: (A) most expensive (B) most diverse (C) least precise (D) least familiar (E) least favorable

6. SAGE: (A) bystander (B) procrastinator (C) fanatic (D) eccentric (E) ignoramus

7. VOUCHSAFE: (A) isolate (B) weaken (C) refuse to grant (D) talk crudely (E) abstain from pleasure

8. CLEMENCY: (A) remorse (B) severity (C) incompetence (D) private opinion (E) careful consideration

9. INTRACTABLE: (A) obvious (B) talented (C) bountiful (D) obedient (E) joyous

10. SUFFRAGE: (A) lack of eloquence (B) lack of franchise (C) lack of pain (D) desire for power (E) desire for retribution

Each sentence below has one or two blanks, each blank indicating that something has been omitted. Beneath the sentence are five lettered words or sets of words. Choose the word or set of words that best fits the meaning of the sentence as a whole.

Example:

Although its publicity has been ----, the film itself is intelligent, well-acted, handsomely produced, and altogether ----.

(A) tasteless. .respectable (B) extensive. .moderate (C) sophisticated. .amateur (D) risqué. .crude (E) perfect. .spectacular

● Ⓑ Ⓒ Ⓓ Ⓔ

11. Only since the 1850's have large numbers of women been able to ---- the scientific community in the United States, and even today they have to ---- lingering male bias.

(A) rescind. .submit to
(B) penetrate. .protect
(C) escape. .combat
(D) enter. .contend with
(E) evaluate. .seek out

12. The attempt to demonstrate that matter can exist in a form too small to be seen by the eye revealed that it is possible to discover truth ----, that is, by a process of inference based on observation.

(A) immediately (B) indirectly (C) momentarily (D) infallibly (E) definitively

13. We cannot endorse developments that make our surroundings more hideous, our culture more ----, or our lives less complete.

(A) viable (B) effectual (C) tolerant (D) provocative (E) tawdry

GO ON TO THE NEXT PAGE

14. Her political thought was developed in a series of essays characterized by a reliance on ----; generalizations and imprecise grand statements ---- her.

(A) universalities. .evaded
(B) minutiae. .disturbed
(C) details. .preoccupied
(D) abstractions. .disconcerted
(E) ambiguities. .infuriated

15. Unfortunately, routine military operations are described ---- in this account of the conflict, whereas analyses of the more significant political considerations are relegated to ---- paragraphs.

(A) concisely. .lavish
(B) summarily. .interminable
(C) exhaustively. .occasional
(D) superficially. .brief
(E) adequately. .ample

Each question below consists of a related pair of words or phrases, followed by five lettered pairs of words or phrases. Select the lettered pair that best expresses a relationship similar to that expressed in the original pair.

Example:

> YAWN : BOREDOM :: (A) dream : sleep
> (B) anger : madness (C) smile : amusement
> (D) face : expression (E) impatience : rebellion
> Ⓐ Ⓑ ● Ⓓ Ⓔ

16. GLAZE : CLAY :: (A) easel : paint
(B) color : chalk (C) varnish : wood
(D) title : book (E) tea : cup

17. FLEET : SHIPS :: (A) dictionary : syllables
(B) committee : people (C) clock : time
(D) photograph : subjects (E) hospital : nurses

18. THREATEN : ATTACK :: (A) cancel : revise
(B) annihilate : defile (C) rehabilitate : discard
(D) promise : deliver (E) assume : doubt

19. SILKWORM : SILK :: (A) oyster : pearl
(B) branch : leaf (C) ant : anthill
(D) moth : wool (E) mosquito : disease

20. SONATA : MUSICAL :: (A) epic : whimsical
(B) novel : literary (C) song : humorous
(D) testimony : rhymed (E) pantomime : vocal

21. CENTRIFUGE : SEPARATION ::
(A) dial : instrumentation
(B) degree : measurement
(C) thermometer : refrigeration
(D) apparatus : filtration
(E) microscope : magnification

22. CATACOMB : CEMETERY ::
(A) subway : railroad (B) dirigible : airplane
(C) elevator : shaft (D) bridge : highway
(E) grotto : cave

23. RED HERRING : MISLEAD ::
(A) smoke screen : obscure
(B) blank check : bewilder
(C) clean slate : condemn
(D) white lie : damage
(E) loan shark : haggle

24. APERTURE : CAMERA :: (A) rope : pulley
(B) window : room (C) piston : engine
(D) eyeglasses : vision (E) wrench : pipe

25. PERCIPIENT : DISCERNMENT ::
(A) ravenous : hunger (B) punctual : tact
(C) heroic : conflict (D) artificial : reality
(E) concerned : indifference

GO ON TO THE NEXT PAGE

Each passage below is followed by questions based on its content. Answer all questions following a passage on the basis of what is stated or implied in that passage.

Despite their seemingly infinite formulations, invisible inks generally fall into one of three categories, depending on the way they are made visible.

First there are organic liquids such as milk, lemon juice, vinegar, and some body fluids. These inks are crude and are detected by heating the paper to which they are applied. Gentle warming actually chars the inks into visibility. Although they can be detected easily, organic inks have the advantage of being always available.

The second category of inks comprises chemical solutions. Colorless when dry, they become visible when treated with an appropriate reagent. Such inks are called "sympathetic inks" because each writing solution requires a specific developing reagent to make the message appear. Of course, the trick with sympathetic inks is to find compounds that are extremely reagent-specific or, better yet, that must be developed in several intermediate steps before color appears.

A third type of ink—radioactive ink—is developed by photographic processes. Solutions of radium D in acetone, for example, have been used to write messages on clothing without raising the suspicion of counterespionage agents who were looking for secret ink on paper. Messages written in this way are developed simply by exposing the clothes to an X-ray film plate.

It is also possible to write messages with plain water and avoid the use of chemicals altogether. Water disturbs paper fibers; the message can be made visible by exposure to iodine vapor. The vapor settles on the paper's surface in the written lines where the fibers have been disturbed.

26. According to the passage, "sympathetic inks" (line 14) are so named because they

(A) have an affinity for various types of writing surfaces
(B) resemble each other in that they leave no color trace when dry
(C) are developed through interaction with a particular substance
(D) can be made visible only for a limited length of time
(E) possess a great degree of internal molecular cohesion

27. It can be inferred from the passage that compounds "that must be developed in several intermediate steps" (lines 18-19) are desirable particularly because

(A) their color definition is improved proportionately
(B) interception of messages is more difficult
(C) complex procedures themselves encourage further technical innovation
(D) legibility increases as an ink requires more developing reagents
(E) such processes facilitate the timely detection of any error

28. It is most likely that the author does not list water as a fourth category of invisible writing fluids because it

(A) does not need a distinct developing process
(B) is so easily made visible as to be of little use
(C) has not yet gained acceptability as an espionage tool
(D) is quickly noticeable even to ordinary citizens
(E) is too elementary a substance to be considered an ink

GO ON TO THE NEXT PAGE

My first glimpse of the flat black stretches of Chicago depressed and dismayed me, mocked all my fantasies. Chicago seemed an unreal city whose mythical houses were built of slabs of black coal wreathed in palls of gray smoke, houses whose foundations were sinking slowly into the dank prairie. Flashes of steam showed intermittently on the wide horizon, gleaming translucently in the winter sun. The din of the city entered my consciousness, entered to remain for years to come. The year was 1927.

What would happen to me here? Would I survive? My expectations were modest. I wanted only a job. Hunger had long been my daily companion. Diversion and recreation, with the exception of reading, were unknown. In all my life–though surrounded by many people–I had not had a single satisfying, sustained relationship with another human being and, not having had any, I did not miss it. I made no demands whatever upon others.

The train rolled into the depot. Aunt Maggie and I got off and walked slowly through the crowds into the station. I looked about to see if there were signs saying: FOR WHITE–FOR COLORED. I saw none. Black people and White people moved about, each seemingly intent upon a private mission. There was no racial fear. And yet, because everything was so new, I began to grow tense again, although it was a different sort of tension than I had known before. I knew that this machine-city was governed by strange laws and I wondered if I would ever learn them.

As I stood in the icy wind waiting for the streetcar, I wanted to talk to Aunt Maggie, to ask her questions, but her tight face made me hold my tongue. I was learning already from the frantic light in her eyes the strain that the city imposed upon its people. I was seized by doubt. Should I have come here? But going back was impossible. I had fled a known terror, and perhaps I could cope with this unknown terror that lay ahead.

The streetcar came. Aunt Maggie motioned for me to get on and pushed me toward a seat in which a White man sat looking blankly out the window. I sat down beside the man and looked straight ahead of me. After a moment I stole a glance at the White man; he was still staring out the window, his mind fastened upon some inward thought. I did not exist for him; I was as far from his mind as the stone buildings that swept past in the street. It would have been illegal for me to sit beside him in the part of the South that I had come from.

29. The passage as a whole is best characterized as

(A) a description of an individual's reactions to a new environment
(B) a portrait of the residents of a city
(C) an illustration of the energy and optimism of youth
(D) an analysis of racial discrimination in an urban setting
(E) a comparison between romantic illusions and mundane reality

30. In the context of the passage, the author's "fantasies" (line 3) most probably have to do with

(A) dreams of great personal wealth and power
(B) memories of scenes and characters from favorite books
(C) theories about the nature of personal relationships
(D) the desire for physical isolation and intellectual independence
(E) notions of the magnificence of the city

31. To the author, Chicago seemed to be all of the following EXCEPT

(A) boring
(B) gloomy
(C) crowded
(D) noisy
(E) unpredictable

32. The author's attitude in lines 38-41 is best described as

(A) deep despair
(B) pretended indifference
(C) calm assurance
(D) apprehensive resolve
(E) excited expectation

33. On the basis of the passage, which of the following statements about Aunt Maggie can most logically be made?

(A) She has just had an argument with the author.
(B) She will find the author a job.
(C) She has become indifferent to the welfare of the author.
(D) She wishes she were anywhere but Chicago.
(E) She feels the pressure of life in Chicago.

GO ON TO THE NEXT PAGE

The chief reason for the development of the medieval Italian into the modern Italian lies in the character of the states of Renaissance Italy including, ironically, even the despotisms. In the Middle Ages both sides of human consciousness—that which was turned within and that which was turned without—lay as though dreaming or half awake beneath a common veil. The veil was woven of faith, illusion, and childlike prepossession, through which the world and history were seen clad in strange hues. Medieval people were conscious of themselves only as members of a race, people, party, family, or corporation—only through some general category. It was in Italy that the veil was first lifted. In Italy there arose an objective treatment and consideration of the state and of all things of this world, and at the same time a subjective side asserted itself with corresponding emphasis. Italians began to recognize themselves as individuals, and they began to behave in accordance with this recognition.

Despotism fostered the utmost individuality not only in the tyrant but also in the persons who were protected or used by the tyrant—the secretaries, ministers, poets, and companions. These people were forced to know all the inward resources of their own nature, the momentary as well as the permanent. Their enjoyment was enhanced and concentrated by the desire to obtain the greatest satisfaction from a period of relative power and influence that held no guarantee of long duration.

34. According to the author, which of the following was a paradox of Renaissance Italy?

(A) Italy was the birthplace of individualism.
(B) Renaissance people perceived the state objectively.
(C) Renaissance people recognized themselves as spiritual individuals.
(D) Renaissance people gained more power as they became more independent.
(E) Despotism helped lead to a greater sense of individuality.

35. Which of the following best describes the style of lines 4-11?

(A) Rambling (B) Satirical (C) Ironic (D) Metaphoric (E) Paradoxical

36. It can be inferred from the passage that those people "who were protected or used by the tyrant" (lines 23-24) were NOT likely to believe that they

(A) should be able to depend on themselves when the need arose
(B) were always in danger of being deprived of their power or influence
(C) ought to make the most of any good fortune that befell them
(D) had identities independent of any group allegiance
(E) could disregard the demands and authority of the despot

GO ON TO THE NEXT PAGE

Confronted by an enigmatic spectacle the writer descends within the self, and in that lonely inward region of stress and strife the writer, if deserving and fortunate, finds the terms of his or her appeal. The appeal is made to our less obvious capacities: to that part of our nature which, because of the warlike conditions of existence, is necessarily kept out of sight within the more resisting and hard qualities—like the vulnerable body within a steel armor. The appeal is less loud, more profound, less distinct, more stirring—and sooner forgotten. Yet its effect endures forever. The changing wisdom of successive generations discards ideas, questions facts, demolishes theories. But the writer appeals to that part of our being which is not dependent on wisdom; to that in us which is a gift and not an acquisition—and, therefore, more permanently enduring. The writer speaks to our capacity for delight and wonder, to the sense of mystery surrounding our lives; to our sense of pity, and beauty, and pain; to the latent feeling of fellowship with all creation—and to the subtle but invincible conviction of solidarity that knits together the loneliness of innumerable hearts, to the solidarity in dreams, in joy, in sorrow, in aspirations, in illusions, in hope, in fear, which binds people to each other, which binds together all humanity—the dead to the living and the living to the yet unborn.

37. According to the passage, if writers are to find the terms of their "appeal" (line 4), they must be which of the following?

I. Clever
II. Worthy
III. Lucky

(A) I only (B) III only (C) I and II only
(D) II and III only (E) I, II, and III

38. The author suggests that a writer appeals to a "part of our nature" (line 6) that is

(A) unsympathetic (B) analytical
(C) innate (D) readily apparent
(E) hard and resisting

39. It can be inferred that the author would most likely describe "wisdom" (lines 12 and 15) as

(A) preeminent (B) mutable (C) timeless
(D) liberating (E) accumulative

40. The author's primary point about writers is that they

(A) descend within themselves to avoid confrontation with the mass of humanity
(B) have an effect that is permanently enduring because they appeal to the wisdom of humanity
(C) address the underlying sense of affinity with others that exists within all human beings
(D) choose to ignore the joys, dreams, sorrows, and fears of other human beings
(E) can foretell what existence will be like for future generations of humans

S T O P

IF YOU FINISH BEFORE TIME IS CALLED, YOU MAY CHECK YOUR WORK ON THIS SECTION ONLY. DO NOT WORK ON ANY OTHER SECTION IN THE TEST.

SECTION 5

Time—30 minutes

35 QUESTIONS

In this section solve each problem, using any available space on the page for scratchwork. Then decide which is the best of the choices given and blacken the corresponding space on the answer sheet.

The following information is for your reference in solving some of the problems.

Circle of radius r: Area $= \pi r^2$; Circumference $= 2\pi r$
The number of degrees of arc in a circle is 360.
The measure in degrees of a straight angle is 180.

Definitions of symbols:

$=$	is equal to	$\leq$	is less than or equal to
$\neq$	is unequal to	$\geq$	is greater than or equal to
$<$	is less than	$\parallel$	is parallel to
$>$	is greater than	$\perp$	is perpendicular to

Triangle: The sum of the measures in degrees of the angles of a triangle is 180.

If $\angle CDA$ is a right angle, then

(1) area of $\triangle ABC = \frac{AB \times CD}{2}$

(2) $AC^2 = AD^2 + DC^2$

Note: Figures which accompany problems in this test are intended to provide information useful in solving the problems. They are drawn as accurately as possible EXCEPT when it is stated in a specific problem that its figure is not drawn to scale. All figures lie in a plane unless otherwise indicated. All numbers used are real numbers.

1. If $a + 2 = 4$, then $2a + 2 =$

(A) 4 (B) 6 (C) 8 (D) 10 (E) 12

Tree	Height (in centimeters)
Cherry	170
Peach	190
Apple	205
Plum	185
Pear	210

2. Exactly how many of the trees listed in the table above are more than 2 meters high? (1 meter = 100 centimeters)

(A) One (B) Two (C) Three
(D) Four (E) Five

3. $2x(3x + 5y) =$

(A) $5x + 7xy$ (B) $6x + 10xy$ (C) $6x^2 + 5y$
(D) $6x^2 + 10y$ (E) $6x^2 + 10xy$

4. Kate and Beth are both members of team X, which played n games in a certain season. Kate played in $\frac{1}{2}$ of the games and Beth played in 12 of the games. If Beth played in fewer games than Kate, which of the following is a possible value for n?

(A) 10 (B) 14 (C) 18 (D) 24 (E) 26

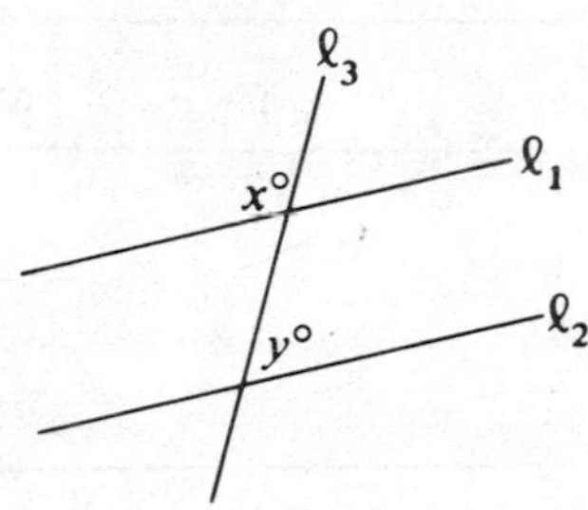

5. If parallel lines ℓ_1 and ℓ_2 are intersected by line ℓ_3, what is the value of $x + y$?

(A) 180 (B) 150 (C) 120 (D) 90
(E) It cannot be determined from the information given.

6. $\frac{27}{1000} + \frac{50}{1000} + \frac{300}{1000} =$

(A) 0.0035 (B) 0.2753 (C) 0.3527
(D) 0.377 (E) 0.72

7. A traffic flow of 1,440 cars during a 24-hour period is equivalent to a rate of how many cars per minute?

(A) 240 (B) 120 (C) 60 (D) 24 (E) 1

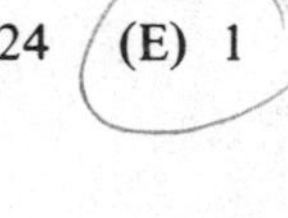

GO ON TO THE NEXT PAGE

Questions 8-27 each consist of two quantities, one in Column A and one in Column B. You are to compare the two quantities and on the answer sheet blacken space

A if the quantity in Column A is greater;
B if the quantity in Column B is greater;
C if the two quantities are equal;
D if the relationship cannot be determined from the information given.

Notes: 1. In certain questions, information concerning one or both of the quantities to be compared is centered above the two columns.
2. In a given question, a symbol that appears in both columns represents the same thing in Column A as it does in Column B.
3. Letters such as x, n, and k stand for real numbers.

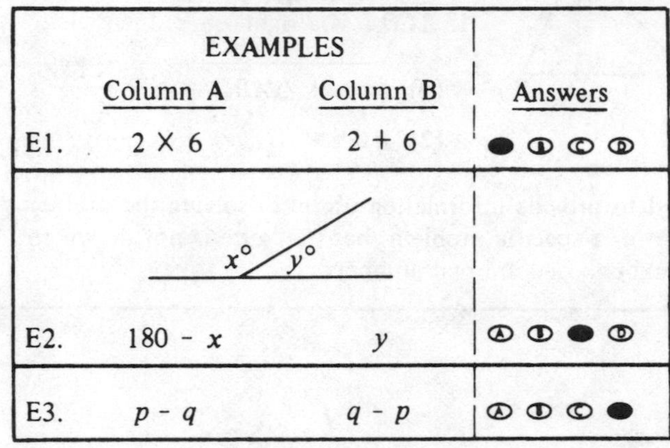

EXAMPLES

	Column A	Column B	Answers
E1.	2×6	$2 + 6$	● Ⓑ Ⓒ Ⓓ
E2.	$180 - x$	y	Ⓐ Ⓑ ● Ⓓ
E3.	$p - q$	$q - p$	Ⓐ Ⓑ Ⓒ ●

	Column A	Column B
8.	$2^2 + 2$	2^3

The total price of 1 apple and 1 peach is 75 cents.

9.	The price of 1 apple	The price of 1 peach
10.	$\frac{1}{\frac{5}{6}}$	1.6

x and y are both positive integers.

$xy = 30$

11.	x	y

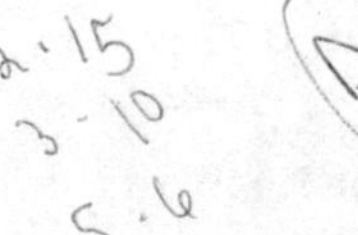

Column A | Column B

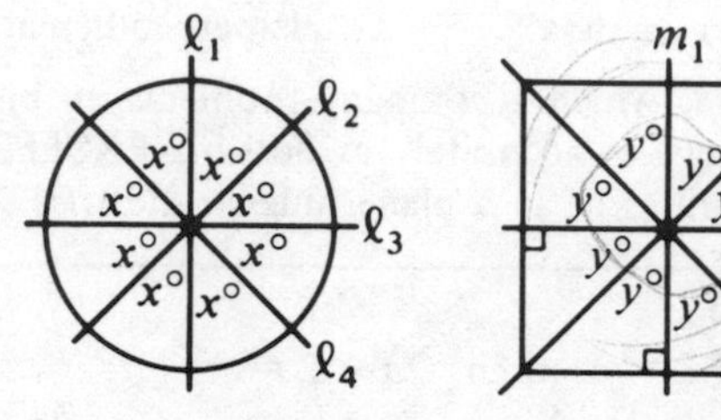

12.	The value of x	The value of y

Car X travels at an average speed of 60 kilometers per hour.

13.	The distance traveled by car X in $\frac{3}{4}$ hour at its average speed	40 kilometers

$x - y > 0$

14.	x	y

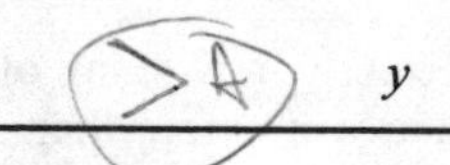

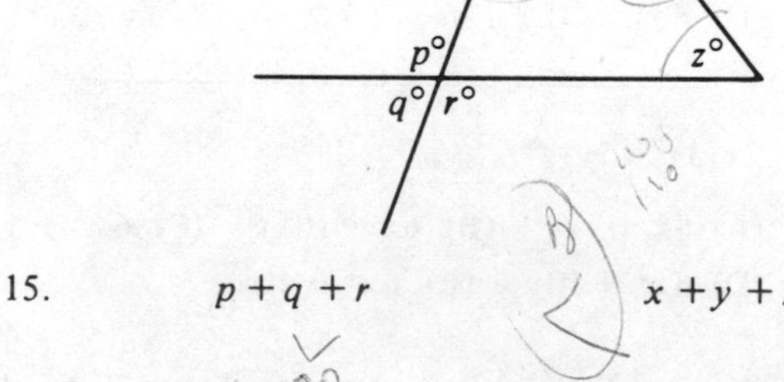

15.	$p + q + r$	$x + y + z$

GO ON TO THE NEXT PAGE

SUMMARY DIRECTIONS FOR COMPARISON QUESTIONS

Answer:
- A if the quantity in Column A is greater;
- B if the quantity in Column B is greater;
- C if the two quantities are equal;
- D if the relationship cannot be determined from the information given.

	Column A	Column B

Last year the gross income of Corporation C was \$5,200,000. This year its gross income was 10 percent higher than last year.

16.	The gross income of Corporation C this year	\$5,700,000

$t < -1$

17.	$(t-1)^2(t+1)^2$	0

$\triangle ABC$ is equilateral.

18.	Length of the altitude to side AB	Length of side AB

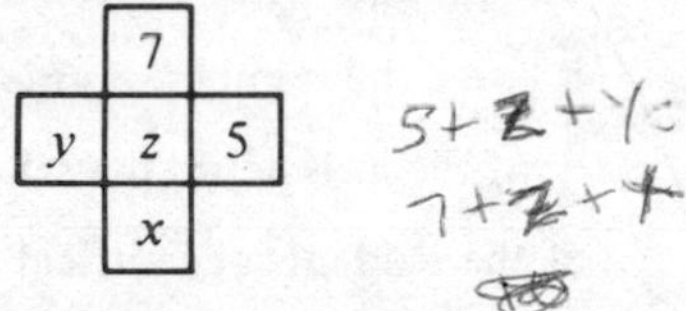

The sum of the numbers in the row is equal to the sum of the numbers in the column.

19.	x	y

$5x + 5y = 30$

20.	The average (arithmetic mean) of x and y	3

A wheel with a radius of 50 centimeters rolls without slipping along a straight line and completes one revolution each second.

21.	Distance along the line that the wheel travels in 2 seconds	400 centimeters

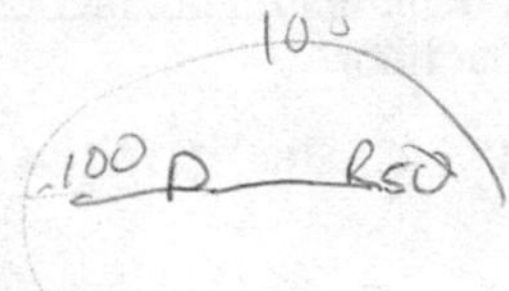

	Column A	Column B

x is a prime number and

$21 < x < 30.$

22.	x	24

23.	The sum of two different odd positive integers each less than 10	The sum of three different even positive integers each less than 10

$2x + y = 7$

$x + 2y = 2$

24.	$x + y$	3

25.	Area of the triangular region bounded by the X-axis, Y-axis, and the graph of the line $x + y = 6$	18

The operation ∇ is defined for all nonzero numbers x and y by the equation $x \nabla y = \left(\frac{x}{y}\right)^2$.

$wz \neq 0$

26.	$w \nabla z$	$w \nabla (-z)$

a and b are positive integers.

27.	$\frac{a}{b}$	$\frac{a+1}{b+1}$

GO ON TO THE NEXT PAGE

5

Solve each of the remaining problems in this section using any available space for scratchwork. Then decide which is the best of the choices given and blacken the corresponding space on the answer sheet.

28. If each time the symbol $\sim$ is used it can represent either of the arithmetic operations $+$ or $\times$, which of the following could be the result of $1 \sim (2 \sim 4)$? (In this expression, the second $\sim$ need not represent the same operation as does the first $\sim$).

I. 7
II. 8
III. 9

(A) I only
(B) II only
(C) I and III only
(D) II and III only
(E) I, II, and III

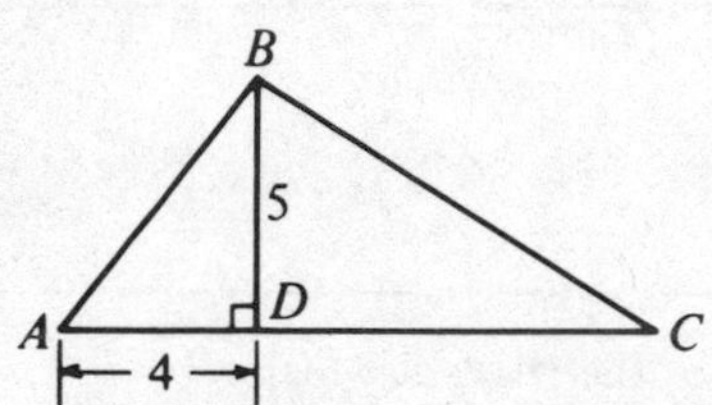

29. In the figure above, if the area of ΔABC is 30, then the area of ΔBDC is

(A) 5 (B) 10 (C) 15 (D) 20 (E) 40

30. What is the thickness, in centimeters, of 1 sheet of paper if the thickness of a uniform pack of 500 such sheets is 2.5 centimeters?

(A) 0.005 (B) 0.02 (C) 0.05
(D) 0.125 (E) 0.2

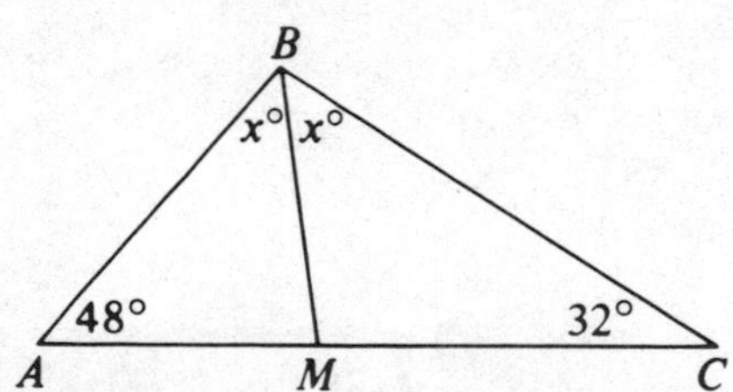

31. In ΔABC above, what is the value of x?

(A) 40 (B) 42 (C) 50 (D) 58
(E) It cannot be determined from the information given.

32. If 12 and 16 each divide N without remainder, what must be the value of N?

(A) 24 (B) 48 (C) 120 (D) 192
(E) It cannot be determined from the information given.

33. In the Lost Dog Kennel there is a total of 25 dogs. Of these, exactly 10 dogs have black spots, exactly 12 dogs have brown spots, and exactly 5 dogs have both brown and black spots. What is the total number of dogs in the kennel that have neither brown spots nor black spots?

(A) 2
(B) 3
(C) 8
(D) 13
(E) 15

34. The number of boys attending Fairfield High School is twice the number of girls. If $\frac{1}{6}$ of the boys and $\frac{1}{4}$ of the girls are in the school band, what fraction of the students at Fairfield are in the school band?

(A) $\frac{5}{36}$
(B) $\frac{7}{36}$
(C) $\frac{2}{9}$
(D) $\frac{7}{24}$
(E) $\frac{5}{12}$

35. A square floor with sides of length 6 meters is to be tiled with square tiles. If each tile has a perimeter of 1 meter, what is the minimum number of such tiles needed to cover the floor?

(A) 12 (B) 24 (C) 36 (D) 144 (E) 576

S T O P

IF YOU FINISH BEFORE TIME IS CALLED, YOU MAY CHECK YOUR WORK ON THIS SECTION ONLY. DO NOT WORK ON ANY OTHER SECTION IN THE TEST.

Correct Answers for Scholastic Aptitude Test Form Code 3F

VERBAL		MATHEMATICAL	
Section 1	Section 3	Section 2	Section 5
1. D	1. D	1. B	1. B
2. D	2. A	2. C	2. B
3. B	3. B	3. D	3. E
4. C	4. B	4. C	4. E
5. C	5. E	5. A	5. A
6. B	6. E	6. D	6. D
7. B	7. C	7. B	7. E
8. E	8. B	8. B	*8. B
9. B	9. D	9. D	*9. D
10. A	10. B	10. E	*10. B
11. C	11. D	11. E	*11. D
12. A	12. B	12. A	*12. C
13. E	13. E	13. D	*13. A
14. C	14. B	14. C	*14. A
15. D	15. C	15. D	*15. C
16. A	16. C	16. E	*16. A
17. A	17. B	17. D	*17. A
18. E	18. D	18. E	*18. B
19. E	19. A	19. A	*19. B
20. B	20. B	20. A	*20. C
21. E	21. E	21. B	*21. A
22. A	22. A	22. B	*22. D
23. D	23. A	23. D	*23. D
24. A	24. B	24. A	*24. C
25. E	25. A	25. C	*25. C
26. E	26. C		*26. C
27. A	27. B		*27. D
28. E	28. E		28. E
29. C	29. A		29. D
30. D	30. E		30. A
31. E	31. A		31. C
32. D	32. D		32. E
33. E	33. E		33. C
34. A	34. E		34. B
35. A	35. D		35. E
36. D	36. E		
37. C	37. D		
38. D	38. C		
39. B	39. B		
40. A	40. C		
41. B			
42. D			
43. B			
44. C			
45. D			

*Indicates four-choice questions. (All of the other questions are five-choice.)

rocess

scoring is done in three steps:

- *nning.* Your answer sheet is "read" by a scanning achine and the oval you filled in for each question is recorded on a computer tape.
- *Scoring.* The computer compares the oval filled in for each question with the correct response. Each correct answer receives one point; omitted questions do not count toward your score. For each wrong answer, a fraction of a point is subtracted to correct for random guessing. For questions with five answer choices, one-fourth of a point is subtracted for each wrong response; for questions with four answer choices, one-third of a point is subtracted for each wrong response. The SAT-verbal test has 85 questions with five answer choices each. If, for example, a student has 44 right, 32 wrong, and 9 omitted, the resulting raw score is determined as follows:

  $$44 \text{ right} - \frac{32 \text{ wrong}}{4} = 44 - 8 = 36 \text{ raw score points}$$

  Obtaining raw scores frequently involves the rounding of fractional numbers to the nearest whole number. For example, a raw score of 36.25 is rounded to 36, the nearest whole number. A raw score of 36.50 is rounded upward to 37.
- *Converting to reported scaled score.* Raw test scores are then placed on the College Board scale of 200 to 800 through a process that adjusts scores to account for minor differences in difficulty among different editions of the test. This process, known as equating, is performed so that a student's reported score is not affected by the edition of the test taken nor by the abilities of the group with whom the student takes the test. As a result of placing SAT scores on the College Board scale, scores earned by students at different times can be compared. For example, an SAT-verbal score of 400 on a test taken at one administration indicates the same level of developed verbal ability as a 400 score obtained on a different edition of the test taken at another time.

How to Score the Test

You can verify the College Board SAT scores reported to you recently by using the information in this booklet along with the copy of your answer sheet. *Before you begin, check that the first two characters (number and letter) of the form code you marked in item 3 on your answer sheet are the same as the form code printed on the front of this booklet.* Compare the responses shown on the copy of your answer sheet with the list of correct answers.

SAT-Verbal Sections 1 and 3

Step A: Count the number of correct answers for *section 1* and record the number in the space provided on the worksheet on the next page. Then do the same for the incorrect answers. (Do not count omitted answers.) To determine subtotal A, use the formula:

$$\text{number correct} - \frac{\text{number incorrect}}{4} = \text{subtotal A}$$

Step B: Count the number of correct answers and the number of incorrect answers for *section 3* and record the numbers in the spaces provided on the worksheet. To determine subtotal B, use the formula:

$$\text{number correct} - \frac{\text{number incorrect}}{4} = \text{subtotal B}$$

Step C: To obtain C, add subtotal A to subtotal B, keeping any decimals. Enter the resulting figure on the worksheet.

Step D: To obtain D, your raw verbal score, round C to the nearest whole number. (For example, any number from 44.50 to 45.49 rounds to 45.) Enter the resulting figure on the worksheet.

Step E: To find your reported SAT-verbal score, look up the total raw verbal score you obtained in step D in the conversion table on the back cover. Enter this figure on the worksheet. (The SAT-verbal score you just recorded and your reported SAT-verbal score should be identical. If not, see the paragraph at the bottom of the next page.)

SAT-Mathematical Sections 2 and 5

Step A: Count the number of correct answers and the number of incorrect answers for *section 2* and record the numbers in the spaces provided on the worksheet. To determine the subtotal A, use the formula:

$$\text{number correct} - \frac{\text{number incorrect}}{4} = \text{subtotal A}$$

Step B: Count the number of correct answers and the number of incorrect answers for the *five-choice questions (questions 1 through 7 and 28 through 35) in section 5* and record the numbers in the spaces provided on the worksheet. To determine the subtotal B, use the formula:

$$\text{number correct} - \frac{\text{number incorrect}}{4} = \text{subtotal B}$$

Step C: Count the number of correct answers and the number of incorrect answers for the *four-choice questions (questions 8 through 27) in section 5* and record the numbers in the spaces provided on the worksheet. To determine the subtotal C, use the formula:

$$\text{number correct} - \frac{\text{number incorrect}}{3} = \text{subtotal C}$$

Step D: To obtain D, add subtotal A, subtotal B, and subtotal C, keeping any decimals. Enter the resulting figure on the worksheet.

Step E: To obtain E, your raw mathematical score, round D to the nearest whole number. (For example, any number from 44.50 to 45.49 rounds to 45.) Enter the resulting figure on the worksheet.

Step F: To find your reported SAT-mathematical score, look up the total raw mathematical score you obtained in E in the conversion table on the back cover. Enter this figure on the worksheet. (The SAT-mathematical score you just recorded and your reported SAT-mathematical score should be identical. If not, see the paragraph at the bottom of the next page.)

SAT-SCORING WORKSHEET

FORM CODE 3F

SAT-Verbal Sections

A. Section 1: ________ no. correct − ¼ (________ no. incorrect) = ________ subtotal A

B. Section 3: ________ no. correct − ¼ (________ no. incorrect) = ________ subtotal B

C. Total unrounded raw score
(Total A + B) ________ C

D. Total rounded raw score
(Rounded to nearest whole number) ________ D

E. SAT-verbal reported scaled score
(See the conversion table on the back cover.) [ ] SAT-verbal score

SAT-Mathematical Sections

A. Section 2: ________ no. correct − ¼ (________ no. incorrect) = ________ subtotal A

B. Section 5:
Questions 1 through 7 and
28 through 35 (5-choice) ________ no. correct − ¼ (________ no. incorrect) = ________ subtotal B

C. Section 5:
Questions 8 through 27
(4-choice) ________ no. correct − ⅓ (________ no. incorrect) = ________ subtotal C

D. Total unrounded raw score
(Total A + B + C) ________ D

E. Total rounded raw score
(Rounded to nearest whole number) ________ E

F. SAT-mathematical reported scaled score
(See the conversion table on the back cover.) [ ] SAT-math score

Should you have any questions on these scoring instructions, you may call the phone number below. If, after following the above scoring directions and checking your work at least twice, your results disagree with the SAT-verbal or SAT-mathematical score reported on your ATP score report, you may request rescoring of your answer sheet. If rescoring confirms that an error had been made (resulting in either higher or lower scores than those originally reported), corrected reports will be sent to all recipients of your original scores. Please send your request to:

College Board ATP
Box 592
Princeton, NJ 08541
Attention: Rescore Request
Telephone: (609) 771-7600

Please indicate whether it is your SAT-verbal or SAT-mathematical score, or both, that you want to be rescored. When you write, please include a copy of this scoring worksheet on which you did your calculations.

Score Conversion Table
Scholastic Aptitude Test
Form Code 3F

Raw Score	College Board Reported Score		Raw Score	College Board Reported Score	
	SAT-Verbal	SAT-Math		SAT-Verbal	SAT-Math
85	800		40	450	610
84	780		39	440	600
83	770		38	440	590
82	760		37	430	580
81	750		36	420	570
80	740		35	420	560
79	730		34	410	550
78	720		33	410	540
77	710		32	400	530
76	700		31	390	520
75	700		30	390	510
74	690		29	380	500
73	680		28	370	490
72	670		27	370	480
71	670		26	360	470
70	660		25	350	460
69	650		24	350	450
68	640		23	340	440
67	640		22	330	430
66	630		21	330	430
65	620		20	320	420
64	610		19	310	410
63	600		18	310	400
62	600		17	300	390
61	590		16	290	380
60	580	800	15	290	370
59	580	780	14	280	360
58	570	770	13	270	360
57	560	760	12	270	350
56	550	750	11	260	340
55	550	740	10	250	330
54	540	730	9	250	320
53	530	720	8	240	320
52	530	710	7	230	310
51	520	710	6	230	300
50	520	700	5	220	290
49	510	690	4	210	290
48	500	680	3	210	280
47	500	670	2	200	270
46	490	660	1	200	260
45	480	650	0	200	250
44	480	640	−1	200	240
43	470	630	−2	200	240
42	460	620	−3	200	230
41	460	610	−4	200	220
			−5	200	210
			−6 or below	200	200

SAT
Form Code 3X

FORM CODE 3X

SECTION 1

Time—30 minutes

45 QUESTIONS

Fallow #11
Execrable #14
Evocative #19
IMMUTABLE #18

For each question in this section, choose the best answer and blacken the corresponding space on the answer sheet.

Each question below consists of a word in capital letters, followed by five lettered words or phrases. Choose the word or phrase that is most nearly opposite in meaning to the word in capital letters. Since some of the questions require you to distinguish fine shades of meaning, consider all the choices before deciding which is best.

Example:

GOOD: (A) sour (B) bad (C) red (D) hot (E) ugly

1. BRITTLE: (A) dim (B) flexible (C) soluble (D) reliable (E) transparent
2. INHOSPITABLE: (A) sensitive (B) healthy (C) inoffensive (D) enduring (E) welcoming
3. COMPRESS: (A) displace (B) entangle (C) expand (D) soothe (E) delay
4. CONVINCE: (A) dissuade (B) reveal (C) impede (D) betray (E) refuse
5. ONLOOKER: (A) seeker (B) failure (C) fugitive (D) participant (E) thinker
6. SLACKEN: (A) enjoy (B) accumulate (C) accelerate (D) set free (E) turn aside
7. INCOMPATIBLE: (A) receptive (B) meticulous (C) harmonious (D) finished (E) fallible
8. FACILITATE: (A) hamper (B) shorten (C) possess (D) equalize (E) anticipate
9. QUAINT: (A) agreeable (B) brave (C) ordinary (D) comfortable (E) affordable
10. WITTICISM: (A) conclusion (B) insult (C) comment (D) rebuttal (E) platitude
11. FALLOW: (A) humid (B) profound (C) undeviating (D) actively cultivated (E) excessively tedious
12. DEFERENCE: (A) abnormality (B) isolation (C) cowardice (D) disrespect (E) pessimism
13. EMBELLISH: (A) revise (B) abbreviate (C) collaborate (D) examine carefully (E) challenge defiantly
14. EXECRABLE: (A) feeble (B) persistent (C) momentous (D) admirable (E) sensible
15. ATROPHY: (A) growth (B) neutralization (C) ambition (D) selection (E) conformity

Each sentence below has one or two blanks, each blank indicating that something has been omitted. Beneath the sentence are five lettered words or sets of words. Choose the word or set of words that best fits the meaning of the sentence as a whole.

Example:

Although its publicity has been ----, the film itself is intelligent, well-acted, handsomely produced, and altogether ----.

(A) tasteless. .respectable (B) extensive. .moderate (C) sophisticated. .amateur (D) risqué. .crude (E) perfect. .spectacular

16. John's back ailment was very painful, but he was not ---- and could manage to complete his performance.

    (A) inconvenienced (B) incapacitated (C) indifferent (D) competitive (E) aggressive

17. To understand the people of another culture, one must not form a ---- impression; one must play the role of the ---- and evaluate all of the evidence carefully.

    (A) distrustful. .skeptic
    (B) sympathetic. .radical
    (C) hasty. .scientist
    (D) graphic. .artist
    (E) biased. .guide

18. One reason for optimism is that the social institutions responsible for our present difficulties are not as ---- as they appear to be.

    (A) immutable (B) harmless (C) flawless (D) divisible (E) improvable

19. All too often in this book ---- conclusions distort illuminating descriptions and tendentious captions spoil ---- photographs.

    (A) illogical. .inane
    (B) pertinent. .irrelevant
    (C) inevitable. .passable
    (D) outlandish. .superfluous
    (E) unjustified. .evocative

20. Humor springs from an unexpected and, more specifically, ---- juxtaposition of ideas so that the audience is surprised into laughter.

    (A) unnecessary (B) common (C) slapstick (D) incongruous (E) deliberate

GO ON TO THE NEXT PAGE

1

Each passage below is followed by questions based on its content. Answer all questions following a passage on the basis of what is stated or implied in that passage.

(This passage was published in 1964.)

The issues of poverty and civil rights are deeply intertwined, presenting the central moral problem of our time. Although it is true that three-quarters of the poor are white, it is a tragic fact that half the nonwhites are poor.

The statistics of poverty bear witness to the results of years of discrimination and apathy on the part of the white majority. In 1962, the average income of a white family was $5,642, that of a black family was $3,023, and that of an American Indian family was $1,500. According to the 1960 census figures, Mexican Americans did not fit into a single classification in which their average family income even approximated $3,000.

Contrary to the widely held belief that American Indians receive some sort of consistent dole from the federal government, they are as dependent on the general economy to provide opportunities and jobs as is the rest of the population. Often unable to gain acceptance in the general community, they tend to stay on the reservations, which cannot provide more than minimal employment at low levels. Forty to fifty per cent, seven to eight times the national average, are unemployed.

Of the approximately 4.5 million Mexican Americans, almost one-quarter become migrant workers, following the harvest from state to state. Because they lack a fixed place of residence and employment, migrant workers are neither protected by federal laws nor eligible for public assistance.

Discrimination costs this country between thirteen and seventeen billion dollars every year in revenue and production. This is more than a fourth of the amount spent for national defense. This does not include the incalculable costs we pay in higher crime rates, poor health, mounting welfare costs, and the countless other indirect costs that flow from discriminatory practices.

A great barrier began to swing aside on the day when the Civil Rights Bill passed—a barrier that for generations had been damming tremendous intellectual resources and incalculable energy and vitality, all lost to the American nation.

I say "began." For if the door is being unlocked, if the door is swinging open, it is only ajar. There will be no miracle wrought overnight. Rather, then will come the real test of the maturity of our people. The test will be whether all people in America can work together to dissolve the barriers that have grown and to develop a healthier sense of community. That task will test the wisdom, courage, patience, and judgment of all of us.

21. The passage primarily concerns

(A) the results of the passage of the Civil Rights Bill
(B) the economic effects of discrimination
(C) the task of building a community-oriented America
(D) the employment practices of impoverished Americans
(E) practical ways of eliminating the burdens of poverty

22. The author indicates that the passage of the Civil Rights Bill should be regarded as

(A) an event whose importance has been overemphasized
(B) a reward for the efforts of all mature Americans
(C) the first step in a long and difficult, but necessary, process
(D) a goal that most Americans have worked toward
(E) the final solution to the dilemmas of poverty and civil rights

23. It can be inferred that the sources of the "energy and vitality" mentioned in lines 44-45 are

(A) branches of the federal government
(B) members of the white majority
(C) politicians who supported the Civil Rights Bill
(D) Americans whose income is less $3,000
(E) minority groups that have suffered from discrimination

24. Which of the following best describes the key that unlocks the "door" mentioned by the author in lines 46-48 ?

(A) The passage of the Civil Rights Bill
(B) The end of poverty for nonwhite Americans
(C) The enormous costs of discrimination
(D) The courage of every American citizen
(E) Opportunities for new jobs for all Americans

25. The author's intention in the last paragraph of the passage is apparently to

(A) suggest specific solutions
(B) warn of unexpected dangers
(C) criticize exaggerated reports
(D) inspire constructive attitudes
(E) soothe agitated tempers

GO ON TO THE NEXT PAGE

The sun has been found surprisingly inconstant both in its rotation and its sunspot activity. Yet it also appears that sunspot occurrences, while irregular, are controlled by a highly precise timer deep within the sun. The intervals between maximum sunspot activity average out to about eleven years, but since magnetic fields on the sun reverse themselves with each cycle, it actually takes about twenty-two years for the sun to return to its original configuration. It has recently been found that the full cycle is controlled by an internal timer that maintains a stable period of 22.27 years, the error margin being only 0.08 year. A possible explanation for the failure of sunspots to adhere to this precise rate may be that the transport of a magnetic field from deep interior to surface is subject to irregularities induced by turbulence in the convective layer, the region in which hot gas rises to the solar surface, cools, and subsides again.

A regularity in climate fluctuations on earth has been attributed to the sunspot cycle. The fluctuations are evident in the varying ratio of deuterium to hydrogen in cellulose extracted from tree rings. The ratio in air moisture seems controlled by atmospheric and sea surface temperature, and evidence of this becomes incorporated into the wood of each annual tree ring. Available data on the formation of tree rings fit the long-term sunspot rhythm, supporting the belief in a link between such activity and the climate.

It is now widely believed that, from 1645 to 1715, virtually no sunspots were evident; the chilling of the climate during this period is known as the "Little Ice Age." The timer deep inside the sun, however, did not miss a beat: when the cycle again became evident, sunspot activity was in step with the earlier rhythm. But it has recently been found that the sun underwent remarkable changes in rotational behavior just before that 70-year intermission, now referred to as the Maunder Minimum. As the minimum and the "Little Ice Age" approached, the rotational velocity of sunspots increased, primarily in the equatorial regions. (The sun, being gaseous, does not rotate as a solid body; normally, the equator rotates every 25 days, the latitudes near the pole every 34.) According to available evidence, the difference between the rotation rate near the equator and that near the poles increased threefold as the minimum approached.

26. According to the author of the passage, the explanation given for the sunspots' failure to adhere to a precise rate of occurrence is

(A) the only credible explanation
(B) a recently documented theory
(C) a highly controversial issue
(D) an unproven hypothesis
(E) a questionable and probably untrue assumption

27. According to the passage, which of the following is (are) true about "the full cycle" (line 11) of sunspot activity?

I. It is repeated approximately once every 22 years.
II. It can be roughly divided into two periods of 11 years.
III. It affects the rotation of the sun.

(A) I only (B) II only (C) I and II only
(D) I and III only (E) I, II, and III

28. It can be inferred from the passage that the word "minimum," as used in "Maunder Minimum" (lines 40-41), probably refers to the decline in the

(A) earth's temperature
(B) number of sunspots
(C) atmospheric ratio of deuterium to hydrogen
(D) relative speed of the sun's rotation
(E) variety of discernible tree rings

29. According to the passage, if in the future the earth were to observe an increase in the rotational velocity of sunspots, we should probably expect which of the following to occur?

I. A general cooling of the earth's climate
II. An increase in the number of sunspots visible on the earth
III. A change in the cycle of the sun's internal timer

(A) I only (B) II only (C) III only
(D) I and II only (E) I and III only

30. The author includes the parenthetical sentence (lines 44-46) for which of the following reasons?

(A) To provide an example supporting a generalization
(B) To state a proposition that is explained in the passage
(C) To present information that clarifies a previous statement
(D) To emphasize the main point of the passage
(E) To shift the description from the abstract to the concrete

GO ON TO THE NEXT PAGE

Select the word or set of words that best completes each of the following sentences.

31. The Mediterranean fruit fly proved to be a ---- to farmers, a pest more ---- to fruits and vegetables than even the Japanese beetle.

(A) delight. .indifferent (B) dilemma. .averse (C) boon. .deadly (D) triumph. .partial (E) nightmare. .harmful

32. The assassination of Zapata had ---- the agrarian movement, but had not ---- it; peasant guerrillas still fought, and an Agrarian Party was founded in Mexico City to defend Zapata's ideals.

(A) destroyed. .deterred
(B) impaired. .ended
(C) generated. .decimated
(D) produced. .exterminated
(E) engendered. .endangered

33. Much in keeping with its ---- start, the cooperative is doing a thriving business and is making plans to expand in the near future.

(A) problematic (B) premature (C) blemished (D) auspicious (E) erratic

34. This book is particularly valuable because it obliges us to ---- our assumption that source material in Central Africa is too meager to allow more than ---- accounts of local history.

(A) devise. .personal (B) defend. .comprehensive (C) disclose. .radical (D) limit. .optional (E) modify. .impressionistic

35. The gaily lit garlands strung across Oxford Street, the enticing shop windows, the crowded theaters—all of these things ---- the ---- of the economic crisis that has come to haunt the country.

(A) bespeak. .severity
(B) underline. .existence
(C) belie. .gravity
(D) protest. .superficiality
(E) malign. .enormity

Each question below consists of a related pair of words or phrases, followed by five lettered pairs of words or phrases. Select the lettered pair that best expresses a relationship similar to that expressed in the original pair.

Example:

YAWN : BOREDOM :: (A) dream : sleep (B) anger : madness (C) smile : amusement (D) face : expression (E) impatience : rebellion

Ⓐ Ⓑ ● Ⓓ Ⓔ

36. TEACHER : FACULTY :: (A) actor : cast (B) student : library (C) painter : mural (D) composer : orchestra (E) soloist : audience

37. DEVOUR : FOOD :: (A) conserve : energy (B) borrow : money (C) sweeten : candy (D) soften : noise (E) guzzle : liquid

38. GHASTLY : HORROR :: (A) soothing : injury (B) momentary : time (C) indifferent : stupidity (D) excruciating : agony (E) feeble : power

39. CREST : WAVE :: (A) trunk : tree (B) shore : lake (C) hub : wheel (D) base : triangle (E) peak : mountain

40. CHAMELEON : LIZARD :: (A) eagle : hawk (B) zebra : camel (C) rainbow : sun (D) blossom : root (E) peacock : bird

41. GULLIBLE : CREDULOUS :: (A) ravenous : voracious (B) overflowing : thirsty (C) secretive : curious (D) frivolous : needy (E) gorgeous : appreciative

42. PERFUNCTORY : ENTHUSIASM ::
(A) persistent : uniformity
(B) tolerant : indecision
(C) impulsive : effectiveness
(D) hesitant : certainty
(E) ambitious : interest

43. NERVE : TEMERITY ::
(A) courage : eminence
(B) skill : finesse
(C) conviction : reliance
(D) foresight : learning
(E) determination : coordination

44. MEDLEY : MUSIC :: (A) panorama : vision (B) tapestry : thread (C) prism : color (D) patchwork : cloth (E) encyclopedia : textbook

45. SHRIVELED : TURGIDITY ::
(A) hoary : decadence
(B) prolific : progeny
(C) ambulatory : motion
(D) comatose : animation
(E) ethereal : inspiration

S T O P

IF YOU FINISH BEFORE TIME IS CALLED, YOU MAY CHECK YOUR WORK ON THIS SECTION ONLY. DO NOT WORK ON ANY OTHER SECTION IN THE TEST.

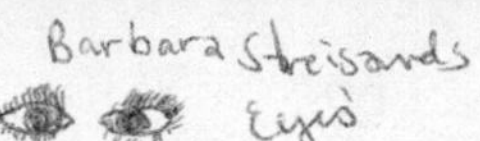

SECTION 2

Time—30 minutes

25 QUESTIONS

In this section solve each problem, using any available space on the page for scratchwork. Then decide which is the best of the choices given and blacken the corresponding space on the answer sheet.

The following information is for your reference in solving some of the problems.

Circle of radius r: Area $= \pi r^2$; Circumference $= 2\pi r$

The number of degrees of arc in a circle is 360.

The measure in degrees of a straight angle is 180.

Definitions of symbols:

$=$	is equal to	$\leq$	is less than or equal to
$\neq$	is unequal to	$\geq$	is greater than or equal to
$<$	is less than	$\parallel$	is parallel to
$>$	is greater than	$\perp$	is perpendicular to

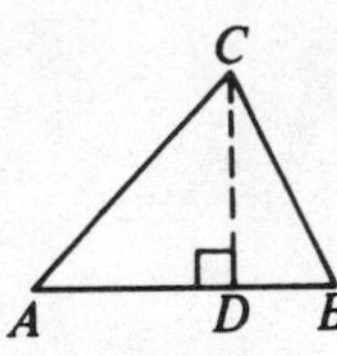

Triangle: The sum of the measures in degrees of the angles of a triangle is 180.

If $\angle CDA$ is a right angle, then

(1) area of $\triangle ABC = \dfrac{AB \times CD}{2}$

(2) $AC^2 = AD^2 + DC^2$

Note: Figures which accompany problems in this test are intended to provide information useful in solving the problems. They are drawn as accurately as possible EXCEPT when it is stated in a specific problem that its figure is not drawn to scale. All figures lie in a plane unless otherwise indicated. All numbers used are real numbers.

---

1. If $\dfrac{x - x + x}{2} = \dfrac{1}{2}$, then $x =$

(A) $\frac{1}{4}$ (B) $\frac{1}{2}$ (C) 1 (D) 2 (E) 4

2. If $\frac{3}{5}$ of n is 30, then $\frac{2}{5}$ of n is

(A) 6
(B) 10
(C) 12
(D) 18
(E) 20

3. If $x \nearrow y$ means that x^2 is less than y^2, then which of the following relations is true?

(A) $\frac{1}{3} \nearrow \frac{1}{2}$ (B) $\frac{1}{3} \nearrow \frac{1}{30}$ (C) $2 \nearrow \frac{1}{2}$

(D) $3 \nearrow 2$ (E) $4 \nearrow 2$

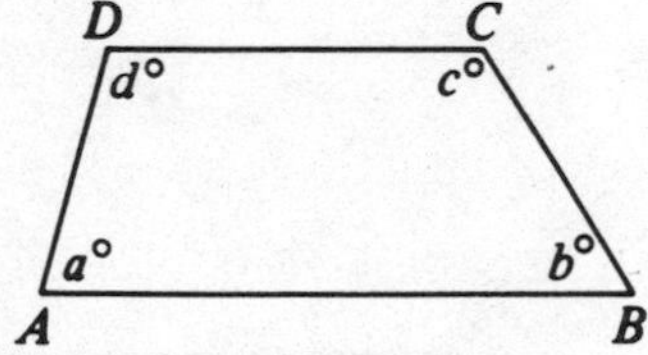

4. In the figure above, AB is parallel to CD. What is the value of $a + b$?

(A) 90 (B) 120 (C) 150 (D) 180

(E) It cannot be determined from the information given.

5. If n is a multiple of 3, which of the following is also a multiple of 3 ?

(A) $n - 2$
(B) $n + 2$
(C) $2n + 6$
(D) $3n - 5$
(E) $3n + 4$

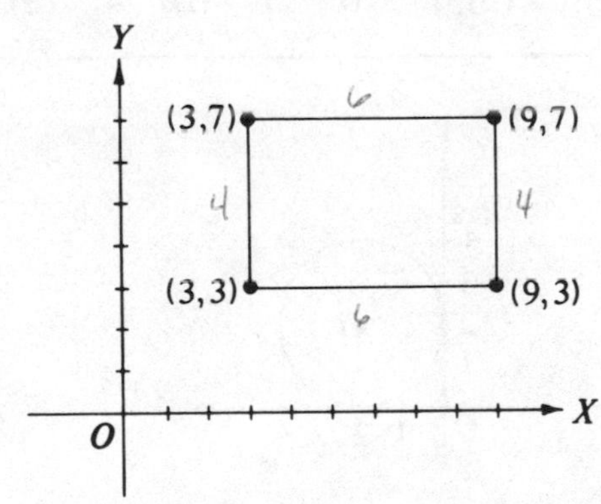

6. In the figure above, the area of the rectangle is

(A) 63 (B) 36 (C) 27 (D) 24 (E) 18

+ +	+ −	− −	− +
− 0	+ +	+ 0	0 −
0 +	0 0	+ −	− 0

7. In the array of pairs of signs above, a pair has value 1 if a + sign is paired with another + sign or with a 0; any other combination has value 0. What is the total value of the array?

(A) 2 (B) 3 (C) 4 (D) 6 (E) 7

8. $3^4 \cdot 3^2 =$

(A) 3^2
(B) 3^6
(C) 3^8
(D) 9^6
(E) 9^8

9. If the perimeter of ΔABC is 50 units and if side AB is 2 units longer than side BC, what is the length of side AC ?

(A) 2
(B) 16
(C) 24
(D) 25
(E) It cannot be determined from the information given.

10. Half of the sum of two numbers is 7. If one of the numbers is 3, then the product of the two numbers is

(A) 10 (B) 15 (C) 21 (D) 24 (E) 33

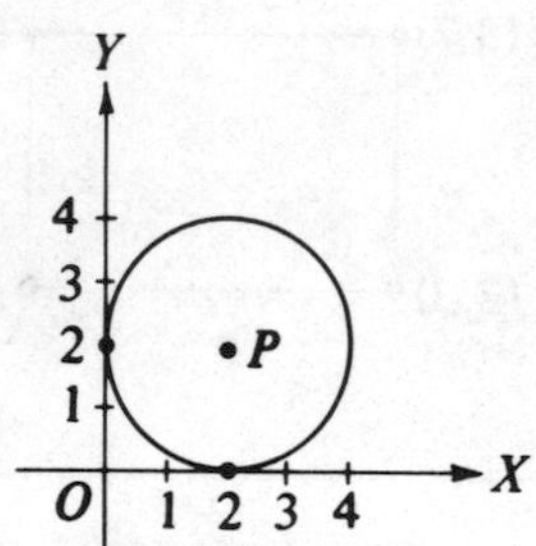

11. If $C(P, r)$ represents a circle with center at the point P and radius r, then the circle in the figure above can be represented as

(A) $C(P, 2)$ (B) $C(P, 1)$ (C) $C(P, 2\sqrt{2})$
(D) $C(P, 4)$ (E) $C(P, 4\pi)$

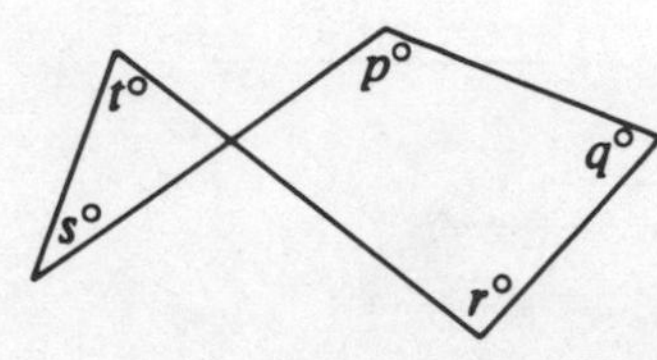

12. Five line segments intersect to form the figure above. If $p + q + r = 285°$, what is the value of $t + s$?

(A) 60
(B) 75
(C) 90
(D) 105
(E) It cannot be determined from the information given.

13. Four empty trucks are on a bridge that has a maximum capacity of 30,000 pounds. If the average (arithmetic mean) weight of three of the trucks is 7,800 pounds, then the greatest possible safe weight of the fourth truck is

(A) 6,000 lb.
(B) 6,600 lb.
(C) 6,800 lb.
(D) 7,600 lb.
(E) 8,000 lb.

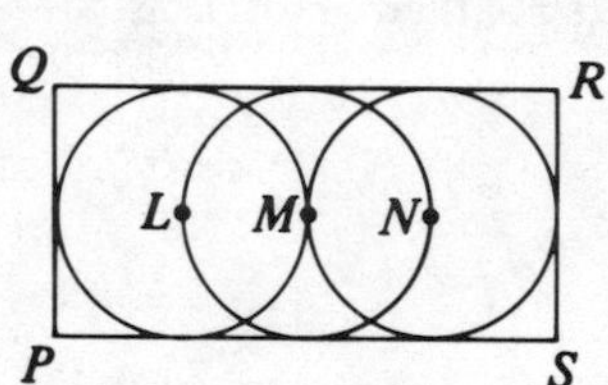

14. In the figure above, circles with centers at L, M, and N each have a radius of 2 and are placed as shown. If $PQRS$ is the smallest rectangle that will enclose the 3 circles, what is the area of $PQRS$?

(A) 8
(B) 12
(C) 16
(D) 32
(E) 48

GO ON TO THE NEXT PAGE

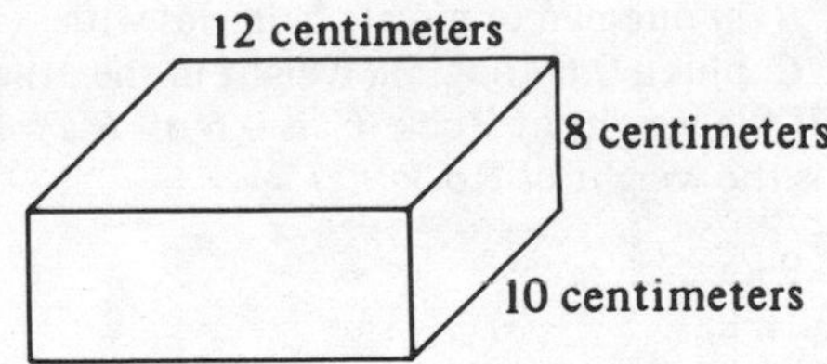

15. How many cubes 2 centimeters on an edge can be packed into the box shown above?

(A) 960 (B) 480 (C) 192
(D) 120 (E) 15

16. If 1 skip equals 3 hops and 1 jump equals 2 skips, how many jumps equal "a hop, a skip, and a jump"?

(A) $1\frac{1}{8}$

(B) $1\frac{2}{3}$

(C) $2\frac{1}{6}$

(D) 3

(E) $3\frac{1}{6}$

17. If x and y are nonzero integers and if $x^2 + y^3 = 0$ and $x^3 + y^5 = 0$, which of the following number lines shows the relative positions of x, y, and 0 ?

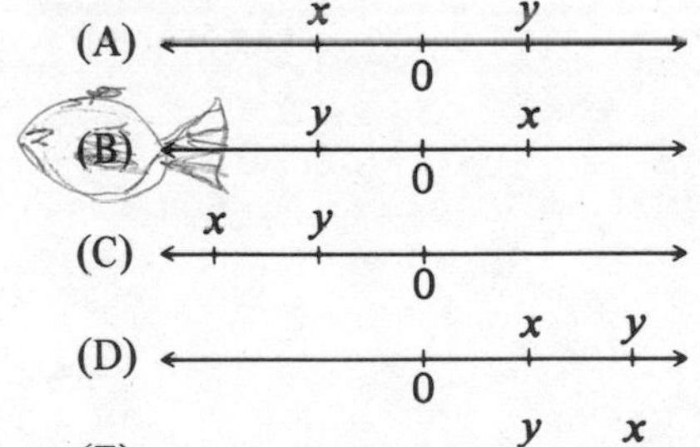

18. A stack of red and blue chips is 5 centimeters high. If the red chips are 0.4 centimeters thick and the blue chips are 0.3 centimeters thick, what is the greatest possible number of blue chips that could be in the stack?

(A) 16
(B) 15
(C) 14
(D) 12
(E) 10

19. What is the maximum number of circles that can be made from a piece of string 100 meters long, if the radius of each circle is 5 meters?

(A) 2
(B) 3
(C) 4
(D) 5
(E) 6

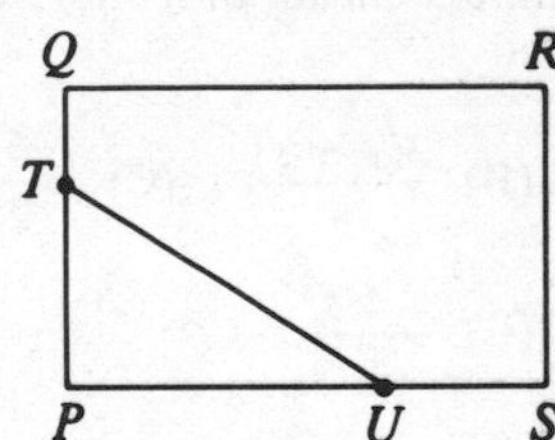

20. If, in rectangle $PQRS$ above, $PT = \frac{2}{3}PQ$ and $PU = \frac{2}{3}PS$, what is the ratio of the area of $\triangle PTU$ to the area of $\square PQRS$?

(A) $\frac{2}{9}$ (B) $\frac{1}{3}$ (C) $\frac{4}{9}$ (D) $\frac{2}{3}$

(E) It cannot be determined from the information given.

Population of Yourtown 1900-1950	
Year	Population
1900	500
1910	700
1920	800
1930	1,000
1940	1,300
1950	1,500

21. In the table above, the percent increase in the population was greatest in which of the following periods?

(A) 1900-1910
(B) 1910-1920
(C) 1920-1930
(D) 1930-1940
(E) 1940-1950

GO ON TO THE NEXT PAGE

22. What are all values of b such that $(b-5)(b+2)$ is negative?

(A) $-5 < b < 2$
(B) $-2 < b < 5$
(C) $2 < b < 5$
(D) $b < -5$ and $b > 2$
(E) $b < -2$ and $b > 5$

23. If $p+q=2(r+s)$, which of the following is the average (arithmetic mean) of $p, q, r,$ and s in terms of r and s?

(A) $r+s$ (B) $\frac{3(r+s)}{4}$ (C) $\frac{r+s}{2}$

(D) $\frac{r+s}{4}$ (E) $\frac{r+s}{8}$

24. Rock B in one pan of a scale balances with Rock C plus a 0.6-kilogram weight in the other pan. If the weight of Rock C is 0.6 of B's weight, what is the weight of Rock C?

(A) 0.9 kg
(B) 0.12 kg
(C) 0.36 kg
(D) 1.0 kg
(E) 1.2 kg

25. In how many different color combinations can 3 balls be painted if each ball is painted one color and there are 3 colors available? (Order is not considered; e.g., red, blue, red is considered the same combination as red, red, blue.)

(A) 4 (B) 6 (C) 9 (D) 10 (E) 27

S T O P

IF YOU FINISH BEFORE TIME IS CALLED, YOU MAY CHECK YOUR WORK ON THIS SECTION ONLY. DO NOT WORK ON ANY OTHER SECTION IN THE TEST.

SECTION 3

Time—30 minutes

40 QUESTIONS

For each question in this section, choose the best answer and blacken the corresponding space on the answer sheet.

Each question below consists of a word in capital letters, followed by five lettered words or phrases. Choose the word or phrase that is most nearly opposite in meaning to the word in capital letters. Since some of the questions require you to distinguish fine shades of meaning, consider all the choices before deciding which is best.

Example:

GOOD: (A) sour (B) bad (C) red (D) hot (E) ugly

1. ACCESSIBLE: (A) impure (B) inactive (C) unimportant (D) purposefully designed (E) difficult to approach

2. INEVITABLE: (A) pleasurable (B) fictitious (C) beneficial (D) avoidable (E) suitable

3. BUNGLE: (A) perform efficiently (B) retire quickly (C) shout angrily (D) energize (E) excuse

4. HYPOTHESIZE:
(A) argue enthusiastically
(B) know with certainty
(C) exaggerate noticeably
(D) plan with care
(E) reflect morally

5. NEGOTIABLE: (A) unpopular (B) illogical (C) unreliable (D) indiscriminate (E) nontransferable

6. REITERATE:
(A) refuse to accept
(B) neglect to examine
(C) fail to repeat
(D) tend to misinterpret
(E) pretend to ignore

7. STEADFASTNESS: (A) lethargy (B) nervousness (C) irresponsibility (D) disorganization (E) irresolution

8. AUTHORITATIVE: (A) partial (B) unscrupulous (C) intelligent (D) submissive (E) fickle

9. INSIPIDNESS:
(A) sweetness and joy
(B) ribaldry and coarseness
(C) indifference and unconcern
(D) spirit and animation
(E) curiosity and acquisitiveness

10. IMPORT: (A) meaninglessness (B) inopportuneness (C) externality (D) negligence (E) humility

Each sentence below has one or two blanks, each blank indicating that something has been omitted. Beneath the sentence are five lettered words or sets of words. Choose the word or set of words that best fits the meaning of the sentence as a whole.

Example:

Although its publicity has been ----, the film itself is intelligent, well-acted, handsomely produced, and altogether ----.

(A) tasteless. .respectable (B) extensive. .moderate (C) sophisticated. .amateur (D) risqué. .crude (E) perfect. .spectacular

11. The body is protected by a natural defense system that acts in the blood to destroy the army of germs ---- our bodies daily.

(A) guarding (B) vacating (C) attracting (D) invading (E) nurturing

12. Annoyed by his seemingly endless attempts to persuade her to his point of view, Nancy wished that Hamilton were just a bit less ----.

(A) vain (B) controlled (C) persistent (D) impressive (E) devious

13. The scientists reported that the pollution in the coastal areas had already ---- their tentative limit of tolerability and that a higher scale of tolerability would have to be postulated.

(A) restored (B) ignored (C) validated (D) surpassed (E) determined

14. Traditional views assume that violence is somehow ---- "masculine" behavior, rather than a way of behaving which may be ---- by either sex in particular circumstances.

(A) naturally. .adopted
(B) inherently. .perceived
(C) acceptably. .described
(D) accidentally. .selected
(E) avoidably. .intensified

15. Smith contends that psychology is bad poetry ---- science, in that many of its theories are based on unexamined ----, such as the mind as a blank slate, a computer, or a camera.

(A) expanding toward. .hypotheses
(B) inimical to. .facts
(C) escaping from. .quandaries
(D) analagous to. .redundancies
(E) masquerading as. .metaphors

GO ON TO THE NEXT PAGE

Each question below consists of a related pair of words or phrases, followed by five lettered pairs of words or phrases. Select the lettered pair that best expresses a relationship similar to that expressed in the original pair.

Example:

YAWN : BOREDOM :: (A) dream : sleep
(B) anger : madness (C) smile : amusement
(D) face : expression (E) impatience : rebellion

Ⓐ Ⓑ ● Ⓓ Ⓔ

16. SEE : INVISIBLE :: (A) correct : inverted
(B) hear : inaudible (C) enjoy : improper
(D) buy : invaluable (E) escape : inaccessible

17. STEAM : GEYSER :: (A) power : generator
(B) atoms : reactor (C) coal : mine
(D) lava : volcano (E) rock : quarry

18. CUSTOMER : SHOPKEEPER :: (A) patron : concert
(B) member : club (C) advocate : policy
(D) peddler : house (E) client : lawyer

19. EPIDERMIS : BODY :: (A) stem : plant
(B) air : diver (C) bark : tree
(D) fur : coat (E) nail : finger

20. OGRE : CRUELTY ::
(A) elf : skepticism
(B) pixie : mischievousness
(C) gnome : punishment
(D) dragon : mythology
(E) goblin : innocence

21. SCRIBBLING : READER :: (A) gibberish : listener
(B) snore : sleeper (C) daub : artist
(D) warble : singer (E) perjury : witness

22. CULMINATION : PROJECT ::
(A) precaution : accident (B) wisdom : judgment
(C) frustration : plan (D) arrival : journey
(E) imitation : idea

23. VERVE : PERFORMANCE :: (A) aspect : feature
(B) valor : courage (C) admiration : talent
(D) imagination : writing (E) sensation : gloom

24. PROMISCUOUS : DISCRIMINATION ::
(A) offensive : aggravation
(B) passive : obedience
(C) impecunious : caution
(D) oblivious : meditation
(E) impulsive : deliberation

25. SATURATE : MOISTEN :: (A) extol : commend
(B) donate : give (C) contaminate : infect
(D) postulate : query (E) assist : hamper

GO ON TO THE NEXT PAGE

COLLEGE BOARD—SCHOLASTIC APTITUDE TEST and Test of Standard Written English Side 1

Use a No. 2 pencil only for completing this answer sheet. Be sure each mark is dark and completely fills the intended space. Completely erase any errors or stray marks.

1. YOUR NAME: (Print) Last First M.I.

SIGNATURE: 3X **DATE:** / /

did verbal section 2 March 2

HOME ADDRESS: (Print) Number and Street

City State Zip Code

CENTER: (Print) City State Center Number

IMPORTANT: Please fill in these boxes exactly as shown on the back cover of your test book.

FOR ETS USE ONLY

2. TEST FORM

3. FORM CODE

4. REGISTRATION NUMBER (Copy from your Admission Ticket.)

5. YOUR NAME

First 4 letters of last name | First Init. | Mid. Init.

6. DATE OF BIRTH

Month | Day | Year

Jan. Feb. Mar. Apr. May June July Aug. Sept. Oct. Nov. Dec.

7. SEX

Male

Female

8. TEST BOOK SERIAL NUMBER

Start with number 1 for each new section. If a section has fewer than 50 questions, leave the extra answer spaces blank.

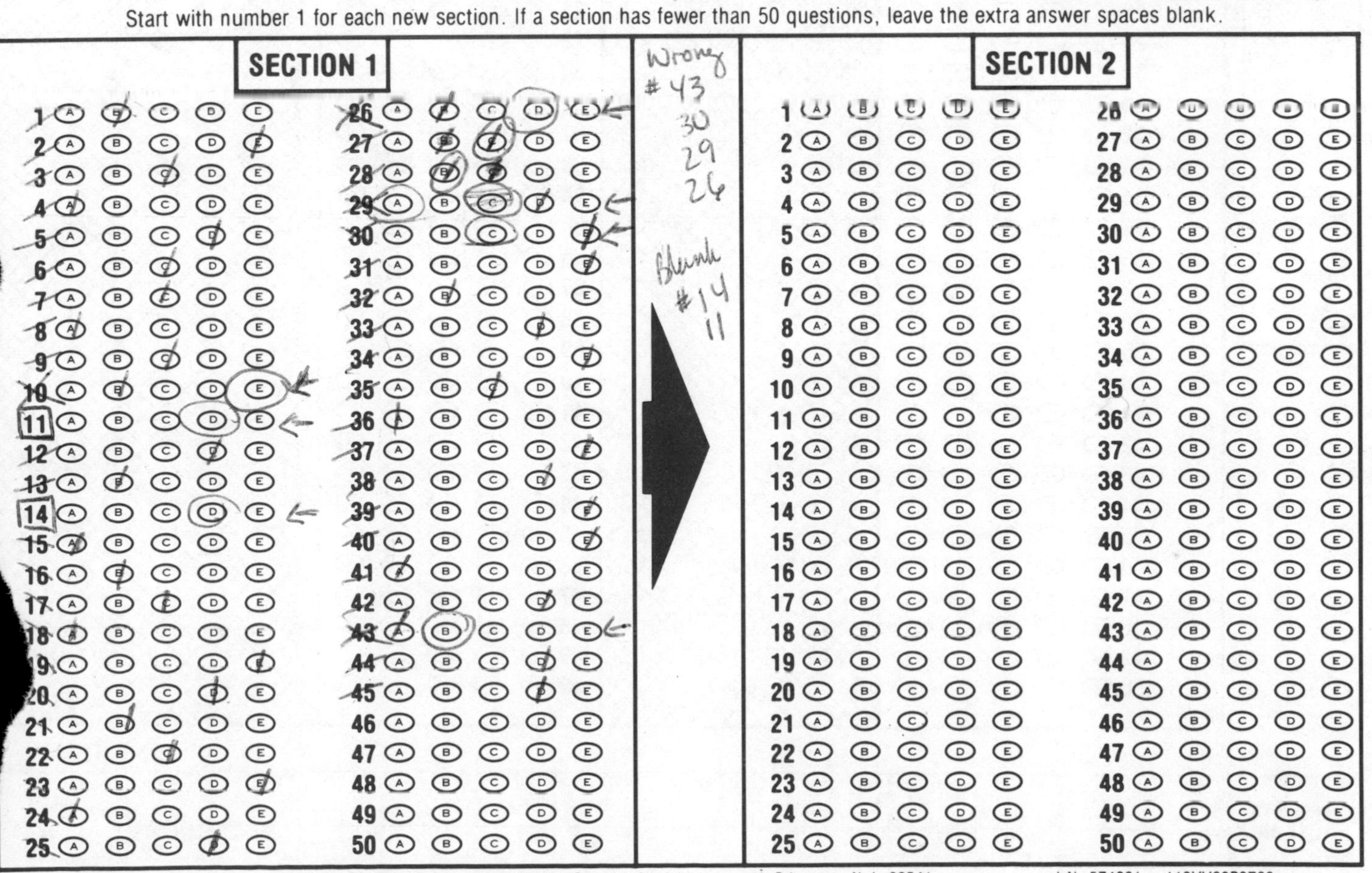

COLLEGE BOARD — SCHOLASTIC APTITUDE TEST and Test of Standard Written English Side 2

Use a No. 2 pencil only for completing this answer sheet. Be sure each mark is dark and completely fills the intended space. Completely erase any errors or stray marks.

Start with number 1 for each new section. If a section has fewer than 50 questions, leave the extra answer spaces blank.

No.	SECTION 3	SECTION 4	SECTION 5	SECTION 6
1	A B C D E	A B C D E	A B C D E	A B C D E
2	A B C D E	A B C D E	A B C D E	A B C D E
3	A B C D E	A B C D E	A B C D E	A B C D E
4	A B C D E	A B C D E	A B C D E	A B C D E
5	A B C D E	A B C D E	A B C D E	A B C D E
6	A B C D E	A B C D E	A B C D E	A B C D E
7	A B C D E	A B C D E	A B C D E	A B C D E
8	A B C D E	A B C D E	A B C D	A B C D E
9	A B C D E	A B C D E	A B C D	A B C D E
10	A B C D E	A B C D E	A B C D	A B C D E
11	A B C D E	A B C D E	A B C D	A B C D E
12	A B C D E	A B C D E	A B C D	A B C D E
13	A B C D E	A B C D E	A B C D	A B C D E
14	A B C D E	A B C D E	A B C D	A B C D E
15	A B C D E	A B C D E	A B C D	A B C D E
16	A B C D E	A B C D E	A B C D	A B C D E
17	A B C D E	A B C D E	A B C D	A B C D E
18	A B C D E	A B C D E	A B C D	A B C D E
19	A B C D E	A B C D E	A B C D	A B C D E
20	A B C D E	A B C D E	A B C D	A B C D E
21	A B C D E	A B C D E	A B C D	A B C D E
22	A B C D E	A B C D E	A B C D	A B C D E
23	A B C D E	A B C D E	A B C D	A B C D E
24	A B C D E	A B C D E	A B C D	A B C D E
25	A B C D E	A B C D E	A B C D	A B C D E
26	A B C D E	A B C D E	A B C D	A B C D E
27	A B C D E	A B C D E	A B C D	A B C D E
28	A B C D E	A B C D E	A B C D E	A B C D E
29	A B C D E	A B C D E	A B C D E	A B C D E
30	A B C D E	A B C D E	A B C D E	A B C D E
31	A B C D E	A B C D E	A B C D E	A B C D E
32	A B C D E	A B C D E	A B C D E	A B C D E
33	A B C D E	A B C D E	A B C D E	A B C D E
34	A B C D E	A B C D E	A B C D E	A B C D E
35	A B C D E	A B C D E	A B C D E	A B C D E
36	A B C D E	A B C D E	A B C D E	A B C D E
37	A B C D E	A B C D E	A B C D E	A B C D E
38	A B C D E	A B C D E	A B C D E	A B C D E
39	A B C D E	A B C D E	A B C D E	A B C D E
40	A B C D E	A B C D E	A B C D E	A B C D E
41	A B C D E	A B C D E	A B C D E	A B C D E
42	A B C D E	A B C D E	A B C D E	A B C D E
43	A B C D E	A B C D E	A B C D E	A B C D E
44	A B C D E	A B C D E	A B C D E	A B C D E
45	A B C D E	A B C D E	A B C D E	A B C D E
46	A B C D E	A B C D E	A B C D E	A B C D E
47	A B C D E	A B C D E	A B C D E	A B C D E
48	A B C D E	A B C D E	A B C D E	A B C D E
49	A B C D E	A B C D E	A B C D E	A B C D E
50	A B C D E	A B C D E	A B C D E	A B C D E

9. SIGNATURE:

FOR ETS USE ONLY	VTR	VTFS	VRR	VRFS	VVR	VVFS	WER	WEFS	M4R	M4FS	M5R	M5FS	MTFS
	VTW	VTCS	VRW	VRCS	VVW	VVCS	WEW	WECS	M4W		M5W		MTCS

Each passage below is followed by questions based on its content. Answer all questions following a passage on the basis of what is stated or implied in that passage.

Above this race of humans stands an immense and tutelary power, which takes upon itself alone to secure their gratification and to watch over their fate. That power is absolute, minute, regular, provident, and mild. It would be like the authority of a parent if, like that authority, its object were to prepare people for adulthood; but it seeks, on the contrary, to keep them in perpetual childhood: it is well content that the people should rejoice, provided they think of nothing but rejoicing. It covers the surface of society with a network of small complicated rules, minute and uniform, through which the most original minds and the most energetic characters cannot penetrate, to rise above the crowd. Such a power does not destroy, but it prevents existence; it does not tyrannize, but it compresses, enervates, extinguishes, and stupefies a people, till each nation is reduced to nothing better than a flock of timid and industrial animals of which the government is shepherd.

26. Which of the following statements summarizes the main idea of the passage?

(A) Creativity finds full expression in a state of anarchy.
(B) Energy not applied toward a specific goal is lost.
(C) Any exercise of power is, by its nature, evil.
(D) Human beings are, by their nature, dependent creatures.
(E) Government is an all-pervasive and inhibiting force.

27. The last sentence suggests that, under the power described, people are kept from all of the following EXCEPT

(A) thinking clearly
(B) acting energetically
(C) working efficiently
(D) creating freely
(E) living fully

28. The author develops the paragraph by means of which of the following?

I. Analogy and metaphor
II. Unsupported generalization
III. Recollected personal experience

(A) I only
(B) I and II only
(C) I and III only
(D) II and III only
(E) I, II, and III

When Samuel Carboy entered through the swinging door, the floor of the stock exchange was in a state of turmoil. The excitement was due to the still unauthenticated but, alas, well-supported rumor that Bonaparte had beaten the Duke of Wellington. The members to a man were trying to sell. Anyone who could get possession of a chair was standing above the crush and repeating the usual formula with frantic vehemence: "I'm here. I'll sell. D'ye hear me? I'll sell. I've got government securities and I've got bank paper and I've got shipping stocks. I'm not going to give these securities away." One member, Roger Gridsby, varied this by shouting: "Come, men, come! You're Englishmen aren't you? Do you want to take advantage of a temporary darkness on the horizon of England? Do you want to traffic in our monetary despair? Have you no feeling of shame? Support the market, if ye're honest Englishmen. D'ye want to drive prices down to nothing?"

A smartly dressed broker came to Samuel Carboy's side and asked in a cautious tone, "What is it to be today?"

The merchant looked down at him and said, "Westerby, I'm going to buy."

"Buy!" The little broker's voice rose almost to a yelp. "Buy, Samuel? You're joking, Samuel."

"Westerby," declared Carboy, "our army could not be beaten by the usurper Bonaparte. I refuse to believe it. Make what you will out of these rumors. I don't believe them. Westerby, I am going to buy."

"But, Samuel, Samuel!" The broker was speaking now in a beseeching voice. "Haven't you heard about Nathan Longman? He came in here looking like a death's head. That's exactly what he looked like. He said just exactly nothing at all. He just kept stamping his hat firmer on his head and looking very sick. And then he turned and walked out. That means he's selling. If he intended to buy he'd stay here and wait for his prices, wouldn't he? It stands to reason, Samuel."

"Westerby, I'm going to buy."

They retired to a relatively quiet corner and Carboy gave the broker his orders. Westerby marked the prices down on slips of paper, making clucking sounds of disapproval. Then, he shoved the little slips into the silver-embroidered pocket of his plum-colored coat. "It may be some time before they get as low as this," he said. "But they'll get there. You'll be ruined in the end, Samuel, mark my words. If you change your mind, get to me fast."

29. For which of the following reasons was there so much activity on the floor of the exchange?

(A) The army was in retreat.
(B) There was talk of the army's defeat.
(C) The pound had been devalued.
(D) A famous bank had gone bankrupt.
(E) There was fear of a military attack on the exchange.

30. It can be inferred that Nathan Longman is

(A) the owner of a bankrupt business
(B) Carboy's long-standing rival
(C) Carboy's business partner
(D) a friend of the Duke of Wellington
(E) a highly respected trader

31. According to the passage, which of the following were written on the slips of paper by the broker?

(A) Comments on the present worth of the stocks
(B) Names of companies certain to fail
(C) Estimates of the dividends Carboy will earn
(D) The prices Carboy wishes to pay for the stocks
(E) Types of stock owned by Carboy

32. This passage was most likely taken from

(A) a history textbook
(B) a treatise on the effects of hysteria on economics
(C) a historical novel
(D) a biography of the life of Nathan Longman
(E) Samuel Carboy's autobiography

33. The primary purpose of the passage is most probably to present

(A) an explanation of an economic depression
(B) a description of the bartering process used in the stock exchange
(C) an important decision in the life of Samuel Carboy
(D) the role and responsibilities of a broker
(E) the story of Wellington and Bonaparte

Since many people are unwilling to accept art for its own sake, they have sought theories that will reduce artistic values to values that are more easily recognized. They seize on doctrines that have been given a limited critical application by serious writers on art and try to make these doctrines the basis of all judgment. Thus we get theories, such as the moralistic view of art in the nineteenth century and the doctrine of functionalism at the present time, which satisfy those who have a craving for explanation but which run counter to the experience of artistically sensitive persons. Art and morals are indeed most closely connected, but the morals of a work of art are to be found less in its ostensible subject matter than in its means of expression. A song may have pious words but a false and wicked tune; a picture may have an improving subject, but the shapes and colors, the very touch of the artist's pencil may be mean and morally revolting. These are truisms, but they were not always present in the mind of even so great a critic as Ruskin and were generally ignored by his contemporaries. The moralistic theory of art suffered when the too crude interpretation of morality that it accompanied was finally brought into popular disfavor. When people ceased to believe that they knew what was good and bad in morals, they were no longer able to discriminate between good and bad in art by the application of moral standards. They had lost faith in everything except material values, values that could be measured. Hence they developed the theory of functionalism, which took its rise from one of several conflicting justifications of Gothic architecture, and began to apply this theory with a kind of desperate simplicity to all the visible arts.

34. The author believes that the connection between art and morality is to be found
    (A) primarily in the views of art critics
    (B) in the subject matter of a work of art
    (C) during periods when people can easily discriminate between good and bad
    (D) in the minds of those who are not artistically sensitive
    (E) in the form of a work of art more than in its content

35. According to the passage, the moralistic view of art and the theory of functionalism are alike in that both
    (A) have been adopted by artistically sensitive persons
    (B) are based on a tenet of Gothic architecture
    (C) are concerned solely with the means of artistic expression
    (D) are justifications of art which go beyond purely artistic values
    (E) marked an abrupt change in the moral values of an era

36. The author of the passage implies that most adherents of the moralistic doctrine demanded that a work of art
    (A) be moral in both its subject matter and its means of expression
    (B) be concerned with some morally improving subject
    (C) have no ostensible subject
    (D) conform to the standards of artistically sensitive persons
    (E) support the material values of the nineteenth century

The "sere and yellow leaf" of autumn is likely to bear a tumor. These tumors, called galls, may develop in any part of a plant—leaf, stem, flower, or root—provided the part contains vascular tissue to keep it supplied with nutrients. The derangement of growth and structure may form a tiny wart or a bulging mass the size of a baseball. Such growths are frequently seen in the fall on the withered stalks of goldenrod.

Plant galls inevitably bring to mind their counterpart in animals: the cancer tumor. In support of this analogy, the gall always contains in its interior a mass of amorphous cells. We know, however, that galls are caused by insects or by viruses, molds, and other microorganisms. The parasite supplies some sort of stimulus to initiate abnormal growth, and the galls seem to grow only so long as the stimulus persists. Many animal cancers appear to grow indefinitely without external stimulation. On the other hand, it may turn out that these tumors too are initiated by viruses or by some other infectious process.

Gall growth can originate when the insect causes tissue to develop into new and different cells and promotes more rapid continued growth than would ordinarily occur. In the insect-induced leaf gall, the parasite provokes its host to grow what is in effect a new organ that is adapted to shelter and nurture the insect egg and larva. The amorphous cells within the gall which feed the larva are enclosed in an intricate structure of supporting tissues covered on the outside by epidermal tissue characteristic of the plant stem. From the cellular point of view, a leaf gall bears some similarity to the stem. The globular gall forms as an appendage to the leaf, a kind of fruit in which the insect embryo takes the place of the plant seed. The insect thus exerts a regulatory power over the growth pattern of the plant that suggests a new line of experimental attack on the secrets of cellular specialization and growth.

37. According to the passage, cancerous growths and galls are alike in that both

(A) contain unspecialized cells
(B) appear to grow indefinitely once they have begun
(C) originate under identical conditions
(D) require external stimulation for continuous growth
(E) are modifications of epidermal tissues

38. In the passage, <u>parasite</u> and <u>host</u> refer, respectively, to the

(A) larva and the plant
(B) gall and the insect
(C) larva and the seed
(D) seed and the fruit
(E) gall and the cancer

39. All of the following are necessary for the initial development of a gall EXCEPT

(A) vascular tissue (B) nutrients
(C) epidermal tissue (D) a host
(E) a parasite

40. The author states that a larva in a gall resembles

(A) a tumor in an animal
(B) an insect in an egg
(C) a seed in a fruit
(D) an embryo in an egg
(E) a cell in a stem

S T O P

IF YOU FINISH BEFORE TIME IS CALLED, YOU MAY CHECK YOUR WORK ON THIS SECTION ONLY. DO NOT WORK ON ANY OTHER SECTION IN THE TEST.

SECTION 5

5

Time—30 minutes

35 QUESTIONS

In this section solve each problem, using any available space on the page for scratchwork. Then decide which is the best of the choices given and blacken the corresponding space on the answer sheet.

The following information is for your reference in solving some of the problems.

Circle of radius r: Area $= \pi r^2$; Circumference $= 2\pi r$
The number of degrees of arc in a circle is 360.
The measure in degrees of a straight angle is 180.

Definitions of symbols:

$=$	is equal to	$\leq$	is less than or equal to
$\neq$	is unequal to	$\geq$	is greater than or equal to
$<$	is less than	$\parallel$	is parallel to
$>$	is greater than	$\perp$	is perpendicular to

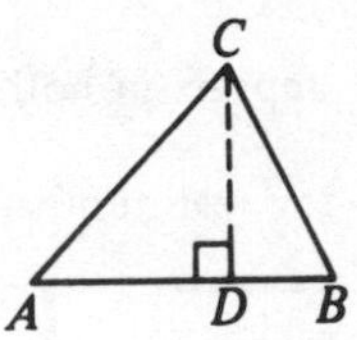

Triangle: The sum of the measures in degrees of the angles of a triangle is 180.

If $\angle CDA$ is a right angle, then

(1) area of $\triangle ABC = \dfrac{AB \times CD}{2}$

(2) $AC^2 = AD^2 + DC^2$

Note: Figures which accompany problems in this test are intended to provide information useful in solving the problems. They are drawn as accurately as possible EXCEPT when it is stated in a specific problem that its figure is not drawn to scale. All figures lie in a plane unless otherwise indicated. All numbers used are real numbers.

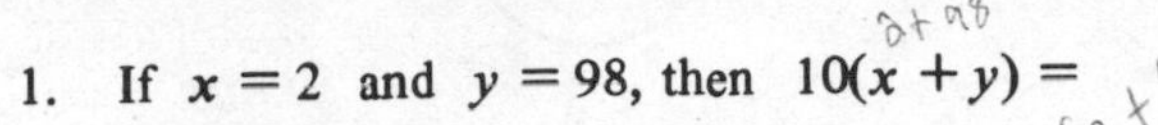

1. If $x = 2$ and $y = 98$, then $10(x + y) =$

   (A) 100 (B) 110 (C) 118
   (D) 980 (E) 1,000

2. If x is 40 percent of y and if z is 30 percent of y, then, when $x \neq 0$, the ratio $\dfrac{z}{x} =$

   (A) 12
   (B) $\dfrac{5}{6}$
   (C) $\dfrac{3}{4}$
   (D) $\dfrac{1}{7}$
   (E) $\dfrac{1}{12}$

3. If the first two terms in a sequence of numbers are 1 and 2 and each succeeding term is formed by adding all of the preceding terms, what is the fifth term in the sequence?

   (A) 5 (B) 10 (C) 12 (D) 15 (E) 24

4. A month with 5 Wednesdays could start on a

   (A) Sunday
   (B) Monday
   (C) Thursday
   (D) Friday
   (E) Saturday

5. $\dfrac{2}{3} \cdot \dfrac{3}{4} \cdot \dfrac{4}{5} \cdot \dfrac{5}{6} \cdot \dfrac{6}{7} \cdot \dfrac{7}{8} \cdot \dfrac{8}{9} \cdot \dfrac{9}{10} \cdot \dfrac{10}{11} \cdot \dfrac{11}{12} =$

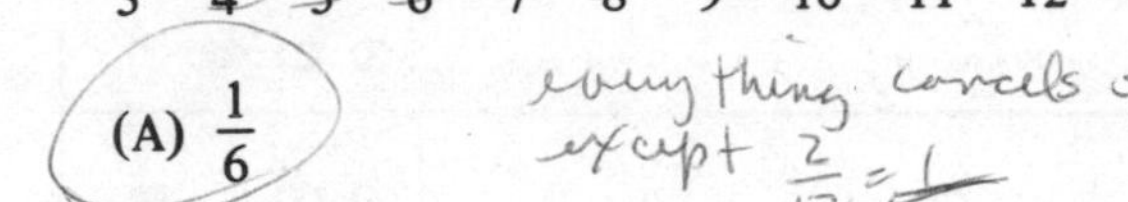

   (A) $\dfrac{1}{6}$
   (B) $\dfrac{11}{36}$
   (C) $\dfrac{11}{18}$
   (D) $\dfrac{2}{3}$
   (E) $\dfrac{11}{12}$

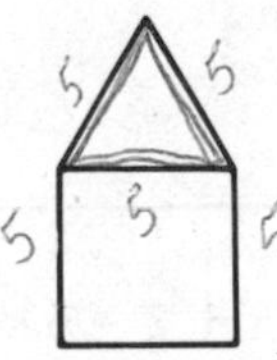

6. In the figure above, the triangle is equilateral and the area of the square is 25. The perimeter of the triangle is

   (A) $\dfrac{25}{2}$ (B) 15 (C) 20 (D) 25 (E) 75

7. If the average (arithmetic mean) of 3, 4, 5, and x is 6, then $x =$

   (A) 0 (B) 6 (C) 12 (D) 24 (E) 60

GO ON TO THE NEXT PAGE

5

Questions 8-27 each consist of two quantities, one in Column A and one in Column B. You are to compare the two quantities and on the answer sheet blacken space

- A if the quantity in Column A is greater;
- B if the quantity in Column B is greater;
- C if the two quantities are equal;
- D if the relationship cannot be determined from the information given.

Notes:
1. In certain questions, information concerning one or both of the quantities to be compared is centered above the two columns.
2. In a given question, a symbol that appears in both columns represents the same thing in Column A as it does in Column B.
3. Letters such as x, n, and k stand for real numbers.

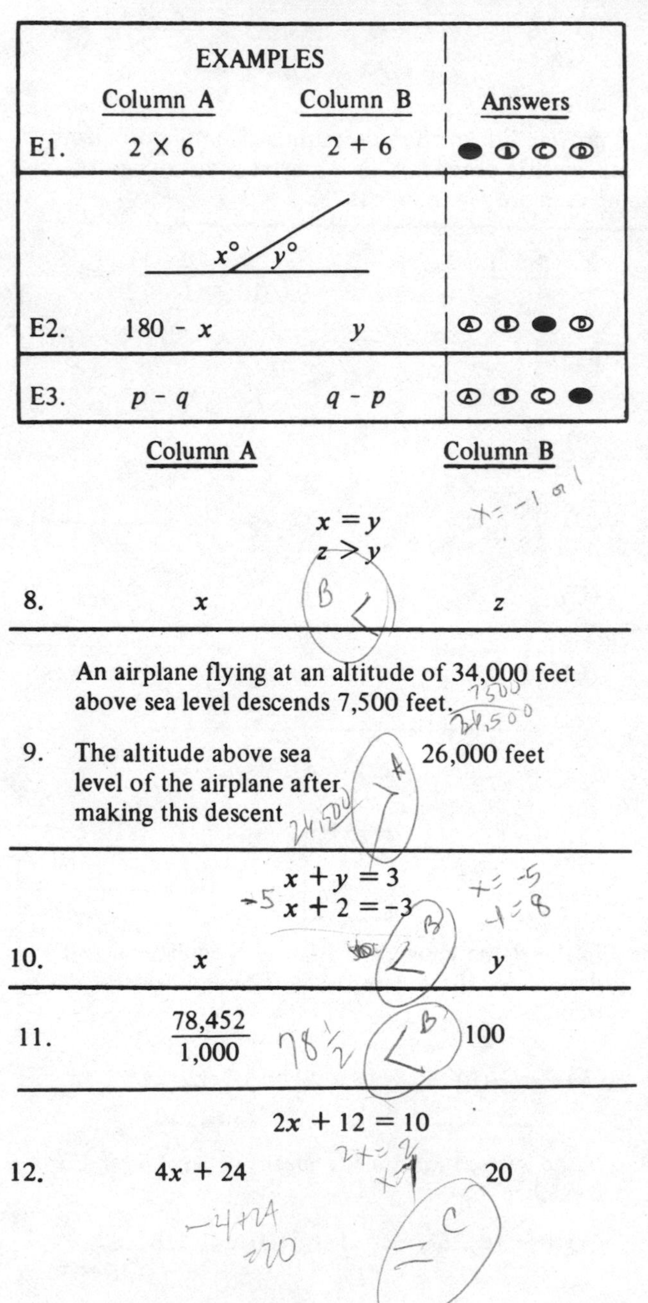

EXAMPLES

	Column A	Column B	Answers
E1.	2×6	$2 + 6$	● Ⓑ Ⓒ Ⓓ
E2.	$180 - x$	y	Ⓐ Ⓑ ● Ⓓ
E3.	$p - q$	$q - p$	Ⓐ Ⓑ Ⓒ ●

	Column A		Column B
		$x = y$ $z > y$	
8.	x		z
	An airplane flying at an altitude of 34,000 feet above sea level descends 7,500 feet.		
9.	The altitude above sea level of the airplane after making this descent		26,000 feet
		$x + y = 3$ $x + 2 = -3$	
10.	x		y
11.	$\frac{78{,}452}{1{,}000}$		100
		$2x + 12 = 10$	
12.	$4x + 24$		20

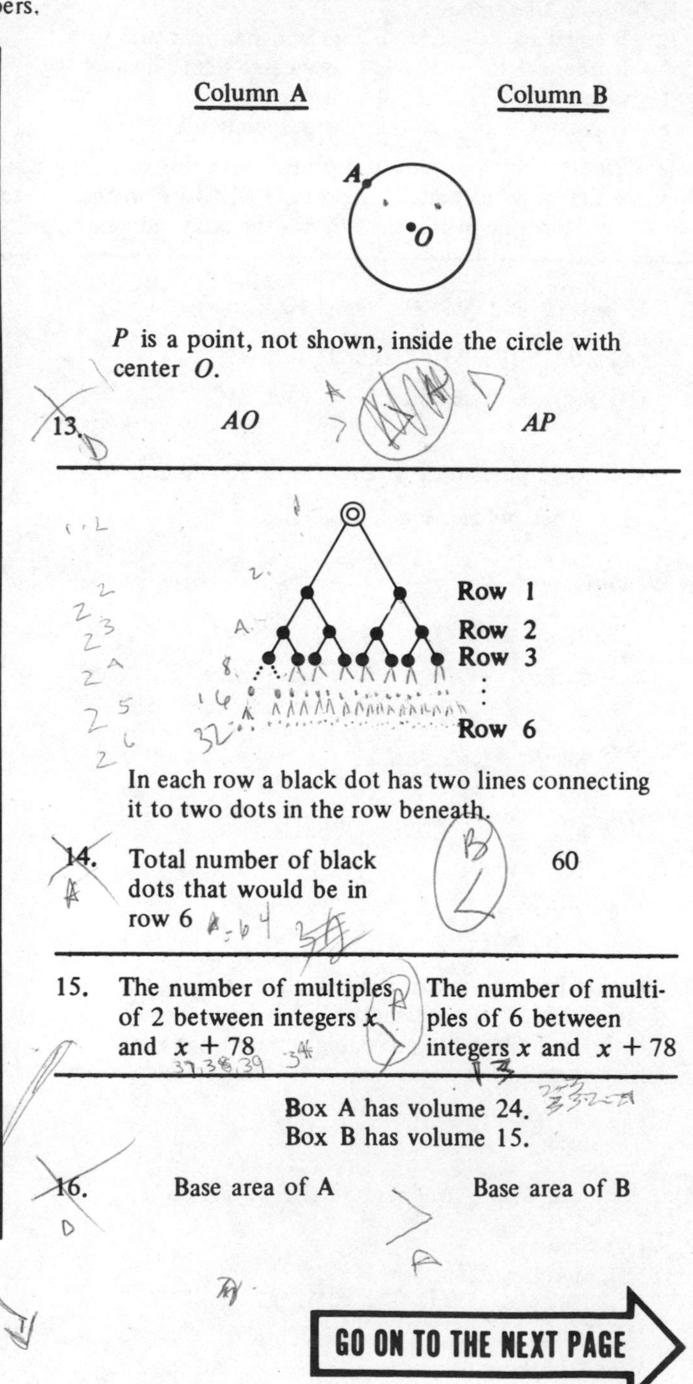

	Column A		Column B
		P is a point, not shown, inside the circle with center O.	
13.	AO		AP
		Row 1, Row 2, Row 3, ..., Row 6 In each row a black dot has two lines connecting it to two dots in the row beneath.	
14.	Total number of black dots that would be in row 6		60
15.	The number of multiples of 2 between integers x and $x + 78$		The number of multiples of 6 between integers x and $x + 78$
		Box A has volume 24. Box B has volume 15.	
16.	Base area of A		Base area of B

GO ON TO THE NEXT PAGE

SUMMARY DIRECTIONS FOR COMPARISON QUESTIONS

Answer: A if the quantity in Column A is greater;
B if the quantity in Column B is greater;
C if the two quantities are equal;
D if the relationship cannot be determined from the information given.

Column A	Column B

Counties A and B are rectangular.

17. Population of County A if there are 10 people per square mile | Population of County B if there are 5 people per square mile

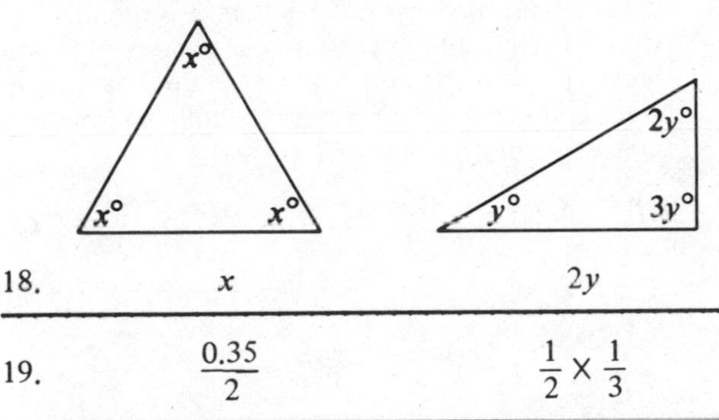

18. x | $2y$

19. $\frac{0.35}{2}$ | $\frac{1}{2} \times \frac{1}{3}$

Tom is now 5 years older than Bill was 3 years ago. Bill is x years old now.

20. $x + 8$ | Tom's age now in years

In a certain game, there are only four types of moves. These moves advance a playing piece 2, 3, 7, or 9 spaces, respectively, in any order.

21. The minimum number of moves required to advance a piece exactly 26 spaces | 4

$$2 + y = 6 + y - 4$$

22. y | 2

23. $\sqrt{x^4 + 4x^2 + 4}$ | $x^2 + 2$

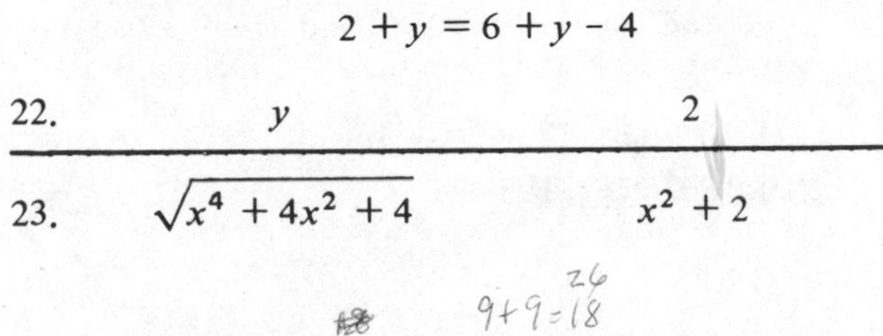

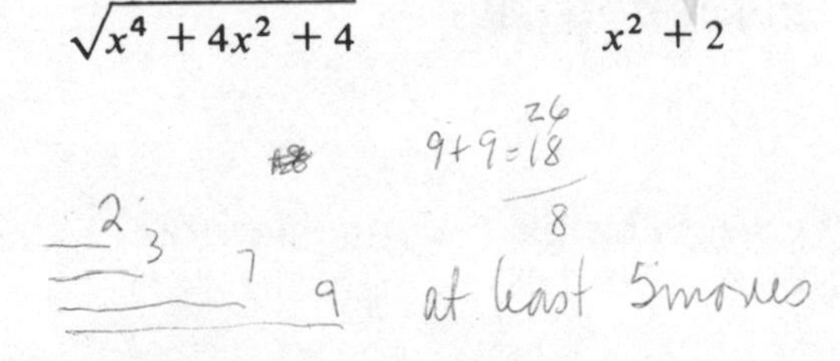

Column A	Column B

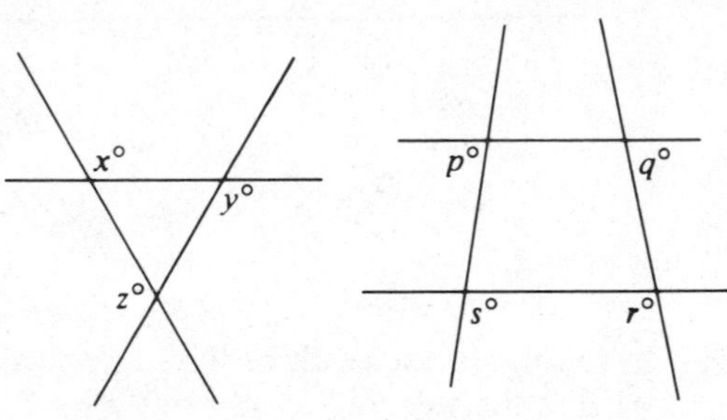

24. $x + y + z$ | $p + q + r + s$

$n < 1$

$n \neq 0$

25. $\frac{1}{n}$ | n

26. $\frac{x^3}{3}$ | $\left(\frac{x}{3}\right)^3$

MACHINE-PART PRODUCTION
July 1

Company	Number Not Defective	Number Defective	Defective as Percent of Total
A	95	5	5%
B	72	x	10%
C	392	y	2%

27. x | y

GO ON TO THE NEXT PAGE

Solve each of the remaining problems in this section using any available space for scratchwork. Then decide which is the best of the choices given and blacken the corresponding space on the answer sheet.

28. If $x > y$ and if $w > z$, which of the following would establish that $y > z$?

I. $x > w$
II. $y = w$
III. $y > w$

(A) I only (B) II only (C) III only
(D) I and II (E) II and III

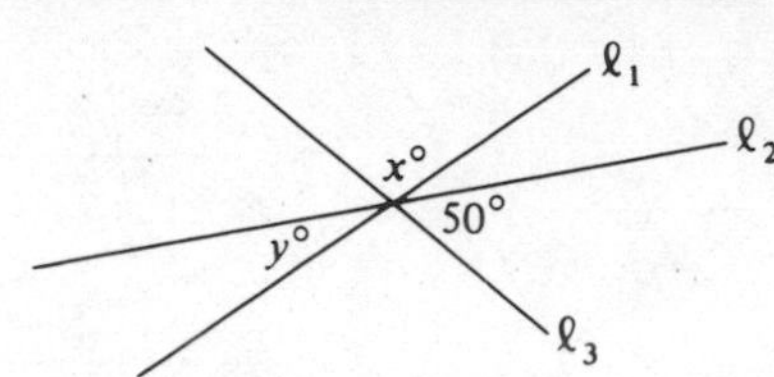

29. In the figure above, three lines intersect in a point. What is the value of x in terms of y ?

(A) $130 - y$ (B) $230 - y$ (C) $260 - 2y$
(D) $310 - 2y$ (E) $50 + y$

30. If two odd integers are prime, which of the following statements must be true?

(A) Their product is an odd integer.
(B) Their sum is prime.
(C) Their sum is an odd integer.
(D) Their product is prime.
(E) The sum of their squares is prime.

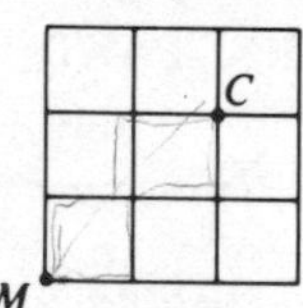

31. A mouse located at point M wants to eat the cheese located at point C. If the mouse can go only up or to the right along the given lines, how many different paths can he take from M to C ?

(A) 12 (B) 10 (C) 8 (D) 6 (E) 4

32. The sum of two positive consecutive integers is x. In terms of x, what is the value of the smaller of these two integers?

(A) $\frac{x}{2} - 1$ (B) $\frac{x-1}{2}$ (C) $\frac{x}{2}$

(D) $\frac{x+1}{2}$ (E) $\frac{x}{2} + 1$

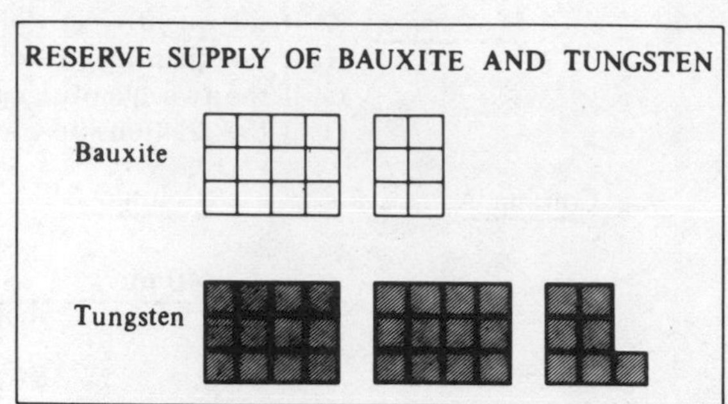

33. In the chart above, the amount represented by each shaded square is twice that represented by each unshaded square. According to the chart, the amount of tungsten in reserve is how many times greater than the amount of bauxite in reserve?

(A) $\frac{9}{31}$ (B) $\frac{31}{36}$ (C) $\frac{36}{31}$ (D) $\frac{11}{6}$ (E) $\frac{31}{9}$

34. A restaurant manager notices that t orders of iced tea, each sold at c cents, are served per hour. If the restaurant is open h hours a day, what is the amount of money in dollars received in 1 day from the sale of iced tea?

(A) $\frac{100tc}{h}$

(B) tch

(C) $\frac{ch}{t}$

(D) $\frac{tch}{100}$

(E) $\frac{tc}{100h}$

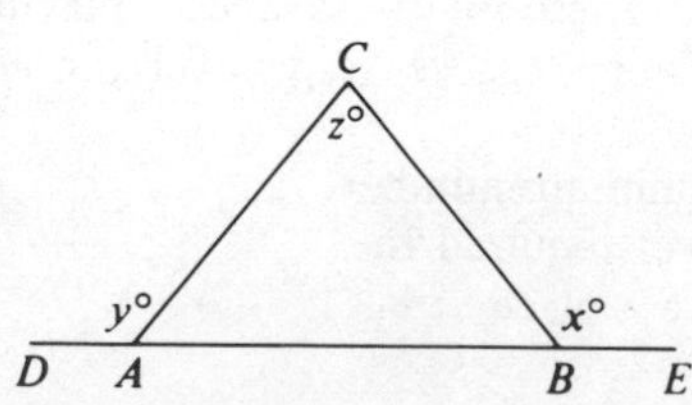

35. In $\triangle ABC$ above, $AC = BC$, and DE is a line segment. If x is 15 less than $2z$, then $y + z =$

(A) 70 (B) 125 (C) 150
(D) 180 (E) 195

S T O P

IF YOU FINISH BEFORE TIME IS CALLED, YOU MAY CHECK YOUR WORK ON THIS SECTION ONLY. DO NOT WORK ON ANY OTHER SECTION IN THE TEST.

Correct Answers for Scholastic Aptitude Test
Form Code 3X

VERBAL		MATHEMATICAL	
Section 1	Section 3	Section 2	Section 5
1. B	1. E	1. C	1. E
2. E	2. D	2. E	2. C
3. C	3. A	3. A	3. C
4. A	4. B	4. E	4. B
5. D	5. E	5. C	5. A
6. C	6. C	6. D	6. B
7. C	7. E	7. C	7. C
8. A	8. D	8. B	*8. B
9. C	9. D	9. E	*9. A
10. E	10. A	10. E	*10. B
11. D	11. D	11. A	*11. B
12. D	12. C	12. D	*12. C
13. B	13. D	13. B	*13. D
14. D	14. A	14. D	*14. A
15. A	15. E	15. D	*15. A
16. B	16. B	16. B	*16. D
17. C	17. D	17. B	*17. B
18. A	18. E	18. C	*18. C
19. E	19. C	19. B	*19. A
20. D	20. B	20. A	*20. A
21. B	21. A	21. A	*21. C
22. C	22. D	22. B	*22. D
23. E	23. D	23. B	*23. C
24. A	24. E	24. A	*24. C
25. D	25. A	25. D	*25. D
26. D	26. E		*26. D
27. C	27. C		*27. C
28. B	28. B		28. E
29. A	29. B		29. A
30. C	30. E		30. A
31. E	31. D		31. D
32. B	32. C		32. B
33. D	33. C		33. E
34. E	34. E		34. D
35. C	35. D		35. E
36. A	36. B		
37. E	37. A		
38. D	38. A		
39. E	39. C		
40. E	40. C		
41. A			
42. D			
43. B			
44. D			
45. D			

*Indicates four-choice questions. (All of the other questions are five-choice.)

The Scoring Process

Machine-scoring is done in three steps:

- *Scanning.* Your answer sheet is "read" by a scanning machine and the oval you filled in for each question is recorded on a computer tape.
- *Scoring.* The computer compares the oval filled in for each question with the correct response. Each correct answer receives one point; omitted questions do not count toward your score. For each wrong answer, a fraction of a point is subtracted to correct for random guessing. For questions with five answer choices, one-fourth of a point is subtracted for each wrong response; for questions with four answer choices, one-third of a point is subtracted for each wrong response. The SAT-verbal test has 85 questions with five answer choices each. If, for example, a student has 44 right, 32 wrong, and 9 omitted, the resulting raw score is determined as follows:

  $$44 \text{ right} - \frac{32 \text{ wrong}}{4} = 44 - 8 = 36 \text{ raw score points}$$

  Obtaining raw scores frequently involves the rounding of fractional numbers to the nearest whole number. For example, a raw score of 36.25 is rounded to 36, the nearest whole number. A raw score of 36.50 is rounded upward to 37.
- *Converting to reported scaled score.* Raw test scores are then placed on the College Board scale of 200 to 800 through a process that adjusts scores to account for minor differences in difficulty among different editions of the test. This process, known as equating, is performed so that a student's reported score is not affected by the edition of the test taken nor by the abilities of the group with whom the student takes the test. As a result of placing SAT scores on the College Board scale, scores earned by students at different times can be compared. For example, an SAT-verbal score of 400 on a test taken at one administration indicates the same level of developed verbal ability as a 400 score obtained on a different edition of the test taken at another time.

How to Score the Test

You can verify the College Board SAT scores reported to you recently by using the information in this booklet along with the copy of your answer sheet. *Before you begin, check that the first two characters (number and letter) of the form code you marked in item 3 on your answer sheet are the same as the form code printed on the front of this booklet.* Compare the responses shown on the copy of your answer sheet with the list of correct answers.

SAT-Verbal Sections 1 and 3

Step A: Count the number of correct answers for *section 1* and record the number in the space provided on the worksheet on the next page. Then do the same for the incorrect answers. (Do not count omitted answers.) To determine subtotal A, use the formula:

$$\text{number correct} - \frac{\text{number incorrect}}{4} = \text{subtotal A}$$

Step B: Count the number of correct answers and the number of incorrect answers for *section 3* and record the numbers in the spaces provided on the worksheet. To determine subtotal B, use the formula:

$$\text{number correct} - \frac{\text{number incorrect}}{4} = \text{subtotal B}$$

Step C: To obtain C, add subtotal A to subtotal B, keeping any decimals. Enter the resulting figure on the worksheet.

Step D: To obtain D, your raw verbal score, round C to the nearest whole number. (For example, any number from 44.50 to 45.49 rounds to 45.) Enter the resulting figure on the worksheet.

Step E: To find your reported SAT-verbal score, look up the total raw verbal score you obtained in step D in the conversion table on the back cover. Enter this figure on the worksheet. (The SAT-verbal score you just recorded and your reported SAT-verbal score should be identical. If not, see the paragraph at the bottom of the next page.)

SAT-Mathematical Sections 2 and 5

Step A: Count the number of correct answers and the number of incorrect answers for *section 2* and record the numbers in the spaces provided on the worksheet. To determine the subtotal A, use the formula:

$$\text{number correct} - \frac{\text{number incorrect}}{4} = \text{subtotal A}$$

Step B: Count the number of correct answers and the number of incorrect answers for the *five-choice questions (questions 1 through 7 and 28 through 35) in section 5* and record the numbers in the spaces provided on the worksheet. To determine the subtotal B, use the formula:

$$\text{number correct} - \frac{\text{number incorrect}}{4} = \text{subtotal B}$$

Step C: Count the number of correct answers and the number of incorrect answers for the *four-choice questions (questions 8 through 27) in section 5* and record the numbers in the spaces provided on the worksheet. To determine the subtotal C, use the formula:

$$\text{number correct} - \frac{\text{number incorrect}}{3} = \text{subtotal C}$$

Step D: To obtain D, add subtotal A, subtotal B, and subtotal C, keeping any decimals. Enter the resulting figure on the worksheet.

Step E: To obtain E, your raw mathematical score, round D to the nearest whole number. (For example, any number from 44.50 to 45.49 rounds to 45.) Enter the resulting figure on the worksheet.

Step F: To find your reported SAT-mathematical score, look up the total raw mathematical score you obtained in E in the conversion table on the back cover. Enter this figure on the worksheet. (The SAT-mathematical score you just recorded and your reported SAT-mathematical score should be identical. If not, see the paragraph at the bottom of the next page.)

SAT-SCORING WORKSHEET

FORM CODE 3X

SAT-Verbal Sections

	no. correct		no. incorrect		
A. Section 1: (out of 45, 2 blank, 4 wrong)	39	− ¼ (	4 = 1)	=	38 subtotal A
B. Section 3:	______ no. correct	− ¼ (	______ no. incorrect)	=	______ subtotal B

C. Total unrounded raw score (Total A + B) ______ C

D. Total rounded raw score (Rounded to nearest whole number) ______ D

E. SAT-verbal reported scaled score (See the conversion table on the back cover.) [ ] SAT-verbal score

SAT-Mathematical Sections

A. Section 2:	______ no. correct	− ¼ (	______ no. incorrect)	=	______ subtotal A
B. Section 5: Questions 1 through 7 and 28 through 35 (5-choice)	______ no. correct	− ¼ (	______ no. incorrect)	=	______ subtotal B
C. Section 5: Questions 8 through 27 (4-choice)	______ no. correct	− ⅓ (	______ no. incorrect)	=	______ subtotal C

D. Total unrounded raw score (Total A + B + C) ______ D

E. Total rounded raw score (Rounded to nearest whole number) ______ E

F. SAT-mathematical reported scaled score (See the conversion table on the back cover.) [ ] SAT-math score

Should you have any questions on these scoring instructions, you may call the phone number below. If, after following the above scoring directions and checking your work at least twice, your results disagree with the SAT-verbal or SAT-mathematical score reported on your ATP score report, you may request rescoring of your answer sheet. If rescoring confirms that an error had been made (resulting in either higher or lower scores than those originally reported), corrected reports will be sent to all recipients of your original scores. Please send your request to:

College Board ATP
Box 592
Princeton, NJ 08541
Attention: Rescore Request
Telephone: (609) 771-7600

Please indicate whether it is your SAT-verbal or SAT-mathematical score, or both, that you want to be rescored. When you write, please include a copy of this scoring worksheet on which you did your calculations.

Score Conversion Table
Scholastic Aptitude Test
Form Code 3X

Raw Score	College Board Reported Score		Raw Score	College Board Reported Score	
	SAT-Verbal	SAT-Math		SAT-Verbal	SAT-Math
85	800		40	440	610
84	780		39	440	600
83	760		38	430	590
82	750		37	420	580
81	740		36	420	570
80	730		35	410	560
79	720		34	400	560
78	710		33	400	550
77	700		32	390	540
76	690		31	380	530
75	680		30	380	520
74	670		29	370	510
73	660		28	360	500
72	650		27	360	490
71	640		26	350	480
70	640		25	340	480
69	630		24	340	470
68	620		23	330	460
67	620		22	320	450
66	610		21	320	440
65	610		20	310	430
64	600		19	300	420
63	590		18	300	410
62	590		17	290	410
61	580		16	280	400
60	570	800	15	280	390
59	570	780	14	270	380
58	560	770	13	260	370
57	550	760	12	260	360
56	550	750	11	250	350
55	540	740	10	250	340
54	530	730	9	240	330
53	530	720	8	230	330
52	520	720	7	230	320
51	510	710	6	220	310
50	510	700	5	210	300
49	500	690	4	210	290
48	490	680	3	200	280
47	490	670	2	200	270
46	480	660	1	200	260
45	470	650	0	200	250
44	470	640	−1	200	250
43	460	640	−2	200	240
42	450	630	−3	200	230
41	450	620	−4	200	220
			−5	200	210
			−6 or below	200	200

SAT
Form Code 0X

FORM CODE 0X

SECTION 1

Time—30 minutes

40 QUESTIONS

For each question in this section, choose the best answer and blacken the corresponding space on the answer sheet.

Each question below consists of a word in capital letters, followed by five lettered words or phrases. Choose the word or phrase that is most nearly opposite in meaning to the word in capital letters. Since some of the questions require you to distinguish fine shades of meaning, consider all the choices before deciding which is best.

Example:

GOOD: (A) sour (B) bad (C) red (D) hot (E) ugly

1. PURIFICATION: (A) heterogeneity (B) negligence (C) contamination (D) experimentation (E) infiltration

2. ABOLISH: (A) stretch (B) soothe (C) refurbish (D) establish (E) straighten

3. RUPTURE: (A) prove (B) regret (C) delay (D) scale down (E) join together

4. DESOLATE: (A) typical (B) populous (C) enormous (D) full of water (E) likely to change

5. ENTHRALLING: (A) incipient (B) boring (C) incomplete (D) minute (E) rejuvenating

6. DESPONDENCY: (A) blithe hopefulness (B) careful attention (C) quick reaction (D) proud dignity (E) bitter jealousy

7. EXPEDITIOUS: (A) protracted (B) pretentious (C) transcendent (D) sensitive and shy (E) slim and graceful

8. PROPRIETY: (A) gentility (B) generosity (C) indecorum (D) servility (E) inability

9. PARSIMONY: (A) formality (B) inhumanity (C) obesity (D) arrogance (E) extravagance

10. RECALCITRANT: (A) repetitious (B) meandering (C) determined (D) indecisive (E) compliant

Each sentence below has one or two blanks, each blank indicating that something has been omitted. Beneath the sentence are five lettered words or sets of words. Choose the word or set of words that best fits the meaning of the sentence as a whole.

Example:

Although its publicity has been ----, the film itself is intelligent, well-acted, handsomely produced, and altogether ----.

(A) tasteless. .respectable (B) extensive. .moderate (C) sophisticated. .amateur (D) risqué. .crude (E) perfect. .spectacular

11. On the assumption that planets and meteors were ---- as a result of the same cosmic catastrophe, their ---- should be roughly similar.
(A) formed. .compositions
(B) discovered. .dates
(C) evolved. .histories
(D) released. .shapes
(E) destroyed. .configurations

12. Advertising alone, no matter how ----, cannot convince people to ---- an item that answers no real and vital need.
(A) stringent. .ignore (B) innocuous. .modify (C) outrageous. .disregard (D) extensive. .purchase (E) enigmatic. .want

13. Perhaps part of the ---- of adolescent behavior is traceable to the violent swing between being dependent and wanting to be independent.
(A) capriciousness (B) predictability (C) reticence (D) irony (E) maturity

14. Self-consciously and ----, but insistently, philosophers keep asking these traditional questions.
(A) confidently (B) diffidently (C) frequently (D) pugnaciously (E) progressively

15. The artistic success of ancient vase painting did not depend entirely on the artist's skill in ---- imitation of observed appearances.
(A) slavish (B) forceful (C) incompetent (D) potential (E) creative

1

Each question below consists of a related pair of words or phrases, followed by five lettered pairs of words or phrases. Select the lettered pair that best expresses a relationship similar to that expressed in the original pair.

Example:

YAWN : BOREDOM :: (A) dream : sleep
(B) anger : madness (C) smile : amusement
(D) face : expression (E) impatience : rebellion

Ⓐ Ⓑ ● Ⓓ Ⓔ

16. PRACTICE : IMPROVEMENT :: (A) memory : event
(B) chaos : arrangement (C) assignment : praise
(D) thought : regret (E) polish : sparkle

17. BREATHE : PANT :: (A) borrow : pay
(B) drop : bounce (C) stride : gallop
(D) spend : save (E) scare : leap

18. LEMON : FRUIT :: (A) author : symposium
(B) branch : tree (C) poetry : prose
(D) hammer : tool (E) partner : syndicate

19. SCRAMBLE : WALK :: (A) race : compete
(B) scrawl : write (C) speak : state
(D) rebel : disagree (E) attack : engage

20. GENE : HEREDITY :: (A) germ : disease
(B) blood : vein (C) cell : nourishment
(D) pain : nerve (E) strength : muscle

21. MERGER : CORPORATIONS ::
(A) budget : finances
(B) indenture : services
(C) marriage : persons
(D) transaction : dealers
(E) annihilation : countries

22. DEBATE : ARGUMENT :: (A) debut : debutante
(B) illness : convalescence (C) campaign : expedition
(D) duel : fight (E) audition : performance

23. INCANTATION : MAGICAL ::
(A) idiom : persuasive
(B) lisp : ungrammatical
(C) phrase : definitional
(D) endearment : affectionate
(E) nomenclature : random

24. MELODEON : ORGANIST ::
(A) reveille : bugler
(B) solo : accompanist
(C) crescendo : pianist
(D) anthem : choirmaster
(E) kettledrum : tympanist

25. LINGUISTICS : LANGUAGE ::
(A) statistics : sociology
(B) ceramics : clay
(C) gymnastics : health
(D) dynamics : motion
(E) economics : warfare

GO ON TO THE NEXT PAGE

Each passage below is followed by questions based on its content. Answer all questions following a passage on the basis of what is stated or implied in that passage.

Archaeology, by its very nature, moves at a slow and deliberate pace, yet it is in the midst of a quiet revolution today. No longer does the study of history confine itself to quests for exotic art objects that glorified rulers in times past. Today, archaeologists are trying to put together a working picture of how ancient societies–particularly the common people in those societies–behaved.

This fresh approach embraces a number of separate strands. Sophisticated instruments developed by physical scientists–computers, nuclear sensors, and even cameras aboard earth satellites–are helping archaeologists to identify and explore promising sites that will yield artifacts for them to interpret. Techniques gleaned from sociology and psychology are supplying archaeologists with reams of statistical data. Some modern archaeologists do not even bother to dig anymore. They prefer to study such relatively modern monuments as gravestones and latter-day examples of primitive peoples like the aborigines of Australia and the Bushmen of Botswana.

The old and the new archaeologists, however, share one fundamental assumption: that modern society can learn from the mistakes of its ancestors. By analyzing how ancient societies coped with such problems as pollution, overpopulation, scarcity of resources, and warfare, archaeologists believe that they can suggest means to help deal with the modern versions of these social scourges.

26. Which of the following would be the most appropriate title for the passage?

(A) Past and Present Archaeological Techniques
(B) The Objectives of Archaeology: Predicting the Future
(C) Critical Attack on the New Archaeology
(D) Finding New Sites for Archaeological Exploration
(E) A New Approach to Archaeology

27. The author provides information that would answer all of the following questions EXCEPT:

(A) Do archaeological studies have implications for scientists dealing with problems of modern-day man?
(B) What sort of studies would an archaeologist following the new approach undertake?
(C) What kind of devices are used to aid the new archaeology?
(D) What are some of the views held by archaeologists on the new archaeology?
(E) What are some of the goals of archaeology?

28. The author's attitude toward the new approach to archaeology would best be described as

(A) sentimental
(B) condescending
(C) approving
(D) pedantic
(E) apathetic

GO ON TO THE NEXT PAGE

Perhaps it is a kind of ethnic chauvinism that is responsible for the fact that many physiologists and nutritionists were surprised to discover that a large percentage of the human adult population is deficient in lactase, the enzyme that breaks down lactose (milk sugar). The few human populations in which lactose tolerance exceeds intolerance include most Northern European and white American ethnic groups.

A period of active investigation of lactose intolerance was initiated at the end of the 1950's. In 1965 investigators who had administered lactose to American blacks and whites reported some startling findings: whereas only fifteen per cent of the whites showed clinical symptoms of lactose intolerance, about seventy per cent of the blacks were lactose intolerant.

In the study various methods of measuring intolerance were used. One was recording the appearance of clinical symptoms after the ingestion of a dose of lactose, which was standardized at two grams of lactose per kilogram of body weight up to a maximum of 100 grams. Another measured low lactase activity, determined through an intestinal biopsy, after ingestion of the lactose. A third recorded the elevation of blood glucose after ingestion of the lactose.

Since clinical symptoms are variable, and the biopsy method is inconvenient for the subject being tested, the blood-glucose method was preferred. It is a direct measure of lactose breakdown, and false negative results are rare if the glucose is measured fifteen minutes after lactose is administered.

By 1970 enough data had been accumulated to indicate that more people all over the world are intolerant to lactose than are tolerant.

29. On the basis of the information in the passage, which of the following conclusions can be made about the participants in the 1965 study?

(A) The majority of the participants were black.
(B) The majority of the participants were white.
(C) None of the participants exhibited clinical symptoms of lactose intolerance.
(D) A majority of the blacks were intolerant to lactose.
(E) A majority of the whites had a lactase deficiency.

30. The main purpose of the passage is to

(A) report on the use of a new technical procedure
(B) challenge the significance of recent experimental data
(C) describe the investigation of a common condition
(D) analyze the reasons for a medical phenomenon
(E) describe the symptoms of a human ailment

31. According to the passage, a person receiving the maximum dosage of lactose would weigh at least

(A) 10 kilograms
(B) 50 kilograms
(C) 100 kilograms
(D) 150 kilograms
(E) 200 kilograms

32. The author suggests that prior to the late 1950's, scientists were unaware of the common occurrence of lactose intolerance in adults because

(A) lactose intolerance was not prevalent among white ethnic groups
(B) they did not know the symptoms of lactose intolerance
(C) they had not identified the function of lactase in human digestion
(D) they did not know the source of lactose in the human diet
(E) it was not yet possible to measure enzyme activities

I call myself a conservationist and am therefore anxious to preserve the environment, particularly my personal environment, and most especially the maple trees in front of my house. One day, sitting in my study, devising strategies of how to deal with "them" when they came on their next, inevitable visit—I heard them. They were here! The snarling of the chain saw was a reality and not just a figment of my imagination.

I leapt from my chair and ran around the corner of the house to the group of men standing around the truck, looking up at the elevated basket that carried the workman with the chain saw. He was cutting branches off my maple trees as if they were so many bunches of bananas.

"What do you think you're doing?"

"Pruning your trees," said a man who looked as if he might be in charge.

"Why?"

He told me that they needed to put an additional set of wires along the poles. "What is it?" I was still shouting. "Another subdivision going up? More houses going to be built? Because if . . ."

"No," he interrupted evenly. "We just need to get more electricity to the houses already here." Defeated, I turned back to the old farmhouse with its electric toothbrush, self-cleaning oven, drier, and electric can opener.

I had met the enemy.

33. The passage suggests that the workmen's primary objective is to

(A) increase the supply of electricity in the narrator's neighborhood
(B) comply with the wishes of the narrator
(C) preserve the trees in the area
(D) provide a source of electricity for a planned housing development
(E) replace the narrator's trees

34. It can be inferred from the passage that the

(A) workmen did not want the narrator to know that they were pruning the trees
(B) man in charge of the work crew sympathized with the narrator
(C) workmen were antagonistic toward the narrator
(D) maple trees had been pruned without the narrator's permission on previous occasions
(E) workman cutting the branches off the trees was planning to cut the trees down

35. The enemy referred to in the last sentence is probably

(A) the workman using the chain saw
(B) the narrator
(C) the narrator's neighbors
(D) builders of new developments
(E) manufacturers of electrical equipment

To emphasize the stagnation and the narrowness of the society depicted in Jane Austen's novels is to take a narrow and mechanical view of them. *Emma* is not a period piece, nor is it what is sometimes called a "comedy of manners." We read it to illuminate not only the past but also the present. And we must face here in both its crudity and its importance a question: Exactly what relevance and helpfulness does *Emma* have for us today? In what sense does a novel dealing skillfully and realistically with a society and its standards, which are dead and gone forever, have value in our very different world today? Stated in such terms, the question itself is unsatisfactory. If *Emma* today captures our imagination and engages our sympathies (as, in fact, it does), then either it has some genuine value for us, or else there is something wrong with the way we give our sympathy and our values are pretty useless.

Put this way, it is clear that anyone who enjoys *Emma* and then remarks "but of course it has no relevance today" is, in fact, debasing the novel, looking at it not as a living, enjoyable work of art but as a mere dead picture of a past society. Such an attitude is fatal both to art and to life. It can be assumed that *Emma* has relevance. The helpful approach is to ask why this novel still has the power to move us today.

What gives *Emma* its power to move us is the realism and depth of feeling behind Jane Austen's attitudes. She examines with a scrupulous yet passionate and critical precision the actual problems of her world. That this world is narrow cannot be denied. But the value of a work of art rests on the depth and truth of the experience it communicates, and such qualities cannot be identified with the breadth of the work's panorama. A conversation between two people in a grocery store may tell us more about a world war than a volume of dispatches from the front. The silliest of all criticisms of Jane Austen is the one that blames her for not writing about the Battle of Waterloo and the French Revolution, which were in the headlines of the newspapers she read. She wrote about what she genuinely understood, and no artist can do more.

36. The main idea of the passage is that
   (A) a constricted view of *Emma* is natural and acceptable
   (B) a novel should not depict a vanished society
   (C) a good novel is an intellectual rather than an emotional experience
   (D) many readers have seen only the comedy in *Emma*
   (E) *Emma* should be read with sensitivity and an open mind

37. The author would probably disagree with those critics or readers who find that the society in Jane Austen's novels is
   (A) unsympathetic (B) uninteresting
   (C) crude (D) authoritarian (E) provincial

38. The author implies that a work of art is properly judged on the basis of its
   (A) universality of human experience truthfully recorded
   (B) popularity and critical acclaim in its own age
   (C) openness to varied interpretations, including seemingly contradictory ones
   (D) avoidance of political and social issues of minor importance
   (E) continued popularity through different eras and with different societies

39. It can be inferred that the author considers the question stated and restated in lines 8-13 to be unsatisfactory because it
   (A) fails to assume that society and its standards are the proper concern of a novel
   (B) neglects to assume that the novel is a definable art form
   (C) suggests that our society and Jane Austen's are quite different
   (D) fails to emphasize Jane Austen's influence on modern writers
   (E) wrongly states the criteria for judging a novel's worth

40. The author's attitude toward someone who "enjoys *Emma* and then remarks 'but of course it has no relevance today' " (lines 21-22) can best be described as one of
   (A) amusement
   (B) astonishment
   (C) disapproval
   (D) resignation
   (E) ambivalence

S T O P

IF YOU FINISH BEFORE TIME IS CALLED, YOU MAY CHECK YOUR WORK ON THIS SECTION ONLY. DO NOT WORK ON ANY OTHER SECTION IN THE TEST.

SECTION 3
Time—30 minutes
25 QUESTIONS

In this section solve each problem, using any available space on the page for scratchwork. Then indicate the one correct answer in the appropriate space on the answer sheet.

The following information is for your reference in solving some of the problems.

Circle of radius r: Area = πr^2; Circumference = $2\pi r$
The number of degrees of arc in a circle is 360.
The measure in degrees of a straight angle is 180.

Definitions of symbols:

$=$	is equal to	$\leqslant$	is less than or equal to
$\neq$	is unequal to	$\geqslant$	is greater than or equal to
$<$	is less than	$\parallel$	is parallel to
$>$	is greater than	$\perp$	is perpendicular to

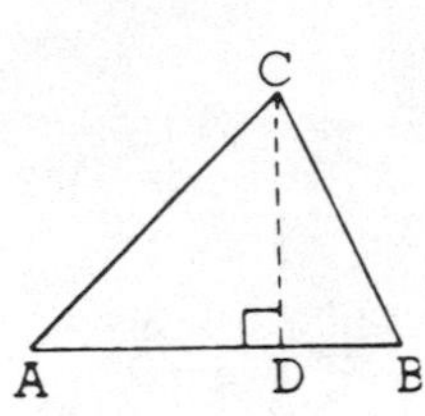

Triangle: The sum of the measures in degrees of the angles of a triangle is 180.

If $\angle CDA$ is a right angle, then

(1) area of $\triangle ABC = \frac{AB \times CD}{2}$

(2) $AC^2 = AD^2 + DC^2$

Note: Figures which accompany problems in this test are intended to provide information useful in solving the problems. They are drawn as accurately as possible EXCEPT when it is stated in a specific problem that its figure is not drawn to scale. All figures lie in a plane unless otherwise indicated. All numbers used are real numbers.

---

1. If $x + y = 2$, then $x + y - 4 =$

(A) -2 (B) 0 (C) 2 (D) 4 (E) 6

2. $14 \div 3\frac{1}{2}$ is

(A) $\frac{1}{49}$

(B) $\frac{1}{4}$

(C) 5

(D) 49

(E) none of the above

3. According to the rules of an organization that has 100 members, no member may serve on more than 3 committees. What is the maximum permissible number of 10-man committees?

(A) 30
(B) 29
(C) 21
(D) 20
(E) 10

4. If n is a positive integer greater than 1 and if the remainders are the same when 9 and 16 are each divided by n, then n =

(A) 2
(B) 5
(C) 6
(D) 7
(E) 8

5. How many tenths of a meter are there in 21.1 meters?

(A) 0.1 (B) 1 (C) 2.11 (D) 21.1 (E) 211

6. Which of the following is NOT equal to the ratio of two whole numbers?

(A) $\frac{1}{3}$

(B) $\frac{3^2}{1}$

(C) 0.3

(D) 3%

(E) $\frac{\sqrt{3}}{1}$

GO ON TO THE NEXT PAGE

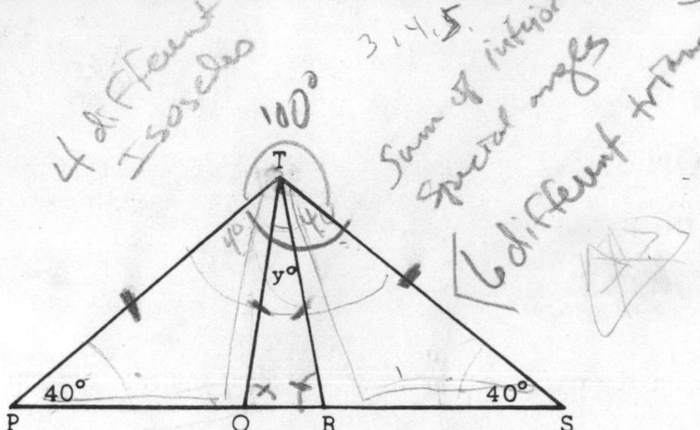

7. In the figure above, if PS is a line segment and PQ = QT = TR = RS, then y =

(A) 10 (B) 20 (C) 30 (D) 40 (E) 50

8. A shipment of 1,680 items is trucked across states M and N. If State M levies a tax of 7 cents for each lot of 7 items and if State N levies a tax of 5 cents for each lot of 5 items, what is the total tax levied by the two states?

(A) $5.76
(B) $33.60
(C) $35.52
(D) $74.00
(E) $576.00

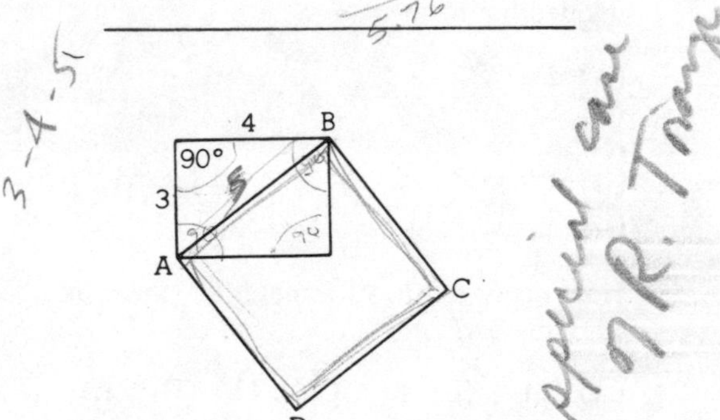

9. In the figure above, what is the length of a side of square ABCD ?

(A) 5 (B) 6 (C) 12 (D) 13 (E) 25

10. Colored banners are strung on a cord to advertise a carnival. If the colors form a repeating pattern starting with white, red, yellow, blue, green, purple; white, red, yellow, blue, green, purple, and so on, what is the color of the 76th banner?

(A) Red
(B) Yellow
(C) Blue
(D) Green
(E) Purple

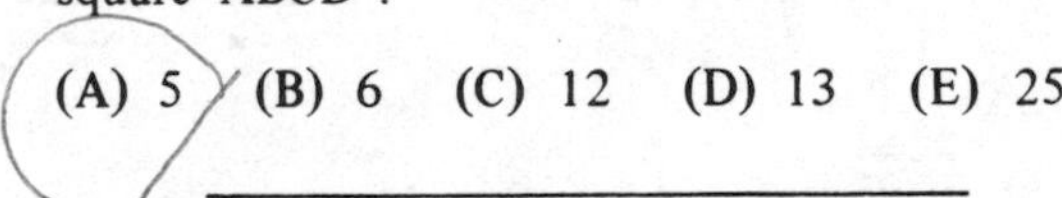

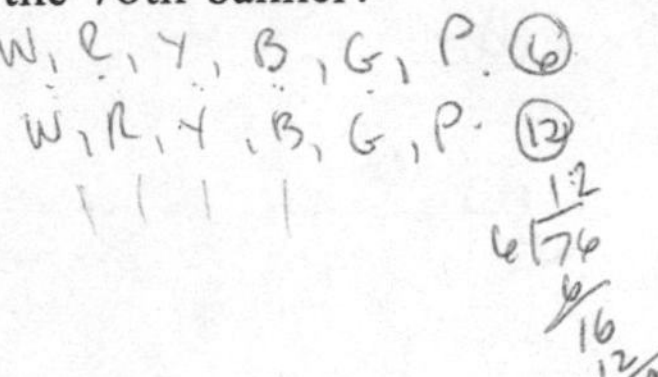

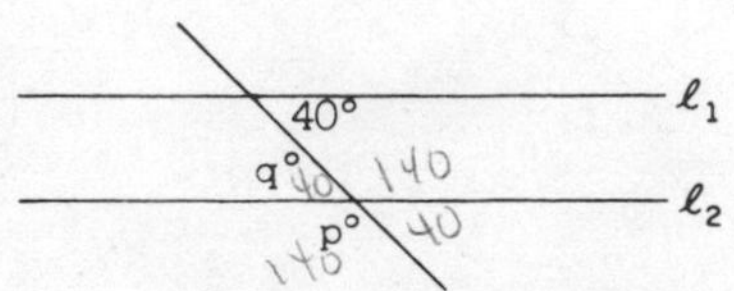

11. In the figure above, if $\ell_1 \parallel \ell_2$, then $p - q =$

(A) 40
(B) 70
(C) 100
(D) 110
(E) 140

12. If x and y are integers and if $x - y > x + y$, which of the following must be true?

(A) $y < 0$
(B) $x < 0$
(C) $x = y$
(D) $y > x$
(E) $x > y$

8
6
P Q R S T
15

Note: Figure not drawn to scale.

13. In the figure above, if R is the midpoint of QS, then PQ =

(A) 1 (B) 2 (C) 3 (D) 4 (E) 5

14. In a set of 24 cubic blocks, each block has pictures on two sides and letters on the remaining sides. How many sides of the entire set have letters?

(A) 24 (B) 48 (C) 72 (D) 96 (E) 144

15. If $p = 27 + t$, $r = 27 - t$, and $t^2 = 9$, then $\frac{pr}{9} =$

(A) 2
(B) 26
(C) 72
(D) 80
(E) 81

GO ON TO THE NEXT PAGE

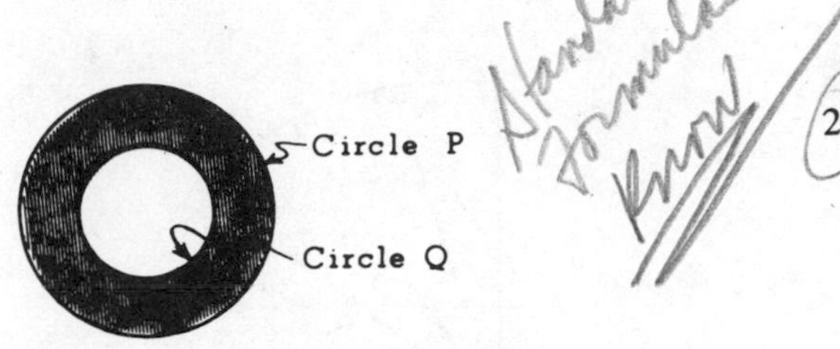

16. In the figure above, if circle P has radius R and circle Q has radius r, the area of the shaded region is

(A) $\pi(R^2 + r^2)$ (B) $\pi(R^2 - r^2)$ (C) $\pi(R - r)^2$
(D) $2\pi(R - r)$ (E) $2\pi(R + r)$

17. In a certain country the ratio of the number of people 30 years of age or under to the number of people over 30 is 3 to 2. What per cent of the population of this country is over 30 ?

(A) 40%

(B) 50%

(C) 60%

(D) $66\frac{2}{3}$%

(E) $88\frac{1}{3}$%

18. Three prizes, with an average value of \$75.00, were offered in a poster contest. However, the judges chose 2 first-place winners and 2 second-place winners and decided to split the prize money so that each first prize was twice as much as each second prize. How much was awarded to each first-place winner?

(A) \$25.00 (B) \$37.50 (C) \$62.50
(D) \$75.00 (E) \$100.00

19. Tom and Joe together earn \$750 per week. If Tom's salary is two-thirds of Joe's, what is three-fourths of Tom's weekly salary?

(A) \$187.50
(B) \$225.00
(C) \$275.00
(D) \$337.50
(E) \$375.00

20. If $\frac{k}{7} = \frac{m}{8}$, $k > 0$, and $m > 0$, which of the following must be true?

(A) $m < k$
(B) $k < m$
(C) $k = 7$, $m = 8$ only
(D) $k = 8$, $m = 7$ only
(E) None of the above

21. If a man reads for 5 hours and x minutes at an average rate of 40 printed pages an hour, then, in terms of x, he will read exactly how many printed pages?

(A) 200x

(B) 200 + 40x

(C) $200 + \frac{2}{3}x$

(D) 200 + 2400x

(E) 12,000 + 40x

22. Which of the following must be greater than N if $0 < N < 1$?

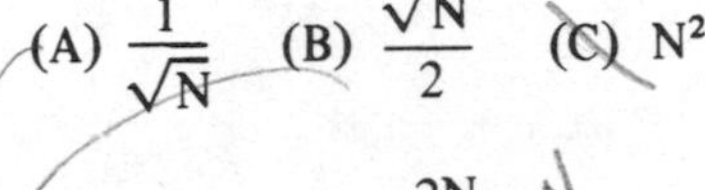

(A) $\frac{1}{\sqrt{N}}$ (B) $\frac{\sqrt{N}}{2}$ (C) N^2

(D) 0.9N (E) $\frac{2N}{3}$

GO ON TO THE NEXT PAGE

23. A polygon with all sides equal is inscribed in a circle with center O. If R and S are adjacent vertices of the polygon, ∠ROS CANNOT equal

(A) 25°
(B) 24°
(C) 15°
(D) 9°
(E) 8°

24. If 125 per cent of m is equal to 80 per cent of n and $n \neq 0$, then $\frac{m}{n}$ =

(A) $\frac{16}{25}$

(B) $\frac{4}{5}$

(C) 1

(D) $\frac{5}{4}$

(E) $\frac{25}{16}$

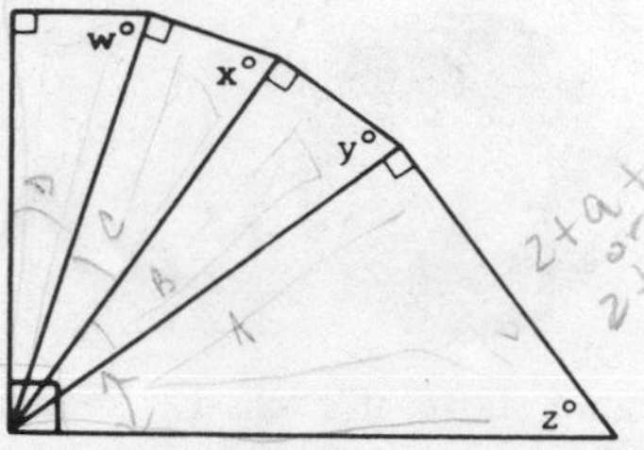

w° x° y° z°

25. In the figure above, w + x + y + z =

(A) 180
(B) 210
(C) 240
(D) 270
(E) 360

S T O P

IF YOU FINISH BEFORE TIME IS CALLED, YOU MAY CHECK YOUR WORK ON THIS SECTION ONLY. DO NOT WORK ON ANY OTHER SECTION IN THE TEST.

SECTION 5

Time—30 minutes

35 QUESTIONS

In this section solve each problem, using any available space on the page for scratchwork. Then indicate the one correct answer in the appropriate space on the answer sheet.

The following information is for your reference in solving some of the problems.

Circle of radius r: Area = πr^2; Circumference = $2\pi r$
The number of degrees of arc in a circle is 360.
The measure in degrees of a straight angle is 180.

Definitions of symbols:

$=$	is equal to	$\leqslant$	is less than or equal to
$\neq$	is unequal to	$\geqslant$	is greater than or equal to
$<$	is less than	$\parallel$	is parallel to
$>$	is greater than	$\perp$	is perpendicular to

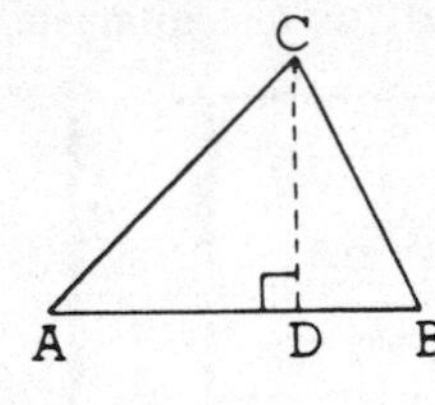

Triangle: The sum of the measures in degrees of the angles of a triangle is 180.

If $\angle CDA$ is a right angle, then

(1) area of $\triangle ABC = \dfrac{AB \times CD}{2}$

(2) $AC^2 = AD^2 + DC^2$

Note: Figures which accompany problems in this test are intended to provide information useful in solving the problems. They are drawn as accurately as possible EXCEPT when it is stated in a specific problem that its figure is not drawn to scale. All figures lie in a plane unless otherwise indicated. All numbers used are real numbers.

---

1. If $3y - 2 = 13$ and $x + y = 4$, then $x =$

(A) -1 (B) $-\frac{1}{3}$ (C) $\frac{1}{3}$ (D) $\frac{23}{3}$ (E) 9

2. What is the average of $\frac{1}{8}, \frac{3}{8}, \frac{5}{8}$, and $\frac{7}{8}$?

(A) $\frac{3}{8}$ (B) $\frac{1}{2}$ (C) $\frac{5}{8}$ (D) 1 (E) 2

3. Which of the following figures can be drawn without lifting the pencil or retracing a segment?

I.

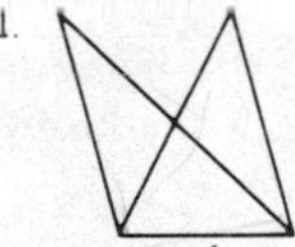

II.

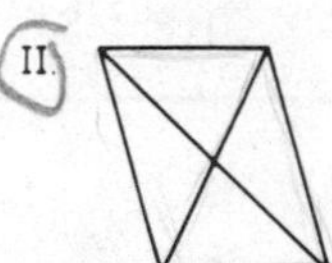

III.

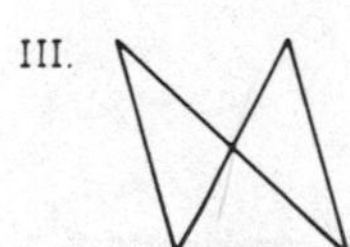

(A) I only (B) II only (C) III only
(D) I and II (E) I and III

4. If p is a whole number such that the only positive divisors of p are 1 and p and if 20p is divisible by 6, then $p =$

(A) 2 (B) 3 (C) 4 (D) 5 (E) 6

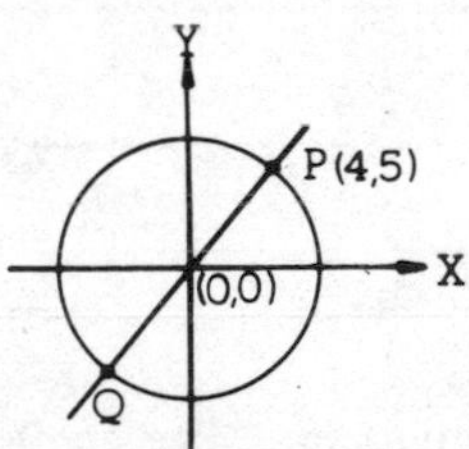

5. In the figure above, the coordinates of point P are (4, 5). If PQ is a diameter of a circle with center (0, 0), what are the coordinates of point Q ?

(A) (−5, −4) (B) (5, 4) (C) (−4, 5)
(D) (4, −5) (E) (−4, −5)

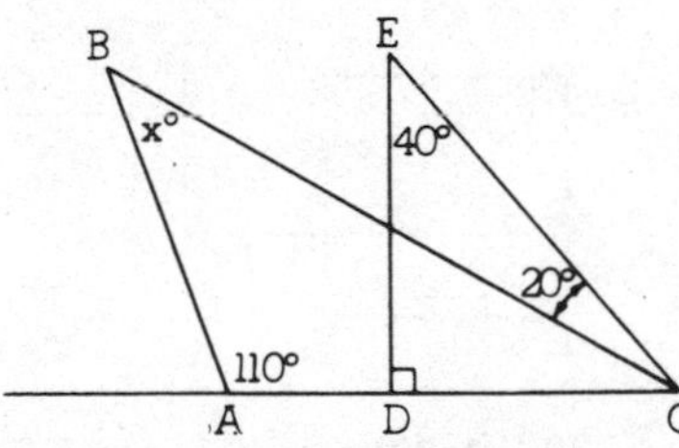

6. In triangles ABC and DEC above, $x =$

(A) 15 (B) 20 (C) 30 (D) 40 (E) 50

---

7. Which of the following is a pair of numbers that are NOT equal?

(A) $\frac{1}{8}$, 0.125 (B) $\frac{3}{7}, \frac{33}{77}$ (C) 2.2, $\frac{11}{5}$

(D) $\frac{21}{63}, \frac{15}{45}$ (E) $\frac{44}{12}, \frac{28}{8}$

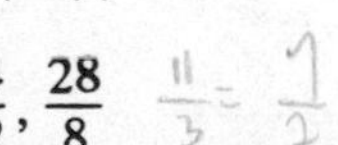

5

Questions 8-27 each consist of two quantities, one in Column A and one in Column B. You are to compare the two quantities and on the answer sheet blacken space

- A if the quantity in Column A is greater;
- B if the quantity in Column B is greater;
- C if the two quantities are equal;
- D if the relationship cannot be determined from the information given.

Notes:
1. In certain questions, information concerning one or both of the quantities to be compared is centered above the two columns.
2. A symbol that appears in both columns represents the same thing in Column A as it does in Column B.
3. Letters such as x, n, and k stand for real numbers.

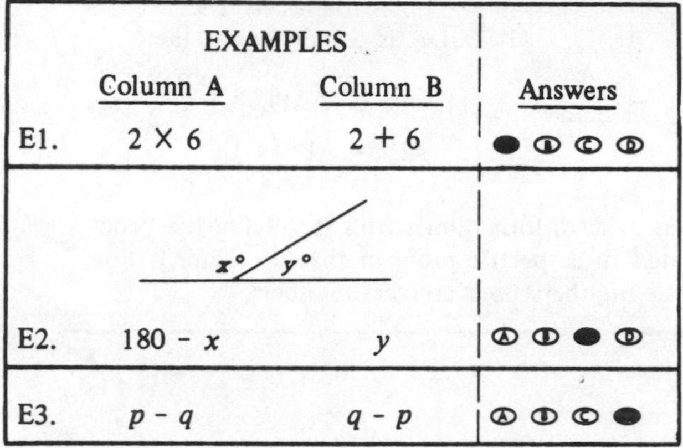

EXAMPLES

	Column A	Column B	Answers
E1.	2×6	$2 + 6$	● Ⓑ Ⓒ Ⓓ
E2.	$180 - x$	y	Ⓐ Ⓑ ● Ⓓ
E3.	$p - q$	$q - p$	Ⓐ Ⓑ Ⓒ ●

	Column A	Column B
8.	The number of hours in a day	The number of days in a month
9.	The value of $3x - 8$ when $x = 8$	The value of $3y - 8$ when $y = -8$

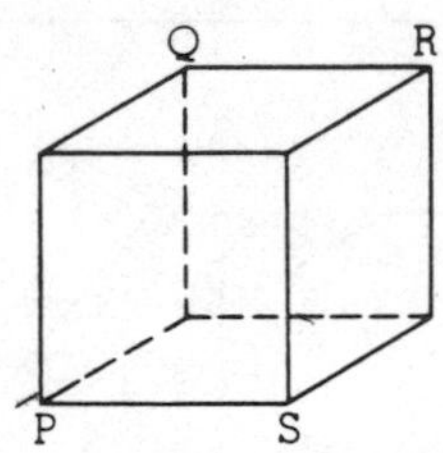

P, Q, R, and S are vertices of the cube.

	Column A	Column B
10.	Length of diagonal PR (not shown)	Length of diagonal QS (not shown)
11.	$0.001 + 8$	$0.008 + 1$

	Column A	Column B

Charge for laying tile is $5 per square meter.

	Column A	Column B
12.	Charge for tiling a rectangular region 32 meters by 20 meters	Charge for tiling a rectangular region 20 meters by 32 meters

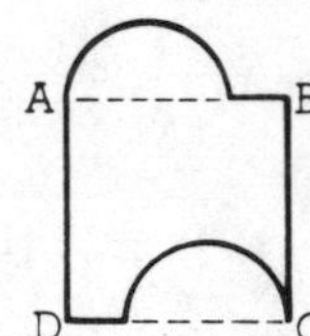

ABCD is a square and the semicircles have equal diameters.

	Column A	Column B
13.	Area of ABCD	Area of the figure outlined with the heavy solid line
14.	$9(7 + 3)$	$(3 \times 3)(2 + 8)$

$$\begin{cases} x + y = 5 \\ x - y = 5 \end{cases}$$

	Column A	Column B
15.	y	5

GO ON TO THE NEXT PAGE

A if the quantity in Column A is greater;
B if the quantity in Column B is greater;
C if the two quantities are equal;
D if the relationship cannot be determined from the information given.

	Column A	Column B

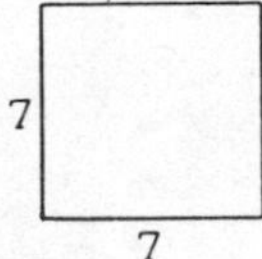

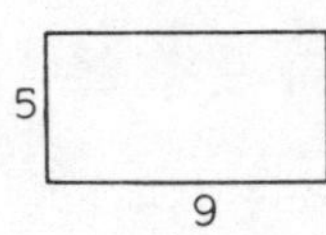

	Column A	Column B
16.	Perimeter of the square	Perimeter of the rectangle

p, q, and r are distinct positive integers.

	Column A	Column B
17.	$p + q + r$	pqr
18.	The length of the hypotenuse of a right triangle with legs of lengths 4 and 2, respectively	5

$y < x < 0$

	Column A	Column B
19.	x	$-2y$

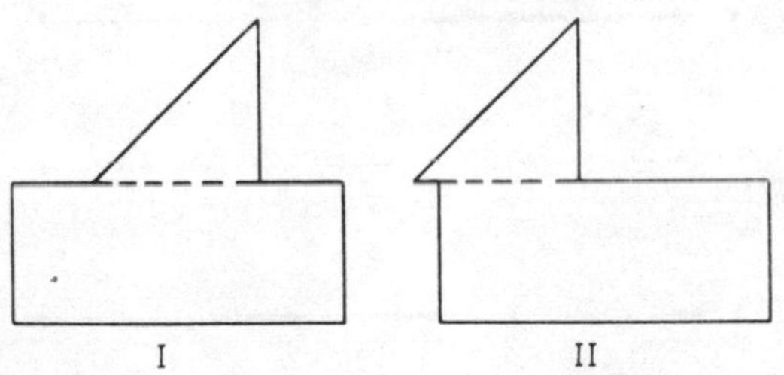

I II

A rectangle and a triangle are arranged without overlapping in the two ways shown.

	Column A	Column B
20.	Perimeter of arrangement I	Perimeter of arrangement II
21.	$1 - \frac{x}{y}$	$\frac{-1}{\frac{y}{y-x}}$

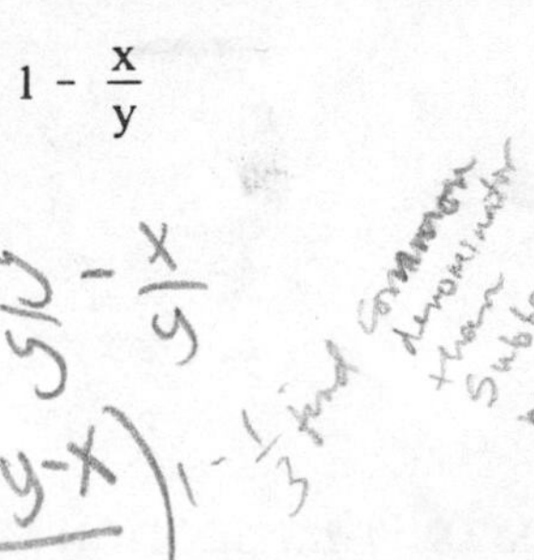

	Column A	Column B

Questions 22-23 refer to the following definition.

For all positive numbers n, $\boxed{n}$ represents the value of n^2 rounded to the nearest integer.

	Column A	Column B
22.	$\boxed{2}$	The product of 4 and $\boxed{1}$
23.	$\boxed{n + 1}$	$\boxed{n} + 1$
24.	$\sqrt{0.049}$	0.07

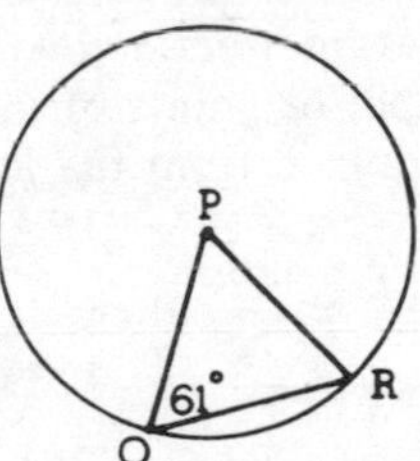

Points Q and R are on the circle with center P.

	Column A	Column B
25.	QR	PQ

$x \neq 1$

	Column A	Column B
26.	$\frac{3x^2 - 3}{x - 1}$	$2x + 2$

The price of a hat increased by 25 per cent and then the new price was decreased by 20 per cent.

	Column A	Column B
27.	The hat's original price	The hat's more recent price

GO ON TO THE NEXT PAGE

5

Solve each of the remaining problems in this section using any available space for scratchwork. Then indicate the one correct answer in the appropriate space on the answer sheet.

28. If x is a number greater than 0, which of the following must be true?

(A) $x \div x = x$
(B) $x \div 1 = 1$
(C) $1 \div x = x$
(D) $1 \div 1 = x$
(E) $x \div x = 1$

29. The centers of two circles are 6 centimeters apart. If the circumference of one of the circles is 4π centimeters and the circumference of the other is 14π centimeters, which of the following is true?

(A) The circles do not intersect and no part of the small circle is within the large circle.
(B) The circles do not intersect and no part of the small circle is outside of the large circle.
(C) The circles intersect at one point only.
(D) The circles intersect at two points only.
(E) The number of points of intersection cannot be determined from the information given.

30. If $\frac{1}{3} + \frac{1}{4} + \frac{1}{5} = \frac{47}{N}$, then all of the following are integers EXCEPT

(A) $\frac{N}{24}$ (B) $\frac{N}{15}$ (C) $\frac{N}{12}$ (D) $\frac{N}{10}$ (E) $\frac{N}{6}$

31. If for all real numbers
$\langle a, b, c \times x, y, z \rangle = ax + by + cz$, then
$\frac{\langle 2, 2, 5 \times 4, 1, 6 \rangle}{\langle -4, -1, -6 \times 2, 2, 5 \rangle} =$

(A) −40
(B) −1
(C) 0
(D) 1
(E) 198

32. If $(2^5 - 2^4)(2^3 - 2^2) = 2^x$, what is x ?

(A) 2
(B) 3
(C) 4
(D) 5
(E) 6

33. A grocer buys m crates of strawberries for q cents per crate. If each crate contains p liters which he sells at c cents per liter and if other expenses are disregarded, which of the following represents his total profit, in cents, on the strawberries?

(A) $\frac{pc}{m} - \frac{q}{m}$

(B) $pc - q$

(C) $\frac{pc}{m} - mq$

(D) $pc - mq$

(E) $mpc - mq$

34. If $xy = -1$ and $(x + y)^2 = 10$, then $x^2 + y^2 =$

(A) 8
(B) 9
(C) 10
(D) 11
(E) 12

35. Which of the following is the graph of all x values such that $x \geq 2$ and $-x \leq -1$?

(A) −2 −1 0 1 2

(B) −2 −1 0 1 2

(C) −2 −1 0 1 2

(D) −2 −1 0 1 2

(E) −2 −1 0 1 2

STOP

IF YOU FINISH BEFORE TIME IS CALLED, YOU MAY CHECK YOUR WORK ON THIS SECTION ONLY. DO NOT WORK ON ANY OTHER SECTION IN THE TEST.

SECTION 6

Time—30 minutes

45 QUESTIONS

For each question in this section, choose the best answer and blacken the corresponding space on the answer sheet.

Each question below consists of a word in capital letters, followed by five lettered words or phrases. Choose the word or phrase that is most nearly opposite in meaning to the word in capital letters. Since some of the questions require you to distinguish fine shades of meaning, consider all the choices before deciding which is best.

Example:

> GOOD: (A) sour (B) bad (C) red (D) hot (E) ugly
> Ⓐ ● Ⓒ Ⓓ Ⓔ

1. VERTICAL: (A) even (B) horizontal (C) straight (D) open (E) parallel

2. SCURRY: (A) dawdle (B) calm (C) align (D) recline (E) capture

3. INNUMERABLE: (A) worthless (B) yielding (C) harsh (D) very few (E) moderately easy

4. IRRATIONAL: (A) curious (B) honest (C) pleasant (D) attentive to detail (E) guided by reason

5. STAGNANT: (A) deep (B) overt (C) crooked (D) flowing (E) tasteless

6. MOTIVATE: (A) deter (B) pester (C) misconstrue (D) alienate (E) minimize

7. DOUR: (A) unable to respond (B) cheerful in appearance (C) youthful (D) crafty (E) clean

8. HARDINESS: (A) vulnerability (B) superficiality (C) skillfulness (D) good fortune (E) poor judgment

9. ENHANCE: (A) vacate (B) insist (C) depreciate (D) volunteer (E) resist

10. AMASS: (A) shut down (B) give away (C) dress up (D) shine forth (E) show off

11. SQUALOR: (A) silence (B) elegance (C) rapidity (D) regularity (E) truthfulness

12. HACKNEYED: (A) liberated (B) fresh (C) afoot (D) logical (E) understood

13. RESCIND: (A) advise (B) falter (C) implement (D) demand (E) predict

14. PAUCITY: (A) ambition (B) eminence (C) intensity (D) hugeness (E) plenty

15. INCORPOREAL: (A) active (B) unusual (C) isolated (D) accurate (E) material

Each sentence below has one or two blanks, each blank indicating that something has been omitted. Beneath the sentence are five lettered words or sets of words. Choose the word or set of words that best fits the meaning of the sentence as a whole.

Example:

> Although its publicity has been ----, the film itself is intelligent, well-acted, handsomely produced, and altogether ----.
>
> (A) tasteless. .respectable (B) extensive. .moderate (C) sophisticated. .amateur (D) risqué. .crude (E) perfect. .spectacular
> ● Ⓑ Ⓒ Ⓓ Ⓔ

16. Common sense tells us that a person's ---- to use certain kinds of words ---- past experiences.

    (A) desire. .recovers (B) refusal. .decides (C) wish. .determines (D) tendency. .reflects (E) inability. .inhibits

17. Only a ---- in the field will comprehend this highly ---- material.

    (A) veteran. .general (B) critic. .complimentary (C) novice. .intricate (D) master. .conventional (E) specialist. .sophisticated

18. The harshness of political struggle ---- Ralph but at the same time fascinated him, so that he could neither ---- the battle nor fully commit himself to it.

    (A) frightened. .dread (B) inspired. .comprehend (C) repelled. .abandon (D) intrigued. .forsake (E) annoyed. .influence

19. By attempting to ---- all the writer's inconsistencies in form, the translator distracts the attention of the general reader, who is not concerned with such close accuracy.

    (A) improve (B) reproduce (C) equalize (D) interpret (E) omit

20. If the world's present known reserves of fossil fuels could be ----, construction of nuclear power plants would doubtless be less ----.

    (A) augmented. .precipitate
    (B) depleted. .expedient
    (C) husbanded. .regulated
    (D) recycled. .reliable
    (E) discovered. .hazardous

GO ON TO THE NEXT PAGE

Each passage below is followed by questions based on its content. Answer all questions following a passage on the basis of what is stated or implied in that passage.

Americans disapproved a preliminary draft of the Declaration of Independence that indicted the king of England for waging "cruel war against human nature itself, violating its most sacred rights of life and liberty in the persons of a distant people who never offended him, captivating and carrying them into slavery in another hemisphere, or to incur miserable death in their transportation thither." The Americans were themselves not ready to abolish slavery and instead used the words "all men are created equal," which did not commit them to any specific action in regard to slavery. This statement represented a goal that some Americans hoped to achieve some day rather than a plan most of them were willing to act upon immediately.

Blacks were at first barred from serving in the revolutionary army although some blacks had already involved themselves in the struggle. Fearing that blacks would enlist in the British army, which welcomed them, and facing a manpower shortage, the Continental army soon began to accept free blacks. Runaway slaves, however, joined the British. More than 30,000 slaves ran away in 1778 alone, preferring military service to slavery. The states started to enroll both free and enslaved blacks, and finally Congress authorized military service for slaves, who were to be emancipated in return for their service.

After the war a few blacks achieved material success and some owned slaves, but the vast majority knew only poverty. Forbidden to settle in some areas and segregated in others, free blacks were targets of prejudice and discrimination. In the South, they were denied freedom of movement, restricted in their choice of occupation, and forbidden to associate with whites or slaves. Whites could legally challenge their freedom at any time, and free blacks lived in constant danger of being enslaved. In both the North and the South, they were denied political power and were regularly the victims of mobs.

Some Americans, Washington and Jefferson among them, advocated the gradual emancipation of slaves, and in the nineteenth century, a movement to abolish slavery grew in importance. A few white abolitionist leaders wanted full equality for blacks, but others sought only to eliminate the institution itself. And some antislavery societies, fearing that the inclusion of black members would unnecessarily offend those who were unsympathetic with abolitionist principles, denied entrance to black abolitionists.

Most Americans were, in fact, against abolishing slavery. They refused to rent their halls for antislavery meetings. They harassed abolitionist leaders who sought to educate white and black children together. They attacked those involved in the movement. Mobs sometimes killed abolitionists and destroyed their property.

21. The author implies that, if the Americans had indicted the king of England according to their original plan, their action would have been

(A) hypocritical (B) underhanded (C) unjustified (D) futile (E) pragmatic

22. The author is primarily concerned with

(A) describing the status of blacks immediately before and after the Revolutionary War
(B) suggesting ways that blacks can help solve the problems of the United States
(C) showing the social and political achievements made by blacks since the founding of the United States
(D) tracing the effect that blacks have had on the development of the United States since the Revolutionary War
(E) showing that the abolitionists were ineffective in their efforts to improve the condition of blacks

23. According to the passage, blacks were denied entrance into antislavery societies because

(A) the black abolitionists were too radical for the whites
(B) such societies were against the law
(C) the abolitionists were afraid of public opinion
(D) most blacks were unwilling to associate with whites
(E) the societies were afraid that white members would misunderstand the presence of black members

24. It can be inferred that in the first half of the nineteenth century under United States law free blacks

(A) could not permanently reside in any one place
(B) had fewer rights than did slaves
(C) could be deported to another country without warning
(D) received as fair treatment as poor whites
(E) could be bound over into slavery

25. According to the author, the words in the Declaration of Independence, "all men are created equal," were meant to represent

(A) an objective (B) a pretext (C) a provocation (D) an overstatement (E) a rationalization

GO ON TO THE NEXT PAGE

Since the days of Copernicus, the greatest change that has occurred in our way of thinking about the universe is the modern conception of the universe as finite. This does not mean merely that there is a finite amount of matter in space, but that space itself is finite. The instant impulse that most lay people have to reject this statement as absurd is really an indication that they are unconsciously dominated by certain assumptions. These assumptions can be isolated and analyzed and shown to be logically arbitrary. The analysis is now about a hundred years old. It began with the invention of the first non-Euclidean geometry.

About a hundred fifty years ago Lobachevski, a Russian, and Bolyai, a Hungarian, found, independently of one another, that Euclid's geometry is not a logical necessity. This is not to say that Euclid's geometry is incorrect. If we start by accepting Euclid's axioms, then we must also accept the whole superstructure Euclid built on them. But the fact is that it is not necessary to accept Euclid's axioms. Quite different axioms can be postulated and a perfectly self-consistent system of geometry can be built on them. It then becomes a matter of experiment to determine which system of geometry best fits our experience.

The invention of the non-Euclidean geometries is one of the most remarkable feats in the intellectual history of humanity. For two thousand years Euclid's axioms had reigned unchallenged. That they were "necessary truths," true even for God, was admitted by all the philosophers. Merely to wonder whether these could be transcended was an effort of extraordinarily imaginative daring. And to translate this skepticism into the creation of a new, coherent, and complete system of geometry was a wonderful and exhilarating achievement of the free human mind.

Gradually the science of deductive geometry has acquired a new status. The question has arisen as to which geometry we are to apply to actual, physical space, the space in which all the millions of stars exist. The question is a matter of measurement. Our measuring instruments may be rods and clocks or rays of light and vibrating atoms. Which geometry best describes the observed behavior of the stars? A particular form of geometry invented by the German geometer Riemann best meets the facts of the case. Einstein was the first to realize this and he applied this geometry with immense success. Scientists are now convinced that we live in a space governed not by the laws of Euclid's geometry, but by the laws of Riemann's geometry.

26. According to the passage, Lobachevski and Bolyai discovered that

(A) there were errors in Euclid's axioms
(B) there is an infinite amount of matter in space
(C) Euclid's axioms could be applied to Copernicus' theories of the universe
(D) Riemann's geometry was applicable to physical space
(E) a consistent system of geometry other than Euclid's could be developed

27. According to the passage, Einstein was the first to recognize the

(A) use of vibrating atoms as measuring devices
(B) logical necessity of Euclid's axioms
(C) absurdity in the theory that the matter in space is finite
(D) possibility that Euclid's axioms could be revised
(E) importance of applying Riemann's geometry to actual, physical space

28. By "this skepticism" (line 35), the author means

(A) denying the existence of non-Euclidean geometries
(B) questioning whether Euclid's axioms were the only possible ones
(C) doubting people's ability to devise new systems of geometry
(D) resisting scientific pressure for the development of new philosophies
(E) criticizing the accuracy of the axioms in Euclid's geometry

29. The content of the passage primarily answers which of the following questions?

(A) How is deductive geometry similar to geometry based on Euclid's axioms?
(B) How did Lobachevski and Bolyai develop new systems of geometry?
(C) Why have people assumed that Euclid's geometry is a logical necessity?
(D) Why has our concept of space changed since the days of Copernicus?
(E) How do the laws of Riemann's geometry apply to the measurement of actual, physical space?

30. We can infer from the passage that Euclidean geometry is

(A) inconsistent
(B) unnecessarily complex
(C) no longer applicable
(D) not completely adequate for describing space
(E) more abstract than other geometries and therefore too restrictive for modern science

GO ON TO THE NEXT PAGE

6

Select the word or set of words that best completes each of the following sentences.

31. From a high-flying jet, the earth appears virtually ----; that is, rolling land is ironed out and the land's general ---- are almost eliminated.

(A) flat. .contours
(B) uninteresting. .colors
(C) round. .markings
(D) unrecognizable. .features
(E) motionless. .guidelines

32. To submit such ---- testimony is to ---- the defendant while pretending to prove his innocence.

(A) arbitrary. .acquit
(B) implausible. .incriminate
(C) airtight. .exonerate
(D) favorable. .sentence
(E) conflicting. .confuse

33. Well-intentioned ---- all too often defeats its basic purpose by destroying the recipient's self-reliance.

(A) benevolence (B) modesty (C) negligence (D) arrogance (E) gratitude

34. A man of great sensibility, the writer ---- the laying bare of his first work; he had put into the book everything he had that was good, true, and beautiful, and it was regarded as ----.

(A) thrilled to. .nonsense
(B) shrank from. .artistry
(C) suffered at. .drivel
(D) glossed over. .caricature
(E) agonized over. .abstraction

35. The union leader made the ---- statement that no union member, not even the maintenance crew, would be allowed to cross the picket line.

(A) discreet (B) ambiguous (C) fallacious (D) obsequious (E) categorical

Each question below consists of a related pair of words or phrases, followed by five lettered pairs of words or phrases. Select the lettered pair that best expresses a relationship similar to that expressed in the original pair.

Example:

YAWN : BOREDOM :: (A) dream : sleep (B) anger : madness (C) smile : amusement (D) face : expression (E) impatience : rebellion

Ⓐ Ⓑ ● Ⓓ Ⓔ

36. SUBMARINE : SHARK :: (A) sled : dog (B) plow : horse (C) caravan : camel (D) airplane : hawk (E) subway : tiger

37. MAGNIFY : SIZE :: (A) pacify : blandness (B) rectify : generosity (C) dignify : wisdom (D) fortify : strength (E) verify : fear

38. FORUM : DISCUSSION :: (A) casino : gambling (B) palette : painting (C) library : printing (D) itinerary : traveling (E) armory : fighting

39. CRUNCH : SNOW :: (A) wade : beach (B) ripple : sand (C) whistle : wind (D) slosh : water (E) drizzle : rain

40. PROTEST : DISCONTENT :: (A) anger : indecision (B) inaction : apathy (C) mockery : contrition (D) sympathy : misery (E) supremacy : anarchy

41. BRAWN : WEIGHT LIFTER :: (A) fame : painter (B) wound : doctor (C) uniform : soldier (D) obedience : pioneer (E) tact : diplomat

42. BRINK : PRECIPICE :: (A) bank : river (B) tree : forest (C) lake : ocean (D) tunnel : mountain (E) whirlpool : waterfall

43. DAREDEVIL : RECKLESS :: (A) virtuoso : careless (B) hostage : lawless (C) brute : helpless (D) prodigal : thriftless (E) wizard : relentless

44. RACONTEUR : ANECDOTE :: (A) orator : speech (B) lecturer : applause (C) actor : monologue (D) operator : message (E) comedian : dialogue

45. APOCRYPHAL : AUTHENTICITY :: (A) absurd : novelty (B) protean : variety (C) unseemly : reality (D) illicit : legality (E) ordained : sanction

IF YOU FINISH BEFORE TIME IS CALLED, YOU MAY CHECK YOUR WORK ON THIS SECTION ONLY. DO NOT WORK ON ANY OTHER SECTION IN THE TEST.

Correct Answers for Scholastic Aptitude Test
Form Code 0X

VERBAL		MATHEMATICAL	
Section 1	**Section 6**	**Section 3**	**Section 5**
1. C	1. B	1. A	1. A
2. D	2. A	2. E	2. B
3. E	3. D	3. A	3. E
4. B	4. E	4. D	4. B
5. B	5. D	5. E	5. E
6. A	6. A	6. E	6. D
7. A	7. B	7. B	7. E
8. C	8. A	8. B	*8. B
9. E	9. C	9. A	*9. A
10. E	10. B	10. C	*10. C
11. A	11. B	11. C	*11. A
12. D	12. B	12. A	*12. C
13. A	13. C	13. D	*13. C
14. B	14. E	14. D	*14. C
15. A	15. E	15. D	*15. B
16. E	16. D	16. B	*16. C
17. C	17. E	17. A	*17. D
18. D	18. C	18. D	*18. B
19. B	19. B	19. B	*19. B
20. A	20. A	20. B	*20. B
21. C	21. A	21. C	*21. D
22. D	22. A	22. A	*22. C
23. D	23. C	23. A	*23. D
24. E	24. E	24. A	*24. A
25. D	25. A	25. D	*25. B
26. E	26. E		*26. D
27. D	27. E		*27. C
28. C	28. B		28. E
29. D	29. D		29. D
30. C	30. D		30. A
31. B	31. A		31. B
32. A	32. B		32. E
33. A	33. A		33. E
34. D	34. C		34. E
35. B	35. E		35. B
36. E	36. D		
37. B	37. D		
38. A	38. A		
39. E	39. D		
40. C	40. B		
	41. E		
	42. A		
	43. D		
	44. A		
	45. D		

*Indicates four-choice questions. (All of the other questions are five-choice.)

The Scoring Process

Machine-scoring is done in three steps:

- *Scanning.* Your answer sheet is "read" by a scanning machine and the oval you filled in for each question is recorded on a computer tape.
- *Scoring.* The computer compares the oval filled in for each question with the correct response. Each correct answer receives one point; omitted questions do not count toward your score. For each wrong answer, a fraction of a point is subtracted to correct for random guessing. For questions with five answer choices, one-fourth of a point is subtracted for each wrong response; for questions with four answer choices, one-third of a point is subtracted for each wrong response. The SAT-verbal test has 85 questions with five answer choices each. If, for example, a student has 44 right, 32 wrong, and 9 omitted, the resulting raw score is determined as follows:

  $$44 \text{ right} - \frac{32 \text{ wrong}}{4} = 44 - 8 = 36 \text{ raw score points}$$

  Obtaining raw scores frequently involves the rounding of fractional numbers to the nearest whole number. For example, a raw score of 36.25 is rounded to 36, the nearest whole number. A raw score of 36.50 is rounded upward to 37.
- *Converting to reported scaled score.* Raw test scores are then placed on the College Board scale of 200 to 800 through a process that adjusts scores to account for minor differences in difficulty among different editions of the test. This process, known as equating, is performed so that a student's reported score is not affected by the edition of the test taken nor by the abilities of the group with whom the student takes the test. As a result of placing SAT scores on the College Board scale, scores earned by students at different times can be compared. For example, an SAT-verbal score of 400 on a test taken at one administration indicates the same level of developed verbal ability as a 400 score obtained on a different edition of the test taken at another time.

How to Score the Test

You can verify the College Board SAT scores reported to you recently by using the information in this booklet along with the copy of your answer sheet. *Before you begin, check that the first two characters (number and letter) of the form code you marked in item 3 on your answer sheet are the same as the form code printed on the front of this booklet.* Compare the responses shown on the copy of your answer sheet with the list of correct answers.

SAT-Verbal Sections 1 and 6

Step A: Count the number of correct answers for *section 1* and record the number in the space provided on the worksheet on the next page. Then do the same for the incorrect answers. (Do not count omitted answers.) To determine subtotal A, use the formula:

$$\text{number correct} - \frac{\text{number incorrect}}{4} = \text{subtotal A}$$

Step B: Count the number of correct answers and the number of incorrect answers for *section 6* and record the numbers in the spaces provided on the worksheet. To determine subtotal B, use the formula:

$$\text{number correct} - \frac{\text{number incorrect}}{4} = \text{subtotal B}$$

Step C: To obtain C, add subtotal A to subtotal B, keeping any decimals. Enter the resulting figure on the worksheet.

Step D: To obtain D, your raw verbal score, round C to the nearest whole number. (For example, any number from 44.50 to 45.49 rounds to 45.) Enter the resulting figure on the worksheet.

Step E: To find your reported SAT-verbal score, look up the total raw verbal score you obtained in step D in the conversion table on the back cover. Enter this figure on the worksheet. (The SAT-verbal score you just recorded and your reported SAT-verbal score should be identical. If not, see the paragraph at the bottom of the next page.)

SAT-Mathematical Sections 3 and 5

Step A: Count the number of correct answers and the number of incorrect answers for *section 3* and record the numbers in the spaces provided on the worksheet. To determine the subtotal A, use the formula:

$$\text{number correct} - \frac{\text{number incorrect}}{4} = \text{subtotal A}$$

Step B: Count the number of correct answers and the number of incorrect answers for the *five-choice questions (questions 1 through 7 and 28 through 35) in section 5* and record the numbers in the spaces provided on the worksheet. To determine the subtotal B, use the formula:

$$\text{number correct} - \frac{\text{number incorrect}}{4} = \text{subtotal B}$$

Step C: Count the number of correct answers and the number of incorrect answers for the *four-choice questions (questions 8 through 27) in section 5* and record the numbers in the spaces provided on the worksheet. To determine the subtotal C, use the formula:

$$\text{number correct} - \frac{\text{number incorrect}}{3} = \text{subtotal C}$$

Step D: To obtain D, add subtotal A, subtotal B, and subtotal C, keeping any decimals. Enter the resulting figure on the worksheet.

Step E: To obtain E, your raw mathematical score, round D to the nearest whole number. (For example, any number from 44.50 to 45.49 rounds to 45.) Enter the resulting figure on the worksheet.

Step F: To find your reported SAT-mathematical score, look up the total raw mathematical score you obtained in E in the conversion table on the back cover. Enter this figure on the worksheet. (The SAT-mathematical score you just recorded and your reported SAT-mathematical score should be identical. If not, see the paragraph at the bottom of the next page.)

SAT SCORING WORKSHEET

FORM CODE 0X

SAT-Verbal Sections

A. Section 1: ________ − ¼ (________) = ________
no. correct — no. incorrect — subtotal A

B. Section 6: ________ − ¼ (________) = ________
no. correct — no. incorrect — subtotal B

C. Total unrounded raw score (Total A + B) ________ C

D. Total rounded raw score (Rounded to nearest whole number) ________ D

E. SAT-verbal reported scaled score (See the conversion table on the back cover.) [ ] SAT-verbal score

SAT-Mathematical Sections

A. Section 3: ________ − ¼ (________) = ________
no. correct — no. incorrect — subtotal A

B. Section 5: Questions 1 through 7 and 28 through 35 (5-choice) ________ − ¼ (________) = ________
no. correct — no. incorrect — subtotal B

C. Section 5: Questions 8 through 27 (4-choice) ________ − ⅓ (________) = ________
no. correct — no. incorrect — subtotal C

D. Total unrounded raw score (Total A + B + C) ________ D

E. Total rounded raw score (Rounded to nearest whole number) ________ E

F. SAT-mathematical reported scaled score (See the conversion table on the back cover.) [ ] SAT-math score

Should you have any questions on these scoring instructions, you may call the phone number below. If, after following the above scoring directions and checking your work at least twice, your results disagree with the SAT-verbal or SAT-mathematical score reported on your ATP Student Report, you may request rescoring of your answer sheet. If rescoring confirms that an error had been made (resulting in either higher or lower scores than those originally reported), corrected reports will be sent to all recipients of your original scores. Please send your request to:

College Board ATP
Box 592
Princeton, NJ 08541
Attention: Rescore Request
Telephone: (609) 883-8500

Please indicate whether it is your SAT-verbal or SAT-mathematical score, or both, that you want to be rescored. When you write, please include a copy of this scoring worksheet on which you did your calculations.

Score Conversion Table
Scholastic Aptitude Test
Form Code 0X

Raw Score	College Board Reported Score		Raw Score	College Board Reported Score	
	SAT-Verbal	SAT-Math		SAT-Verbal	SAT-Math
85	800		40	460	610
84	790		39	450	600
83	780		38	440	590
82	770		37	440	590
81	760		36	430	580
80	760		35	420	570
79	750		34	420	560
78	740		33	410	550
77	730		32	400	540
76	720		31	400	530
75	720		30	390	530
74	710		29	380	520
73	700		28	380	510
72	690		27	370	500
71	680		26	360	490
70	680		25	350	480
69	670		24	350	470
68	660		23	340	460
67	650		22	330	460
66	640		21	330	450
65	640		20	320	440
64	630		19	310	430
63	620		18	310	420
62	610		17	300	410
61	600		16	290	400
60	600	800	15	290	400
59	590	790	14	280	390
58	580	780	13	270	380
57	580	770	12	260	370
56	570	760	11	260	360
55	560	750	10	250	350
54	560	740	9	240	340
53	550	730	8	240	330
52	540	720	7	230	330
51	530	710	6	220	320
50	530	700	5	220	310
49	520	690	4	210	300
48	510	680	3	200	290
47	510	670	2	200	280
46	500	660	1	200	270
45	490	660	0	200	270
44	490	650	−1	200	260
43	480	640	−2	200	250
42	470	630	−3	200	240
41	470	620	−4	200	230
			−5	200	220
			−6	200	210
			−7 or below	200	200

SAT
Form Code 7G027

FORM CODE 7G027

1

SECTION 1

Time—30 minutes

45 QUESTIONS

For each question in this section, choose the best answer and blacken the corresponding space on the answer sheet.

Each question below consists of a word in capital letters, followed by five lettered words or phrases. Choose the word or phrase that is most nearly opposite in meaning to the word in capital letters. Since some of the questions require you to distinguish fine shades of meaning, consider all the choices before deciding which is best.

Example:

GOOD: (A) sour (B) bad (C) red (D) hot (E) ugly

1. FLABBY: (A) fertile (B) taut (C) radiant (D) fortunate (E) miniature
2. CONCLUSIVE: (A) debatable (B) tactless (C) obvious (D) aggravating (E) noisy
3. INERT: (A) exact (B) dry (C) active (D) congenital (E) hopeful
4. HEARTEN: (A) assume (B) dismay (C) imitate (D) confide in (E) sympathize with
5. OBSCURITY: (A) prominence (B) continuity (C) reliability (D) gentleness (E) resistance
6. ADULTERATE: (A) unite (B) conclude (C) polish (D) purify (E) impute
7. ZENITH: (A) slow progress (B) hidden side (C) distant object (D) revealed truth (E) lowest point
8. CHERUBIC: (A) ecstatic (B) provincial (C) very colorful (D) highly potent (E) fiendish
9. ARTFUL: (A) forlorn (B) attentive (C) guileless (D) oppressive (E) stubborn
10. GRIEVOUS: (A) minor (B) visible (C) incomplete (D) inevitable (E) genuine
11. AMITY: (A) animosity (B) tragedy (C) poverty (D) sobriety (E) ordeal
12. AMELIORATE: (A) aggravate (B) forget (C) refuse (D) hesitate (E) amputate
13. EPHEMERAL: (A) valiant (B) legible (C) apathetic (D) predestined (E) eternal
14. BROACH: (A) devalue (B) close (C) reprove (D) affirm (E) heed
15. IRASCIBLE: (A) honorable (B) fickle (C) delectable (D) stubborn (E) impassive

Each sentence below has one or two blanks, each blank indicating that something has been omitted. Beneath the sentence are five lettered words or sets of words. Choose the word or set of words that best fits the meaning of the sentence as a whole.

Example:

Although its publicity has been ----, the film itself is intelligent, well-acted, handsomely produced, and altogether ----.

(A) tasteless. .respectable (B) extensive. .moderate (C) sophisticated. .amateur (D) risqué. .crude (E) perfect. .spectacular

16. Because mist is a magician, even the ---- object may appear beautiful under certain atmospheric conditions.

    (A) largest (B) heaviest (C) ugliest (D) simplest (E) strongest

17. The great voyages of discovery that expanded people's geographic vision served to ---- their intellectual horizons as well.

    (A) engulf (B) immobilize (C) clarify (D) broaden (E) fragment

18. Rebecca's ---- of ---- in all its forms was consistent with her commitment to reason and moderation.

    (A) dismissal. .doubt
    (B) suspicion. .fanaticism
    (C) disparagement. .frailty
    (D) tolerance. .intemperance
    (E) exaggeration. .courtesy

19. Some critics maintain that Mahler's music is uneven, running the gamut from the ---- to the great.

    (A) unprecedented (B) monumental (C) essential (D) sublime (E) banal

20. The foreign correspondent portrayed the leaders of both warring factions so sympathetically that he was ---- by both sides for his blindness to the enemy's ----.

    (A) admonished. .virtue
    (B) censured. .affability
    (C) commended. .integrity
    (D) vilified. .baseness
    (E) revered. .innocence

GO ON TO THE NEXT PAGE

Each passage below is followed by questions based on its content. Answer all questions following a passage on the basis of what is stated or implied in that passage.

Can poverty in the United States be abolished within the limits of the welfare state?

The answer is clear enough. The government's own figures demonstrate that the current antipoverty programs are basically inadequate. I do not, however, want to dismiss completely the government's antipoverty programs. Current serious discussion of poverty in this country is a gain which one owes in part to that program. But there is no point in pretending that a little more welfarism will do away with a national shame.

Today's poor are different from the pre-Second World War poor. The "old" poor lived at a time when economic opportunity was the national trend, when the net income from the growth of American manufacturing increased by 4,500 per cent. It was the "old" poor, mostly Eastern European immigrants unified by language and culture, who created the big-city political machines and participated in the organization of unions and the political struggle for the New Deal. They had objective, realistic reason for hope.

An analysis of the first phase and second phase of the New Deal of the Roosevelt administration is quite relevant at this point. The first phase of the New Deal, supported by American business and dominated by the National Recovery Act, gave recognition to an old corporate dream—economy planned by business. The second phase of the New Deal (the source of today's welfare theory and antipoverty wisdom) moved away from the concept of planning and toward a "free market." The assumption was that in its intervention the government should not plan but should stimulate the economy and that the private sector and initiative would continue to be the mainspring of progress.

After the Second World War, the government started emphasizing training programs because some workers were not participating in the general economic advance. However, these training programs have missed the fundamental problem. The novelty of impoverishment today is that it takes place in a time of automation. The government offers education and training and at the same time admits that the jobs for its graduates are obsolete. Such hypocrisy reinforces the cynicism and resistance to organization which characterizes poor communities.

It is therefore crucial that the federal government generate jobs and create an environment of economic hope. The essence of the "third phase" of the New Deal would be social investment, a conscious and political allocation of resources to meet public needs. This New Deal would be dependent upon a coalition, which would include, but not be confined to, the poor, that would see to it that planning and social investment were extended in a democratic way.

21. It can be inferred that the first phase of the New Deal
    - (A) discouraged investment in industry
    - (B) was the source of today's welfare theory
    - (C) stimulated the growth of big-city political machines
    - (D) provided programs to prepare workers for jobs in automated industry
    - (E) gave business an opportunity to extend control over the economy

22. The author credits the government's antipoverty program with which of the following?
    - (A) Encouraging serious discussions on national poverty
    - (B) Promoting a new welfare system
    - (C) Establishing programs to generate jobs
    - (D) Eliminating a national shame
    - (E) Involving the poor in plans for social reform

23. The primary purpose of the passage is to
    - (A) expose those who support government antipoverty programs
    - (B) distinguish between the pre- and p[illegible] World War poor
    - (C) argue for social investment by the federal government to alleviate poverty
    - (D) reveal the practices of society that perpetuate poverty
    - (E) distinguish among the first, second, and third New Deal approaches to reducing unemployment

24. According to the passage, today's poor differ from the "old" poor in which of the following ways?
    - I. The "old" poor enjoyed a higher average income.
    - II. The "old" poor had a realistic hope for economic opportunity.
    - III. The "old" poor were better educated.

    (A) II only (B) III only (C) I and III only (D) II and III only (E) I, II, and III

25. The author's attitude toward the government's current poverty program can best be described as
    - (A) unqualified appreciation
    - (B) fundamental dissatisfaction
    - (C) apathetic acceptance
    - (D) self-righteous pomposity
    - (E) violent indignation

GO ON TO THE NEXT PAGE

The reading passages in this test are brief excerpts or adaptations of excerpts from published material. The ideas contained in them do not necessarily represent the opinions of the College Board or Educational Testing Service. To make the text suitable for testing purposes, we may in some cases have altered the style, contents, or point of view of the original.

Scientists studying choriocarcinoma, a kind of cancer developing out of fetal tissue, are inevitably students of the fetus-mother relationship and of the phenomenon by which a mother's body suppresses normal rejection of foreign tissue such as the fetus itself. Many scientists feel that the trophoblast is responsible for this phenomenon. The trophoblast that gives rise to choriocarcinoma first appears as a layer of cells covering the blastocyst (an early stage of the embryo) that is located on the surface of the placenta. It penetrates and erodes the surface tissue of the uterine wall with the result that the blastocyst becomes attached to the uterus. Moreover, the eroding action of the trophoblast damages and thus opens up some of the uterine blood vessels, providing a source of nourishment for the fetus. It appears obvious that the trophoblast has some peculiar property which permits its toleration by the mother's body. Especially important may be the noncellular substance called fibrinoid (or the layer of Nitabuch) covering the cells of the trophoblast. It has recently been hypothesized that the layer of Nitabuch, known for at least a hundred years, may be a barrier to prevent the escape of antigens from the embryonic tissues so that the mother's immune response cannot be stimulated into taking action against the foreign tissue growing in her uterus.

There is a lot of evidence to suggest that in the normal rejection process some sort of direct cell-to-cell contact must occur, and that the host cell making direct contact with the foreign tissue is a white blood cell—the lymphocyte. What the lymphocyte does when it establishes contact is not clear. Some message goes back to the lymph gland in the area, with the result that there is a proliferation of lymphocytes in the lymph gland. These are specialized lymphocytes that can then move in to attack the foreign tissue; and there may also be a secondary process in which antibodies are produced. But if the lymphocyte (which has a fairly high net negative surface charge) opposed a cell that also had a high negative surface charge, then it might not be possible for the lymphocyte to make the appropriate contact, since negative charges repel. It is difficult to measure the electrical charge of the trophoblast cell, but it is likely that it has a high net negative charge, perhaps due to the layer of Nitabuch. If the lymphocyte is prevented from making contact with the cell of the foreign body, then the foreign body—be it fetus or the fetus-originated choriocarcinoma—will not be rejected.

26. Which of the following can be inferred about choriocarcinoma?

(A) Only embryos are immune to its attack.
(B) It is most commonly associated with pregnancy.
(C) It is the type of cancer which has been most extensively studied.
(D) It is the only type of cancer for which the body's rejection process is important.
(E) It is the only type of cancer for which a cure has been found.

27. The author states that foreign tissue will not be rejected by the host if

(A) the layer of Nitabuch has been damaged
(B) the cells of the host are positively charged
(C) the host is already fighting off other foreign cells
(D) direct contact between a lymphocyte and a foreign cell is prevented
(E) the structure of the foreign cells resembles that of the host cells

28. The author provides information to answer which of the following questions?

(A) Where do the body's lymphocytes originate?
(B) What is the process by which antibodies are produced?
(C) What does a lymphocyte do after making contact with a foreign cell?
(D) What is the mechanism by which the layer of Nitabuch prevents the escape of antigens from embryonic tissue?
(E) What are the issues on which scientists disagree concerning the role of the trophoblast?

29. The author's discussion suggests that

(A) cancer research has accomplished very little
(B) much of the explanation he offers is only tentative
(C) current cancer research emphasizes prevention rather than cure
(D) he is not qualified to judge the significance of the research he describes
(E) many scientists have overemphasized study of the fetus-mother relationship to the exclusion of other aspects of cancer research

30. Which of the following titles best describes the content of the passage?

(A) The Layer of Nitabuch—Cause of Choriocarcinoma
(B) The Lymphocyte and Its Ways of Defeating Disease
C) The Mutually Beneficial Relationship of the Trophoblast and the Blastocyst
(D) Some Discoveries Revealing Possible Cures for Choriocarcinoma
(E) Some Speculations as to Why the Mother's Body Fails to Reject Choriocarcinoma

GO ON TO THE NEXT PAGE

1

Select the word or set of words that best completes each of the following sentences.

31. Many great dramatic parts make such heavy --- the physical and spiritual resources of the chief performers that eight performances a week are an ---- strain.

(A) impositions on. .appropriate
(B) requirements on. .invigorating
(C) overtures to. .ultimate
(D) demands on. .unbearable
(E) competition for. .unmitigated

32. In their search for artifacts, archaeologists are often ----, not because a suspected site is remote and isolated but because it is ----.

(A) misled. .verified
(B) undeterred. .unearthed
(C) belittled. .undespoiled
(D) venerated. .sacred
(E) frustrated. .urbanized

33. The ---- of the individual's desire for freedom despite constant efforts to destroy it does not mean that freedom will triumph; at best, it suggests that the desire for it is ----.

(A) repudiation. .enviable
(B) vacillation. .insatiable
(C) emasculation. .universal
(D) reassertion. .unforeseen
(E) persistence. .indestructible

34. The ---- of erecting arbitrary barriers between the sciences is clearly demonstrated in the study of sensory processes, where progress has been made through the ---- efforts of many specialists.

(A) efficacy. .qualified
(B) utility. .united
(C) possibility. .diverse
(D) irrationality. .combined
(E) practice. .immense

35. Naturally his course brought down on him the --- of both leftists and moderates, and he had long since ---- the conservative elements of the population.

(A) admiration. .reactivated
(B) anger. .appeased
(C) malediction. .misdirected
(D) respect. .alienated
(E) distrust. .estranged

Each question below consists of a related pair of words or phrases, followed by five lettered pairs of words or phrases. Select the lettered pair that best expresses a relationship similar to that expressed in the original pair.

Example:

YAWN : BOREDOM :: (A) dream : sleep (B) anger : madness (C) smile : amusement (D) face : expression (E) impatience : rebellion

Ⓐ Ⓑ ● Ⓓ Ⓔ

36. SEED : SPROUT :: (A) lava : volcano (B) bud : bloom (C) fish : minnow (D) pollen : bee (E) vine : tree

37. RUMOR : FACT :: (A) myth : history (B) guess : assumption (C) science : knowledge (D) fiction : story (E) inference : intuition

38. SNARL : ANGRY :: (A) bite : pensive (B) growl : humble (C) purr : contented (D) search : defensive (E) pounce : secretive

39. DERIVATION : WORD :: (A) ancestry : person (B) nomenclature : term (C) address : family (D) validation : document (E) relationship : brother

40. LONESOME : COMPANIONSHIP :: (A) nervous : agitation (B) bored : stimulation (C) clumsy : determination (D) suspicious : caution (E) arrogant : ambition

41. NEEDLE : SEW :: (A) padlock : enter (B) picture : draw (C) gauge : measure (D) sound : fear (E) rope : knot

42. EMENDATION : TEXT :: (A) introduction : speech (B) boundary : territory (C) alteration : garment (D) sketch : painting (E) dilapidation : building

43. HEMORRHAGE : BLOOD :: (A) battle : wound (B) deterrence : aggression (C) consensus : opinion (D) opulence : wealth (E) effusion : emotion

44. UNREMITTING : CESSATION :: (A) unique : corruption (B) irrelevant : distraction (C) uniform : diversity (D) unbecoming : permanence (E) indisputable : certainty

45. DISFRANCHISEMENT : RIGHTS ::
(A) corruption : ability
(B) emancipation : freedom
(C) imitation : originality
(D) organization : individuality
(E) enervation : strength

S T O P

IF YOU FINISH BEFORE TIME IS CALLED, CHECK YOUR WORK ON THIS SECTION ONLY. DO NOT WORK ON ANY OTHER SECTION IN THE TEST.

SECTION 2

Time—30 minutes

25 QUESTIONS

In this section solve each problem, using any available space on the page for scratchwork. Then indicate the one correct answer in the appropriate space on the answer sheet.

The following information is for your reference in solving some of the problems.

Circle of radius r: Area $= \pi r^2$; Circumference $= 2\pi r$
The number of degrees of arc in a circle is 360.
The measure in degrees of a straight angle is 180.

Definitions of symbols:

$=$	is equal to	$\leq$	is less than or equal to
$\neq$	is unequal to	$\geq$	is greater than or equal to
$<$	is less than	$\parallel$	is parallel to
$>$	is greater than	$\perp$	is perpendicular to

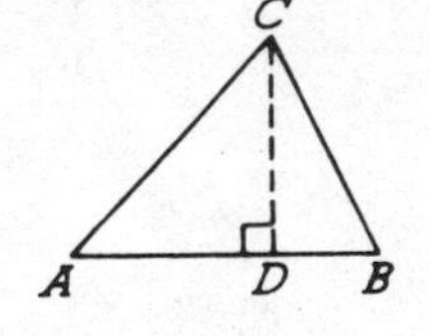

Triangle: The sum of the measures in degrees of the angles of a triangle is 180.

If $\angle CDA$ is a right angle, then

(1) area of $\triangle ABC = \dfrac{AB \times CD}{2}$

(2) $AC^2 = AD^2 + DC^2$

Note: Figures which accompany problems in this test are intended to provide information useful in solving the problems. They are drawn as accurately as possible EXCEPT when it is stated in a specific problem that its figure is not drawn to scale. All figures lie in a plane unless otherwise indicated. All numbers used are real numbers.

---

1. The cost of 900 items at \$1.65 per 100 is

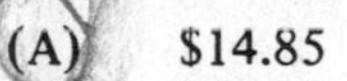

(A) \$14.85
(B) \$18.30
(C) \$148.50
(D) \$183.00
(E) \$1,485.00

2. 51(52 + 53 + 54) is equal to all of the following EXCEPT

(A) 51(52) + 51(53 + 54)
(B) 51(52) + 51(53) + 51(54)
(C) (54 + 53 + 52)51
(D) (54 + 53)51 + 52(51)
(E) 51 + (52)(53)(54)

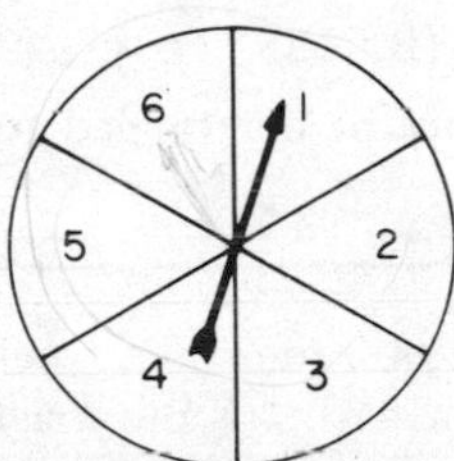

3. In a certain game, a player gets an additional spin if, when he spins the arrow on the disc shown above, the arrowhead stops in the region numbered 6. On a given spin, what is the chance that he will get an additional spin? (All regions are of equal size.)

(A) 1 in 36
(B) 1 in 6
(C) 1 in 5
(D) 1 in 3
(E) 1 in 2

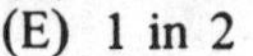

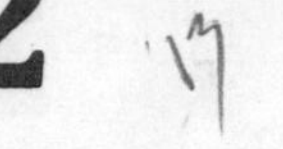

4. If $y - 4 = 9$, then $y + 4 =$

(A) 4 (B) 8 (C) 9 (D) 13 (E) 17

5. If $x > 0$ and $x^2 - 1 = 15 \times 17$, then $x =$

(A) 11
(B) 14
(C) 15
(D) 16
(E) 17

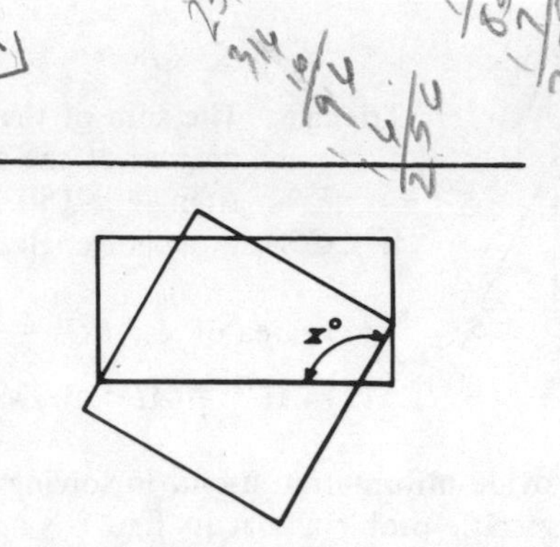

6. In the figure above, a square and a rectangle overlap. Which of the following is equal to x ?

(A) 120 (B) 135 (C) 140 (D) 150
(E) It cannot be determined from the information given.

7. A load of 1,000 tons on a truck is increased by one per cent. What is the weight, in tons, of the adjusted load?

(A) 1,001
(B) 1,010
(C) 1,100
(D) 1,110
(E) 1,111

8. If $6 + x + y = 20$ and if $x + y = k$, then $20 - k$ is equal to

(A) 14 (B) 9 (C) 6 (D) $3\frac{2}{3}$

(E) none of the above

D G H C
IV III
V II
VI I
A E F B

9. $ABCD$ is a rectangle and squares I through VI have equal areas. If $EF = 2AE$, the area of one of the squares is what fraction of the area of rectangle $ABCD$?

(A) $\frac{1}{12}$ (B) $\frac{1}{6}$ (C) $\frac{1}{4}$ (D) $\frac{1}{3}$ (E) $\frac{2}{3}$

10. Which of the following fractions is the greatest?

(A) $\frac{16}{17}$

(B) $\frac{8}{9}$

(C) $\frac{14}{15}$

(D) $\frac{9}{10}$

(E) $\frac{11}{12}$

11. A woman made 5 payments on a loan with each payment being twice the amount of the preceding one. If the total of all 5 payments was \$465, how much was the first payment?

(A) \$5
(B) \$15
(C) \$31
(D) \$93
(E) \$155

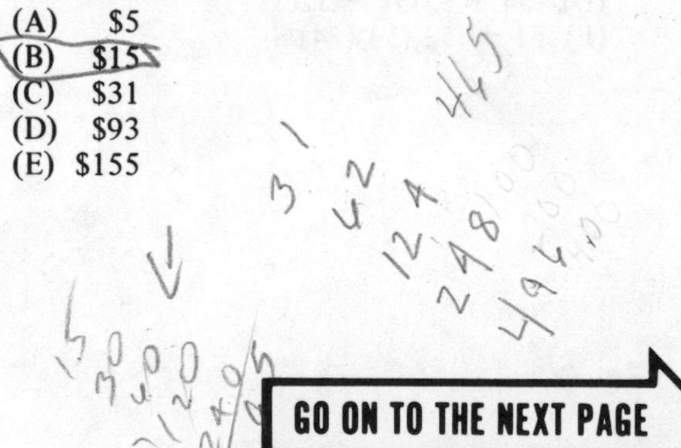

GO ON TO THE NEXT PAGE

12. If $20 \cdot 3{,}000 = 6 \cdot 100^{x}$, then $x =$

(A) 2 (B) 3 (C) 4 (D) 5 (E) 6

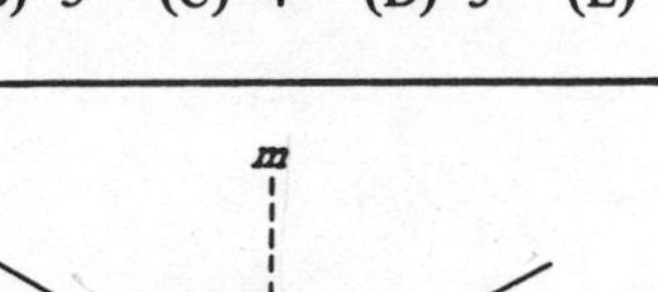

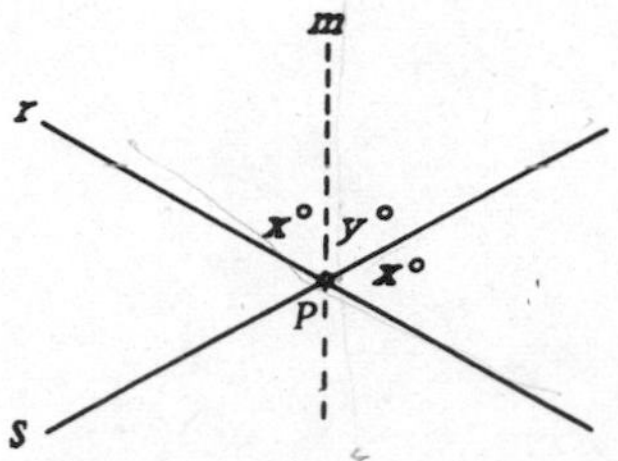

13. In the figure above, line r intersects line s at P. If another line m is drawn through P with angles formed as indicated in the figure, then what is the value of y in terms of x ?

(A) 60 (B) x (C) $2x$
(D) $180 - x$ (E) $180 - 2x$

14. If $k = \frac{n}{12} + \frac{n}{12} + \frac{n}{12}$, then the least positive integer n for which k is an integer is

(A) 2
(B) 3
(C) 4
(D) 6
(E) 8

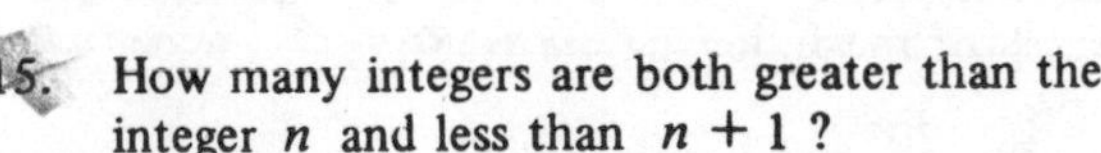

15. How many integers are both greater than the integer n and less than $n + 1$?

(A) None
(B) One
(C) n
(D) $n + 1$
(E) It cannot be determined from the information given.

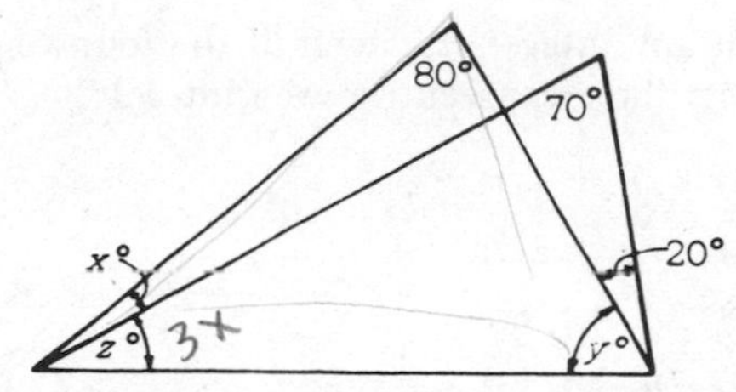

16. In the figure above, if $z = 3x$, then $y =$

(A) 30 (B) 60 (C) 70 (D) 80 (E) 90

17. If N is the least positive integer for which $3N$ is both an even integer and equal to the square of an integer, then $N =$

(A) 3 (B) 4 (C) 6 (D) 12 (E) 18

18. Bud now weighs 9 kilograms more than he did a year ago. If his weight then, in kilograms, was $\frac{9}{10}$ of his present weight, what is his present weight?

(A) 72 kg
(B) 81 kg
(C) 90 kg
(D) 99 kg
(E) 108 kg

19. The volume of a cube with edge $\sqrt{2}$ is how many times the volume of a cube with edge $\sqrt[3]{2}$?

(A) $\sqrt[3]{2}$
(B) $\sqrt{2}$
(C) 2
(D) $2\sqrt{2}$
(E) 4

GO ON TO THE NEXT PAGE

20. For any integer n, which of the following represents three consecutive even integers?

(A) $n, n + 1, n + 2$
(B) $n, n + 2, n + 4$
(C) $2n, 4n, 6n$
(D) $2n, 2n + 1, 2n + 2$
(E) $2n, 2n + 2, 2n + 4$

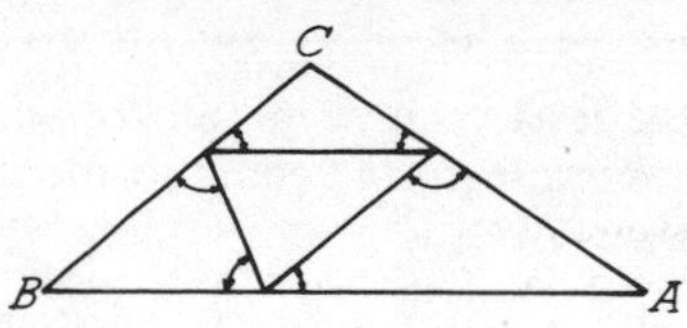

21. In the figure above, if ABC is a triangle, what is the sum of the degree measures of the marked angles?

(A) 180°
(B) 270°
(C) 360°
(D) 450°
(E) It cannot be determined from the information given.

---

22. The height of triangle T is 50 per cent of the width of rectangle R, and the length of the base of triangle T is 40 per cent of the length of rectangle R. If the area of triangle T is 3, what is the area of rectangle R ?

(A) 1
(B) 10
(C) 15
(D) 20
(E) 30

23. If 3 blots equal 4 bleets and 5 bleets equal 6 blits, what is the ratio of one blit to one blot?

(A) $\frac{1}{2}$
(B) $\frac{5}{8}$
(C) $\frac{2}{3}$
(D) $\frac{8}{5}$
(E) $\frac{2}{1}$

24. The average of 10 students' test scores is 72. When the 2 highest and 2 lowest scores are eliminated, the average of the remaining scores is 68. What is the average (arithmetic mean) of those eliminated?

(A) 64
(B) 76
(C) 78
(D) 80
(E) It cannot be determined from the information given.

25. If N is a positive whole number, let N^* equal the sum of all whole numbers from 1 to N, inclusive; for example, $6^* = 6 + 5 + 4 + 3 + 2 + 1 = 21$. Which of the following are true?

I. 20^* is an odd number.
II. If P is an odd whole number, then P^* is odd.
III. $(R + 1)^* - R^*$ [illegible] to $R + 1$.

(A) None
(B) I only
(C) II only
(D) III only
(E) II and III

S T O P

IF YOU FINISH BEFORE TIME IS CALLED, CHECK YOUR WORK ON THIS SECTION ONLY. DO NOT WORK ON ANY OTHER SECTION IN THE TEST.

SECTION 4

Time—30 minutes

40 QUESTIONS

For each question in this section, choose the best answer and blacken the corresponding space on the answer sheet.

Each question below consists of a word in capital letters, followed by five lettered words or phrases. Choose the word or phrase that is most nearly opposite in meaning to the word in capital letters. Since some of the questions require you to distinguish fine shades of meaning, consider all the choices before deciding which is best.

Example:

GOOD: (A) sour (B) bad (C) red (D) hot (E) ugly

Ⓐ ● Ⓒ Ⓓ Ⓔ

1. PERISHABLE:
(A) immobile
(B) inexcusable
(C) unable to advance
(D) unlikely to deteriorate
(E) unaccustomed to routine

2. DRAWBACK: (A) similarity (B) advantage (C) prediction (D) evidence (E) introduction

3. OUTPOST: (A) central location (B) large crowd (C) strong defense (D) vital fact (E) active leadership

4. PULVERIZE: (A) mold together (B) gain weight (C) make narrow (D) use force (E) push aside

5. DAWDLE: (A) liberate (B) soothe (C) brighten (D) solidify (E) rush

6. GRAPHIC: (A) politely refused (B) gracefully executed (C) poorly delineated (D) unintentional (E) modest

7. SQUANDER: (A) idealize (B) economize (C) classify (D) move rapidly (E) agree meekly

8. REVERE: (A) despise (B) restrain (C) misunderstand (D) conceal deliberately (E) leave unchanged

9. SACCHARINE: (A) taciturn (B) elated (C) vitriolic (D) amicable (E) squalid

10. RECALCITRANT: (A) obedient (B) energetic (C) temporary (D) perceptive (E) conservative

Each sentence below has one or two blanks, each blank indicating that something has been omitted. Beneath the sentence are five lettered words or sets of words. Choose the word or set of words that best fits the meaning of the sentence as a whole.

Example:

Although its publicity has been ----, the film itself is intelligent, well-acted, handsomely produced, and altogether ----.

(A) tasteless. .respectable (B) extensive. .moderate (C) sophisticated. .amateur (D) risqué. .crude (E) perfect. .spectacular

● Ⓑ Ⓒ Ⓓ Ⓔ

11. When, in 1972, the Indian government found that there were only 1,827 tigers left, the shooting of tigers was ----, and steps were taken to preserve their ----.
(A) prohibited. .habitats
(B) limited. .examination
(C) investigated. .multiplication
(D) reduced. .nature
(E) legalized. .well-being

12. Ms. Cartright's arguments are so well organized, clearly expressed, and extensively documented that even the most zealous of her opponents have ---- the ---- of her stance.
(A) recognized. .fallacy
(B) minimized. .legitimacy
(C) garbled. .frankness
(D) acknowledged. .merit
(E) modified. .ambiguity

13. Neither Green nor Simmons had particularly ---- ambitions; both seem to have been concerned more with the ---- of their audience than with the pursuit of truth.
(A) humanitarian. .virtues
(B) laudable. .plaudits
(C) philanthropic. .needs
(D) ignoble. .blandishments
(E) materialistic. .treasures

GO ON TO THE NEXT PAGE

14. There is an effort afoot among dissatisfied scientists to ---- what has clearly been an imbalance in the fields chosen for intensive research.

(A) augment (B) endorse (C) underbid (D) reinstate (E) redress

15. His characteristic dogmatism is occasionally --- by his ability to see merit in the ideas of others.

(A) rationalized (B) intensified (C) substantiated (D) disqualified (E) redeemed

---

Each question below consists of a related pair of words or phrases, followed by five lettered pairs of words or phrases. Select the lettered pair that best expresses a relationship similar to that expressed in the original pair.

Example:

> YAWN : BOREDOM :: (A) dream : sleep (B) anger : madness (C) smile : amusement (D) face : expression (E) impatience : rebellion
>
> Ⓐ Ⓑ ● Ⓓ Ⓔ

16. COMPOSER : PERFORMER :: (A) painter : wall (B) poet : posterity (C) intellectual : lowbrow (D) playwright : actor (E) philosopher : eternity

17. CAPILLARY : ARTERY :: (A) bridge : gorge (B) bank : river (C) ebb : flow (D) twig : branch (E) blood : heart

18. TASKMASTER : CREW :: (A) director : cast (B) soloist : chorus (C) observer : crowd (D) prisoner : jury (E) truant : class

19. PAINSTAKING : CAREFUL :: (A) restive : destructive (B) generous : polite (C) punctual : busy (D) engrossed : disturbed (E) fastidious : neat

20. DAM : WATER :: (A) ramp : turnpike (B) tunnel : mountain (C) dock : ships (D) roadblock : traffic (E) balloon : air

21. ADJOINING : LOCATION :: (A) consecutive : time (B) coincidental : error (C) occasional : duration (D) accidental : purpose (E) vacant : space

22. LARCENY : PROPERTY :: (A) arson : building (B) libel : slander (C) plagiarism : ideas (D) counterfeit : evidence (E) forgery : pen

23. LABYRINTH : CONFUSION :: (A) deadlock : arbitration (B) catalyst : delay (C) treadmill : boredom (D) pattern : chaos (E) riddle : solution

24. PARENTHESIS : PARAGRAPH :: (A) illness : sanity (B) conclusion : experiment (C) stage : dialogue (D) knowledge : wisdom (E) digression : argument

25. PARIAH : SOCIETY :: (A) novice : sport (B) exile : country (C) leper : colony (D) tyrant : dictatorship (E) chairman : committee

Each passage below is followed by questions based on its content. Answer all questions following a passage on the basis of what is stated or implied in that passage.

We were four companions. Unforeseen chance had joined us together on a large sugar plantation on the Peruvian coast. We worked at different occupations during the day and met during the evening. Not being Englishmen, we did not play cards. Instead our constant discussions led to disputes. These didn't stop us from wanting to see each other the next night, however, to continue the interrupted debates and support them with new arguments. Nor did the rough sentences of the preceding wrangles indicate a lessening of affection, of which we assured ourselves reciprocally with the clasping of hands. On Sundays we used to go on hunting parties. We roamed the fertile glens, stalking, generally with poor results, the game of the warm region around the coast.

We came to be tireless wanderers and excellent marksmen. What attracted us was the trans-Andean region: fertile plateaus extending on the other side of the range in the direction of the Atlantic toward the immense land of Brazil. It was as if primitive nature called us to her breast. The vigor of the fertile, untouched jungles promised to rejuvenate our minds, the same vigor which rejuvenates the strength and thickness of the trees each year. At times we devised crazy plans. As with all things that are given a lot of thought, these schemes generally materialized. Ultimately nature and events are largely what our imaginations make them out to be. At the end of the year, with arranged vacations, accumulated money, good rifles, and four hammocks, our caravan descended the Andean slopes leading to the endless green ocean.

26. The four companions in the passage are discussed primarily in terms of

(A) the topics they discussed
(B) their mutual activities
(C) their interaction with others
(D) the characteristics of the land in which they lived
(E) the different personalities of each

27. It can be inferred from the passage that the acquaintanceship among the four companions developed because they

(A) held similar views on most issues
(B) were all of the same nationality
(C) worked in the same general location
(D) had trained in the same profession
(E) had traveled together previously

28. The companions seemed to view the jungle as a source of

(A) mysterious danger
(B) impassive peace
(C) lucrative profits
(D) inconsequential diversion
(E) refreshing vitality

The assumption that chlorofluorocarbons would be innocuous in the environment because they were chemically inert might have gone unchallenged for some time, but at a conference someone mentioned their curious persistence in the atmosphere to F. Sherwood Rowland, a chemist, who began to wonder what ultimately became of the synthetic compounds. In 1973, Rowland got a research grant to study the question, and he and his associate, Mario J. Molina, set out to prove that chlorofluorocarbons must be floating unchanged to the stratosphere, where the strong ultraviolet rays in sunlight would cause them to release chlorine atoms. These atoms would act as catalysts to destroy ozone, with each chlorine atom capable of setting off a chain reaction involving thousands of ozone molecules. These ozone molecules are part of the atmospheric ozone layer that protects the earth from solar ultraviolet rays. It is thought that if this layer is depleted, the results could be increased incidences of skin cancer, damage to plant life, and even global climatic changes.

Even though the depletion of the ozone layer would be lessened if production of the compounds ceased immediately, Rowland and Molina concluded that a twenty to forty per cent reduction of the layer was a strong possibility. The most disturbing conclusion was that the full effect of chlorofluorocarbons already in the atmosphere would not be felt for at least a decade, since the gases floated up and down until they gradually ascended to the ozone layer. "There was no moment of triumph," Rowland recalled. "I just came home one night and told my wife, 'The work is going very well, but it looks like the end of the world.'"

29. The passage primarily concerns the

(A) effects of ozone on plant and animal life
(B) interaction of ultraviolet rays with ozone
(C) potentially dangerous uses for chlorofluorocarbons
(D) discovery of the effect of chlorofluorocarbons on the ozone layer
(E) variety of gases in the atmosphere surrounding the earth

30. It can be inferred that before the publication of the study of Rowland and Molina, it was widely assumed that chlorofluorocarbons in the environment

(A) were harmless
(B) absorbed ultraviolet rays
(C) reacted with ozone
(D) were rapidly increasing
(E) could not be reproduced in a laboratory

31. According to the hypothesis of Rowland and Molina, the chlorofluorocarbons would release chlorine atoms when

(A) the ozone broke up the chlorofluorocarbon molecules
(B) they were subjected to the lowered air pressure of the stratosphere
(C) they were exposed to strong ultraviolet rays in the stratosphere
(D) they floated down from the stratosphere closer to the earth's surface
(E) the amount of ozone in the stratosphere was more than twenty per cent

Present-day Chicanos are the fulfillment of a cosmic cycle from ancient Aztlán (what is now the southwestern part of the United States), the seed ground of the great civilizations of Anahuac, to modern Aztlán. We have rediscovered Aztlán in ourselves. This knowledge provides the dynamic principle on which to build a deep unity and brotherhood among Chicanos. Ties much more profound than even language, birthplace, or culture bind us together—Aztlán represents the unifying force of our nonmaterial heritage.

References to Aztlán as the place of origin of the Mexican Indian peoples are negligible in North American chronicles. Two of the most easily obtainable texts by historians of the United States are Prescott's *History of the Conquest of Mexico* (1843) and Josephy's *The Indian Heritage of America* (1968). Prescott, in reviewing the various histories compiled for the most part by priest-scholars, suggested that the American peoples were descended from one of the lost tribes of Israel. He wrote:

> The theory of an Asiatic origin for Aztec civilizations derives strong confirmation from tradition. Traditions concerning their origin were found among the tribes, and were preserved both orally and in hieroglyphical maps, where the different stages of their migration are carefully noted. But who at this day shall read them? They are admitted to agree, however, in representing the populous North as the prolific hive of the American races. In this quarter were placed their Aztlán and their Huehuetlapallan, the abodes of their ancestors.

In a footnote, he says of the maps, "But as they are all within the boundaries of New Spain, indeed, south of the Rio Gila, they throw little light, of course, on the vexed question of the primitive abodes of the Aztecs."

It so happens that the Rio Gila is part of a convergence of rivers and cultures as significant as the confluence of the Tigris and Euphrates. Yet Prescott would have us seek a more distant source.

In a comprehensive study of the Indians of the Americas, Josephy recounts the settling of the Mexica tribe on the site of today's Mexico City. He says that the Mexica took the name Aztec from Aztlán, whence they had come, "somewhere vaguely to the Northwest and perhaps even in the present-day United States Southwest."

Mexican scholars clearly identify Aztec and Mexican origins with the southwestern United States. However, aside from the two sources cited, further reference to Aztlán is difficult to find in United States histories. It has obviously been of little consequence to anyone except the Chicano. We still know very little about our ancient origins.

32. According to the author, Aztlán today can be described as which of the following?

    I. A unifying force
    II. An abstract principle
    III. An actual location

    (A) I only (B) III only (C) I and II only
    (D) II and III only (E) I, II, and III

33. According to the passage, Prescott's information about Aztlán was derived primarily from his own
    (A) interviews with Mexican Indians
    (B) careful reading of Aztec hieroglyphics
    (C) study of the writings of earlier historians
    (D) field work done in the American Southwest
    (E) studies of Indian life-styles

34. The author mentions the works of Prescott and Josephy chiefly because
    (A) they are among the few sources that mention Aztlán
    (B) their authors are particularly knowledgeable about North American Indians
    (C) they stress the significance of Aztlán for the Chicano
    (D) they are the texts commonly used in North American schools
    (E) they provide the most comprehensive treatments of North American history

35. The tone of Josephy's statement about the location of Aztlán (lines 49-51) can best be described as one of
    (A) apologetic regret
    (B) disguised irony
    (C) cautious speculation
    (D) dramatic revelation
    (E) philosophical resignation

36. The information in the passage suggests that the author is most likely
    (A) a historian who is concerned about the validity of his sources
    (B) a Chicano who is interested in bringing the Chicanos together
    (C) a literary critic who questions the conclusions of historians
    (D) an educator primarily concerned with the future of Chicano children
    (E) a researcher who is interested in discovering new facts about the Mexican Indians

GO ON TO THE NEXT PAGE

If we are to understand the impact of Aristotle on subsequent thought, we must remember some curious facts connected with the transmission of his writings. When Aristotle died in 322 B.C., he left a very extensive body of writings that consisted of two completely different groups. The first group of writings included a large number of dialogues and other popular treatises, which had been published during his lifetime and which continued to be widely read through many centuries until they were finally lost toward the end of antiquity. These popular writings of Aristotle were praised for their literary elegance, and apparently the most famous among them were composed in Aristotle's earlier years and were comparatively close to Plato in their philosophical opinions. The second group of Aristotle's writings, which is the one that has come down to us, represents a collection of lecture courses that he delivered in his school in Athens. These courses served no immediate literary purpose, but instead are highly technical in character, very detailed in their reasoning and in the information supplied, and fairly systematic in their overall arrangement, forming a vast encyclopedia of philosophical and scientific knowledge. These lectures of Aristotle were not published by him or his immediate successors; they remained for several centuries in the library of his school, where they were accessible to its professors but not to the general public or to the members of other schools of philosophy.

37. Which of the following best summarizes the "curious facts" (lines 2-3) that the author focuses on in the passage?

(A) Few of Aristotle's contemporaries were and no modern scholars are familiar with both groups of his writings.
(B) Aristotle's academic lectures were no less elegantly written than were his more famous dialogues and treatises.
(C) The content of Aristotle's popular dialogues is contradicted in the lecture courses he delivered in his school.
(D) The popularity of Aristotle's writings ceased when he died and it was not revived for many centuries.
(E) The content of Aristotle's academic lectures was popularized not by his followers but by members of other Athenian schools of philosophy.

38. It can be inferred that by "transmission" (line 3) the author means

(A) inspiration or motivation for action
(B) analysis or interpretation of theory
(C) alteration or modification of material
(D) communication or dissemination of information
(E) relocation or replacement of evidence

39. The author appears most certain of the answer to which of the following questions?

(A) Why were copies of Aristotle's popular treatises lost?
(B) How is the influence of Plato evident in Aristotle's earlier treatises?
(C) What was the content of the lecture courses given by Aristotle at his school?
(D) Why did Aristotle not publish the lectures he gave at his school?
(E) What was the content of Aristotle's popular treatises?

40. The author's attitude toward Aristotle's writings is best described as one of

(A) unqualified endorsement
(B) apologetic approval
(C) analytical objectivity
(D) skeptical reserve
(E) scholarly dissatisfaction

S T O P

**IF YOU FINISH BEFORE TIME IS CALLED, CHECK YOUR WORK ON THIS SECTION ONLY.
DO NOT WORK ON ANY OTHER SECTION IN THE TEST.**

SECTION 5

5

Time—30 minutes

35 QUESTIONS

In this section solve each problem, using any available space on the page for scratchwork. Then indicate the one correct answer in the appropriate space on the answer sheet.

The following information is for your reference in solving some of the problems.

Circle of radius r: Area $= \pi r^2$; Circumference $= 2\pi r$
The number of degrees of arc in a circle is 360.
The measure in degrees of a straight angle is 180.

Definitions of symbols:

$=$	is equal to	$\leq$	is less than or equal to
$\neq$	is unequal to	$\geq$	is greater than or equal to
$<$	is less than	$\parallel$	is parallel to
$>$	is greater than	$\perp$	is perpendicular to

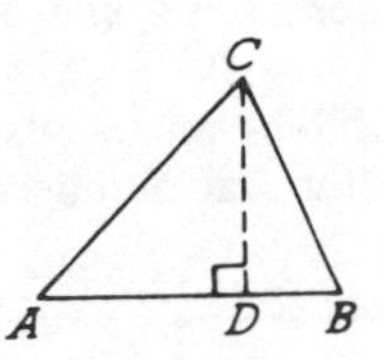

Triangle: The sum of the measures in degrees of the angles of a triangle is 180.

If $\angle CDA$ is a right angle, then

(1) area of $\triangle ABC = \dfrac{AB \times CD}{2}$

(2) $AC^2 = AD^2 + DC^2$

Note: Figures which accompany problems in this test are intended to provide information useful in solving the problems. They are drawn as accurately as possible EXCEPT when it is stated in a specific problem that its figure is not drawn to scale. All figures lie in a plane unless otherwise indicated. All numbers used are real numbers.

---

1. If $x = 8$ and $y = 6$, then $\dfrac{\frac{x}{2} + \frac{y}{3}}{\frac{xy}{4}} =$

(A) 3

(B) 2

(C) $\frac{4}{5}$

(D) $\frac{1}{2}$

(E) $\frac{17}{36}$

2. Three bananas cost as much as 2 pears. If bananas cost 18 cents each, what is the cost of each pear?

(A) 12¢ (B) 18¢ (C) 24¢
(D) 27¢ (E) 36¢

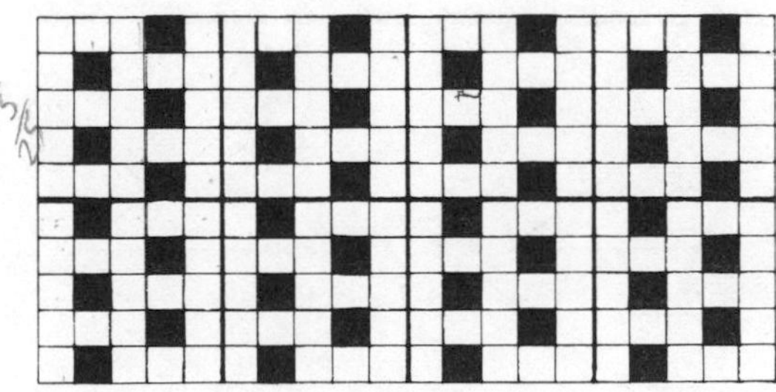

3. In the figure above, what per cent of the entire figure is shaded?

(A) 5% (B) 20% (C) 25%
(D) 40% (E) $66\frac{2}{3}$%

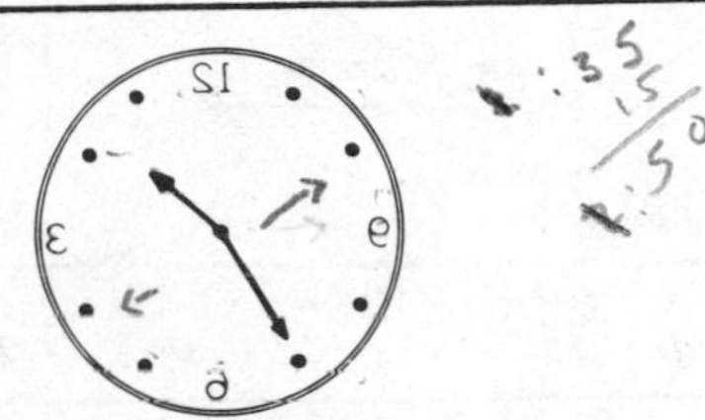

4. If the figure above is the mirror image of an accurate clock, what time will it be 15 minutes after the time shown?

(A) 1:50 (B) 1:40 (C) 1:10
(D) 10:40 (E) 10:05

5. If the sum of 6 consecutive integers is 75, what is the least of these integers?

(A) 8 (B) 9 (C) 10 (D) 11 (E) 12

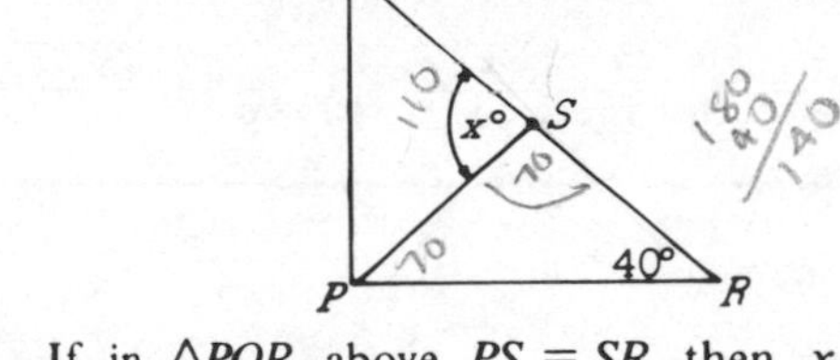

6. If, in $\triangle PQR$ above, $PS = SR$, then $x =$

(A) 50 (B) 80 (C) 90 (D) 100 (E) 110

7. If a rectangular sheet of paper is repeatedly folded in half until the area of the exposed side is $\frac{1}{16}$ of the original area exposed, how many times was the paper folded?

(A) Three (B) Four (C) Five
(D) Six (E) Eight

GO ON TO THE NEXT PAGE

5

Questions 8-27 each consist of two quantities, one in Column A and one in Column B. You are to compare the two quantities and on the answer sheet blacken space

A if the quantity in Column A is greater;
B if the quantity in Column B is greater;
C if the two quantities are equal;
D if the relationship cannot be determined from the information given.

Notes: 1. In certain questions, information concerning one or both of the quantities to be compared is centered above the two columns.
2. A symbol that appears in both columns represents the same thing in Column A as it does in Column B.
3. Letters such as x, n, and k stand for real numbers.

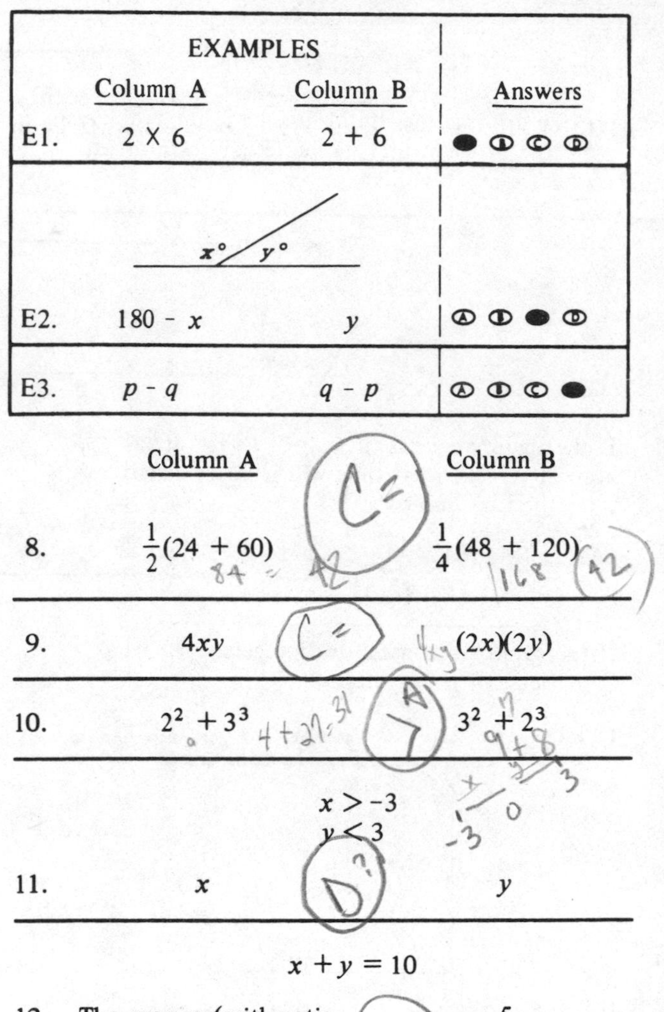

	EXAMPLES Column A	Column B	Answers
E1.	2×6	$2 + 6$	● Ⓑ Ⓒ Ⓓ
E2.	$180 - x$	y	Ⓐ Ⓑ ● Ⓓ
E3.	$p - q$	$q - p$	Ⓐ Ⓑ Ⓒ ●

	Column A	Column B
8.	$\frac{1}{2}(24 + 60)$	$\frac{1}{4}(48 + 120)$
9.	$4xy$	$(2x)(2y)$
10.	$2^2 + 3^3$	$3^2 + 2^3$

$x > -3$
$y < 3$

11.	x	y

$x + y = 10$

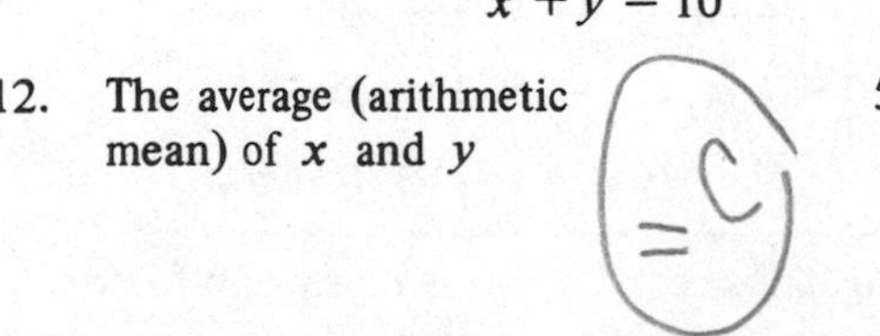

12.	The average (arithmetic mean) of x and y	5

Column A	Column B

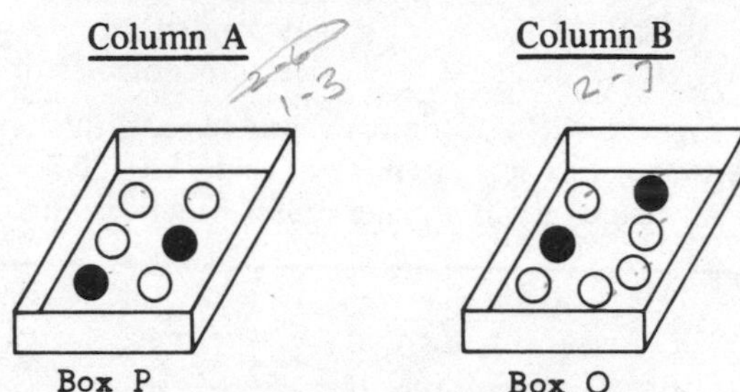

While blindfolded, Jill picked a marble from Box P and a marble from Box Q.

13.	The chance that Jill picked a black marble from Box P	The chance that Jill picked a black marble from Box Q

$X = \{0.98, 0.098, 0.09\}$
$Y = \{0.089, 0.89, 0.9\}$

14.	The greatest number in set X	The greatest number in set Y

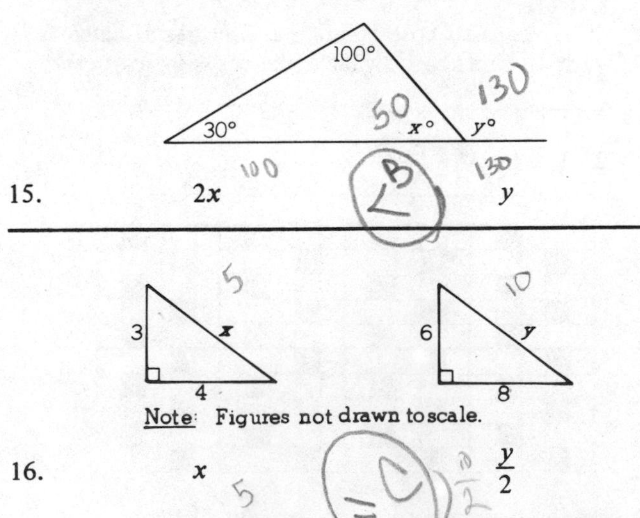

15.	$2x$	y

Note: Figures not drawn to scale.

16.	x	$\frac{y}{2}$

GO ON TO THE NEXT PAGE

SUMMARY DIRECTIONS FOR COMPARISON QUESTIONS

Answer:
- A if the quantity in Column A is greater;
- B if the quantity in Column B is greater;
- C if the two quantities are equal;
- D if the relationship cannot be determined from the information given.

	Column A	Column B

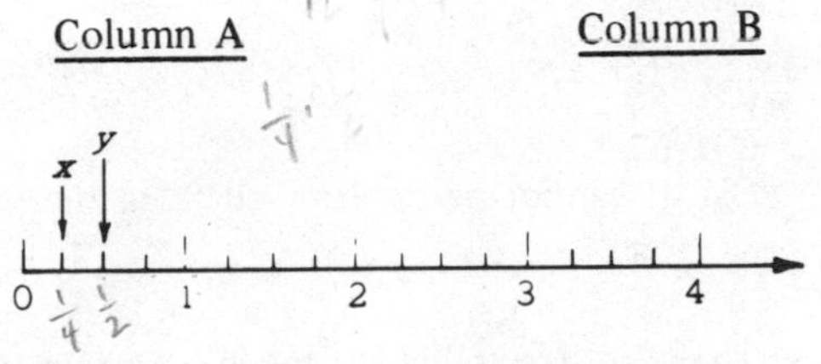

x and y are points on the number line.

	Column A	Column B
17.	$x \cdot y \cdot 2 \cdot 3 \cdot 4$	4

On a certain day, 80 per cent of the girls and 75 per cent of the boys were present in a mathematics class.

	Column A	Column B
18.	The number of girls absent	The number of boys absent
19.	Surface area of a sphere of radius 5	Area of a circle of radius 5

Questions 20-21 refer to the following definition of $\boxed{x}$ where x is any real number.

$$\boxed{x} = (x-1)^4 + (x-1)^2 + 1$$

	Column A	Column B
20.	$\boxed{1}$	1
21.	$\boxed{10}$	$\boxed{-10}$
22.	$\sqrt{5} + \sqrt{11}$	$\sqrt{16}$

$xy > 0$

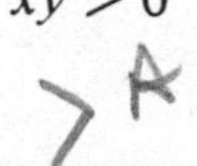

	Column A	Column B
23.	$x + y$	$x - y$

Two circles each with radius 4 overlap in such a way that their respective centers P and Q lie in the interior of both circular regions.

	Column A	Column B
24.	Length of segment PQ	4

$x^2 - y^2 = 0$

	Column A	Column B
25.	x	y

x per cent of y is z.

$z \neq 0$

	Column A	Column B
26.	100	$\frac{xy}{z}$

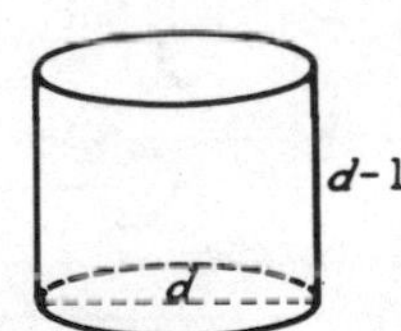

The diameter of the cylinder is d, where $d > 1$, and the height is $d - 1$.

	Column A	Column B
27.	The radius of the largest sphere that will fit completely inside the cylinder	$\frac{d}{2}$

GO ON TO THE NEXT PAGE

Solve each of the remaining problems in this section using any available space for scratchwork. Then indicate the <u>one</u> correct answer in the appropriate space on the answer sheet.

28. Dividing a number by $\frac{1}{4}$ gives the same result as multiplying by

(A) $\frac{1}{4}$ (B) 0.4 (C) 25% (D) 2 (E) 4

29. Of the following, the closest approximation to $\frac{14{,}995{,}844}{2{,}987}$ is

(A) 500
(B) 700
(C) 5,000
(D) 7,000
(E) 50,000

30. In a certain class of 30 students 18 are girls. If $\frac{2}{3}$ of the girls are either 16 years old or younger, what fractional part of the class is girls over 16 ?

(A) $\frac{2}{15}$

(B) $\frac{1}{5}$

(C) $\frac{1}{3}$

(D) $\frac{2}{5}$

(E) $\frac{1}{2}$

	Scale I	Scale II
Boiling	200°	500°
Freezing	0°	100°

31. The table above shows boiling and freezing points of the same liquid measured under the same conditions on two temperature scales. If the numbers on each of the scales are equally spaced, 50° on scale I would correspond to how many degrees on scale II ?

(A) 125
(B) 150
(C) 200
(D) 225
(E) 250

32. Points P, Q, R, and S lie on a straight line in the order given. The ratio of PQ to QR is 4 to 5 and the ratio of QR to RS is 3 to 7. If $PQ = 12$, what is the length of PS ?

(A) 36
(B) 48
(C) 50
(D) 62
(E) It cannot be determined from the information given.

33. There are 6 baseball teams in a certain league. If in one month each of the 6 teams played exactly 2 games with each of the other teams, how many games were played in the league that month?

(A) 12
(B) 15
(C) 30
(D) 36
(E) 60

34. A metal ball is rolled down a street. Without hitting any bumps, it can travel 200 meters. However, every 20 meters the ball hits a bump and each time the remaining distance it can travel is cut in half. How many bumps will the ball hit before stopping?

(A) 2
(B) 3
(C) 4
(D) 5
(E) 6

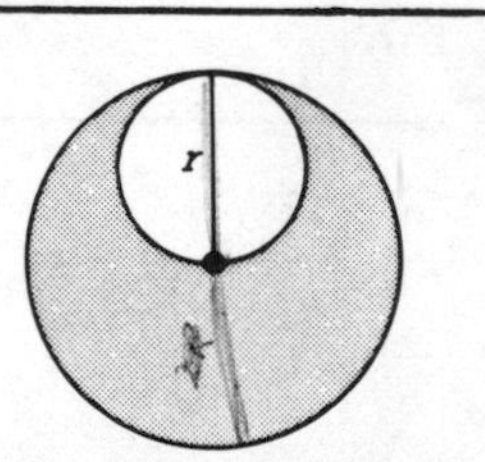

35. In the figure above, if one circle has radius r and the other has diameter r, what is the area of the shaded region?

(A) $\frac{\pi}{2}$ (B) $\frac{3\pi r}{4}$ (C) $\frac{\pi r}{2}$

(D) $\frac{\pi r^2}{2}$ (E) $\frac{3\pi r^2}{4}$

S T O P

IF YOU FINISH BEFORE TIME IS CALLED, CHECK YOUR WORK ON THIS SECTION ONLY. DO NOT WORK ON ANY OTHER SECTION IN THE TEST.

Correct Answers for Scholastic Aptitude Test
Form Code 7G027

VERBAL		MATHEMATICAL	
Section 1	**Section 4**	**Section 2**	**Section 5**
1. B	1. D	1. A	1. D
2. A	2. B	2. E	2. D
3. C	3. A	3. B	3. B
4. B	4. A	4. E	4. A
5. A	5. E	5. D	5. C
6. D	6. C	6. E	6. B
7. E	7. B	7. B	7. B
8. E	8. A	8. C	*8. C
9. C	9. C	9. A	*9. C
10. A	10. A	10. A	*10. A
11. A	11. A	11. B	*11. D
12. A	12. D	12. A	*12. C
13. E	13. B	13. E	*13. A
14. B	14. E	14. C	*14. A
15. E	15. E	15. A	*15. B
16. C	16. D	16. B	*16. C
17. D	17. D	17. D	*17. B
18. B	18. A	18. C	*18. D
19. E	19. E	19. B	*19. A
20. D	20. D	20. E	*20. C
21. E	21. A	21. C	*21. B
22. A	22. C	22. E	*22. A
23. C	23. C	23. B	*23. D
24. A	24. E	24. C	*24. B
25. B	25. B	25. D	*25. D
26. B	26. B		*26. C
27. D	27. C		*27. B
28. A	28. E		28. E
29. B	29. D		29. C
30. E	30. A		30. B
31. D	31. C		31. C
32. E	32. E		32. D
33. E	33. C		33. C
34. D	34. A		34. B
35. E	35. C		35. E
36. B	36. B		
37. A	37. A		
38. C	38. D		
39. A	39. C		
40. B	40. C		
41. C			
42. C			
43. E			
44. C			
45. E			

*Indicates four-choice questions. (All of the other questions are five-choice.)

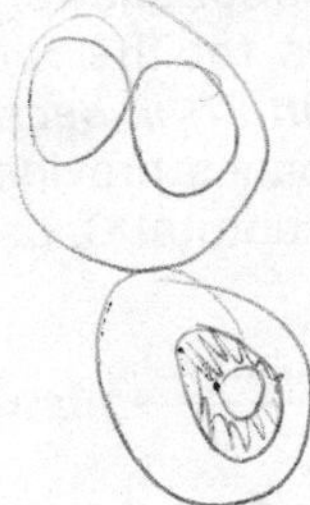

Scoring Process

Machine-scoring is done in three steps:

- *Scanning.* Your answer sheet is "read" by a scanning machine and the oval you filled in for each question is recorded on a computer tape.
- *Scoring.* The computer compares the oval filled in for each question with the correct response. Each correct answer receives one point; omitted questions do not count toward your score. For each wrong answer, a fraction of a point is subtracted to correct for random guessing. For questions with five answer choices, one-fourth of a point is subtracted for each wrong response; for questions with four answer choices, one-third of a point is subtracted for each wrong response. For example, the SAT-verbal test has 85 questions with five answer choices each, and if a student has 44 right, 32 wrong, and 9 omitted, the resulting raw score is determined as follows:

  $$44 \text{ right} - \frac{32 \text{ wrong}}{4} = 44 - 8 = 36 \text{ raw score points}$$

  Obtaining raw scores frequently involves the rounding of fractional numbers to the nearest whole number. For example, a raw score of 36.25 is rounded to 36, the nearest whole number. A raw score of 36.50 is rounded upward to 37.
- *Converting to reported scaled score.* Raw test scores are then placed on the College Board scale of 200 to 800 through a process that adjusts scores to account for minor differences in difficulty between different editions of the test. This process, known as equating, is performed so that a student's reported score is not affected by the edition of the test taken nor by the abilities of the group with whom the student takes the test. As a result of placing ATP scores on the College Board scale, scores earned by students at different times can be compared. For example, an SAT-verbal score of 400 on a test taken at one administration indicates the same level of developed verbal ability as a 400 score obtained on a different edition of the test taken at another time.

How to Score the Test

You can verify the College Board SAT scores reported to you recently by using the information in this booklet along with the copy of your answer sheet. *Before you begin, check that the form code you marked in item 3 on your answer sheet is the same as the one printed on the front of this booklet.* Compare the responses shown on the copy of your answer sheet with the list of correct answers.

SAT-Verbal Sections 1 and 4

Step A: Count the number of correct answers for *section 1* and record the number in the space provided on the worksheet on the opposite page. Then do the same for the incorrect answers. (Do not count omitted answers.) To determine subtotal A, use the formula:

$$\text{number correct} - \frac{\text{number incorrect}}{4} = \text{subtotal A}$$

Step B: Count the number of correct answers and the number of incorrect answers for *section 4* and record the numbers in the spaces provided on the worksheet. To determine subtotal B, use the formula:

$$\text{number correct} - \frac{\text{number incorrect}}{4} = \text{subtotal B}$$

Step C: To obtain C, add subtotal A to subtotal B, keeping any decimals.

Step D: To obtain D, your raw verbal score, round C to the nearest whole number. (For example, any number from 44.50 to 45.49 rounds to 45.)

Step E: To find your reported SAT-verbal score, look up the total raw verbal score you obtained in step D in the conversion table on the back cover.

SAT-Mathematical Sections 2 and 5

Step A: Count the number of correct answers and the number of incorrect answers for section 2 and record the numbers in the spaces provided on the worksheet. To determine the subtotal A, use the formula:

$$\text{number correct} - \frac{\text{number incorrect}}{4} = \text{subtotal A}$$

Step B: Count the number of correct answers and the number of incorrect answers for the *five-choice questions (questions 1 through 7 and 28 through 35) in section 5* and record the numbers in the spaces provided on the worksheet. To determine the subtotal B, use the formula:

$$\text{number correct} - \frac{\text{number incorrect}}{4} = \text{subtotal B}$$

Step C: Count the number of correct answers and the number of incorrect answers for the *four-choice questions (questions 8 through 27) in section 5* and record the numbers in the spaces provided on the worksheet. To determine the subtotal C, use the formula:

$$\text{number correct} - \frac{\text{number incorrect}}{3} = \text{subtotal C}$$

Step D: To obtain D, add subtotal A, subtotal B, and subtotal C, keeping any decimals.

Step E: To obtain E, your raw mathematical score, round D to the nearest whole number. (For example, any number from 44.50 to 45.49 rounds to 45.)

Step F: To find your reported SAT-mathematical score, look up the total raw mathematical score you obtained in E in the conversion table on the back cover.

FORM CODE 7G027

SAT-Verbal Worksheet

A. Section 1:	______ no. correct	− ¼	(______) no. incorrect	=	______ subtotal A
B. Section 4:	______ no. correct	− ¼	(______) no. incorrect	=	______ subtotal B

C. Total unrounded raw score (Total A + B) ______ C

D. Total rounded raw score (Rounded to nearest whole number) ______ D

E. Reported SAT-verbal score (See the conversion table on the back cover.) [ ] SAT-Verbal

SAT-Mathematical Worksheet

A. Section 2:	______ no. correct	− ¼	(______) no. incorrect	=	______ subtotal A
B. Section 5: Questions 1 through 7 and 28 through 35 (5-choice)	______ no. correct	− ¼	(______) no. incorrect	=	______ subtotal B
C. Section 5: Questions 8 through 27 (4-choice)	______ no. correct	− ⅓	(______) no. incorrect	=	______ subtotal C

D. Total unrounded raw score (Total A + B + C) ______ D

E. Total rounded raw score (Rounded to nearest whole number) ______ E

F. Reported SAT-mathematical score (See the conversion table on the back cover.) [ ] SAT-Math

If you have any questions on these scoring instructions, you may call the phone number below.

If, after following the above scoring directions and checking your work carefully, your results disagree with the verbal or mathematical score reported on your ATP Student Report, you may request a hand scoring of your answer sheet by writing or calling:

College Board ATP
Box 592
Princeton, NJ 08541
Attention: Rescore Request
Telephone: (609) 883-8500

Please indicate whether it is your verbal or mathematical score, or both, that you want to be rescored. When you write, please include a copy of this scoring worksheet on which you did your calculations.

Score Conversion Table
Scholastic Aptitude Test
Form Code 7G027

Raw Score	College Board Reported Score		Raw Score	College Board Reported Score	
	SAT-Verbal	SAT-Math		SAT-Verbal	SAT-Math
85	800		40	460	610
84	790		39	450	600
83	780		38	450	590
82	770		37	440	580
81	760		36	430	580
80	750		35	430	570
79	740		34	420	560
78	730		33	410	550
77	720		32	410	540
76	710		31	400	530
75	710		30	390	520
74	700		29	390	510
73	690		28	380	510
72	680		27	370	500
71	680		26	370	490
70	670		25	360	480
69	660		24	350	470
68	650		23	350	460
67	650		22	340	450
66	640		21	330	440
65	630		20	330	430
64	620		19	320	430
63	620		18	320	420
62	610		17	310	410
61	600		16	300	400
60	590	800	15	300	390
59	590	790	14	290	380
58	580	780	13	280	370
57	570	770	12	280	360
56	570	760	11	270	360
55	560	750	10	260	350
54	550	740	9	260	340
53	550	730	8	250	330
52	540	720	7	240	320
51	530	710	6	240	310
50	530	700	5	230	300
49	520	690	4	220	290
48	510	680	3	220	290
47	510	670	2	210	280
46	500	660	1	200	270
45	490	650	0	200	260
44	490	650	– 1	200	250
43	480	640	– 2	200	240
42	470	630	– 3	200	230
41	470	620	– 4	200	220
			– 5	200	210
			– 6	200	210
			– 7 or below	200	200

SAT
Form Code 8B210

(Cut here to detach.)

COLLEGE BOARD—SCHOLASTIC APTITUDE TEST and Test of Standard Written English — Side 1

Use a No. 2 pencil only for completing this answer sheet. Be sure each mark is dark and completely fills the intended space. Completely erase any errors or stray marks.

1.

YOUR NAME: ______________________ (Print) Last First M.I.

SIGNATURE: ______________________ **DATE:** ___ / ___ / ___

HOME ADDRESS: ______________________ (Print) Number and Street

______________________ City State Zip Code

CENTER: ______________________ (Print) City State Center Number

IMPORTANT: Please fill in these boxes exactly as shown on the back cover of your test book.

FOR ETS USE ONLY

2. TEST FORM

3. FORM CODE

0 1 2 3 4 5 6 7 8 9; A B C D E F G H I; J K L M N O P Q R; S T U V W X Y Z; 0–9; 0–9; 0–9

4. REGISTRATION NUMBER (Copy from your Admission Ticket.)

0–9 (seven columns)

5. YOUR NAME

First 4 letters of last name | First Init. | Mid. Init.

A–Z (each column)

6. DATE OF BIRTH

Month	Day		Year	
Jan.				
Feb.				
Mar.	0	0	0	0
Apr.	1	1	1	1
May	2	2	2	2
June	3	3	3	3
July		4	4	4
Aug.		5	5	5
Sept.		6	6	6
Oct.		7	7	7
Nov.		8		8
Dec.		9		9

7. SEX

Male

Female

8. TEST BOOK SERIAL NUMBER

Start with number 1 for each new section. If a section has fewer than 50 questions, leave the extra answer spaces blank.

SECTION 1

Questions	Choices
1–50	A B C D E

SECTION 2

Questions	Choices
1–7	A B C D E
8–25	A B C D
26–27	A B C D
28–50	A B C D E

Q1205

I.N. 574001—110VV33P2723

COLLEGE BOARD — SCHOLASTIC APTITUDE TEST and Test of Standard Written English **Side 2**

Use a No. 2 pencil only for completing this answer sheet. Be sure each mark is dark and completely fills the intended space. Completely erase any errors or stray marks.

Start with number 1 for each new section. If a section has fewer than 50 questions, leave the extra answer spaces blank.

	SECTION 3	SECTION 4	SECTION 5	SECTION 6
1	A B C D E	A B C D E	A B C D E	A B C D E
2	A B C D E	A B C D E	A B C D E	A B C D E
3	A B C D E	A B C D E	A B C D E	A B C D E
4	A B C D E	A B C D E	A B C D E	A B C D E
5	A B C D E	A B C D E	A B C D E	A B C D E
6	A B C D E	A B C D E	A B C D E	A B C D E
7	A B C D E	A B C D E	A B C D E	A B C D E
8	A B C D E	A B C D E	A B C D E	A B C D E
9	A B C D E	A B C D E	A B C D E	A B C D E
10	A B C D E	A B C D E	A B C D E	A B C D E
11	A B C D E	A B C D E	A B C D E	A B C D E
12	A B C D E	A B C D E	A B C D E	A B C D E
13	A B C D E	A B C D E	A B C D E	A B C D E
14	A B C D E	A B C D E	A B C D E	A B C D E
15	A B C D E	A B C D E	A B C D E	A B C D E
16	A B C D E	A B C D E	A B C D E	A B C D E
17	A B C D E	A B C D E	A B C D E	A B C D E
18	A B C D E	A B C D E	A B C D E	A B C D E
19	A B C D E	A B C D E	A B C D E	A B C D E
20	A B C D E	A B C D E	A B C D E	A B C D E
21	A B C D E	A B C D E	A B C D E	A B C D E
22	A B C D E	A B C D E	A B C D E	A B C D E
23	A B C D E	A B C D E	A B C D E	A B C D E
24	A B C D E	A B C D E	A B C D E	A B C D E
25	A B C D E	A B C D E	A B C D E	A B C D E
26	A B C D E	A B C D E	A B C D E	A B C D E
27	A B C D E	A B C D E	A B C D E	A B C D E
28	A B C D E	A B C D E	A B C D E	A B C D E
29	A B C D E	A B C D E	A B C D E	A B C D E
30	A B C D E	A B C D E	A B C D E	A B C D E
31	A B C D E	A B C D E	A B C D E	A B C D E
32	A B C D E	A B C D E	A B C D E	A B C D E
33	A B C D E	A B C D E	A B C D E	A B C D E
34	A B C D E	A B C D E	A B C D E	A B C D E
35	A B C D E	A B C D E	A B C D E	A B C D E
36	A B C D E	A B C D E	A B C D E	A B C D E
37	A B C D E	A B C D E	A B C D E	A B C D E
38	A B C D E	A B C D E	A B C D E	A B C D E
39	A B C D E	A B C D E	A B C D E	A B C D E
40	A B C D E	A B C D E	A B C D E	A B C D E
41	A B C D E	A B C D E	A B C D E	A B C D E
42	A B C D E	A B C D E	A B C D E	A B C D E
43	A B C D E	A B C D E	A B C D E	A B C D E
44	A B C D E	A B C D E	A B C D E	A B C D E
45	A B C D E	A B C D E	A B C D E	A B C D E
46	A B C D E	A B C D E	A B C D E	A B C D E
47	A B C D E	A B C D E	A B C D E	A B C D E
48	A B C D E	A B C D E	A B C D E	A B C D E
49	A B C D E	A B C D E	A B C D E	A B C D E
50	A B C D E	A B C D E	A B C D E	A B C D E

9. SIGNATURE: ______________________

FOR ETS USE ONLY	VTR	VTFS	VRR	VRFS	VVR	VVFS	WER	WEFS	M4R	M4FS	M5R	M5FS	MTFS
	VTW	VTCS	VRW	VRCS	VVW	VVCS	WEW	WECS	M4W		M5W		MTCS

FORM CODE 8B210

SECTION 1

1

Time—30 minutes

40 QUESTIONS

For each question in this section, choose the best answer and blacken the corresponding space on the answer sheet.

Each question below consists of a word in capital letters, followed by five lettered words or phrases. Choose the word or phrase that is most nearly opposite in meaning to the word in capital letters. Since some of the questions require you to distinguish fine shades of meaning, consider all the choices before deciding which is best.

Example:

GOOD: (A) sour (B) bad (C) red (D) hot (E) ugly

Ⓐ ● Ⓒ Ⓓ Ⓔ

1. TOUGH: (A) neatly garbed (B) quietly stated (C) greatly improved (D) easily chewed (E) extremely clean

2. FEROCITY: (A) mildness (B) inaccuracy (C) originality (D) awkwardness (E) uselessness

3. ALLY: (A) miser (B) dictator (C) amateur (D) opponent (E) daredevil

4. GRACIOUS: (A) surly (B) vague (C) elderly (D) anonymous (E) miraculous

5. FIREBRAND: (A) genius (B) impostor (C) sentinel (D) spendthrift (E) peacemaker

6. GALL: (A) revive (B) murmur (C) soothe (D) prohibit disagreement (E) evaluate performance

7. FLAGRANT: (A) inferior (B) unnoticeable (C) infallible (D) conclusive (E) rancid

8. UNDULATING: (A) level (B) profuse (C) fragmentary (D) pompous (E) buoyant

9. EXTRICATE: (A) ripen (B) deceive (C) decrease (D) snare (E) invent

10. PLATITUDE: (A) valid criticism (B) dishonest approach (C) novel utterance (D) mammoth undertaking (E) significant progress

Each sentence below has one or two blanks, each blank indicating that something has been omitted. Beneath the sentence are five lettered words or sets of words. Choose the word or set of words that best fits the meaning of the sentence as a whole.

Example:

Although its publicity has been ----, the film itself is intelligent, well-acted, handsomely produced, and altogether ----.

(A) tasteless..respectable (B) extensive..moderate (C) sophisticated..amateur (D) risqué..crude (E) perfect..spectacular

● Ⓑ Ⓒ Ⓓ Ⓔ

11. The castles of the feudal lords were primarily forts and therefore were constructed more for ---- than for ----.

(A) privacy..seclusion
(B) protection..comfort
(C) convenience..security
(D) permanence..preservation
(E) retaliation..defense

12. Those who ---- the use of force by labor unions should realize that management cannot be depended on to ---- a program of reform voluntarily.

(A) laud..initiate (B) ignore..discard (C) censure..deprecate (D) promote..effect (E) deplore..inaugurate

13. Standing up quietly for her rights, the heroine of Dickens' novel ---- bigots and ---- innumerable affronts to her personal dignity.

(A) denounced..replaced (B) converted..caused (C) trusted..expanded (D) shamed..weathered (E) insulted..inflicted

14. As if to ---- the towering buildings that now dominate our landscape, biographies of modern American authors depend on sheer ---- to compel authority.

(A) embody..intelligence (B) dismantle..ability (C) emulate..size (D) echo..talent (E) disregard..strength

15. Simmons could no longer be ----; with unusual ---- he castigated the council members for their persistent pettiness and provincialism.

(A) abusive..outrage (B) forbearing..venom (C) diplomatic..tact (D) polite..courtesy (E) censorious..scorn

The reading passages in this test are brief excerpts or adaptations of excerpts from published material. To make the text suitable for testing purposes, we may in some cases have altered the style, contents, or point of view of the original.

1

Each question below consists of a related pair of words or phrases, followed by five lettered pairs of words or phrases. Select the lettered pair that best expresses a relationship similar to that expressed in the original pair.

Example:

YAWN : BOREDOM :: (A) dream : sleep
(B) anger : madness (C) smile : amusement
(D) face : expression (E) impatience : rebellion

Ⓐ Ⓑ ● Ⓓ Ⓔ

16. MOTH : CLOTHING :: (A) woodpecker : hole
(B) bear : trap (C) lamb : wool
(D) puncture : tire (E) termite : house

17. FILTER : LIQUID :: (A) melt : ice
(B) grind : solid (C) sift : powder
(D) inflate : air (E) chisel : rock

18. ANNULMENT : MARRIAGE ::
(A) nullification : contract
(B) negation : opinion
(C) refutation : authority
(D) invalidation : discovery
(E) denial : permission

19. FRAME : PAINTING :: (A) orchestra : violin
(B) shore : lake (C) stage : balcony
(D) window : wall (E) lock : cell

20. HIJACK : GOODS :: (A) embezzle : bank
(B) slander : reputation (C) trespass : boundary
(D) forge : document (E) kidnap : person

21. CONSERVATORY : MUSIC :: (A) anthology : books
(B) aerie : birds (C) bivouac : army
(D) seminary : religion (E) arbor : grapes

22. HOMOGENEOUS : KIND :: (A) contemporary : age
(B) enigmatic : force (C) precipitous : length
(D) superficial : surface (E) suitable : form

23. MAGICIAN : PRESTIDIGITATION ::
(A) masquerader : conspiracy
(B) matador : peccadillo
(C) gymnast : omnipotence
(D) clown : pugilism
(E) mimic : imitation

24. PRATTLE : DISCOURSE :: (A) trinket : treasure
(B) epithet : effigy (C) halo : crown
(D) shot : volley (E) answer : response

25. DOUBLE-DEALER : DUPLICITY ::
(A) profligate : dissipation
(B) insurgent : oppression
(C) perjurer : negligence
(D) counterfeiter : authenticity
(E) authoritarian : disobedience

GO ON TO THE NEXT PAGE

Each passage below is followed by questions based on its content. Answer all questions following a passage on the basis of what is stated or implied in that passage.

(The passages for this test have been adapted from published material. The ideas contained in them do not necessarily represent the opinions of the College Board or Educational Testing Service.)

In past days Captain Bailey had handled many thousands of pounds of his employers' money and of his own; he had attended faithfully, as by law a shipmaster is expected to do, to the conflicting interests of owners, charterers, and underwriters. He had never lost a ship or consented to a shady transaction. He had buried his wife, had married off his daughter to a man of her unlucky choice, and had lost much in the crash of the notorious Travanacore and Deccan Banking Corporation, whose downfall had shaken the East like an earthquake. And he was sixty-seven years old.

His age sat lightly on him, and of his ruin he was not ashamed. He had not been alone in believing in the stability of the Banking Corporation. Men whose judgment in matters of finance was as expert as his seamanship had commended the prudence of his investments, and had themselves lost much money in the great failure. The only difference between him and them was that he had lost his all and yet not his all. There remained to him from his lost fortune a very pretty little barque, Fair Maid, which he had bought to occupy his leisure as a retired sailor.

He had formally declared himself tired of the sea the year preceding his daughter's marriage. But after the young couple had gone to settle in Melbourne, he found that he could not make himself happy on shore. He was too much of a merchant sea-captain for mere yachting to satisfy him. He wanted the illusion of affairs, and his acquisition of Fair Maid preserved continuity in his life. He introduced her to his acquaintances in various ports as "my last command." When he grew too old to be trusted with a ship, he would lay her up and go ashore and be buried, leaving directions in his will to have the barque towed out and scuttled on the day of the funeral. His daughter would not begrudge him the satisfaction of knowing that no stranger would handle his last command after him. All this would be said with a jocular twinkle in his eye: the vigorous old man had too much vitality for the sentimentalism of regret; and yet a little wistfully because he was at home in life, taking genuine pleasure in its feelings and possessions, in the dignity of his reputation, in his love for his daughter, and in his satisfaction with the ship—the plaything of his lonely leisure.

26. The passage primarily concerns

(A) Captain Bailey's memories of his career at sea
(B) the events that contributed to Captain Bailey's success as a shipmaster
(C) Captain Bailey's actions and attitudes after retirement
(D) the conditions that caused the loss of Captain Bailey's fortune
(E) the experiences shared by Captain Bailey and Fair Maid

27. The expression "his ruin" (line 13) refers to Captain Bailey's

(A) physical condition
(B) discredited reputation
(C) loss of his fortune
(D) isolation from his former friends
(E) departure from his job as shipmaster

28. It can be inferred that Captain Bailey's employers believed that, as a shipmaster, he was

(A) loyal but unambitious
(B) competent and ethical
(C) talented but undependable
(D) eccentric and unpopular
(E) restless and erratic

29. Captain Bailey wished to have Fair Maid sunk on the day of his funeral because he

(A) knew that no one else could handle the boat
(B) resented the boat's seductive power over him
(C) realized that maintaining the boat would be a burden for his daughter
(D) did not want the boat to be under any command but his own
(E) feared that the boat would fall into the hands of his creditors

30. Captain Bailey regarded Fair Maid with

(A) weary resignation
(B) casual indifference
(C) sentimental regret
(D) awe-struck fascination
(E) affectionate delight

GO ON TO THE NEXT PAGE

Any survey of medieval town life delights in the color of guild organizations: the broiders and glovers, the shipwrights and upholsters, each with its guild hall, its distinctive livery, and its elaborate set of rules. But if life in the guilds and at the fairs provides a sharp contrast with the stodgy life on the manor, we must not be misled by surface resemblances into thinking that guild life represented a foretaste of modern life in medieval dress. It is a long distance from guilds to modern business firms, and it is well to fix in mind some of the differences.

In the first place, the guild was much more than just an institution for organizing production. Whereas most of its regulations concerned wages and conditions of work and specifications of output, they also dwelt at length on noneconomic matters: on a member's civic role, on his appropriate dress, and even on his daily deportment. Guilds were the regulators not only of production but of social conduct.

Between guilds and modern business firms there is a profound gulf. Unlike modern firms, the purpose of guilds was not first and foremost to make money. Rather, it was to preserve a certain orderly way of life—a way which envisaged a decent income for the master craftsmen but which was certainly not intended to allow any of them to become "big" businessmen. On the contrary, guilds were specifically designed to ward off any such outcome of an uninhibited struggle among their members. The terms of service and wages were fixed by custom. So, too, were the terms of sale: a guild member who cornered the supply of an item or bought wholesale to sell at retail was severely punished. Competition was strictly limited and profits were held to prescribed levels. Advertising was forbidden, and even technical progress in advance of one's fellow guildsmen was considered disloyal.

Surely the guilds represent a more "modern" aspect of feudal life than the manor, but the whole temper of guild life was still far removed from the goals and ideals of modern business enterprise. There was no free competition and no restless probing for advantage. Existing on the margin of a relatively moneyless society, the guilds were organizations that sought to take the risks out of their slender enterprises. As such, they were as drenched in the medieval atmosphere as the manors.

31. The author is primarily concerned with

(A) analyzing the origins of the guild system
(B) explaining the relationships between manors, fairs, and modern business firms
(C) depicting the weaknesses of the guilds' business practices
(D) stressing the historical evolution of guilds to modern business firms
(E) discussing some differences between medieval and modern business practices

32. According to the passage, which of the following would LEAST likely be found in a guild handbook?

(A) The fees a master guildsman should charge
(B) The bonus a member would receive for record sales
(C) The maximum number of hours a guildsman would be expected to work
(D) The steps a new shipwright would follow to become a master craftsman
(E) The organizations to which a member should contribute as an upstanding citizen

33. According to the passage, modern business enterprises, compared to the medieval guilds, are

(A) more concerned with increasing profits
(B) influenced more by craftsmen than by tradesmen
(C) more subordinate to the demands of consumers
(D) less progressive in financial dealings
(E) less interested in quantity than quality

34. It can be inferred that the guilds were organized as they were because

(A) life on the manors was boring and drab
(B) technical improvements were still improbable
(C) they stressed preservation and stability, not progress
(D) people in medieval times were interested in advancing individual liberty
(E) social status was determined by income

35. With which of the following statements concerning modern business firms would the author be most likely to agree?

(A) They make rules concerning appropriate business practices for employees.
(B) They permit the free play of price in terms of service and sales.
(C) Their main concern is the stability of profit levels.
(D) Their aim is to discourage competition among independent manufacturers.
(E) They are organized in such a way that co-operating monopolies will develop.

GO ON TO THE NEXT PAGE

All migrating birds must guide their flight by means of some aspect of their environment which is related in a reasonably reliable fashion to the direction of the goal. We must also take as certain, unless we are to fall back on extrascientific theories, that this environmental cue must be perceived by the birds; it must stimulate some sense organ or receptor cells, for these are the only functional contacts between a bird's nervous system and its outside environment. Our problem, then, is to find the environmental cue, and also to find the sensory mechanism by which this cue is recognized and channeled into the central nervous system, where it can result in the appropriate actions to move the bird in the right direction.

Some investigators have tried to account for bird navigation in terms of the known sensory mechanisms, which are the same in all higher vertebrates. For example, some have suggested that migrants are guided by visual landmarks. But the overwater routes such as those of the golden plover are devoid of topography for hundreds of miles. Others feel that wind direction may offer a guiding cue, but winds are notoriously changeable. Only if the bird knew the wind direction characteristic of each type of air mass and weather condition along its route could it guide itself from the arctic to the tropics.

On the other side, we find a variety of ingenious theories hung up on formidable objections from the point of view of the sensory physiologist. Best known, perhaps, are a number of theories based on the idea that birds have the equivalent of a magnetic compass— that they can perceive the earth's magnetic field in some manner and guide their migrations accordingly. Those who subscribe to these theories must face the fact, however, that no one has been able to show that birds can sense a magnetic field as weak as the earth's, any more than we ourselves can.

A really new theory was advanced recently, namely that birds orient themselves by means of mechanical forces arising from the earth's rotation. One of the forms such forces may take is an increase in the apparent weight of a flying bird depending on the direction of its flight. This effect is of a type which might be within the range of a bird's sense organs, since it involves mechanical acceleration for which the bird has specialized receptors in the inner ear labyrinth. But the difficulties in the way of the bird's being able to make the necessary quantitative distinctions are enormous. The variation in weight is only one part in several thousand, and it could easily be masked by the much larger accelerations resulting from the flight itself, to say nothing of the slightest turbulence of the air, or even the bird's own breathing and heartbeat. Thus this hypothesis seems scarcely more plausible than the magnetic theories.

36. Which of the following best describes the passage?

(A) A comprehensive account of each of the theories that has been developed to explain bird navigation
(B) A description of a theory of bird navigation followed by specific supporting evidence
(C) An account of the different methods of navigation used by different varieties of birds
(D) A statement of the general problem of explaining bird navigation followed by examples of attempted solutions
(E) An account of the findings of research in bird navigation conducted by the author

37. Which of the following is an assumption made by the author?

(A) Most migrating birds navigate in the same manner.
(B) The sensory mechanism used by birds in navigation is common to all higher vertebrates.
(C) Migrating birds can fly in the correct direction without aid from environmental clues.
(D) Birds have more highly developed sense organs than most other animals.
(E) Birds have no specific goal in mind when they begin a migration.

38. Which of the following best states the author's opinion of the theories discussed in the last two paragraphs?

(A) The theories are not themselves complete explanations of bird navigation, but they are steps in the right direction.
(B) The theories are essentially extrascientific and not worthy of the attention of serious scientists.
(C) The theories are very clever and interesting, but they are probably untrue.
(D) The theories are untrue, since they are contradicted by the known facts of bird physiology.
(E) The theories are probably true, but they do not really explain bird navigation.

39. The author's objection to the theory that birds navigate by means of forces arising from the earth's rotation is based primarily on the fact that

(A) the environmental cue is weak relative to other forces that affect the bird in a similar manner
(B) the receptors through which the bird perceives mechanical acceleration are not sufficiently sensitive
(C) a bird is not heavy enough to be affected by the earth's rotation
(D) the effects of the earth's rotation on a bird are not related to direction of flight
(E) birds are not intelligent enough to determine their direction relative to the earth's rotation

40. The author's objection to the "magnetic" theory of bird navigation is based on which of the following?

I. The environmental cue is not related reliably to the direction of the goal.
II. There is no known sensory mechanism by which the environmental cue can be perceived.
III. The weak effects of the earth's magnetic field are masked by other forces acting on the bird.

(A) I only
(B) II only
(C) III only
(D) I and II only
(E) II and III only

S T O P

IF YOU FINISH BEFORE TIME IS CALLED, CHECK YOUR WORK ON THIS SECTION ONLY.
DO NOT WORK ON ANY OTHER SECTION IN THE TEST.

SECTION 2

Time—30 minutes

35 QUESTIONS

In this section solve each problem, using any available space on the page for scratchwork. Then indicate the one correct answer in the appropriate space on the answer sheet.

The following information is for your reference in solving some of the problems.

Circle of radius r: Area = πr^2; Circumference = $2\pi r$
The number of degrees of arc in a circle is 360.
The measure in degrees of a straight angle is 180.

Definitions of symbols:

= is equal to	≦ is less than or equal to
≠ is unequal to	≧ is greater than or equal to
< is less than	∥ is parallel to
> is greater than	⊥ is perpendicular to

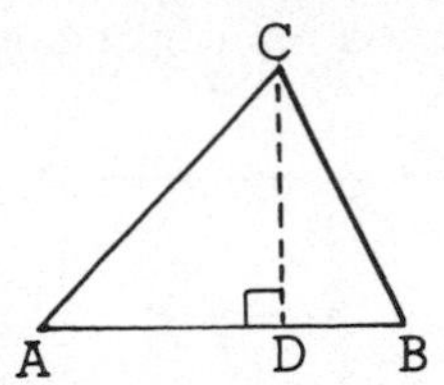

Triangle: The sum of the measures in degrees of the angles of a triangle is 180

If ∠CDA is a right angle, then

(1) area of $\triangle ABC = \frac{AB \times CD}{2}$

(2) $AC^2 = AD^2 + DC^2$

Note: Figures which accompany problems in this test are intended to provide information useful in solving the problems. They are drawn as accurately as possible EXCEPT when it is stated in a specific problem that its figure is not drawn to scale. All figures lie in a plane unless otherwise indicated. All numbers used are real numbers.

---

1. $\frac{1}{2} + \frac{2}{3} + \frac{3}{4} =$

(A) $\frac{1}{4}$ (B) $\frac{3}{5}$ (C) $\frac{10}{7}$ (D) $\frac{17}{10}$ (E) $\frac{23}{12}$

2. If $N \div 6 = K$, which of the following statements must be true?

(A) $K \div 6 = N$

(B) $6 \div K = N$

(C) $6 \times N = K$

(D) $6 \times K = N$

(E) $N \times K = 6$

3. If $\frac{2}{3}$ the perimeter of an equilateral triangle is 6, what is its perimeter?

(A) 4 (B) 8 (C) 9 (D) 12 (E) 18

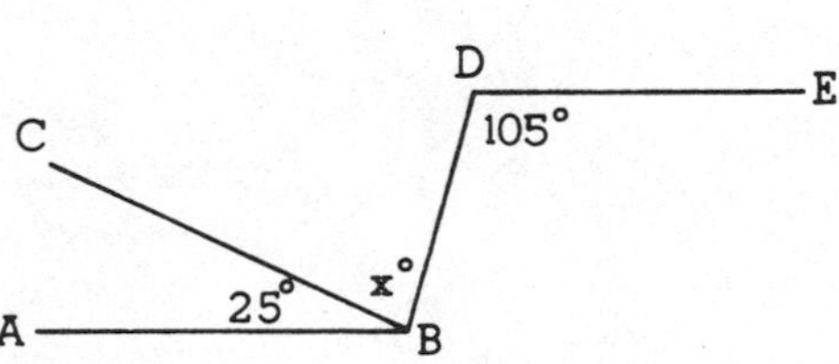

4. In the figure above, if AB is parallel to DE, then x =

(A) 105 (B) 90 (C) 80 (D) 75 (E) 65

5. If the sum of t − 1, t − 2, t − 3 is 0, then t =

(A) −2 (B) −1 (C) 0 (D) 1 (E) 2

6. In 1969 a seaport handled 120,000 tons of cargo. If it handled 180,000 tons in 1973, the average annual increase in tons handled was

(A) 12,000
(B) 15,000
(C) 18,000
(D) 20,000
(E) 45,000

7. If p, q, r, s, and t are different numbers and each is equal to one of the numbers 1, 2, 4, 8, and 16 and if $4p = \frac{1}{2}q = 8r = s = 2t$, then q =

(A) 1
(B) 2
(C) 4
(D) 8
(E) 16

GO ON TO THE NEXT PAGE

2

Questions 8-27 each consist of two quantities, one in Column A and one in Column B. You are to compare the two quantities and on the answer sheet blacken space

- A if the quantity in Column A is greater;
- B if the quantity in Column B is greater;
- C if the two quantities are equal;
- D if the relationship cannot be determined from the information given.

Notes: 1. In certain questions, information concerning one or both of the quantities to be compared is centered above the two columns.
2. A symbol that appears in both columns represents the same thing in Column A as it does in Column B.
3. Letters such as x, n, and k stand for real numbers.

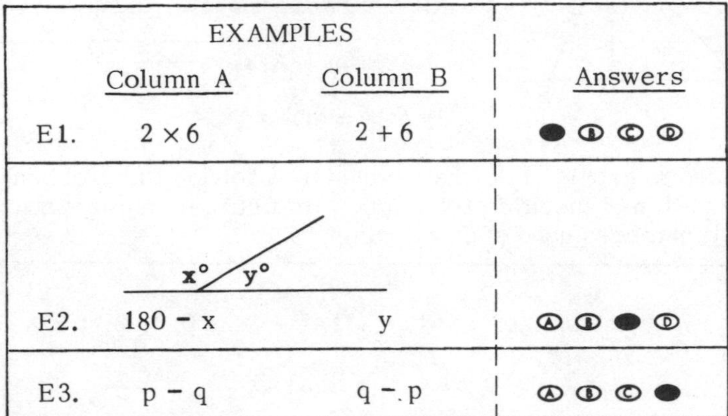

EXAMPLES

	Column A	Column B	Answers
E1.	2×6	$2 + 6$	● Ⓑ Ⓒ Ⓓ
E2.	$180 - x$	y	Ⓐ Ⓑ ● Ⓓ
E3.	$p - q$	$q - p$	Ⓐ Ⓑ Ⓒ ●

	Column A	Column B
8.	$e(f + e)$	$(e + f)e$

Three years ago, Gina was 2 centimeters taller than Tina.

9.	Tina's height today	Gina's height today

25% of $x = 60$

10.	50% of x	120
11.	The average (arithmetic mean) of x and y	x
12.	The number of odd integers greater than 2 and less than 10	The number of prime integers greater than 2 and less than 10

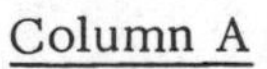

	Column A	Column B
13.	Sum of any two negative numbers	Sum of any two positive numbers

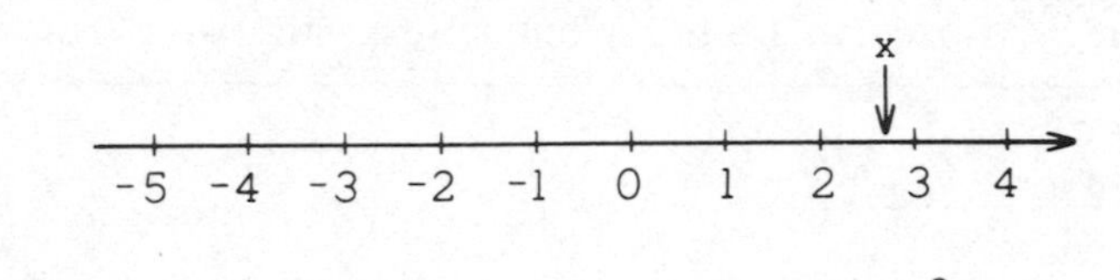

14.	$2 - x$	0
15.	The greatest integer x such that $x^2 < 65$	The greatest integer y such that $y^3 < 65$

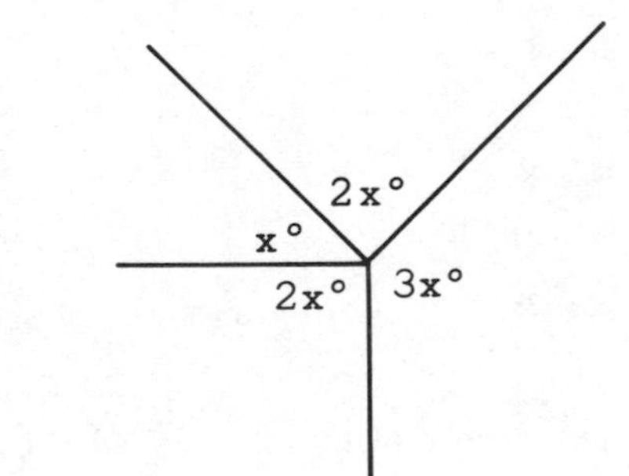

16.	x	45

$$\begin{cases} x + 2y = 10 \\ 2x - 2y = 5 \end{cases}$$

17.	x	y

GO ON TO THE NEXT PAGE

SUMMARY DIRECTIONS FOR COMPARISON QUESTIONS

Answer: A if the quantity in Column A is greater;
B if the quantity in Column B is greater;
C if the two quantities are equal;
D if the relationship cannot be determined from the information given.

	Column A	Column B

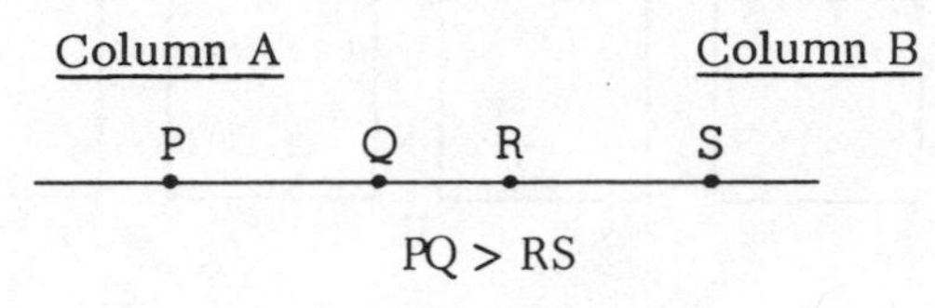

PQ > RS

18. PR — QS

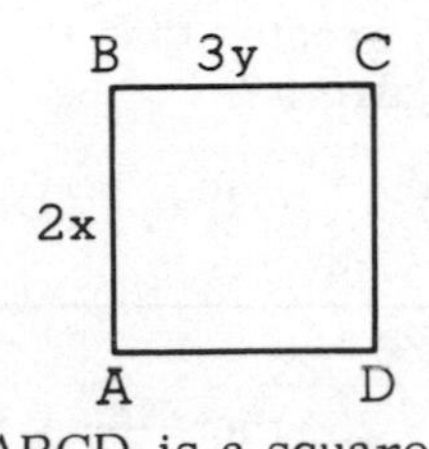

ABCD is a square.

19. $4x^2$ — $9y^2$

$s \neq 0$

20. $\frac{r}{s}$ — rs

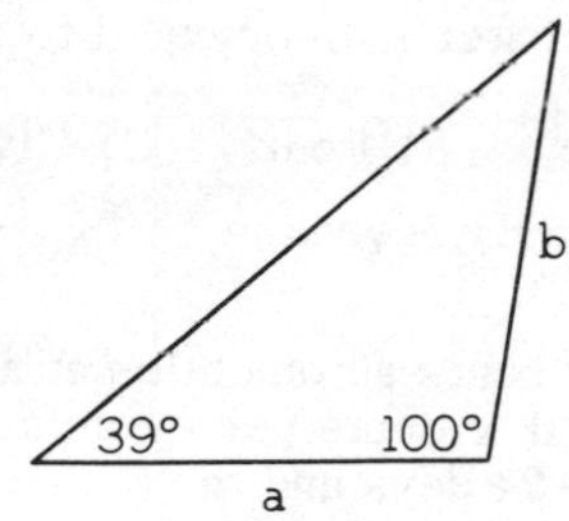

21. a — b

$2x < 4$
$3y < 9$

22. x — y

Let n* be defined by the equation $n^* = (n-1)(n)(n+1)$ where n is an integer.

23. $\frac{6^*}{3^*}$ — 2^*

	Column A	Column B

24. The square of $\frac{13}{19}$ — The square root of $\frac{13}{19}$

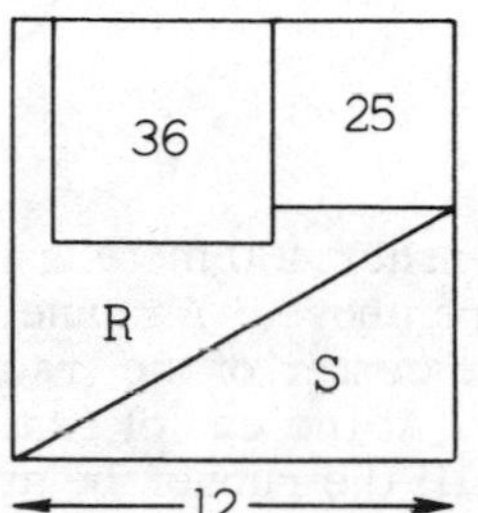

The square with side 12 above is divided into squares with areas 36 and 25 and two nonoverlapping regions with areas R and S.

25. R — S

$\frac{1}{2}, \frac{2}{3}, \frac{3}{5}, \frac{5}{8}, \frac{8}{13}$

26. The greatest fraction shown — The product of the least fraction shown and $\frac{4}{3}$

$x - y = 5$

27. $\frac{1}{x} - \frac{1}{y}$ — $\frac{1}{5}$

GO ON TO THE NEXT PAGE

2

Solve each of the remaining problems in this section using any available space for scratchwork. Then indicate the one correct answer in the appropriate space on the answer sheet.

28. If $\frac{k}{2}$ is an even number and $\frac{k}{4}$ is an odd number, then k could equal

(A) 24 (B) 20 (C) 16 (D) 10 (E) 8

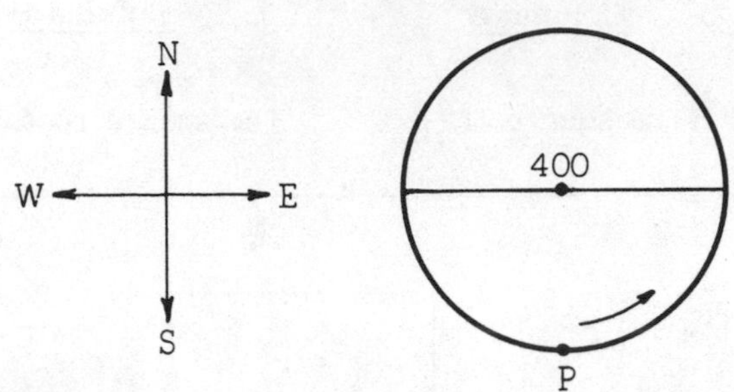

29. A circular track 400 meters in diameter is shown in the figure above. A runner starts at P, directly south of the center of the track, and runs counter-clockwise. At the end of exactly how many meters of travel will the runner be at the point where he is traveling directly north?

(A) 25π (B) 100π (C) 400π
(D) 800π (E) $1,000\pi$

30. If x ranges in value from 0.0001 to 0.01 and y ranges in value from 0.001 to 0.1, what is the maximum value of $\frac{x}{y}$?

(A) 0.001 (B) 0.1 (C) 1
(D) 10 (E) 1,000

31. Jane owes Bill \$20, Bill owes George \$30, and George owes Jane \$40. All of these debts may be settled if

(A) Bill and George each pay Jane \$10
(B) Bill pays George \$10 and George pays Jane \$10
(C) George pays Jane and Bill \$10 each
(D) George pays Jane \$20
(E) Jane pays George \$20

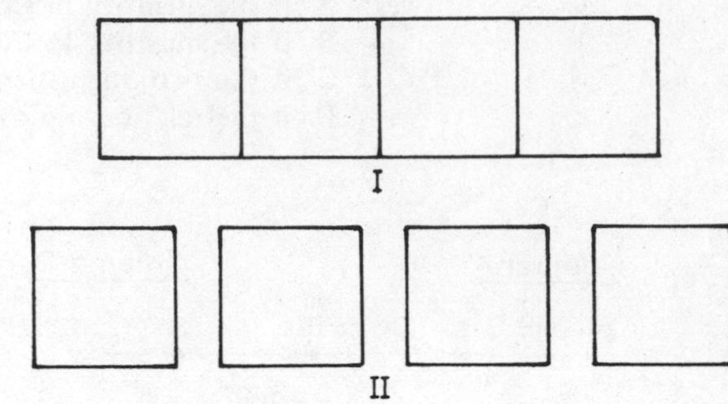

32. All of the squares above are equal in area; the total area of the four squares in each figure is 36. The total length of the line segments that form figure II is how much greater than the total length of those that form figure I ?

(A) 0 (B) 3 (C) 6 (D) 9 (E) 12

33. If $\left(x + \frac{1}{x}\right)^2 = 25$, then $\frac{1}{x^2} + x^2 =$

(A) 23
(B) 24
(C) 25
(D) 27
(E) 624

34. What is the maximum number of points that can be located within or on the sides of a square of side 2 if the distance between any two of the points is to be greater than or equal to $\sqrt{2}$?

(A) Three (B) Four (C) Five
(D) Six (E) Seven

35. An agency rents automobiles at a rate of d dollars per day and x cents per kilometer. If a car was rented for 24 days and the odometer showed an addition of 1800 kilometers traveled, then the amount, in dollars, due the agency was

(A) $\frac{24(d + 75x)}{100}$ (B) $\frac{6(3d + 400x)}{100}$ (C) $24(d + 75x$

(D) $6(3d + 4x)$ (E) $6(4d + 3x)$

S T O P

IF YOU FINISH BEFORE TIME IS CALLED, CHECK YOUR WORK ON THIS SECTION ONLY. DO NOT WORK ON ANY OTHER SECTION IN THE TEST.

SECTION 4 **4**

Time—30 minutes

45 QUESTIONS

For each question in this section, choose the best answer and blacken the corresponding space on the answer sheet.

Each question below consists of a word in capital letters, followed by five lettered words or phrases. Choose the word or phrase that is most nearly opposite in meaning to the word in capital letters. Since some of the questions require you to distinguish fine shades of meaning, consider all the choices before deciding which is best.

Example:

GOOD: (A) sour (B) bad (C) red (D) hot (E) ugly

Ⓐ ● Ⓒ Ⓓ Ⓔ

1. DISTRIBUTE: (A) unveil (B) repay (C) collect (D) burden (E) refute

2. GRATIFYING: (A) inexpensive (B) unsatisfying (C) stultifying (D) unappetizing (E) pessimistic

3. HIDEOUS: (A) timid (B) genuine (C) fragile (D) obvious (E) lovely

4. FLOWER: (A) wither (B) envelop (C) soften (D) simplify (E) challenge

5. BOISTEROUS: (A) courageous (B) skillful (C) tolerant (D) serene (E) supernatural

6. GOUGE: (A) hold up (B) fill in (C) eat slowly (D) disengage (E) mount

7. HILARITY: (A) rivalry (B) obscurity (C) cleverness (D) viciousness (E) downheartedness

8. CORRUGATED: (A) distended (B) refined (C) uninsulated (D) smooth (E) honest

9. CIRCUITOUS: (A) involuntary (B) straightforward (C) lily-livered (D) dog-eared (E) homely

10. COALESCE: (A) disrupt (B) disprove (C) disperse (D) disown (E) dislike

11. LEVITY: (A) seriousness (B) indifference (C) purity (D) uniformity (E) incoherence

12. COGNIZANT: (A) practical (B) ignorant (C) hostile (D) unattractive (E) silent

13. DEARTH: (A) power (B) liveliness (C) serious attempt (D) adequate supply (E) persuasive personality

14. UNWITTING: (A) intelligent (B) conscious (C) disappointing (D) overly curious (E) in plain sight

15. ASSUAGE: (A) intensify (B) promote (C) trust (D) mislead (E) isolate

Each sentence below has one or two blanks, each blank indicating that something has been omitted. Beneath the sentence are five lettered words or sets of words. Choose the word or set of words that best fits the meaning of the sentence as a whole.

Example:

Although its publicity has been ----, the film itself is intelligent, well-acted, handsomely produced, and altogether ----.

(A) tasteless..respectable (B) extensive..moderate (C) sophisticated..amateur (D) risqué..crude (E) perfect..spectacular

● Ⓑ Ⓒ Ⓓ Ⓔ

16. No longer is it enough to ---- our present resources; somehow we must find ways to replace what we have lost.

(A) squander (B) conserve (C) belittle (D) eliminate (E) utilize

17. Stability in a culture does not mean inertia; even the most ---- culture is marked by constant ----.

(A) mobile..inflexibility
(B) materialistic..uncertainty
(C) progressive..failure
(D) advanced..variety
(E) conservative..change

18. Williams rather likes the present tenure policy and would be distressed if it were ----.

(A) emulated (B) tolerated (C) nurtured (D) extolled (E) superseded

19. Crawford is unnecessarily ---- in assessing the views of others; he often describes the conclusions of respected scholars as "not worthy of being refuted."

(A) contrite (B) verbose (C) disparaging (D) diligent (E) hesitant

20. You have only to study the intricate thoughts of the great philosophers to see that it is possible to express with ---- the most ---- reflections.

(A) incisiveness..clear-cut
(B) refinement..pleasant
(C) unanimity..disagreeable
(D) emotion..banal
(E) lucidity..subtle

GO ON TO THE NEXT PAGE

Each passage below is followed by questions based on its content. Answer all questions following a passage on the basis of what is stated or implied in that passage.

(The passages for this test have been adapted from published material. The ideas contained in them do not necessarily represent the opinions of the College Board or Educational Testing Service.)

William H. Johnson's best paintings, which express great warmth and humanity, represent a significant contribution by a black American to modern art. Johnson has been described, though somewhat inadequately, as an American primitive painter. Unlike the true primitive, Johnson deliberately chose a naïve approach; his relationship to naïve art is similar to the relationship of some expressionists to African sculpture. He borrows the forms in order to express new ideas.

Johnson spent his early years in Scandinavia painting impressionistic landscapes, which are technically competent but of little artistic interest. However, it is in his later religious art, using primitive techniques, that William H. Johnson finds his true expression. His pictures from the life of Christ embody the simplicity and sincerity of the Negro spiritual and are extremely moving. The secular pictures of this primitive period, however, usually fail to achieve any emotional depth. His "Two Sisters," for example, is a decorative, attractive picture, but the artist does not transcend the primitive medium he has deliberately chosen. Again, in the "Funeral," the self-conscious primitivism is obvious and awkward. The facial expressions are empty; the large gestures are melodramatic and somewhat posterlike.

In his series of works from the life of Christ, Johnson develops a far greater sensitivity. How infinitely delicate is his drawing of the baby Christ in his "Nativity"; how movingly sincere and pious the simple gestures of the parents. Here the naïve approach is used to good purpose. A more sophisticated approach to perspective, anatomy, texture, light and shade, etc., would have detracted from the pure, simple emotion the artist wants to portray.

Johnson's treatment of hands is extremely expressive. They are usually very large, and sometimes, as in Christ's hands in "Let Little Children Come unto Me," their ecstatic gestures dominate the entire composition. In the "Entombment," his treatment of feet is equally expressive. The feet here not only produce the gentle rhythm and movement of the picture but also express sorrow. Johnson uses his particular forms of distortion and simplification to express simplicity and sincerity, and he also achieves a feeling of great intimacy.

Occasionally he produces works of unusual intensity. His "Crucifixion I" is a picture of great power. In its heightened expression of pain, particularly in the contorted pain of Mary, the picture is reminiscent of Grünewald's famous Isenheim altar.

21. It can be inferred that Johnson's early impressionistic work was

(A) artistically undistinguished
(B) stylistically innovative
(C) emotionally sensitive
(D) generally underrated
(E) belatedly popular

22. The author is mainly concerned with Johnson's

(A) life story (B) artistic style
(C) reasons for painting (D) religious beliefs
(E) technical training

23. According to the passage, Johnson's treatment of feet expressed sorrow in which of the following works?

(A) "Funeral"
(B) "Nativity"
(C) "Let Little Children Come unto Me"
(D) "Entombment"
(E) "Crucifixion I"

24. The author describes the gestures depicted in which of the following paintings as "posterlike" (line 27) ?

(A) "Two Sisters" (B) "Funeral" (C) "Nativity"
(D) "Entombment" (E) "Crucifixion I"

25. It can be inferred that the author finds the description of Johnson as an American primitive to be somewhat inadequate because Johnson has

(A) produced abstract paintings, whereas American primitive art is generally representational
(B) built his reputation as an impressionistic painter
(C) used primitive techniques only in his very early works
(D) produced profane pictures, whereas American primitive painting is entirely religious
(E) expressed new ideas by means of the primitive artistic approach

GO ON TO THE NEXT PAGE

The people of the United States have the undoubted right to change their form of government and to renounce established customs or longstanding policies whenever in their wisdom they see fit to do so. As a believer in democratic government, I readily acknowledge the right of the people to make in an orderly fashion such changes as may be approved in their judgment at any time. I contend, moreover, that when radical and important departures from established national policies are proposed, the people ought to be consulted.

There has been proposed what to my mind is the most radical departure from our policies that has ever been proposed at any time since our government was established. I think even the advocates of this program agree with me that it is a pronounced departure from all the policies we have heretofore obtained. It may be wise, as they contend; nevertheless, it involves a different course of conduct on the part of the government and of our people for the future, and the people are entitled to pass judgment on the advisability of such a course.

Certainly questions of this kind ought to be submitted to a plebiscite, a vote of the people. We are merely agents of the people, and it will not be contended that we have received any authority from the principal, the people, to proceed along this line. It is a greater responsibility than an agent ought to assume without express authority or approval from his principal. Preliminary to a discussion of this question, therefore, I want to declare my belief that we should arrange the machinery for taking a vote of the people of the United States upon this stupendous program. I am aware that the processes by which that may be accomplished involve some difficulties; but they are not insurmountable, and they are by no means to be compared in their difficulty with the importance of being right and in harmony with the judgment of the people before we proceed to the final approval. We should have the specific endorsement of those whose agents we are for the fearful responsibility we propose to assume. If we can effectuate this change now proposed without direct authority from the people, I cannot think of a question of sufficient moment to call for their endorsement.

26. The author's primary purpose is apparently to

(A) persuade citizens to make full use of their voting privileges
(B) suggest needed changes in the manner of voting for government officials
(C) deter legislators from making unnecessary changes in national policies
(D) convince the public that a proposed program is detrimental to the nation
(E) urge that the public be consulted before radical changes in national policy are made

27. The author implies that those who believe that the proposed program involves substantial changes in national policy include

(A) only the conservative legislators
(B) only the opponents of the program
(C) only the advocates of the program
(D) both the opponents and the advocates of the program
(E) both the legislators and the populace

28. It can be inferred that the author's concern with the proposed program is that of

(A) an irate citizen
(B) an uninformed commentator
(C) a wary opponent
(D) an approving legislator
(E) a bitter and critical historian

29. Which of the following best describes the author's attitude in the last sentence of the passage?

(A) Enthusiastic optimism
(B) Sympathetic encouragement
(C) Momentary doubt
(D) Solemn apprehension
(E) Flippant sarcasm

30. According to the author, the effort of taking a nation-wide vote on the proposed program would be

(A) meaningless and unsuccessful
(B) necessary and uncomplicated
(C) advisable but impossible
(D) arduous but worthwhile
(E) unwieldy and futile

GO ON TO THE NEXT PAGE

4

Select the word or set of words that best completes each of the following sentences.

31. This probing and startling analysis challenges us to ---- our ---- attitudes and look at the world in a totally new way.

(A) defend..immutable
(B) discard..preconceived
(C) shelve..novel
(D) affirm..conventional
(E) waive..innovative

32. Many people believe that malnutrition and its ill effects occur only in developing countries, but the fact is that our own population is far from ----.

(A) healthy (B) informed (C) nutritious
(D) susceptible (E) impoverished

33. The admiral's tolerance of ---- among the officers was ---- by his desire for loyalty from all.

(A) flattery..offset
(B) dissent..tempered
(C) compliance..undermined
(D) defiance..intensified
(E) discipline..corrupted

34. Hinckle tried to explain the differences between those controversies that demand an absolutist, moralistic approach and those that call for a pragmatic, ---- solution.

(A) conciliatory (B) permanent (C) immoderate
(D) categorical (E) inexpedient

35. Generally ---- the opportunity to join the gentry and live the aristocratic life, the British scientists of this period brought to their laboratories a devotion to their calling akin in its intensity to ---- asceticism.

(A) pursuing..medieval
(B) exploiting..orthodox
(C) eschewing..monastic
(D) coveting..intellectual
(E) flaunting..hypocritical

Each question below consists of a related pair of words or phrases, followed by five lettered pairs of words or phrases. Select the lettered pair that best expresses a relationship similar to that expressed in the original pair.

Example:

YAWN : BOREDOM :: (A) dream : sleep
(B) anger : madness (C) smile : amusement
(D) face : expression (E) impatience : rebellion

36. INTERMISSION : PERFORMANCE ::
(A) break : work (B) backlog : shipping
(C) solo : melody (D) union : strike
(E) skirmish : fighting

37. SNIP : SCISSORS :: (A) chop : ax
(B) darn : socks (C) flow : river
(D) pedal : bicycle (E) puff : pipe

38. TITTER : LAUGHTER :: (A) patter : stumbling
(B) paddle : canoeing (C) flipper : swimming
(D) ladder : height (E) whisper : speech

39. QUARREL : DEBATE :: (A) marathon : victory
(B) invasion : compromise (C) brawl : duel
(D) riot : defeat (E) permit : license

40. POACHER : GAME :: (A) sentry : fort
(B) archer : quiver (C) fugitive : clue
(D) swindler : truth (E) pickpocket : wallet

41. UNIQUE : DUPLICATE :: (A) substantial : base
(B) resonant : tone (C) abstract : merit
(D) eternal : end (E) poetic : rhythm

42. LEAN : EMACIATED :: (A) weary : exhausted
(B) large : expanded (C) ill : cured
(D) swollen : shrunken (E) narrow : enclosed

43. PREEMINENT : WORTH :: (A) eccentric : popularity
(B) insolvent : funds (C) complacent : efficiency
(D) optimistic : wealth (E) noble : character

44. TACITURN : CHATTER ::
(A) clever : think
(B) ascetic : indulge
(C) benevolent : donate
(D) authoritative : administer
(E) inquisitive : inquire

45. FLUSTERED : COMPOSURE ::
(A) lukewarm : enthusiasm (B) jealous : elegance
(C) sluggish : endurance (D) boring : patience
(E) aggressive : activity

S T O P

IF YOU FINISH BEFORE TIME IS CALLED, CHECK YOUR WORK ON THIS SECTION ONLY.
DO NOT WORK ON ANY OTHER SECTION IN THE TEST.

5

SECTION 5

Time—30 minutes

25 QUESTIONS

In this section solve each problem, using any available space on the page for scratchwork. Then indicate the one correct answer in the appropriate space on the answer sheet.

The following information is for your reference in solving some of the problems.

Circle of radius r: Area = πr^2; Circumference = $2\pi r$
The number of degrees of arc in a circle is 360.
The measure in degrees of a straight angle is 180.

Definitions of symbols:

=	is equal to	≦	is less than or equal to
≠	is unequal to	≧	is greater than or equal to
<	is less than	∥	is parallel to
>	is greater than	⊥	is perpendicular to

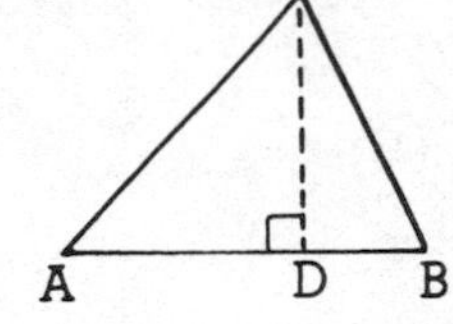

Triangle: The sum of the measures in degrees of the angles of a triangle is 180

If ∠CDA is a right angle, then

(1) area of $\triangle ABC = \frac{AB \times CD}{2}$

(2) $AC^2 = AD^2 + DC^2$

Note: Figures which accompany problems in this test are intended to provide information useful in solving the problems. They are drawn as accurately as possible EXCEPT when it is stated in a specific problem that its figure is not drawn to scale. All figures lie in a plane unless otherwise indicated. All numbers used are real numbers.

---

1. If $11 + xy = 12 + 11$, then the pair x, y could be any of the following EXCEPT

(A) 12, 1
(B) 6, 6
(C) 4, 3
(D) 3, 4
(E) 2, 6

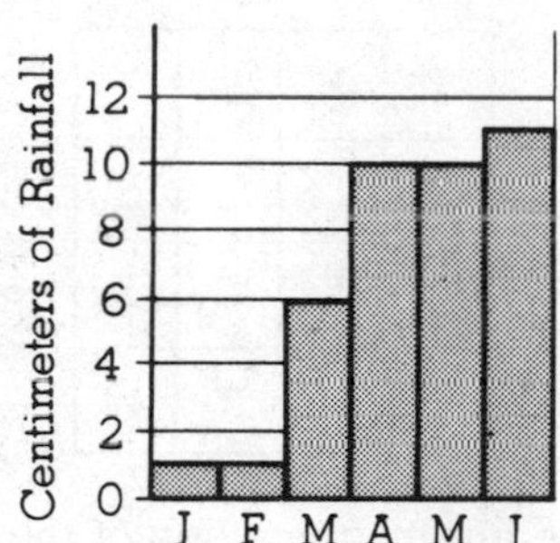

2. The graph above shows the monthly rainfall for a six-month period in a region of Ghana. What was the total rainfall in centimeters for this period?

(A) 28
(B) 29
(C) 38
(D) 39
(E) 40

3. A woman sailed 1 kilometer east and then 1 kilometer south. In what direction would she have to go to return directly to her starting point?

(A) North (B) Northeast (C) Northwest
(D) Southeast (E) Southwest

4. If the measure of one acute angle of a right triangle is 35°, then the measure of the other acute angle is

(A) 35° (B) 55° (C) 65° (D) 90° (E) 145°

5. The formula for the power P of an electric appliance is P = EI where E is the number of volts and I the number of amperes of current. What is I when P = 1,620 and E = 120 ?

(A) 13.5
(B) 19.4
(C) 135
(D) 19,440
(E) 194,400

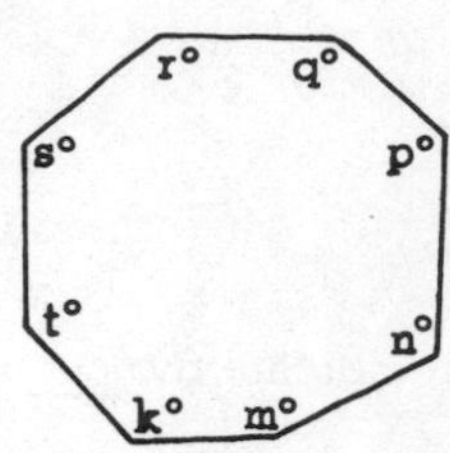

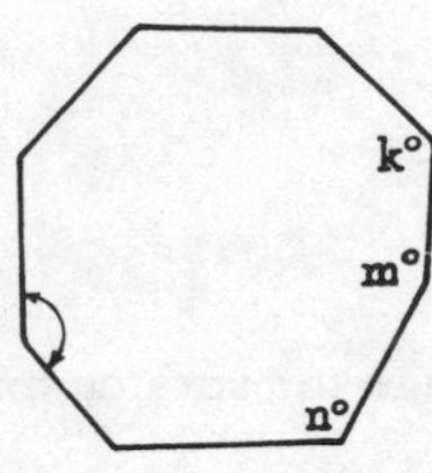

6. If the octagon on the left above is turned over and placed in the position indicated by the angle measures in the octagon on the right, what is the measure of the marked angle?

(A) p° (B) t° (C) q° (D) s° (E) r°

7. The following are the dimensions of five boxes. All have equal volume EXCEPT the one that is

(A) 8 by 3 by 5
(B) 2 by 12 by 5
(C) 2 by 3 by 20
(D) 4 by 6 by 5
(E) 3 by 4 by 14

8. Which of the following conditions will make $x - y$ a positive number?

(A) $0 < y$
(B) $y < x$
(C) $x < 0$
(D) $x < y$
(E) $x = y$

9. What is half of the perimeter of a square of area 36 ?

(A) 3 (B) 6 (C) 12 (D) 18 (E) 24

10. If $x(3y) = (5)(3)$, then $xy - 1 =$

(A) 4 (B) 5 (C) 14 (D) 15 (E) 39

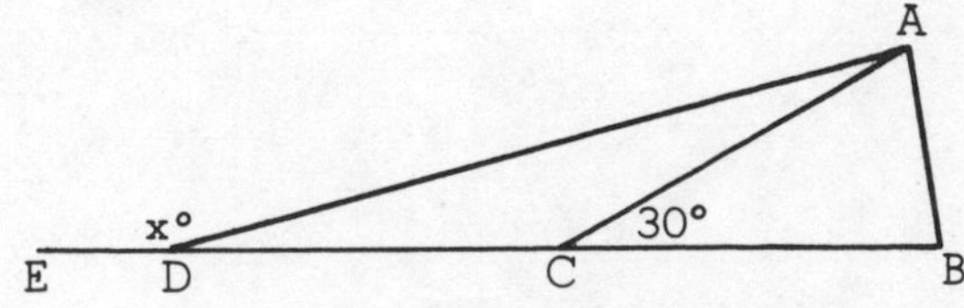

11. In the figure above, if AC = CD, then x =

(A) 105
(B) 120
(C) 135
(D) 150
(E) 165

12. If $abe = 0$, $bcd = 1$, and $bce = 0$, which of the following must equal 0 ?

(A) a (B) b (C) c (D) d (E) e

13. Container R is full of water and has twice the volume of container S, which is empty. If $\frac{1}{4}$ of the water in R is poured into S, what fraction of the volume of S is occupied by water?

(A) 1 (B) $\frac{1}{2}$ (C) $\frac{1}{4}$ (D) $\frac{1}{8}$

(E) None of the above

2	X	14	Y
X	14	Y	2
14	Y	2	X
Y	2	X	14

14. In the figure above, the sums of the numbers in each row, column, and main diagonal are the same. What is the value of X ?

(A) 2
(B) 8
(C) 12
(D) 14
(E) 16

GO ON TO THE NEXT PAGE

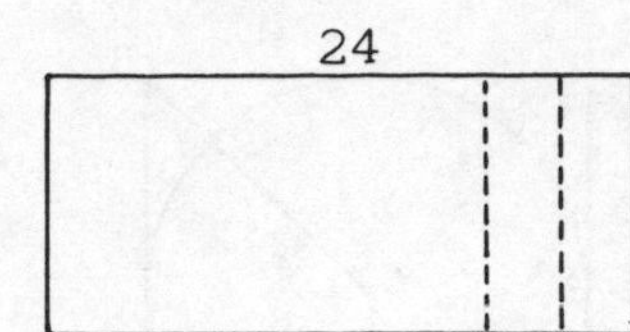

15. In the figure above, a rectangular piece of paper with length 24 is cut into strips of equal width as indicated by the dotted lines. If the area of two of these strips is 25 per cent of the area of the rectangle, how wide is each strip?

(A) 8 (B) 6 (C) 4 (D) 3 (E) 2

---

16. If $3x + 2y + xy + 6 = 0$ and $x + 2 = 5$, then $3 + y =$

(A) −15 (B) −3 (C) 0 (D) 3 (E) 15

17. P, Q, R, S, and T are five distinct lines in a plane. If $P \perp Q$, $Q \perp R$, $S \perp T$, and $R \parallel S$, then all of the following are true EXCEPT

(A) $P \parallel R$ (B) $P \parallel S$ (C) $P \perp T$
(D) $S \perp Q$ (E) $Q \perp T$

18. What is the difference between the greatest and least of all three-digit positive integers, each of whose digits is a different nonzero multiple of 3 ?

(A) 324 (B) 540 (C) 567 (D) 594 (E) 604

<u>Questions 19-20</u> refer to the following definition.

$$\overline{\underline{a / b / c}} = \frac{\frac{a}{b}}{c}$$ for all nonzero real numbers b and c.

19. $\overline{\underline{3 / 5 / 6}} =$

(A) $\frac{1}{10}$ (B) $\frac{1}{6}$ (C) $\frac{1}{5}$ (D) $\frac{1}{3}$ (E) $\frac{1}{2}$

20. $\overline{\underline{8 / 16 / 8}}$ is equal to which of the following?

(A) $\overline{\underline{1 / 2 / 1}}$ (B) $\overline{\underline{2 / 16 / 2}}$ (C) $\overline{\underline{8 / 2 / 8}}$
(D) $\overline{\underline{16 / 8 / 16}}$ (E) $\overline{\underline{4 / 1 / 1}}$

---

21. Three line segments have lengths $2x - 1$, $x + 2$, and $3x - 4$, respectively. If the average length of the line segments is 9, how much longer is the longest segment than the shortest?

(A) 3
(B) 4
(C) 5
(D) 7
(E) 11

GO ON TO THE NEXT PAGE

22. The lines with equations $x = 1$, $x = 6$, $y = -1$, $y = 3$ form a rectangle. What is the area of this rectangle?

(A) 10
(B) 12
(C) 15
(D) 18
(E) 20

23. A class of 35 students took a test that was scored from 0 to 100. Exactly 20 students received scores greater than or equal to 70. If A is the class average score, which of the following is the LOWEST possible value of A ?

(A) 20 (B) 40 (C) 50 (D) 70 (E) 80

24. A store which formerly sold peppers at 3 pounds for $1.00 changed the price to 2 pounds for $0.75. What is the per cent increase in the price per pound?

(A) 25% (B) 20% (C) $16\frac{2}{3}$% (D) $12\frac{1}{2}$% (E) $6\frac{2}{3}$%

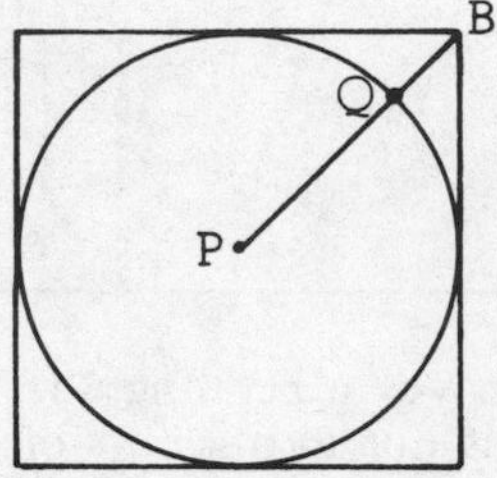

25. In the square above, Q is the intersection of segment PB and the circle with center P. What is the ratio of the length of QB to the length of PQ ?

(A) $\sqrt{2} - 1$
(B) $\frac{\sqrt{2}}{2}$
(C) $\sqrt{2}$
(D) $\sqrt{2} + 1$
(E) $2\sqrt{2}$

S T O P

IF YOU FINISH BEFORE TIME IS CALLED, CHECK YOUR WORK ON THIS SECTION ONLY.
DO NOT WORK ON ANY OTHER SECTION IN THE TEST.

Correct Answers for Scholastic Aptitude Test
Form Code 8B210

VERBAL		MATHEMATICAL	
Section 1	Section 4	Section 2	Section 5
1. D	1. C	1. E	1. B
2. A	2. B	2. D	2. D
3. D	3. E	3. C	3. C
4. A	4. A	4. C	4. B
5. E	5. D	5. E	5. A
6. C	6. B	6. B	6. C
7. B	7. E	7. E	7. E
8. A	8. D	*8. C	8. B
9. D	9. B	*9. D	9. C
10. C	10. C	*10. C	10. A
11. B	11. A	*11. D	11. E
12. E	12. B	*12. A	12. E
13. D	13. D	*13. B	13. B
14. C	14. B	*14. B	14. B
15. B	15. A	*15. A	15. D
16. E	16. B	*16. C	16. C
17. C	17. E	*17. A	17. E
18. A	18. E	*18. A	18. D
19. B	19. C	*19. C	19. A
20. E	20. E	*20. D	20. B
21. D	21. A	*21. A	21. B
22. A	22. B	*22. D	22. E
23. E	23. D	*23. A	23. B
24. A	24. B	*24. B	24. D
25. A	25. E	*25. B	25. A
26. C	26. E	*26. C	
27. C	27. D	*27. D	
28. B	28. C	28. B	
29. D	29. D	29. B	
30. E	30. D	30. D	
31. E	31. B	31. A	
32. B	32. A	32. D	
33. A	33. B	33. A	
34. C	34. A	34. C	
35. B	35. C	35. E	
36. D	36. A		
37. A	37. A		
38. C	38. E		
39. A	39. C		
40. B	40. E		
	41. D		
	42. A		
	43. E		
	44. B		
	45. A		

*Indicates four-choice questions. (All of the other questions are five-choice.)

The Scoring Process

Machine-scoring is done in three steps:

- *Scanning.* Your answer sheet is "read" by a scanning machine and the oval you filled in for each question is recorded on a computer tape.
- *Scoring.* The computer compares the oval filled in for each question with the correct response. Each correct answer receives one point; omitted questions do not count toward your score. For each wrong answer, a fraction of a point is subtracted to correct for random guessing. For questions with five answer choices, one-fourth of a point is subtracted for each wrong response; for questions with four answer choices, one-third of a point is subtracted for each wrong response. For example, the SAT-verbal test has 85 questions with five answer choices each, and if a student has 44 right, 32 wrong, and 9 omitted, the resulting raw score is determined as follows:

  $$44 \text{ right} - \frac{32 \text{ wrong}}{4} = 44 - 8 = 36 \text{ raw score points}$$

  Obtaining raw scores frequently involves the rounding of fractional numbers to the nearest whole number. For example, a raw score of 36.25 is rounded to 36, the nearest whole number. A raw score of 36.50 is rounded upward to 37.
- *Converting to reported scaled score.* Raw test scores are then placed on the College Board scale of 200 to 800 through a process that adjusts scores to account for minor differences in difficulty between different editions of the test. This process, known as equating, is performed so that a student's reported score is not affected by the edition of the test taken nor by the abilities of the group with whom the student takes the test. As a result of placing ATP scores on the College Board scale, scores earned by students at different times can be compared. For example, an SAT-verbal score of 400 on a test taken at one administration indicates the same level of developed verbal ability as a 400 score obtained on a different edition of the test taken at another time.

How to Score the Test

You can verify the College Board SAT scores reported to you recently by using the information in this booklet along with the copy of your answer sheet. *Before you begin, check that the form code you marked in item 3 on your answer sheet is the same as the one printed on the front of this booklet.* Compare the responses shown on the copy of your answer sheet with the list of correct answers.

SAT-Verbal Sections 1 and 4

Step A: Count the number of correct answers for *section 1* and record the number in the space provided on the worksheet on the opposite page. Then do the same for the incorrect answers. (Do not count omitted answers.) To determine subtotal A, use the formula:

$$\text{number correct} - \frac{\text{number incorrect}}{4} = \text{subtotal A}$$

Step B: Count the number of correct answers and the number of incorrect answers for *section 4* and record the numbers in the spaces provided on the worksheet. To determine subtotal B, use the formula:

$$\text{number correct} - \frac{\text{number incorrect}}{4} = \text{subtotal B}$$

Step C: To obtain C, add subtotal A to subtotal B, keeping any decimals.

Step D: To obtain D, your raw verbal score, round C to the nearest whole number. (For example, any number from 44.50 to 45.49 rounds to 45.)

Step E: To find your reported SAT-verbal score, look up the total raw verbal score you obtained in step D in the conversion table on the back cover.

SAT-Mathematical Sections 2 and 5

Step A: Count the number of correct answers and the number of incorrect answers for the *four-choice questions (questions 8 through 27) in section 2* and record the numbers in the spaces provided on the worksheet. To determine the subtotal A, use the formula:

$$\text{number correct} - \frac{\text{number incorrect}}{3} = \text{subtotal A}$$

Step B: Count the number of correct answers and the number of incorrect answers for the *five-choice questions (questions 1 through 7 and 28 through 35) in section 2* and record the numbers in the spaces provided on the worksheet. To determine the subtotal B, use the formula:

$$\text{number correct} - \frac{\text{number incorrect}}{4} = \text{subtotal B}$$

Step C: Count the number of correct answers and the number of incorrect answers for section 5 and record the numbers in the spaces provided on the worksheet. To determine the subtotal C, use the formula:

$$\text{number correct} - \frac{\text{number incorrect}}{4} = \text{subtotal C}$$

Step D: To obtain D, add subtotal A, subtotal B, and subtotal C, keeping any decimals.

Step E: To obtain E, your raw mathematical score, round D to the nearest whole number. (For example, any number from 44.50 to 45.49 rounds to 45.)

Step F: To find your reported SAT-mathematical score, look up the total raw mathematical score you obtained in E in the conversion table on the back cover.

SAT-Verbal Worksheet

A. Section 1: ______ – ¼ (______) = ______
no. correct — no. incorrect — subtotal A

B. Section 4: ______ – ¼ (______) = ______
no. correct — no. incorrect — subtotal B

C. Total unrounded raw score
(Total A + B) ______ C

D. Total rounded raw score
(Rounded to nearest whole number) ______ D

E. Reported SAT-verbal score
(See the conversion table on the back cover.) [ ] SAT-Verbal

SAT-Mathematical Worksheet

A. Section 2:
Questions 8 through 27
(4-choice) ______ – ⅓ (______) = ______
no. correct — no. incorrect — subtotal A

B. Section 2:
Questions 1 through 7 and
28 through 35 (5-choice) ______ – ¼ (______) = ______
no. correct — no. incorrect — subtotal B

C. Section 5: ______ – ¼ (______) = ______
no. correct — no. incorrect — subtotal C

D. Total unrounded raw score
(Total A + B + C) ______ D

E. Total rounded raw score
(Rounded to nearest whole number) ______ E

F. Reported SAT-mathematical score
(See the conversion table on the back cover.) [ ] SAT-Math

If you have any questions on these scoring instructions, you may call the phone number below.

If, after following the above scoring directions and checking your work carefully, your results disagree with the verbal or mathematical score reported on your ATP Student Report, you may request a hand scoring of your answer sheet by writing or calling:

College Board ATP
Box 592
Princeton, NJ 08541
Attention: Rescore Request
Telephone: (609) 883-8500

Please indicate whether it is your verbal or mathematical score, or both, that you want to be rescored. When you write, please include a copy of the scoring worksheet in this booklet on which you did your calculations.

Score Conversion Table
Scholastic Aptitude Test
Form Code 8B210

Raw Score	College Board Reported Score		Raw Score	College Board Reported Score	
	SAT-Verbal	SAT-Math		SAT-Verbal	SAT-Math
85	800		40	470	600
84	790		39	460	590
83	780		38	450	590
82	770		37	450	580
81	760		36	440	570
80	760		35	430	560
79	750		34	430	550
78	740		33	420	540
77	730		32	410	540
76	720		31	410	530
75	720		30	400	520
74	710		29	390	510
73	700		28	390	500
72	690		27	380	490
71	690		26	370	490
70	680		25	370	480
69	670		24	360	470
68	660		23	350	460
67	650		22	350	450
66	650		21	340	440
65	640		20	330	430
64	630		19	330	430
63	620		18	320	420
62	610		17	310	410
61	610		16	310	400
60	600	800	15	300	390
59	590	780	14	290	380
58	590	770	13	290	380
57	580	760	12	280	370
56	570	750	11	270	360
55	570	740	10	270	350
54	560	730	9	260	340
53	550	720	8	250	330
52	550	710	7	250	330
51	540	700	6	240	320
50	530	690	5	230	310
49	530	680	4	220	300
48	520	670	3	220	290
47	510	660	2	210	280
46	510	650	1	200	280
45	500	640	0	200	270
44	490	640	−1	200	260
43	490	630	−2	200	250
42	480	620	−3	200	240
41	470	610	−4	200	230
			−5	200	220
			−6	200	220
			−7	200	210
			−8 or below	200	200

SAT
Form Code 8G071

SECTION 1

Time—30 minutes

40 QUESTIONS

For each question in this section, choose the best answer and blacken the corresponding space on the answer sheet.

Each question below consists of a word in capital letters, followed by five lettered words or phrases. Choose the word or phrase that is most nearly opposite in meaning to the word in capital letters. Since some of the questions require you to distinguish fine shades of meaning, consider all the choices before deciding which is best.

Example:

GOOD: (A) sour (B) bad (C) red (D) hot (E) ugly

Ⓐ ● Ⓒ Ⓓ Ⓔ

1. SOOTHE: (A) praise (B) promise (C) provoke (D) join together (E) conceal quickly

2. DECELERATION: (A) increased speed (B) regular occurrence (C) additional cost (D) different approach (E) greater productivity

3. LINGER: (A) inflate (B) detest (C) attempt to win (D) thrust in deeper (E) hasten to depart

4. INCONSPICUOUS: (A) blameworthy (B) glaring (C) possible (D) beneficial (E) desperate

5. FRACTURE: (A) knit (B) disencumber (C) entangle (D) render inactive (E) pull taut

6. ACCESSORY:
(A) logical argument
(B) persistent questioner
(C) inconclusive evidence
(D) primary component
(E) distinguished predecessor

7. DISPASSIONATE: (A) isolated (B) prejudiced (C) unfortunate (D) irreconcilable (E) disgraceful

8. SUPERCILIOUS: (A) fatal (B) acute (C) extreme (D) servile (E) precocious

9. DESECRATE: (A) refurbish (B) construct (C) moisten (D) rejoice (E) hallow

10. TANTAMOUNT:
(A) unclear in meaning
(B) impractical in design
(C) undesirable in effect
(D) immeasurable in size
(E) unlike in significance

GO ON TO THE NEXT PAGE

1

Each sentence below has one or two blanks, each blank indicating that something has been omitted. Beneath the sentence are five lettered words or sets of words. Choose the word or set of words that best fits the meaning of the sentence as a whole.

Example:

> Although its publicity has been ----, the film itself is intelligent, well-acted, handsomely produced, and altogether ----.
>
> (A) tasteless. .respectable (B) extensive. .moderate (C) sophisticated. .amateur (D) risqué. .crude (E) perfect. .spectacular
>
> ● Ⓑ Ⓒ Ⓓ Ⓔ

11. Lee knows the jungle and loves it, having the explorer's ---- to ---- discomfort for the sake of knowledge gained through the senses.
    (A) zeal. .lessen
    (B) resolve. .display
    (C) willingness. .endure
    (D) disinclination. .discover
    (E) fervor. .overestimate

12. Some scientists argue against ---- any microbe, suggesting that even the smallpox virus, which is now nearly ----, might be preserved in a kind of microbial museum.
    (A) conserving. .isolated
    (B) exterminating. .extinct
    (C) eradicating. .immunized
    (D) fertilizing. .virulent
    (E) infecting. .controlled

13. People who insist that some particular injustice is not their responsibility sooner or later become unable to ---- any injustice.
    (A) condone (B) excuse (C) permit (D) ignore (E) resent

14. The Modernists were people of the strongest ---- propensities: they gloried in their refusal to ---- bourgeois sentiments and relationships.
    (A) altruistic. .wink at
    (B) radical. .cast off
    (C) puritanical. .preside over
    (D) antisocial. .traffic in
    (E) conservative. .abide by

15. The establishment of a center here has been held up by insistent fears that local ---- would be undermined by state control.
    (A) autonomy (B) officials (C) buildings (D) recreation (E) funds

Each question below consists of a related pair of words or phrases, followed by five lettered pairs of words or phrases. Select the lettered pair that best expresses a relationship similar to that expressed in the original pair.

Example:

> YAWN : BOREDOM :: (A) dream : sleep (B) anger : madness (C) smile : amusement (D) face : expression (E) impatience : rebellion
>
> Ⓐ Ⓑ ● Ⓓ Ⓔ

16. PADDLE : CANOE :: (A) runner : sled (B) pedal : bicycle (C) hangar : airplane (D) track : train (E) dock : boat

17. TELESCOPE : ASTRONOMER ::
    (A) binoculars : oculist
    (B) stethoscope : chemist
    (C) periscope : aviator
    (D) horoscope : astrologer
    (E) microscope : biologist

18. SHOPLIFTER : MERCHANT ::
    (A) burglar : homeowner (B) pickpocket : thief (C) defendant : juror (D) colleague : employer (E) browser : customer

19. MIST : DAMPNESS :: (A) ice : slipperiness (B) hail : heat (C) snow : winter (D) climate : humidity (E) wind : thaw

20. BRAGGART : BOAST ::
    (A) censor : obscenity (B) heckler : compliment (C) liar : falsehood (D) flatterer : grievance (E) conspirator : confession

21. ANESTHETIC : PAIN :: (A) sandpaper : friction (B) alloy : durability (C) fan : ventilation (D) preservative : decay (E) spark : electricity

22. SUSPICIOUS : DOUBT :: (A) happy : laughter (B) apprehensive : fear (C) guilty : conscience (D) angry : violence (E) imaginative : fiction

23. REVERIE : DAYDREAMER :: (A) plot : conspirator (B) audience : actor (C) sleep : insomniac (D) crime : detective (E) perfection : bungler

24. MAVERICK : HERD :: (A) boss : workers (B) dissenter : group (C) duck : flock (D) hero : army (E) expert : mass

25. EPICURE : FASTIDIOUS ::
    (A) ascetic : abstemious (B) stoic : volatile (C) spartan : extravagant (D) gourmet : greedy (E) truant : insubordinate

GO ON TO THE NEXT PAGE

Each passage below is followed by questions based on its content. Answer all questions following a passage on the basis of what is stated or implied in that passage.

There was a young girl of nineteen in a small town of north Germany who had a strong bent for research; but when her brother went to the University of Gōttingen, she, according to the customs of her country, remained at home. Agnes Pockels had observed the streaming of currents when salts were put into solution and, by attaching a float to a balance, had found that salts increased the pull of the surface of the fluid. In other words, she had discovered surface tension. This was in 1881. She did not know whether anyone else had ever observed this phenomenon. Through her brother, she brought her work to the attention of the professor of physics at Gōttingen. He failed to grasp its significance. For ten years she went on studying the properties of solutions. Then, when the renowned English physicist, Lord Rayleigh, began to publish on this subject, Agnes wrote to him about her work. Lord Rayleigh sent a translation of her letter to the English journal Nature asking that it be published. He wrote that the first part of her letter covered nearly the same ground as his own recent work and that with very "homely appliances" she had arrived at valuable results respecting the behavior of contaminated water surfaces. (Interestingly, this same "homely device" is still used to measure surface tension.) For a few years Lord Rayleigh arranged for the publication of all Agnes Pockels' work in English until, in 1898, her discoveries were accepted for publication in her own language.

26. Which of the following best describes the content of the passage?

(A) An explanation of the means by which surface tension may be observed and measured
(B) An analysis of the events which led to the discovery of surface tension
(C) An evaluation of the significance of Agnes Pockels' discovery of surface tension
(D) An account of Agnes Pockels' discovery of surface tension and how her work became known to the world
(E) An account of Agnes Pockels' efforts to attend a university and of her reaction to the fame her discovery brought

27. It can be inferred that Lord Rayleigh arranged for the publication of Agnes Pockels' work primarily because he wanted to

(A) reveal the crudity of her equipment
(B) challenge the accuracy of her results
(C) show others the major influences on his own work
(D) assume responsibility for having inspired her first efforts
(E) inform other scientists of the significance of her discoveries

28. It can be inferred that a scientist today would most probably describe the device Agnes Pockels used to measure surface tension as

(A) overly complex
(B) clever but inaccurate
(C) still very effective
(D) of historical value only
(E) difficult to reconstruct

GO ON TO THE NEXT PAGE

The reading passages in this test are brief excerpts or adaptations of excerpts from published material. The ideas contained in them do not necessarily represent the opinions of the College Board or Educational Testing Service. To make the text suitable for testing purposes, we may in some cases have altered the style, contents, or point of view of the original.

Environments spoiled by smogs, pesticides, or strip mining are not destroyed thereby but rather become different by evolving in new ecological directions determined by these stresses. We may not like the aesthetic and economic consequences of these alterations, but we can be sure that the disturbed environments will eventually achieve some new kind of biological equilibrium, as has repeatedly occurred in the past after great ecological disasters. Stable communities are in fact exceptional in nature, and they are all but impossible wherever there is human activity. Every form of agriculture, even the most primitive, involves the creation of new ecosystems. Since most of the temperate world has been transformed by agriculture, it now constitutes a man-made ecosystem.

The conservationist's attitude toward changes in nature finds its scientific justification in the fact that it is difficult, if not impossible, to predict the long-range consequences of human interventions into natural ecosystems. Experience has shown indeed that the consequences can be disastrous. Furthermore, the progressive destruction of wilderness tends to decrease biological diversity, and this in turn renders ecological systems less stable and less likely to remain suitable for a variety of species, including man. But these scientific reasons are not likely to have much weight for many human beings. Man is adventurous and he has been endlessly taking ecological risks. His motto may well be "catastrophe rather than boredom" and, irrespective of dangers, he is likely to continue upsetting his ecosystems.

29. The most important point that the author wishes to make regarding smogs, pesticides, or strip mining is that they

(A) produce new ecosystems
(B) spoil our natural environment
(C) threaten the stability of nature
(D) have an adverse effect upon agriculture
(E) are aesthetically offensive and economically harmful

30. The author's attitude toward humanity's continued willingness to disturb ecosystems appears to be one of

(A) alarm (B) resignation (C) bewilderment
(D) encouragement (E) disappointment

31. The author implies that the only scientifically defensible objection to causing environmental changes is that such changes

(A) can deprive man of important natural resources
(B) will increase the variety of biological species
(C) can encourage man to take greater ecological risks
(D) run counter to man's instinct for stability
(E) can have unpredictable consequences

32. The primary point of the passage is that

(A) most of the ecosystems in the world have been transformed by agriculture
(B) there are many differences between "natural" and "man-made" ecosystems
(C) man's nature makes most arguments to leave natural environments alone futile
(D) human beings are able to survive even great ecological disasters
(E) science has advanced man's love of adventure and his willingness to take risks

GO ON TO THE NEXT PAGE

Dylan Thomas' outward life as a poet was not, at first, in spite of his (very few) champions, easy. Following the publication of his second book, a furious attack on him developed in letters addressed to one of the two principal London newspapers. It was my privilege and pride to give the attackers more than as good as they gave. The air still seems to reverberate with the wooden sound of numskulls being soundly hit.

Although the occasion was supremely important to me, I cannot remember the exact date of our first meeting–knowing only that it was before the attack. I had reviewed his second book and had written to him; so when I arrived in London, he came to see me. It seems now, though I am so much his senior, that he and his great poetry were always a part of my life.

I have never known anyone more capable of endearing himself to others. And this was not only the result of his great charm, warmth, and touching funniness. I have never known anyone with a more holy and childlike innocence of mind. He loved humanity, and had contempt only for the cruel, the unkind (these are not always identical), and the mean. He was most generous in his enthusiasms and most loyal in his friendships. Alas, that some of the people who crowded round him were unworthy of that noble nature. But these I will leave to their shame. For he is dead. And there is nothing to be done.

33. "The wooden sound of numskulls being soundly hit" (lines 8-9) refers to the

(A) narrator's attack on those who criticized Dylan Thomas' work
(B) critics' reviews of Dylan Thomas' second book
(C) important occasion of the narrator's first meeting with Dylan Thomas
(D) holy and childlike innocence of Dylan Thomas
(E) unworthiness of some of the people who surrounded Dylan Thomas

34. It can be assumed from the passage that the narrator's review of Dylan Thomas' second book was

(A) favorable (B) explosive (C) charming (D) funny (E) angry

35. According to the passage, Dylan Thomas scorned those who lacked

(A) courage (B) humility (C) compassion (D) artistic sensitivity (E) a sense of humor

GO ON TO THE NEXT PAGE

Like the redwood which thinks the marigold may dry up its roots, Americans in the 1920's sealed their borders to most foreigners. It is ironic that the exception was the English, against whose laws we once rebelled. We were proud of our vast country, but prouder still of ourselves. The oppressed became oppressors.

It is a commentary on our institutions that it took 144 years to impose racial restrictions on a broad scale. Only in the last 44 years have attempts been made to remove them. Now that we are mending the "melting pot," we can admit that the pot had a serious crack which drained America of talent and dissipated a source of energy. The defect in the melting pot has been the restrictive immigration laws. These had their origins in sparks of xenophobia set in the 1850's and rekindled by xenophobic lobbies of the twenties. The laws were based on the national origins theory: each country was assigned a quota based on a ratio between that country's immigrants already here and the total population of the United States. Supporters of the system justified it by noting that it mirrored our society: to each country an allowance according to its prior contribution of people. But the mirror was flawed: Asians and Afro-Americans were not reflected at all.

During the presidential campaign of 1856, Lincoln said, "If the Know-Nothings obtain control, the Constitution will read: 'All men are created equal except Negroes, foreigners, and Catholics.' I shall prefer emigrating to some country where they make no pretense of loving liberty."

Not only was there an unrealistic quota system, but also problems concerning aid to needy immigrants. After the Civil War, certain states began to aid them on a small scale. To this end, the New York Board of Emigration collected a $1.50-per-passenger fee from shipowners transporting aliens. In lieu of that fee, the owner of the vessel could pay a bond on only those immigrants deemed "likely to become public charges." But any such fee did, in fact, threaten the shipowners' property rights. Thus, the Supreme Court ruled that since Congress had exclusive power to regulate foreign commerce, the states must desist. The administration of immigrant charities fell, therefore, into private hands with predictable results.

36. According to the author, a major flaw in the national origins theory was that

(A) it halted the flow of immigration
(B) it threatened property rights
(C) it created a homogeneous society
(D) certain groups were not included
(E) talented people were forced to emigrate

37. The passage is primarily concerned with

(A) explaining the background of a new law
(B) deploring a historical phenomenon
(C) formulating a theory about popular prejudice
(D) expressing doubts about the strength of liberal attitudes
(E) suggesting a revision of immigration laws

38. The author states that advocates of the quota system defended it on the grounds that it

(A) protected the fundamental principles on which the United States was founded
(B) fostered friendly ties with Western Europe
(C) prevented overpopulation and unemployment
(D) deterred the immigration of persons who were likely to become public charges
(E) reflected the existing ethnic composition of American society

39. According to the passage, the administration of immigrant charities was turned over to private agencies because

(A) the burden of administration was too great for one state agency
(B) xenophobic lobbies wished to curtail assistance to immigrants
(C) public charities were considered suspect by the populace
(D) the flow of immigration had been checked by the quota system
(E) the state administered levy was judged unconstitutional

40. The tone of Lincoln's remarks in lines 29-31 is best described as

(A) ironic (B) patronizing (C) tentative (D) defensive (E) sentimental

S T O P

IF YOU FINISH BEFORE TIME IS CALLED, CHECK YOUR WORK ON THIS SECTION ONLY.
DO NOT WORK ON ANY OTHER SECTION IN THE TEST.

SECTION 2

Time—30 minutes

35 QUESTIONS

In this section solve each problem, using any available space on the page for scratchwork. Then indicate the one correct answer in the appropriate space on the answer sheet.

The following information is for your reference in solving some of the problems.

Circle of radius r: Area = πr^2; Circumference = $2\pi r$
The number of degrees of arc in a circle is 360.
The measure in degrees of a straight angle is 180.

Definitions of symbols:

=	is equal to	$\leq$	is less than or equal to
$\neq$	is unequal to	$\geq$	is greater than or equal to
<	is less than	$\parallel$	is parallel to
>	is greater than	$\perp$	is perpendicular to

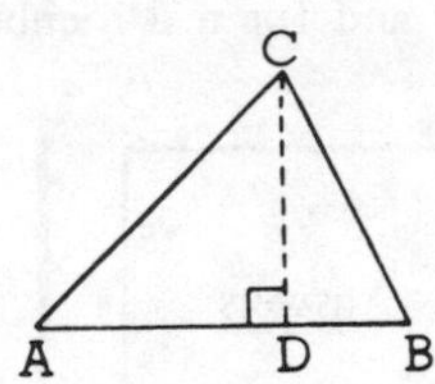

Triangle: The sum of the measures in degrees of the angles of a triangle is 180.

If $\angle CDA$ is a right angle, then

(1) area of $\Delta ABC = \frac{AB \times CD}{2}$

(2) $AC^2 = AD^2 + DC^2$

Note: Figures which accompany problems in this test are intended to provide information useful in solving the problems. They are drawn as accurately as possible EXCEPT when it is stated in a specific problem that its figure is not drawn to scale. All figures lie in a plane unless otherwise indicated. All numbers used are real numbers.

---

1. If $2x + 9 = -12$, then $x =$

(A) -21 (B) $-\frac{21}{2}$ (C) $-\frac{3}{2}$ (D) 3 (E) $\frac{21}{2}$

2. $\frac{473}{3} =$

(A) $\frac{470}{2} + \frac{3}{1}$

(B) $\frac{400}{1} + \frac{70}{1} + \frac{3}{1}$

(C) $\frac{473}{1} + \frac{473}{1} + \frac{473}{1}$

(D) $\frac{473}{2} + \frac{473}{1}$

(E) $\frac{400}{3} + \frac{70}{3} + \frac{3}{3}$

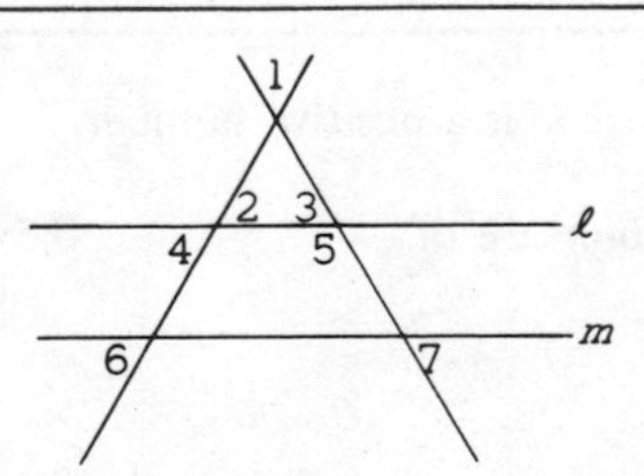

3. In the figure above, $\ell \parallel m$. Which of the following pairs of angles must be equal?

(A) 1 and 3
(B) 2 and 3
(C) 3 and 5
(D) 4 and 6
(E) 5 and 7

4. If water flowed into a 70-liter tank and filled half the tank in 10 minutes, what was the rate of flow in liters per minute?

(A) 3.5 (B) 7 (C) 35 (D) 70 (E) 210

5. If the perimeter of square A is double that of square B, then the area of A is how many times the area of B ?

(A) $\frac{1}{2}$ (B) 1 (C) 2 (D) 3 (E) 4

6. What is the average of $\frac{1}{5}$ and $\frac{1}{7}$?

(A) $\frac{1}{12}$

(B) $\frac{1}{6}$

(C) $\frac{6}{35}$

(D) $\frac{12}{35}$

(E) $\frac{36}{35}$

7. How many numbers between 1 and 99 are divisible by both 2 and 7 ?

(A) 7 (B) 8 (C) 14 (D) 20 (E) 49

2

Questions 8-27 each consist of two quantities, one in Column A and one in Column B. You are to compare the two quantities and on the answer sheet blacken space

A if the quantity in Column A is greater;
B if the quantity in Column B is greater;
C if the two quantities are equal;
D if the relationship cannot be determined from the information given.

Notes: 1. In certain questions, information concerning one or both of the quantities to be compared is centered above the two columns.
2. A symbol that appears in both columns represents the same thing in Column A as it does in Column B.
3. Letters such as x, n, and k stand for real numbers.

EXAMPLES

	Column A	Column B	Answers
E1.	2×6	$2 + 6$	● Ⓑ Ⓒ Ⓓ
	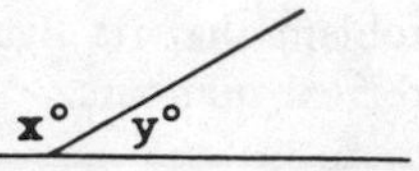		
E2.	$180 - x$	y	Ⓐ Ⓑ ● Ⓓ
E3.	$p - q$	$q - p$	Ⓐ Ⓑ Ⓒ ●

	Column A	Column B
8.	$\frac{63{,}000{,}000}{3{,}000}$	20,000

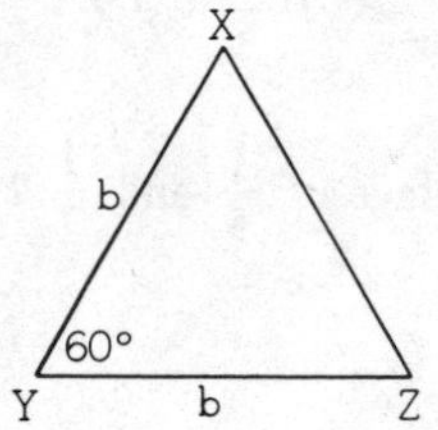

9.	Number of angles with equal measure in ΔXYZ	3
10.	$\frac{40}{9}$	4.5

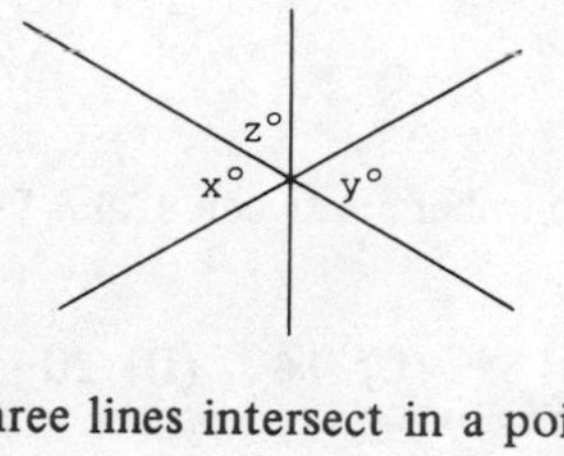

Three lines intersect in a point.

Column A	Column B
$x + z$	$y + z$

	Column A	Column B
	$a \neq 0$	
12.	$a + (-a)$	$a \cdot \frac{1}{a}$
	$k \neq 0$	
13.	$\frac{1}{k^2}$	$\left(\frac{1}{k}\right)^2$
14.	a^4b^2	a^2b^4

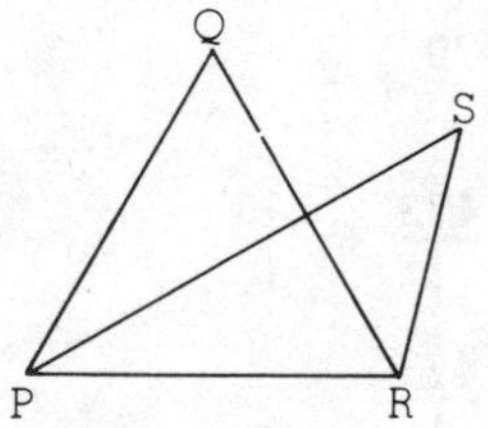

Perimeter of ΔPQR = Perimeter of ΔPSR

15.	$PQ + QR$	$PS + SR$
	x is a positive number.	
16.	x plus an increase of 50% of x	0.5x

GO ON TO THE NEXT PAGE

SUMMARY DIRECTIONS FOR COMPARISON QUESTIONS

Answer: A if the quantity in Column A is greater;
B if the quantity in Column B is greater;
C if the two quantities are equal;
D if the relationship cannot be determined from the information given.

	Column A	Column B
17.	Area of a circle with radius 1	Area of a square with side 1

1 skedallion = 4.6 skippers
2 phantoms = 9.3 skippers

18.	Value of one skedallion	Value of one phantom

$x^2 + 8x + 15 = 0$

19.	$x^2 + 8x$	15

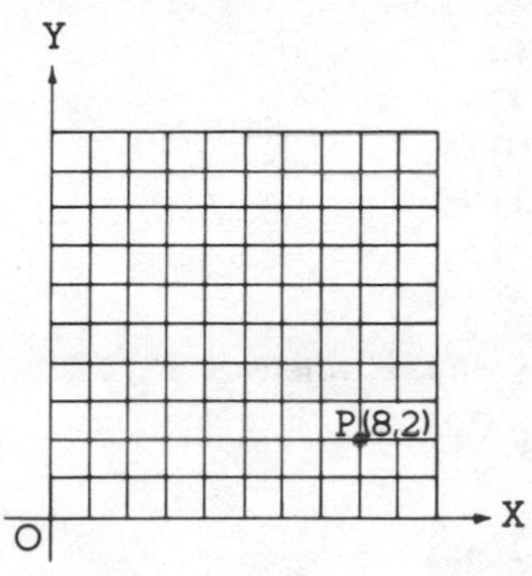

A point Q to be placed on the grid above has x-coordinate of 6.

20.	Distance OP	Distance OQ

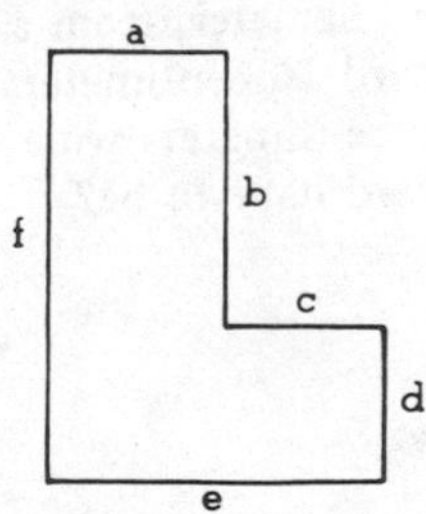

In the figure above, all segments intersect at right angles and the segments have lengths a, b, c, d, e, and f as shown.

21.	$a + b + c + d$	$e + f$

	Column A	Column B
22.	The number of men in an all-man division if there are 15 patrols in the division, 14 squads in each patrol, and 4 men in each squad	The number of women in an all-woman division if there are 12 patrols in the division, 10 squads in each patrol, and 7 women in each squad
23.	$x^2 - y^2 + 2y(y + x)$	$(x + y)^2$

$-2 < x < -1$

24.	$\frac{1}{x}$	x

x and y are integers with $8 \leqq x \leqq 12$ and $2 \leqq y \leqq 10$.

25.	Maximum possible value of $x - y$	9

A B C D E

Note: Figure not drawn to scale.

$AC = 11$, $BD = 7$, $CE = 5$

26.	AD	BE

On a certain test, the average score for the juniors was 87 and the average score for the sophomores was 81.

27.	The average score for the total group	84

GO ON TO THE NEXT PAGE

2

Solve each of the remaining problems in this section using any available space for scratchwork. Then indicate the one correct answer in the appropriate space on the answer sheet.

28. In a certain language, a "word" is defined as any 5-letter combination in which the position of at least one letter in the "word" is in the same position in which it is found in the English alphabet. For example "dbaec" is a word, because of the placement of the letter b, but "bdaac" is not. Which of the following is a word in this language?

(A) cddcd (B) cdddc (C) ccdcc
(D) dcdcc (E) dddcd

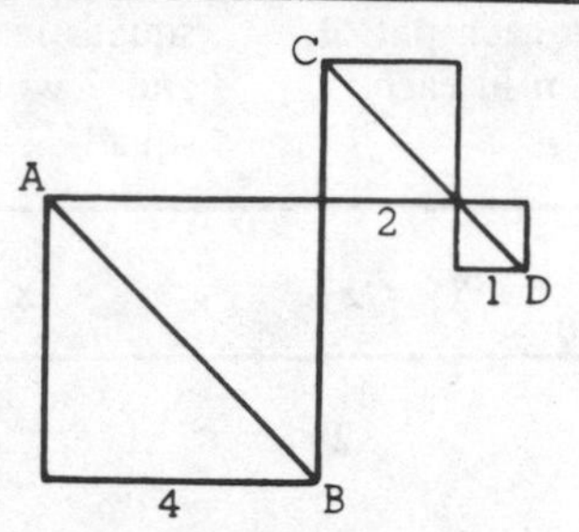

29. In the three squares above, what is the ratio $\frac{\text{length of segment CD}}{\text{length of segment AB}}$?

(A) $\frac{3}{16}$ (B) $\frac{3\sqrt{2}}{16}$ (C) $\frac{5}{16}$

(D) $\frac{3}{4\sqrt{2}}$ (E) $\frac{3}{4}$

30. A machine began knitting a row of 100 stitches by making 3 knit stitches and 2 purl stitches and repeated the same pattern thereafter. What is the order in which it knitted the 77th, 78th, 79th, and 80th stitches in the row?

(A) 2 knit, 2 purl
(B) 1 knit, 2 purl, 1 knit
(C) 3 knit, 1 purl
(D) 2 purl, 2 knit
(E) 1 purl, 2 knit, 1 purl

31. If a car travels x kilometers in t hours and 20 minutes, what is its average speed in kilometers per hour?

(A) $\frac{x}{t + 20}$ (B) $\frac{t + 20}{x}$ (C) $x\left(t + \frac{1}{3}\right)$

(D) $\frac{t + \frac{1}{3}}{x}$ (E) $\frac{x}{t + \frac{1}{3}}$

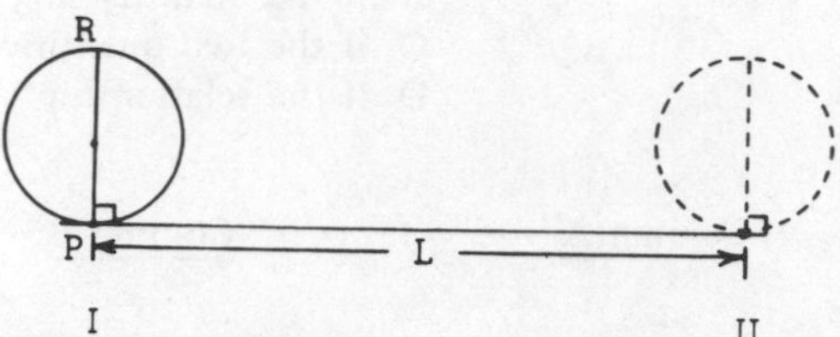

32. In the figure above, the circle at I with diameter PR is rolled one revolution along a plane until it reaches II as shown. The ratio $\frac{PR}{L}$ =

(A) $\frac{1}{\pi}$ (B) $\frac{1}{3}$ (C) 2 (D) 3 (E) π

33. The operation $*$ is defined on ordered pairs of numbers in the following way: $(a, b) * (c, d) = (ac + bd, ad + bc)$. If $(a, b) * (x, y) = (a, b)$, then (x, y) =

(A) (0, 0)
(B) (0, 1)
(C) (1, 0)
(D) (1, 1)
(E) (1, −1)

34. For all x and y where $x \neq 2y$,
$\frac{x - 2y}{2y - x} + \frac{2y - x}{x - 2y} =$

(A) $2(x - 2y)$
(B) $2y - x$
(C) 1
(D) 0
(E) −2

35. If a person were to cut seven circles, each 4 centimeters in diameter, from a rectangular piece of cardboard 16 centimeters long, at least how many centimeters wide would the piece of cardboard have to be?

(A) $2 + 2\sqrt{3}$
(B) $4 + \sqrt{3}$
(C) $4 + 2\sqrt{3}$
(D) 6
(E) 8

S T O P

IF YOU FINISH BEFORE TIME IS CALLED, CHECK YOUR WORK ON THIS SECTION ONLY. DO NOT WORK ON ANY OTHER SECTION IN THE TEST.

SECTION 4

4

Time—30 minutes

45 QUESTIONS

For each question in this section, choose the best answer and blacken the corresponding space on the answer sheet.

Each question below consists of a word in capital letters, followed by five lettered words or phrases. Choose the word or phrase that is most nearly opposite in meaning to the word in capital letters. Since some of the questions require you to distinguish fine shades of meaning, consider all the choices before deciding which is best.

Example:

GOOD: (A) sour (B) bad (C) red (D) hot (E) ugly

Ⓐ ● Ⓒ Ⓓ Ⓔ

1. COUPLE: (A) contain (B) separate (C) cover (D) increase (E) win

2. OBSOLETE: (A) indefinite (B) fertile (C) updated (D) prestigious (E) lenient

3. FLOURISH: (A) ingrain (B) wither (C) impede (D) turn pale (E) make peace

4. GRISLY: (A) rugged (B) nervous (C) modern (D) attractive (E) haughty

5. DEPENDENT: (A) self-reliant (B) intangible (C) conclusive (D) resilient (E) offensive

6. MELLOW: (A) angular (B) dry (C) clean (D) harsh (E) ragged

7. RESERVE: (A) confusion (B) admiration (C) gratitude (D) immaturity (E) boldness

8. IMPEL: (A) scatter (B) cease (C) taper off (D) turn away (E) hold back

9. PREMATURE: (A) explicit (B) perfidious (C) belated (D) punctual (E) induced

10. DILATION: (A) refraction (B) cohesion (C) vacillation (D) constriction (E) enervation

11. CONTRITE: (A) inarticulate (B) disoriented (C) unrepentant (D) infinite (E) impatient

12. MALADROIT: (A) healthful (B) zestful (C) adept (D) invigorating (E) discreet

13. IRASCIBLE: (A) imperturbable (B) curious (C) unconventional (D) unorganized (E) ordinary

14. BANE: (A) unanswerable question (B) benign influence (C) useless information (D) compilation (E) singularity

15. ERUDITION: (A) tolerance (B) crudeness (C) loyalty (D) cowardice (E) ignorance

Each sentence below has one or two blanks, each blank indicating that something has been omitted. Beneath the sentence are five lettered words or sets of words. Choose the word or set of words that best fits the meaning of the sentence as a whole.

Example:

Although its publicity has been ----, the film itself is intelligent, well-acted, handsomely produced, and altogether ----.

(A) tasteless. .respectable (B) extensive. .moderate (C) sophisticated. .amateur (D) risqué. .crude (E) perfect. .spectacular

● Ⓑ Ⓒ Ⓓ Ⓔ

16. More Americans might remain unmarried if society afforded other means of obtaining regular ----, or else valued ---- more highly.

(A) meals. .malnutrition
(B) companionship. .solitude
(C) lodging. .poverty
(D) conversation. .nonsense
(E) advice. .irresponsibility

17. The very young child has no concept of death: it is too ---- an idea, too ---- his or her experience.

(A) abstract. .removed from
(B) frightening. .thrilling for
(C) real. .close to
(D) recognizable. .irrelevant for
(E) familiar. .new to

18. Before burdening us with more of his ---- conclusions, he would do well to read a few scholarly books on the subject and brush up on the fundamentals of logic.

(A) valid (B) shrewd (C) edifying (D) superficial (E) impervious

19. An organism's energies are not called forth in some ---- fashion; rather, there are certain situations to which it invariably reacts.

(A) reasonable (B) hypothetical (C) indiscriminate (D) interacting (E) orderly

20. The book contains too much ---- material, such as extensive data about people ---- to events and unintegrated anecdotes about minor characters.

(A) erroneous. .momentous
(B) extraneous. .tangential
(C) vital. .contemporary
(D) irrelevant. .critical
(E) incontrovertible. .unattached

GO ON TO THE NEXT PAGE

Each passage below is followed by questions based on its content. Answer all questions following a passage on the basis of what is stated or implied in that passage.

The debilitating effects of poverty are not only the result of lack of money but are also the result of powerlessness, of being subject to one's social situation instead of being able to affect it through action, that is, through behavior that flows from an individual's decisions and plans. In other words, when social scientists have reported on the psychological consequences of poverty, it seems reasonable to believe that they have described the psychological consequences of powerlessness. The solution to poverty most frequently suggested is to help the poor secure more money without otherwise changing present power relationships. This appears to implement the idea of equality while avoiding any necessary threat to established centers of power. But, since the consequences of poverty are related to powerlessness, not to the absolute supply of money available to the poor, and since the amount of power purchasable with a given supply of money decreases as a society acquires a larger supply of goods and services, the solution of raising the incomes of the poor is likely, unless accompanied by other measures, to be ineffective in an affluent society.

In order to reduce poverty-related psychological and social problems in the United States, the major community will have to change its relationship to neighborhoods of poverty in such fashion that families in the neighborhoods have a greater stake in the broader society and can more successfully participate in the decision-making process of the surrounding community. Social action to help the poor should have the following characteristics: the poor should see themselves as the source of the action; the action should affect in major ways the preconceptions of institutions and persons defining the poor; the action should demand much in effort or skill; the action should be successful; and the successful self-originated important action should increase the feeling of potential worth and individual power of individuals who are poor.

The only initial resource which a community should provide to neighborhoods of poverty should be on a temporary basis and should consist of organizers who will enable the neighborhoods quickly to create powerful, independent, democratic organizations of the poor. Through such organizations, the poor will then negotiate with outsiders for resources and opportunities without having to submit to concurrent control from outside.

21. According to the passage, the primary role of the major community in assisting neighborhoods of poverty should be to
   (A) lend experienced advice to help in the formation of democratic self-help organizations
   (B) solicit public support for the business ventures of the poor
   (C) provide assistance to help the poor advance socially
   (D) suggest legislation to further the interests of the poor
   (E) implement projects that improve conditions in the neighborhood

22. The author's main purpose is apparently to
   (A) criticize present methods of helping the poor
   (B) discuss various types of power and how they can be used by the poor
   (C) describe the various causes of poverty
   (D) propose a way in which the poor can be more effectively helped
   (E) describe the psychological and social effects of power

23. The author implies that what might appear to be a lack of ambition in the poor can be ascribed to their feeling that
   (A) other people succeed without working
   (B) they have no friends who will support them
   (C) they are unable to buy the things they want
   (D) there is no one they can trust
   (E) they lack control over the circumstances of their lives

24. Which of the following statements best illustrates the author's ideas about money?
   (A) Self-reliance is a blessing money cannot buy.
   (B) Love of money is the root of all evil.
   (C) A penny saved is a penny earned.
   (D) No chains enslave so well as money.
   (E) Wine maketh merry but money answereth all things.

25. When speaking of power in this passage, the author is referring primarily to power as
   (A) force of will
   (B) authority in one's own affairs
   (C) control over others
   (D) energy necessary to succeed
   (E) strength to resist pressure

GO ON TO THE NEXT PAGE

The quality of science that, above all else, enriches the spirits of those who pursue science is the manner in which it enables us to glimpse the orderliness of nature. One of the most thrilling experiences for the students of chemistry is their exposure to the periodic table of elements and its revelation of the systematic structure of all matter.

A comparable disclosure in astronomy grew, in large measure, out of an ambitious, laborious, and seemingly pedantic project at Harvard. Since the stars are too remote to be seen except as diffuse points of light, our knowledge of them depends heavily on their spectra. The Italian astronomer Father Angelo Secchi had already found that he could sort stars into certain spectral categories, somewhat as the first walker in a forest might pick out oaks, maples, birches, and pines. Even though the stellar types shade more into one another than tree species, Father Secchi found that they clearly fit into a succession of pigeonholes. In 1890, Harvard published a preliminary catalog of 10,351 stars, classified according to their spectra, and by 1949 the entries in the catalog had grown to 359,082.

Astronomers at Harvard soon guessed that star types reflected temperature differences, but it remained for the Indian, Meghnad Saha, to decipher the specific messages contained in the spectra of each group. The stars classed by the letter O displayed the spectral lines of highly ionized helium, silicon, and nitrogen, and thus were the hottest. The types were listed in order of decreasing temperature, as follows:

O, B, A, F, G, K, M

Then, Russell at Princeton and Hertzsprung in Europe came upon another striking pattern in star classification. If the inherent brightness, or luminosity, of the stars is plotted on a graph against their types, arranged in order of temperature, some ninety per cent of all stars lie along a narrow band that has come to be called the main sequence. The hotter a star is, if it lies on the main sequence, the brighter it is, the larger it is, and the shorter is its lifetime. The graph that displays this relationship between luminosity and star type is known as the Hertzsprung-Russell diagram. When it was formulated on the eve of the First World War, Russell viewed the main sequence as a highway along which stars travel in their long journey from birth to death. A different interpretation is now placed on the main sequence, but the Hertzsprung-Russell diagram has come to be for astronomers a testimony of order in the universe.

26. The author is primarily concerned with

(A) evaluating various schemes for classifying stars
(B) pointing out the worldwide nature of interest in astronomy
(C) explaining a basic distinction between chemistry and astronomy
(D) describing a number of projects carried on at Harvard
(E) presenting an instance of the orderly nature of the universe

27. The author compares stars with trees (lines 13-21) primarily in order to suggest that

(A) discoveries in one field may lead to new findings in another
(B) there are more classes of stars than of trees
(C) stars fall into categories that can be identified
(D) Father Secchi was primarily interested in the study of botany
(E) stars, like trees, can be classified only by experts

28. According to the passage, which of the following statements about a star classed as O is FALSE?

(A) It is likely to be brighter than a star classed as B.
(B) It is likely to be larger than a star classed as B.
(C) It is likely to be found on the main sequence.
(D) Its spectrum is likely to include lines of ionized helium, silicon, and nitrogen.
(E) It is likely to have a longer life cycle than a star classed as B.

29. Which of the following titles best summarizes the content of the passage?

(A) Measuring the Temperature of the Stars
(B) How to Determine the Luminosity of Stars
(C) The Evolution of Stars from Birth to Death
(D) The Genesis of the Hertzsprung-Russell Diagram
(E) A New Interpretation of the Hertzsprung-Russell Diagram

30. The author's tone suggests that his attitude toward the orderliness of nature is one of

(A) enthusiastic appreciation
(B) casual interest
(C) aloof disinterest
(D) anxious concern
(E) skeptical suspicion

GO ON TO THE NEXT PAGE

4

Select the word or set of words that best completes each of the following sentences.

31. The scientist, motivated by an abhorrence of excessively ---- explanations, usually makes a ---- attempt to reduce all phenomena to only a few known principles.

(A) convoluted. .determined
(B) simple. .futile
(C) succinct. .detailed
(D) popularized. .casual
(E) axiomatic. .redundant

32. The statesmen and politicians who found his genius ---- to their designs ---- courted his favor through four stormy decades of history.

(A) vital. .inadvertently
(B) detrimental. .languidly
(C) superfluous. .incessantly
(D) inadequate. .resolutely
(E) indispensable. .sedulously

33. This ---- law will make little difference to the ---- drug companies whose standards are already high.

(A) economical. .prosperous
(B) stringent. .scrupulous
(C) invariable. .mediocre
(D) protective. .fraudulent
(E) mitigating. .conscientious

34. Only when one approaches ---- of availability of personnel, funds, or facilities does one have to consider seriously ---- among research programs.

(A) an understanding. .disharmony
(B) an overabundance. .inadequacies
(C) a discovery. .developments
(D) a disparity. .rivalries
(E) a ceiling. .priorities

35. Modern writers, ---- to drape reality with pretty phrases, show us everything, putrid and pure, with a grim ----.

(A) aspiring. .austerity
(B) hesitating. .discretion
(C) disdaining. .objectivity
(D) purporting. .omniscience
(E) endeavoring. .naturalism

Each question below consists of a related pair of words or phrases, followed by five lettered pairs of words or phrases. Select the lettered pair that best expresses a relationship similar to that expressed in the original pair.

Example:

YAWN : BOREDOM :: (A) dream : sleep
(B) anger : madness (C) smile : amusement
(D) face : expression (E) impatience : rebellion

Ⓐ Ⓑ ● Ⓓ Ⓔ

36. SIPPING : GULPING :: (A) whispering : shouting
(B) inhaling : exhaling (C) dieting : eating
(D) inspecting : examining (E) smiling : sighing

37. OVERDUE : DEADLINE ::
(A) incorrect : error (B) surrounded : boundary
(C) accurate : measurement (D) excessive : limit
(E) luxurious : extravagance

38. GILL : SALMON :: (A) egg : chicken
(B) plume : parrot (C) lung : sparrow
(D) feather : ostrich (E) talon : eagle

39. PROPOSAL : MARRIAGE :: (A) employment : work
(B) rule : law (C) candidate : nomination
(D) truce : war (E) bid : contract

40. BIBLIOGRAPHY : PUBLICATIONS ::
(A) textbook : subject (B) museum : paintings
(C) store : goods (D) directory : names
(E) legislature : legislation

41. UNETHICAL : MORALITY ::
(A) remedial : education (B) absurd : reason
(C) exorbitant : price (D) incorrigible : freedom
(E) abstract : art

42. MIRED : MUD :: (A) soaked : skin
(B) snared : trap (C) nourished : food
(D) rescued : danger (E) extinguished : fire

43. TACITURN : SILENCE :: (A) implicated : concern
(B) suave : humility (C) compassionate : blame
(D) pompous : courtesy (E) querulous : complaint

44. MEANING : NUANCE :: (A) subtlety : nicety
(B) difference : distinction (C) form : style
(D) color : shade (E) brilliance : hue

45. DOTARD : SAGE :: (A) proxy : voter
(B) dolt : prodigy (C) student : tutor
(D) sorcerer : genius (E) mentor : counselor

S T O P

IF YOU FINISH BEFORE TIME IS CALLED, CHECK YOUR WORK ON THIS SECTION ONLY. DO NOT WORK ON ANY OTHER SECTION IN THE TEST.

SECTION 5

Time—30 minutes

25 QUESTIONS

In this section solve each problem, using any available space on the page for scratchwork. Then indicate the one correct answer in the appropriate space on the answer sheet.

The following information is for your reference in solving some of the problems.

Circle of radius r: Area = πr^2; Circumference = $2\pi r$
The number of degrees of arc in a circle is 360.
The measure in degrees of a straight angle is 180.

Definitions of symbols:

$=$	is equal to	$\leq$	is less than or equal to
$\neq$	is unequal to	$\geq$	is greater than or equal to
$<$	is less than	$\parallel$	is parallel to
$>$	is greater than	$\perp$	is perpendicular to

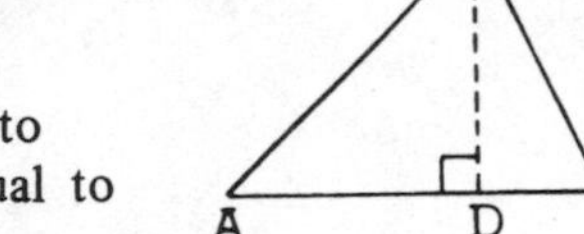

Triangle: The sum of the measures in degrees of the angles of a triangle is 180.

If $\angle CDA$ is a right angle, then

(1) area of $\triangle ABC = \frac{AB \times CD}{2}$

(2) $AC^2 = AD^2 + DC^2$

Note: Figures which accompany problems in this test are intended to provide information useful in solving the problems. They are drawn as accurately as possible EXCEPT when it is stated in a specific problem that its figure is not drawn to scale. All figures lie in a plane unless otherwise indicated. All numbers used are real numbers.

---

1. In a certain dart game, Don scored 25 per cent more points than Craig. If Craig scored 100 points, how many points did Don score?

(A) 225 (B) 125 (C) 100 (D) 80 (E) 75

2. For which of the following blocks could the top face viewed from the top look like the front face viewed from the front?

(A) 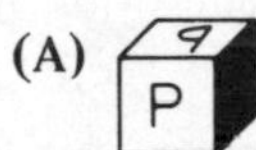

(B) 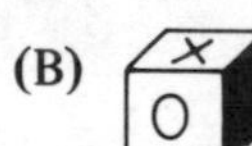

(C) 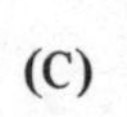 

(D) 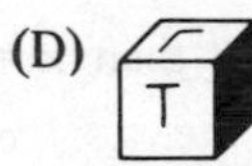

(E) 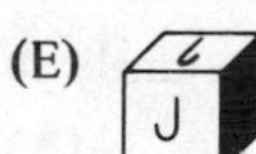

---

3. A polygon is NOT a triangle if it has exactly

(A) three sides
(B) three angles
(C) one angle which measures 135°
(D) two perpendicular sides
(E) two parallel sides

4. $2\frac{1}{2} - \left(\frac{1}{4} + \frac{1}{4} + \frac{1}{4} - \frac{1}{3}\right) =$

(A) $1\frac{5}{6}$ (B) 2 (C) $2\frac{1}{12}$ (D) $2\frac{1}{6}$ (E) $2\frac{5}{12}$

5. If the freshman class has 28 students of whom $\frac{1}{2}$ are women and the sophomore class has 24 students of whom $\frac{2}{3}$ are women, which of the following gives the total number of women in both classes?

(A) $\left(\frac{1}{2}\right) + \left(\frac{2}{3}\right)\left(\frac{24 + 28}{2}\right)$

(B) $2\left(\frac{1}{2} + \frac{2}{3}\right)(24 + 28)$

(C) $\left(\frac{1}{2}\right)\left(\frac{2}{3}\right)(24 + 28)$

(D) $\frac{2}{3}(28) + \frac{1}{2}(24)$

(E) $\frac{1}{2}(28) + \frac{2}{3}(24)$

6. A roll of plastic 250 meters long costs \$26. If it takes a length of $2\frac{1}{2}$ meters of this plastic to cover a certain machine, how much will it cost to buy the exact length of plastic needed to cover 600 such machines?

(A) \$62
(B) \$65
(C) \$156
(D) \$1,550
(E) \$1.560

GO ON TO THE NEXT PAGE

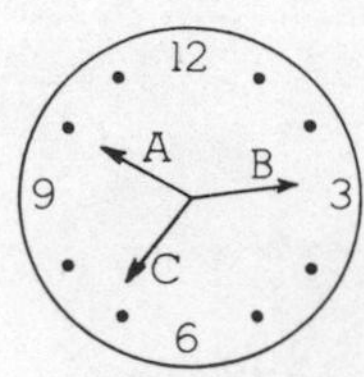

7. The clock above is accurate, but the minute, hour, and second hands are drawn the same length. If the time shown is between 2:45 and 3:00, which of the three lettered hands could be the second hand?

(A) A only
(B) B only
(C) C only
(D) Either A or C
(E) Either B or C

8. If the two middle digits of 4,579 are interchanged the resulting number is

(A) 18 less than 4,579
(B) 180 less than 4,579
(C) equal to 4,579
(D) 18 more than 4,579
(E) 180 more than 4,579

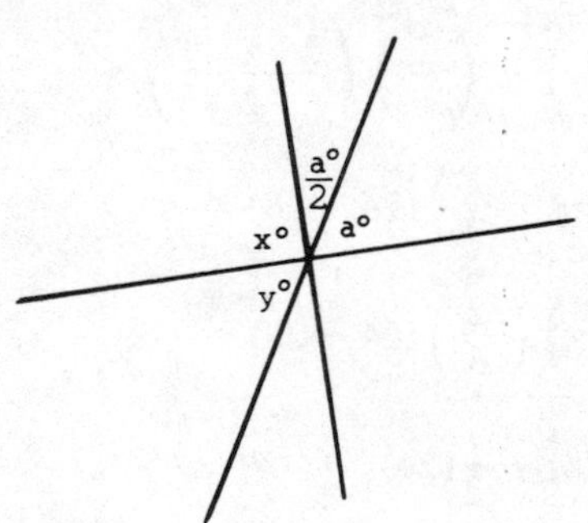

9. If three lines intersect in a point to form the angles shown above, then $x + y =$

(A) $\frac{a}{2} - 180$ (B) $180 - \frac{a}{2}$ (C) $180 - \frac{5a}{2}$

(D) $180 - a$ (E) $a - 180$

10. If $x^2 = 1$, then x^3 is equal to

(A) -3 (B) -1 only (C) 1 only

(D) 3 (E) -1 or 1

11. If $x = 2a$ and $y = \frac{1}{4a + 2}$, what is y in terms of x ?

(A) $\frac{1}{2x + 2}$

(B) $\frac{1}{2x + 4}$

(C) $\frac{2}{x + 4}$

(D) $\frac{1}{8x + 2}$

(E) $\frac{1}{8x + 4}$

12. A certain bleach is to be diluted with water so that the ratio of bleach to water will be $\frac{1}{8}$. If 3 bottles of bleach, each containing 0.5 liters, are to be used, how many liters of water should be used to obtain this same ratio?

(A) 4
(B) 6
(C) 12
(D) 18
(E) 24

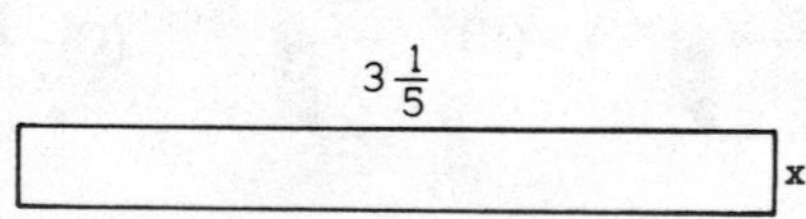

13. If the area of the rectangle above is 1, then $x =$

(A) $\frac{5}{16}$ (B) $\frac{3}{5}$ (C) $\frac{5}{3}$ (D) $\frac{16}{5}$ (E) 5

14. If a and b are integers and $a - b$ is a multiple of 5, which of the following must also be a multiple of 5 ?

(A) a (B) b (C) $a + b$ (D) $b - a$ (E) ab

GO ON TO THE NEXT PAGE

15. If $x > 0$, which of the following is greatest?

(A) $\frac{1}{x}$

(B) $\sqrt{x}$

(C) x

(D) x^2

(E) It cannot be determined from the information given.

16. In the figure above, if an edge of each small cube has length 2, what is the volume of the entire rectangular solid?

(A) 192 (B) 144 (C) 72 (D) 52 (E) 48

17. If 5 per cent of 50 per cent of x is 75, then $x =$

(A) 250 (B) 300 (C) 750
(D) 2,500 (E) 3,000

18. In a class of 39 students, the number b of boys is twice the number g of girls. Which of the following accurately describes this situation?

(A) $\begin{cases} b + 2g = 39 \\ b - g = 39 \end{cases}$

(B) $\begin{cases} b - 2g = 0 \\ b + g = 39 \end{cases}$

(C) $\begin{cases} 2b - g = 0 \\ b + g = 39 \end{cases}$

(D) $\begin{cases} b + g = 39 \\ b + 2g = 0 \end{cases}$

(E) $\begin{cases} b + 2g = 39 \\ b - 2g = 0 \end{cases}$

$$s = \frac{3}{2}r$$

$$r = \frac{1}{2}w$$

$$w = 3z$$

$$x = 2y$$

$$y = \frac{3}{4}z$$

19. Given the table above, x is equal to which of the following?

(A) r
(B) s
(C) w
(D) y
(E) z

20. If a and b are positive integers such that $\frac{a}{b} < 1$, which of the following is (are) true?

I. $a < b$

II. $\frac{1}{b} < \frac{1}{a}$

III. $\frac{a-1}{b} < 0$

(A) None (B) I only (C) III only
(D) I and II only (E) I, II, and III

21. A teacher gave a test to 30 students and the average score was x. Scores on the test ranged from 0 to 90, inclusive. If the average score for the first 10 papers graded was 60, what is the difference between the greatest and least possible values of x ?

(A) 20 (B) 30 (C) 40 (D) 50 (E) 60

GO ON TO THE NEXT PAGE

$$x^2 + xy^2 + 2y^3 = k$$
$$y^2 + yx^2 + 2x^3 = m$$

22. In the equations above, x is an odd integer and y is an even integer. Which of the following expressions must be even?

I. $m^2 + mk^2 + 2k^3$
II. $3k^3 + 3m^3 + 3k^3$
III. $k^2 + km^2 + 2m^3$

(A) I only
(B) II only
(C) III only
(D) I and II only
(E) I and III only

---

23. A triangle with one side 5 and another side 10 has perimeter P. What are the least and greatest possible integer values of P ?

(A) 21 and 29
(B) 21 and 24
(C) 16 and 39
(D) 16 and 24
(E) 6 and 29

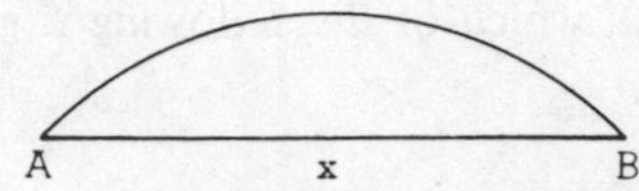

24. If arc AB is $\frac{1}{4}$ of the circumference of a certain circle and if the length of chord AB is x, what is the diameter of the circle?

(A) $\frac{\sqrt{2}}{2}x$

(B) $\frac{\pi}{4}x$

(C) $\sqrt{2}x$

(D) $\frac{\pi}{2}x$

(E) $2\sqrt{2}x$

---

25. On a 300-kilometer trip, a motorcyclist drove the first 100 kilometers at 40 kilometers per hour, the second 100 kilometers at 50 kilometers per hour, and the third 100 kilometers at 60 kilometers per hour. For what fraction of the time spent driving the 300 kilometers did the cyclist drive at 40 kilometers per hour?

(A) $\frac{4}{15}$ (B) $\frac{1}{3}$ (C) $\frac{2}{5}$ (D) $\frac{15}{37}$ (E) $\frac{11}{15}$

S T O P

IF YOU FINISH BEFORE TIME IS CALLED, CHECK YOUR WORK ON THIS SECTION ONLY. DO NOT WORK ON ANY OTHER SECTION IN THE TEST.

Correct Answers for Scholastic Aptitude Test Form Code 8G071

VERBAL		MATHEMATICAL	
Section 1	**Section 4**	**Section 2**	**Section 5**
1. C	1. B	1. B	1. B
2. A	2. C	2. E	2. C
3. E	3. B	3. D	3. E
4. B	4. D	4. A	4. C
5. A	5. A	5. E	5. E
6. D	6. D	6. C	6. C
7. B	7. E	7. A	7. C
8. D	8. E	*8. A	8. E
9. E	9. C	*9. C	9. B
10. E	10. D	*10. B	10. E
11. C	11. C	*11. C	11. A
12. B	12. C	*12. B	12. C
13. E	13. A	*13. C	13. A
14. D	14. B	*14. D	14. D
15. A	15. E	*15. C	15. E
16. B	16. B	*16. A	16. A
17. E	17. A	*17. A	17. E
18. A	18. D	*18. B	18. B
19. A	19. C	*19. B	19. A
20. C	20. B	*20. D	20. D
21. D	21. A	*21. C	21. E
22. B	22. D	*22. C	22. D
23. A	23. E	*23. C	23. A
24. B	24. A	*24. A	24. C
25. A	25. B	*25. A	25. D
26. D	26. E	*26. D	
27. E	27. C	*27. D	
28. C	28. E	28. B	
29. A	29. D	29. E	
30. B	30. A	30. A	
31. E	31. A	31. E	
32. C	32. E	32. A	
33. A	33. B	33. C	
34. A	34. E	34. E	
35. C	35. C	35. C	
36. D	36. A		
37. B	37. D		
38. E	38. C		
39. E	39. E		
40. A	40. D		
	41. B		
	42. B		
	43. E		
	44. D		
	45. B		

*Indicates four-choice questions. (All of the other questions are five-choice.)

The Scoring Process

Machine-scoring is done in three steps:

- *Scanning.* Your answer sheet is "read" by a scanning machine and the oval you filled in for each question is recorded on a computer tape.
- *Scoring.* The computer compares the oval filled in for each question with the correct response. Each correct answer receives one point; omitted questions do not count toward your score. For each wrong answer, a fraction of a point is subtracted to correct for random guessing. For questions with five answer choices, one-fourth of a point is subtracted for each wrong response; for questions with four answer choices, one-third of a point is subtracted for each wrong response. For example, the SAT-verbal test has 85 questions with five answer choices each, and if a student has 44 right, 32 wrong, and 9 omitted, the resulting raw score is determined as follows:

  $$44 \text{ right} - \frac{32 \text{ wrong}}{4} = 44 - 8 = 36 \text{ raw score points}$$

  Obtaining raw scores frequently involves the rounding of fractional numbers to the nearest whole number. For example, a raw score of 36.25 is rounded to 36, the nearest whole number. A raw score of 36.50 is rounded upward to 37.
- *Converting to reported scaled score.* Raw test scores are then placed on the College Board scale of 200 to 800 through a process that adjusts scores to account for minor differences in difficulty between different editions of the test. This process, known as equating, is performed so that a student's reported score is not affected by the edition of the test taken nor by the abilities of the group with whom the student takes the test. As a result of placing ATP scores on the College Board scale, scores earned by students at different times can be compared. For example, an SAT-verbal score of 400 on a test taken at one administration indicates the same level of developed verbal ability as a 400 score obtained on a different edition of the test taken at another time.

How to Score the Test

You can verify the College Board SAT scores reported to you recently by using the information in this booklet along with the copy of your answer sheet. *Before you begin, check that the form code you marked in item 3 on your answer sheet is the same as the one printed on the front of this booklet.* Compare the responses shown on the copy of your answer sheet with the list of correct answers.

SAT-Verbal Sections 1 and 4

Step A: Count the number of correct answers for *section 1* and record the number in the space provided on the worksheet on the opposite page. Then do the same for the incorrect answers. (Do not count omitted answers.) To determine subtotal A, use the formula:

$$\text{number correct} - \frac{\text{number incorrect}}{4} = \text{subtotal A}$$

Step B: Count the number of correct answers and the number of incorrect answers for *section 4* and record the numbers in the spaces provided on the worksheet. To determine subtotal B, use the formula:

$$\text{number correct} - \frac{\text{number incorrect}}{4} = \text{subtotal B}$$

Step C: To obtain C, add subtotal A to subtotal B, keeping any decimals.

Step D: To obtain D, your raw verbal score, round C to the nearest whole number. (For example, any number from 44.50 to 45.49 rounds to 45.)

Step E: To find your reported SAT-verbal score, look up the total raw verbal score you obtained in step D in the conversion table on the back cover.

SAT-Mathematical Sections 2 and 5

Step A: Count the number of correct answers and the number of incorrect answers for the *four-choice questions (questions 8 through 27) in section 2* and record the numbers in the spaces provided on the worksheet. To determine the subtotal A, use the formula:

$$\text{number correct} - \frac{\text{number incorrect}}{3} = \text{subtotal A}$$

Step B: Count the number of correct answers and the number of incorrect answers for the *five-choice questions (questions 1 through 7 and 28 through 35) in section 2* and record the numbers in the spaces provided on the worksheet. To determine the subtotal B, use the formula:

$$\text{number correct} - \frac{\text{number incorrect}}{4} = \text{subtotal B}$$

Step C: Count the number of correct answers and the number of incorrect answers for section 5 and record the numbers in the spaces provided on the worksheet. To determine the subtotal C, use the formula:

$$\text{number correct} - \frac{\text{number incorrect}}{4} = \text{subtotal C}$$

Step D: To obtain D, add subtotal A, subtotal B, and subtotal C, keeping any decimals.

Step E: To obtain E, your raw mathematical score, round D to the nearest whole number. (For example, any number from 44.50 to 45.49 rounds to 45.)

Step F: To find your reported SAT-mathematical score, look up the total raw mathematical score you obtained in E in the conversion table on the back cover.

FORM CODE 8G071

SAT-Verbal Worksheet

A. Section 1:	________ no. correct	− ¼	(________ no. incorrect)	=	________ subtotal A
B. Section 4:	________ no. correct	− ¼	(________ no. incorrect)	=	________ subtotal B
C. Total unrounded raw score (Total A + B)					________ C
D. Total rounded raw score (Rounded to nearest whole number)					________ D
E. Reported SAT-verbal score (See the conversion table on the back cover.)					[ ] SAT-Verbal

SAT-Mathematical Worksheet

A. Section 2: Questions 8 through 27 (4-choice)	________ no. correct	− ⅓	(________ no. incorrect)	=	________ subtotal A
B. Section 2: Questions 1 through 7 and 28 through 35 (5-choice)	________ no. correct	− ¼	(________ no. incorrect)	=	________ subtotal B
C. Section 5:	________ no. correct	− ¼	(________ no. incorrect)	=	________ subtotal C
D. Total unrounded raw score (Total A + B + C)					________ D
E. Total rounded raw score (Rounded to nearest whole number)					________ E
F. Reported SAT-mathematical score (See the conversion table on the back cover.)					[ ] SAT-Math

If you have any questions on these scoring instructions, you may call the phone number below.

If, after following the above scoring directions and checking your work carefully, your results disagree with the verbal or mathematical score reported on your ATP Student Report, you may request a hand scoring of your answer sheet by writing or calling:

College Board ATP
Box 592
Princeton, NJ 08541
Attention: Rescore Request
Telephone: (609) 883-8500

Please indicate whether it is your verbal or mathematical score, or both, that you want to be rescored. When you write, please include a copy of this scoring worksheet on which you did your calculations.

Score Conversion Table
Scholastic Aptitude Test
Form Code 8G071

Raw Score	College Board Reported Score		Raw Score	College Board Reported Score	
	SAT-Verbal	SAT-Math		SAT-Verbal	SAT-Math
85	800		40	450	600
84	780		39	450	590
83	770		38	440	580
82	760		37	430	570
81	750		36	430	570
80	740		35	420	560
79	720		34	410	550
78	710		33	410	540
77	700		32	400	530
76	690		31	400	520
75	680		30	390	520
74	670		29	380	510
73	660		28	380	500
72	660		27	370	490
71	650		26	360	480
70	640		25	360	470
69	640		24	350	470
68	630		23	340	460
67	630		22	340	450
66	620		21	330	440
65	610		20	330	430
64	610		19	320	420
63	600		18	310	420
62	590		17	310	410
61	590		16	300	400
60	580	800	15	290	390
59	570	780	14	290	380
58	570	770	13	280	370
57	560	760	12	270	370
56	560	750	11	270	360
55	550	740	10	260	350
54	540	730	9	260	340
53	540	720	8	250	330
52	530	710	7	240	320
51	520	700	6	240	320
50	520	690	5	230	310
49	510	680	4	220	300
48	500	670	3	220	290
47	500	660	2	210	280
46	490	650	1	200	270
45	490	640	0	200	270
44	480	630	– 1	200	260
43	470	620	– 2	200	250
42	470	620	– 3	200	240
41	460	610	– 4	200	230
			– 5	200	220
			– 6	200	220
			– 7	200	210
			– 8 or below	200	200

SAT
Form Code 0B023

(Cut here to detach.)

COLLEGE BOARD—SCHOLASTIC APTITUDE TEST and Test of Standard Written English

Side 1

Use a No. 2 pencil only for completing this answer sheet. Be sure each mark is dark and completely fills the intended space. Completely erase any errors or stray marks.

1.

YOUR NAME: (Print) ____ Last ____ First ____ M.I.

SIGNATURE: ____ **DATE:** __/__/__

HOME ADDRESS: (Print) ____ Number and Street

____ City ____ State ____ Zip Code

CENTER: (Print) ____ City ____ State ____ Center Number

IMPORTANT: Please fill in these boxes exactly as shown on the back cover of your test book.

FOR ETS USE ONLY

2. TEST FORM

3. FORM CODE

0	A	J	S	0	0	0
1	B	K	T	1	1	1
2	C	L	U	2	2	2
3	D	M	V	3	3	3
4	E	N	W	4	4	4
5	F	O	X	5	5	5
6	G	P	Y	6	6	6
7	H	Q	Z	7	7	7
8	I	R		8	8	8
9				9	9	9

4. REGISTRATION NUMBER
(Copy from your Admission Ticket.)

0	0	0	0	0	0	0
1	1	1	1	1	1	1
2	2	2	2	2	2	2
3	3	3	3	3	3	3
4	4	4	4	4	4	4
5	5	5	5	5	5	5
6	6	6	6	6	6	6
7	7	7	7	7	7	7
8	8	8	8	8	8	8
9	9	9	9	9	9	9

5. YOUR NAME

First 4 letters of last name				First Init.	Mid. Init.
A	A	A	A	A	A
B	B	B	B	B	B
C	C	C	C	C	C
D	D	D	D	D	D
E	E	E	E	E	E
F	F	F	F	F	F
G	G	G	G	G	G
H	H	H	H	H	H
I	I	I	I	I	I
J	J	J	J	J	J
K	K	K	K	K	K
L	L	L	L	L	L
M	M	M	M	M	M
N	N	N	N	N	N
O	O	O	O	O	O
P	P	P	P	P	P
Q	Q	Q	Q	Q	Q
R	R	R	R	R	R
S	S	S	S	S	S
T	T	T	T	T	T
U	U	U	U	U	U
V	V	V	V	V	V
W	W	W	W	W	W
X	X	X	X	X	X
Y	Y	Y	Y	Y	Y
Z	Z	Z	Z	Z	Z

6. DATE OF BIRTH

Month	Day		Year	
Jan.				
Feb.				
Mar.	0	0	0	0
Apr.	1	1	1	1
May	2	2	2	2
June	3	3	3	3
July		4	4	4
Aug.		5	5	5
Sept.		6	6	6
Oct.		7	7	7
Nov.		8		8
Dec.		9		9

7. SEX

Male

Female

8. TEST BOOK SERIAL NUMBER

Start with number 1 for each new section. If a section has fewer than 50 questions, leave the extra answer spaces blank.

SECTION 1

1 A B C D E
2 A B C D E
3 A B C D E
4 A B C D E
5 A B C D E
6 A B C D E
7 A B C D E
8 A B C D E
9 A B C D E
10 A B C D E
11 A B C D E
12 A B C D E
13 A B C D E
14 A B C D E
15 A B C D E
16 A B C D E
17 A B C D E
18 A B C D E
19 A B C D E
20 A B C D E
21 A B C D E
22 A B C D E
23 A B C D E
24 A B C D E
25 A B C D E
26 A B C D E
27 A B C D E
28 A B C D E
29 A B C D E
30 A B C D E
31 A B C D E
32 A B C D E
33 A B C D E
34 A B C D E
35 A B C D E
36 A B C D E
37 A B C D E
38 A B C D E
39 A B C D E
40 A B C D E
41 A B C D E
42 A B C D E
43 A B C D E
44 A B C D E
45 A B C D E
46 A B C D E
47 A B C D E
48 A B C D E
49 A B C D E
50 A B C D E

SECTION 2

1 A B C D E
2 A B C D E
3 A B C D E
4 A B C D E
5 A B C D E
6 A B C D E
7 A B C D E
8 A B C D
9 A B C D
10 A B C D
11 A B C D
12 A B C D
13 A B C D
14 A B C D
15 A B C D
16 A B C D
17 A B C D
18 A B C D
19 A B C D
20 A B C D
21 A B C D
22 A B C D
23 A B C D
24 A B C D
25 A B C D
26 A B C D
27 A B C D
28 A B C D E
29 A B C D E
30 A B C D E
31 A B C D E
32 A B C D E
33 A B C D E
34 A B C D E
35 A B C D E
36 A B C D E
37 A B C D E
38 A B C D E
39 A B C D E
40 A B C D E
41 A B C D E
42 A B C D E
43 A B C D E
44 A B C D E
45 A B C D E
46 A B C D E
47 A B C D E
48 A B C D E
49 A B C D E
50 A B C D E

COLLEGE BOARD — SCHOLASTIC APTITUDE TEST and Test of Standard Written English Side 2

Use a No. 2 pencil only for completing this answer sheet. Be sure each mark is dark and completely fills the intended space. Completely erase any errors or stray marks.

Start with number 1 for each new section. If a section has fewer than 50 questions, leave the extra answer spaces blank.

SECTION 3	SECTION 4	SECTION 5	SECTION 6
1 A B C D E	1 A B C D E	1 A B C D E	1 A B C D E
2 A B C D E	2 A B C D E	2 A B C D E	2 A B C D E
3 A B C D E	3 A B C D E	3 A B C D E	3 A B C D E
4 A B C D E	4 A B C D E	4 A B C D E	4 A B C D E
5 A B C D E	5 A B C D E	5 A B C D E	5 A B C D E
6 A B C D E	6 A B C D E	6 A B C D E	6 A B C D E
7 A B C D E	7 A B C D E	7 A B C D E	7 A B C D E
8 A B C D E	8 A B C D E	8 A B C D E	8 A B C D E
9 A B C D E	9 A B C D E	9 A B C D E	9 A B C D E
10 A B C D E	10 A B C D E	10 A B C D E	10 A B C D E
11 A B C D E	11 A B C D E	11 A B C D E	11 A B C D E
12 A B C D E	12 A B C D E	12 A B C D E	12 A B C D E
13 A B C D E	13 A B C D E	13 A B C D E	13 A B C D E
14 A B C D E	14 A B C D E	14 A B C D E	14 A B C D E
15 A B C D E	15 A B C D E	15 A B C D E	15 A B C D E
16 A B C D E	16 A B C D E	16 A B C D E	16 A B C D E
17 A B C D E	17 A B C D E	17 A B C D E	17 A B C D E
18 A B C D E	18 A B C D E	18 A B C D E	18 A B C D E
19 A B C D E	19 A B C D E	19 A B C D E	19 A B C D E
20 A B C D E	20 A B C D E	20 A B C D E	20 A B C D E
21 A B C D E	21 A B C D E	21 A B C D E	21 A B C D E
22 A B C D E	22 A B C D E	22 A B C D E	22 A B C D E
23 A B C D E	23 A B C D E	23 A B C D E	23 A B C D E
24 A B C D E	24 A B C D E	24 A B C D E	24 A B C D E
25 A B C D E	25 A B C D E	25 A B C D E	25 A B C D E
26 A B C D E	26 A B C D E	26 A B C D E	26 A B C D E
27 A B C D E	27 A B C D E	27 A B C D E	27 A B C D E
28 A B C D E	28 A B C D E	28 A B C D E	28 A B C D E
29 A B C D E	29 A B C D E	29 A B C D E	29 A B C D E
30 A B C D E	30 A B C D E	30 A B C D E	30 A B C D E
31 A B C D E	31 A B C D E	31 A B C D E	31 A B C D E
32 A B C D E	32 A B C D E	32 A B C D E	32 A B C D E
33 A B C D E	33 A B C D E	33 A B C D E	33 A B C D E
34 A B C D E	34 A B C D E	34 A B C D E	34 A B C D E
35 A B C D E	35 A B C D E	35 A B C D E	35 A B C D E
36 A B C D E	36 A B C D E	36 A B C D E	36 A B C D E
37 A B C D E	37 A B C D E	37 A B C D E	37 A B C D E
38 A B C D E	38 A B C D E	38 A B C D E	38 A B C D E
39 A B C D E	39 A B C D E	39 A B C D E	39 A B C D E
40 A B C D E	40 A B C D E	40 A B C D E	40 A B C D E
41 A B C D E	41 A B C D E	41 A B C D E	41 A B C D E
42 A B C D E	42 A B C D E	42 A B C D E	42 A B C D E
43 A B C D E	43 A B C D E	43 A B C D E	43 A B C D E
44 A B C D E	44 A B C D E	44 A B C D E	44 A B C D E
45 A B C D E	45 A B C D E	45 A B C D E	45 A B C D E
46 A B C D E	46 A B C D E	46 A B C D E	46 A B C D E
47 A B C D E	47 A B C D E	47 A B C D E	47 A B C D E
48 A B C D E	48 A B C D E	48 A B C D E	48 A B C D E
49 A B C D E	49 A B C D E	49 A B C D E	49 A B C D E
50 A B C D E	50 A B C D E	50 A B C D E	50 A B C D E

9. SIGNATURE: ____________

FOR ETS USE ONLY	VTR	VTFS	VRR	VRFS	VVR	VVFS	WER	WEFS	M4R	M4FS	M5R	M5FS	MTFS	
	VTW	VTCS	VRW	VRCS	VVW	VVCS	WEW	WECS	M4W		M5W		MTCS	

FORM CODE 0B023

SECTION 1

Time—30 minutes

40 QUESTIONS

For each question in this section, choose the best answer and blacken the corresponding space on the answer sheet.

Each question below consists of a word in capital letters, followed by five lettered words or phrases. Choose the word or phrase that is most nearly opposite in meaning to the word in capital letters. Since some of the questions require you to distinguish fine shades of meaning, consider all the choices before deciding which is best.

Example:

GOOD: (A) sour (B) bad (C) red (D) hot (E) ugly

Ⓐ ● Ⓒ Ⓓ Ⓔ

1. EXPEL: (A) await (B) adapt (C) loiter (D) disturb (E) admit

2. LENIENCY: (A) disdain (B) hostility (C) severity (D) persistence (E) stinginess

3. COMBUSTIBLE: (A) unlikely to break (B) unable to burn (C) reluctant to play (D) expected to fail (E) forced to open

4. DISAPPROVAL: (A) concern (B) security (C) cooperation (D) endorsement (E) tastelessness

5. SQUANDER: (A) agree (B) cleanse (C) conserve (D) treat fairly (E) speak eloquently

6. MULTIFARIOUS: (A) absorbent (B) clumsy (C) limited in variety (D) causing dissension (E) unintentionally harmful

7. PHILISTINE: (A) cultured (B) courageous (C) arrogant (D) generous (E) witty

8. BALEFUL: (A) vain (B) solid (C) benign (D) common (E) incessant

9. DISINTERMENT: (A) penetration (B) burial (C) denunciation (D) perseverance (E) construction

10. GLUT: (A) dearth (B) change (C) disparity (D) refinement (E) correction

Each sentence below has one or two blanks, each blank indicating that something has been omitted. Beneath the sentence are five lettered words or sets of words. Choose the word or set of words that best fits the meaning of the sentence as a whole.

Example:

Although its publicity has been ----, the film itself is intelligent, well-acted, handsomely produced, and altogether ----.

(A) tasteless..respectable (B) extensive..moderate (C) sophisticated..amateur (D) risqué..crude (E) perfect..spectacular

● Ⓑ Ⓒ Ⓓ Ⓔ

11. Although most people have one explanation or another for what happened, the event remains ----.

(A) old-fashioned (B) unpopular (C) frightening (D) accidental (E) mysterious

12. The basic purpose of advertising is the announcement of products, prices, new equipment, and special sales and is, therefore, entirely ---- since such announcements ---- needed useful information.

(A) useless..duplicate
(B) benevolent..confirm
(C) suspect..insinuate
(D) defensible..eliminate
(E) reasonable..provide

13. Good health is ---- with a high degree of resistance to bacterial attack; any influence that lowers one's general health also ---- one's resistance to such an attack.

(A) associated..activates
(B) balanced..secures
(C) allied..increases
(D) synonymous..reduces
(E) confused..diminishes

GO ON TO THE NEXT PAGE

The reading passages in this test are brief excerpts or adaptations of excerpts from published material. To make the text suitable for testing purposes, we may in some cases have altered the style, contents, or point of view of the original.

14. MacDougall theorizes that in human history order has tended to arise from chaos and, similarly, that social forces will do almost anything to ---- anarchy.

(A) prolong (B) avert (C) instill (D) imitate (E) instigate

15. Few politicians are so ---- asinine as to adopt a stance that is morally ---- and then boast of it.

(A) furtively. .precarious
(B) scrupulously. .laudable
(C) egregiously. .untenable
(D) surreptitiously. .tolerable
(E) transparently. .indisputable

Each question below consists of a related pair of words or phrases, followed by five lettered pairs of words or phrases. Select the lettered pair that best expresses a relationship similar to that expressed in the original pair.

Example:

YAWN : BOREDOM :: (A) dream : sleep (B) anger : madness (C) smile : amusement (D) face : expression (E) impatience : rebellion

Ⓐ Ⓑ ● Ⓓ Ⓔ

16. OLDTIMER : NEWCOMER :: (A) host : party (B) imitator : copy (C) veteran : inductee (D) fable : legend (E) ancestor : relative

17. MARGIN : PAGE :: (A) envelope : letter (B) crust : bread (C) grass : field (D) tide : ocean (E) country : nation

18. DISMISS : EMPLOYEE :: (A) evict : tenant (B) harass : enemy (C) dislike : food (D) load : baggage (E) betray : friend

19. YARDSTICK : LENGTH :: (A) meter : capacity (B) plateau : elevation (C) meridian : longitude (D) hourglass : time (E) humidifier : moisture

20. SMILE : HAPPINESS :: (A) pallor : health (B) laughter : pun (C) grimace : condolence (D) frown : puzzlement (E) shout : contentment

21. LOW : CATTLE :: (A) wool : sheep (B) fodder : horses (C) cluck : chickens (D) nest : robins (E) litter : puppies

22. ABEYANCE : ACTIVITY :: (A) petition : request (B) intermission : concert (C) exploit : adventure (D) rebuttal : denial (E) rehearsal : drama

23. SANCTUARY : PROTECTION ::
(A) quagmire : difficulty
(B) labyrinth : circularity
(C) treadmill : variety
(D) apotheosis : ennui
(E) conundrum : lucidity

24. PALEONTOLOGY : FOSSILS ::
(A) philology : words (B) philosophy : adages (C) oceanography : ships (D) meteorology : stars (E) ontology : plants

25. LIMPID : MUDDINESS :: (A) eerie : fear (B) ambiguous : doubt (C) iridescent : color (D) chaotic : confusion (E) harmonious : discord

GO ON TO THE NEXT PAGE

Each passage below is followed by questions based on its content. Answer all questions following a passage on the basis of what is stated or implied in that passage.

(The passages for this test have been adapted from published material. The ideas contained in them do not necessarily represent the opinions of the College Board or Educational Testing Service.)

Compared with modern cities, cities of the Italian Renaissance were not large. In traveling from one side of the city to another, citizens could not avoid the main thoroughfares. They became accustomed to the same faces. In one way or another, citizens were always on show.

Citizens measured one another accordingly. There was no separation between the private and public lives of the citizens. The world of the individual was permeated with the values of the society. Parish and guild, family and neighborhood were the vessels from which the citizen drew identity and security.

We know too little about the values of the very poor. The record, such as it is, indicates that the poor constantly drifted in a quest for lower rents and higher wages. But, for the members of the tenacious and prosperous middle and upper classes, attachment to neighborhood and family was profound.

Hence, we can begin to understand why exile from one's native city was an agonizing experience. The effects of such estrangement were most acutely felt by members of the ruling class. They were the best known citizens in the city. They were born and bred to politics until the triumph of one-man rule transformed such grooming into a preparation for service to a prince.

Not surprisingly, the Aristotelian stress on people as political animals found an approving audience in the intelligentsia. Humanity seemed to have no reality outside a civil context.

26. Which of the following best summarizes the author's main point?

(A) Individual and social identity were one during the Italian Renaissance.
(B) Social class distinctions were at their height during the Italian Renaissance.
(C) Politicians of the Italian Renaissance were bred for their roles in the public sphere.
(D) The notion of man as a political animal was an Aristotelian ideal.
(E) Life in the cities of the Italian Renaissance was crowded and hectic.

27. According to the passage, exile from an Italian Renaissance city was an especially painful experience for members of the ruling class because they

(A) were poorly informed about customs in territories beyond their own city
(B) derived their identity from interaction with others in their community
(C) would have difficulty adjusting to an alien intellectual atmosphere
(D) had been taught to regard other princes as enemies
(E) would find it difficult to survive financially in a new place

28. It can be inferred that the history of the poor in the cities of the Italian Renaissance

(A) has been carefully suppressed
(B) is a record of discontent and rebellion
(C) deals mostly with their economic impact
(D) is chiefly an account of their migrations
(E) has been inadequately recorded

29. The passage is probably intended to

(A) argue an unpopular point of view
(B) present a nostalgic view of the period
(C) provide information about the cities
(D) suggest the weaknesses of the small city
(E) refute legends about the golden age of the Italian Renaissance

GO ON TO THE NEXT PAGE

One great group of seed-producing plants, the angiosperms (commonly known as flowering plants), is both the largest group in number of genera, species, and individuals, and the most recent to develop on earth. The angiosperms differ from gymnospermous seed plants in that their ovules and seeds are enclosed within the pistil, or megasporophyll, which later becomes a seed-bearing fruit. The structure of the pistil in certain primitive angiosperms suggests that the enclosure of the seeds may have come about by the evolutionary folding of a leaflike, ovule-bearing megasporophyll.

The angiosperms exceed all other vascular plants in range of diversity of plant body and habitat, and in their utility to mankind. Both woody and herbaceous angiosperms exist, and among the latter especially there is considerable diversity of vegetative structure, exemplified by bulbous hyacinths, onions, lilies, rhizomatous *Iris*, and many grasses. Diversity of habitat is demonstrated by such aquatics as water lilies, *Elodea*, and duckweed, or *Lemna*; such xerophytic genera as cacti; and such epiphytes as "Spanish moss," orchids, and bromeliads. In mature cacti, the leaves are either much reduced or absent.

Woody angiosperms are used extensively as lumber and fuel and as the source of commercial cork, while herbaceous types are important sources of food, beverages, textiles, drugs, and vegetable oils. Both the vegetative and reproductive portions of angiosperms are used as foods. Sweet potatoes, carrots, turnips, beets, and parsnips are examples of fleshy roots that are important foods; white or "Irish"potatoes and asparagus are stems. Various greens, such as spinach, turnip greens, chard, and lettuce are leaves. One eats the immense terminal buds of cabbages and head lettuce, whereas it is the fleshy petioles of rhubarb and celery that are eaten. Examples of the reproductive organs of angiosperms–flowers, fruits, and seeds–used as food are even more abundant. In both cauliflower and broccoli, we eat groups of flowers, called inflorescences. National cultures and economies are based on the use for food of such fruits as the grains of corn, rice, wheat, and rye. Indeed, fruits used as food are too numerous to list completely, but among them we may cite citrus fruits, squashes and melons, tomatoes, grapes, bananas, apples, pears, and various berries. The preceding list contains examples, such as tomatoes and squash, of fruits that laymen frequently classify as "vegetables."

30. According to the passage, which of the following can be inferred about squash?

(A) The edible parts of squash are called inflorescences.
(B) The edible parts of squash are derived from the reproductive organs of the plant.
(C) Like sweet potatoes, the edible parts of squash are roots.
(D) Squash is considered a woody angiosperm.
(E) Squash is often inaccurately classified as a fruit.

31. It can be inferred that which of the following was discussed in the paragraphs immediately preceding the passage?

(A) Plants that do not produce seeds
(B) The differences between woody and herbaceous angiosperms
(C) Blights that attack angiosperms
(D) Types of flowers produced by angiosperms
(E) Gymnospermous seed plants

32. The author mentions *Elodea*, cacti, and orchids primarily in order to emphasize the

(A) differences between woody and herbaceous angiosperms
(B) uses to which mankind has put angiosperms
(C) diversity of structure among angiosperms
(D) diversity of habitat among angiosperms
(E) similarity between xerophytic genera and epiphytes

33. The author's primary purpose in the passage is to

(A) give practical advice about growing angiosperms
(B) detail new discoveries in horticulture
(C) discuss the diversity of a particular group of plants
(D) question existing theories in botanical evolution
(E) trace evolutionary developments of gymnosperms

GO ON TO THE NEXT PAGE

People, once they have provided for their immediate needs, seem always to turn toward some form of creative expression. Yet strong feelings of guilt can often be found lurking somewhere in the background, based on many cultures' glorification of "practical" work. We need to know, I think, that our need to create is as valid as our need to maintain ourselves. If poetry (or any art form) has a function in society, it may be to serve as visible, audible evidence that creativity is a universal and timeless characteristic.

34. We can infer that the author would consider sculpture evidence of

(A) humanity's practical need for useful objects
(B) a means of escape from universal guilt feelings
(C) humanity's need to create
(D) realistic documentation of the differences in various cultures
(E) an entertaining diversion for those who must work at difficult tasks

35. According to the passage, people often feel guilty when they

(A) create works of art
(B) toil without enjoying it
(C) criticize those who are creative
(D) fail to help others meet their needs
(E) overemphasize the importance of practical tasks

Both conventional and continuous steelmaking begin with the melting of pig iron and scrap steel, together with fluxing, alloying, and purifying agents, in a furnace. It is in the shaping and solidifying of the molten metal that continuous casting offers its great economies in plant investment and in operation and energy costs. In the conventional procedure, the full ladle is moved to a casting pit where, supported by an overhead crane, it is tapped into a series of individual ingot molds standing upright on rail cars. When the surface of the ingots has solidified so that they can stand alone, the molds are stripped off. The ingots are then transferred to another furnace, the soaking pit, where they are heated to uniform temperature for the rolling to follow.

The hot ingots are first sent through the primary, or breakdown, mill: a series of massive rollers that squeeze the ingots down to the cross section appropriate to the type of product that is being made in that particular plant. The products of the primary mill are classified according to size and shape as slabs, blooms, and billets. Slabs have an oblong cross section; if they are destined to be rolled into plate or sheet, this cross section is usually larger than three by twelve inches. Blooms have a square cross section greater than five inches; billets are blooms that have been reduced to a smaller cross section.

Continuous-casting methods are not all the same, but they are enough alike to fit a generalized description. The ladle of molten steel is transported by a vehicle or crane to a platform above the casting machine, where it is teemed, or discharged, into a rectangular trough called a tundish. From the vessel the steel flows into a casting "strand," the heart of which is a bottomless vertical mold that receives and confines the molten metal, partially shaping it into the desired cross section as it passes through. Just below the upper surface of the metal a thin skin forms on the surfaces adjacent to the inner walls of the mold; this skin thickens as the metal is pulled through the mold.

The steel continues to solidify as the billet is withdrawn, and to hasten cooling it is usually passed through a secondary cooling chamber where it is sprayed with water from an array of nozzles. The solid billet, still at red heat, is pulled by rollers that are synchronized with the level of liquid metal in the mold in order to ensure that the billet is formed in a steady manner. Beyond the withdrawal mechanism the continuous billet is cut into convenient lengths for subsequent reduction. In short, continuous casting eliminates the pouring, molding, transporting, and reheating of ingots.

GO ON TO THE NEXT PAGE

36. The style of the passage can best be described as

(A) argumentative
(B) explanatory
(C) contemplative
(D) rhetorical
(E) scholarly

37. It can be inferred that steel is shaped into the final product at which stage of the casting process?

(A) When it has cooled in the molds in the casting pits
(B) When it has been formed into slabs, blooms, and billets
(C) When the billets have been cut and cooled completely
(D) Before it leaves the secondary cooling chamber
(E) After the stages described in the passage

38. The author provides information that answers which of the following questions?

I. In what ways does the continuous method differ from the conventional method of casting steel?
II. In what ways do the various methods of continuous casting differ from each other?
III. In what ways does the continuous-casting method provide economic benefit to the steel manufacturer?

(A) I only
(B) III only
(C) I and II only
(D) I and III only
(E) I, II, and III

39. According to the passage, in what way are the soaking pit and the secondary cooling chamber alike?

(A) In both, water is sprayed on the steel.
(B) In both, the steel is cooled and solidified.
(C) In both, steel is heated before passing through a series of rollers.
(D) Both receive steel in a partially solidified form.
(E) Both are stages in the conventional method of casting steel.

40. The passage is concerned primarily with

(A) presenting a complete picture of the ways in which steel is produced and molded into usable forms
(B) proving that there is little difference between the conventional and the continuous methods of steel production
(C) comparing the various methods of continuous casting of steel in order to present a generalized description
(D) tracing the development of the continuous-casting method of steel production as an outgrowth and modification of the conventional process
(E) demonstrating the advantages of continuous casting of steel by contrasting this process with the conventional method of steelmaking

S T O P

IF YOU FINISH BEFORE TIME IS CALLED, CHECK YOUR WORK ON THIS SECTION ONLY. DO NOT WORK ON ANY OTHER SECTION IN THE TEST.

SECTION 2

Time—30 minutes

35 QUESTIONS

In this section solve each problem, using any available space on the page for scratchwork. Then indicate the one correct answer in the appropriate space on the answer sheet.

The following information is for your reference in solving some of the problems.

Circle of radius r: Area $= \pi r^2$; Circumference $= 2\pi r$
The number of degrees of arc in a circle is 360.
The measure in degrees of a straight angle is 180.

Definitions of symbols:

$=$	is equal to	$\leq$	is less than or equal to
$\neq$	is unequal to	$\geq$	is greater than or equal to
$<$	is less than	$\parallel$	is parallel to
$>$	is greater than	$\perp$	is perpendicular to

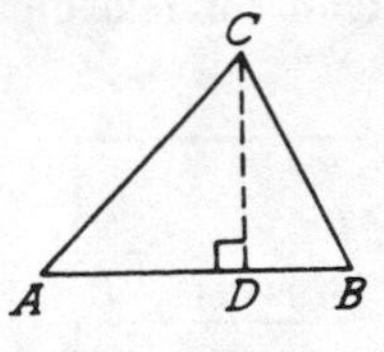

Triangle: The sum of the measures in degrees of the angles of a triangle is 180.

If $\angle CDA$ is a right angle, then

(1) area of $\triangle ABC = \dfrac{AB \times CD}{2}$

(2) $AC^2 = AD^2 + DC^2$

Note: Figures which accompany problems in this test are intended to provide information useful in solving the problems. They are drawn as accurately as possible EXCEPT when it is stated in a specific problem that its figure is not drawn to scale. All figures lie in a plane unless otherwise indicated. All numbers used are real numbers.

---

1. If 2 out of every 5 students in a class of 35 intend to go to summer school, how many intend to go to summer school?

   (A) 5 (B) 7 (C) 10 (D) 14 (E) 21

2. If $2x = 5$ and $3y = 6$, then $6xy =$

   (A) 30 (B) 15 (C) 11 (D) $\frac{24}{5}$ (E) $\frac{12}{5}$

3. If $x + y = 6$ and $y + z = 9$, what is the value of z?

   (A) 2
   (B) 3
   (C) 6
   (D) 7
   (E) It cannot be determined from the information given.

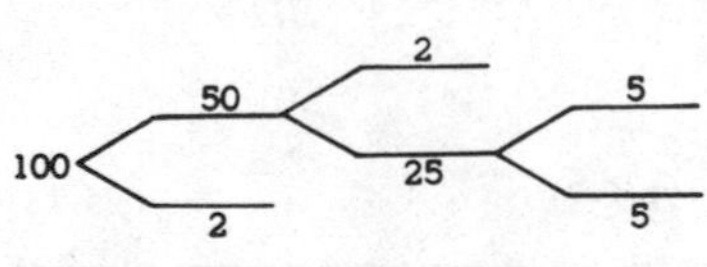

Figure I

Figure II

4. Figure I is an example of a "factor diagram" of 100. What is the value of N if Figure II is a "factor diagram" of N?

   (A) 70 (B) 120 (C) 150
   (D) 240 (E) 300

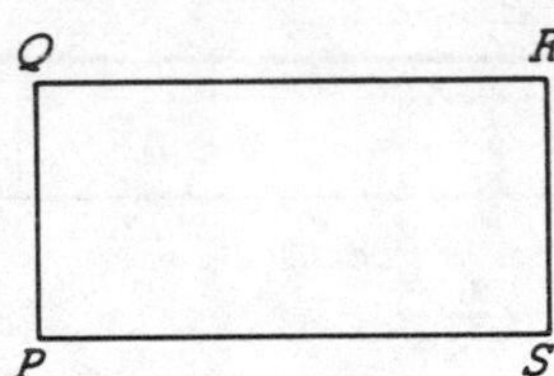

5. In the rectangle above, $PQ = x$ and $QR = 2x$. What per cent of the perimeter of the rectangle is the sum $PQ + QR + RS$?

   (A) 50% (B) $66\frac{2}{3}$% (C) 75%
   (D) 80% (E) $83\frac{2}{3}$%

6. If 45 cards can be copied in 30 minutes, how many hours will it take to copy 540 such cards at the same rate?

   (A) 3
   (B) 6
   (C) 12
   (D) 18
   (E) 24

7. Ms. Smith is S years old and is 3 years older than Ms. Lopez. In terms of S, how many years old was Ms. Lopez 2 years ago?

   (A) $S - 5$ (B) $S - 3$ (C) $S - 2$
   (D) $S - 1$ (E) $S + 1$

GO ON TO THE NEXT PAGE

2

Questions 8-27 each consist of two quantities, one in Column A and one in Column B. You are to compare the two quantities and on the answer sheet blacken space

- A if the quantity in Column A is greater;
- B if the quantity in Column B is greater;
- C if the two quantities are equal;
- D if the relationship cannot be determined from the information given.

Notes:
1. In certain questions, information concerning one or both of the quantities to be compared is centered above the two columns.
2. A symbol that appears in both columns represents the same thing in Column A as it does in Column B.
3. Letters such as x, n, and k stand for real numbers.

EXAMPLES

	Column A	Column B	Answers
E1.	2×6	$2 + 6$	● Ⓑ Ⓒ Ⓓ
	$x°$ $y°$		
E2.	$180 - x$	y	Ⓐ Ⓑ ● Ⓓ
E3.	$p - q$	$q - p$	Ⓐ Ⓑ Ⓒ ●

	Column A	Column B
8.	$\frac{6}{15}$	$\frac{11}{30}$

$y = x^2 - 1$
$z = w^2 - 1$

9.	y when $x = 3$	z when $w = -3$

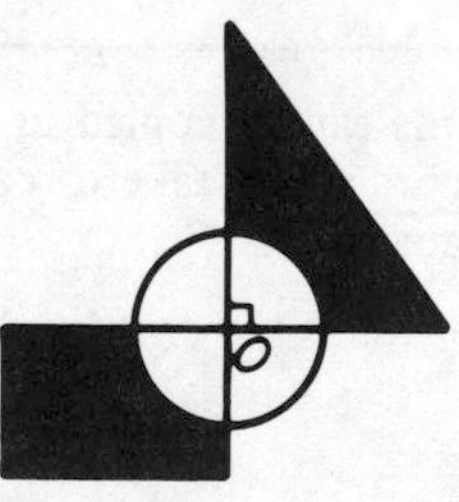

The total area of the rectangle is equal to the total area of the triangle. O is the center of the circle.

10.	The area of the shaded region in the rectangle	The area of the shaded region in the triangle

	Column A	Column B
11.	3,560 rounded to the nearest hundred	3,546 rounded to the nearest hundred

$\frac{x}{2} = 15$

12.	$\frac{x}{3}$	15

$x < y < 0$

13.	x	xy

$w, x, y,$ and z are integers.
$x \div 5 = y + 3$ and $w \div 5 = z + 2$

14.	x	w

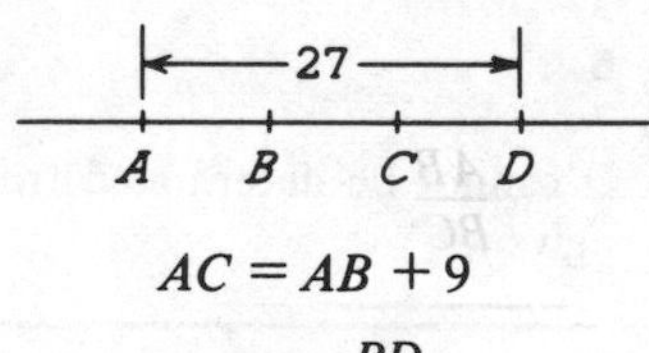

$AC = AB + 9$

$BC = \frac{BD}{2}$

15.	AB	CD

The positive whole number divisors of 6 are 1, 2, 3, and 6.

16.	The number of positive whole number divisors of 20	5

GO ON TO THE NEXT PAGE

SUMMARY DIRECTIONS FOR COMPARISON QUESTIONS

Answer: A if the quantity in Column A is greater;
B if the quantity in Column B is greater;
C if the two quantities are equal;
D if the relationship cannot be determined from the information given.

	Column A	Column B

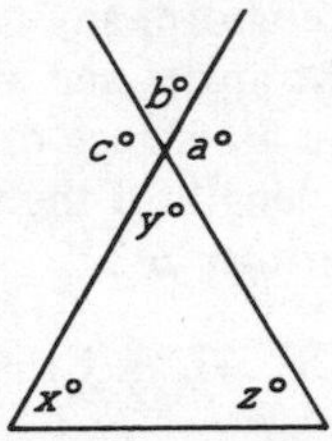

17. $a + b + c$ | $x + y + z$

$2x + 3 = y$

18. $20x + 20$ | $10y$

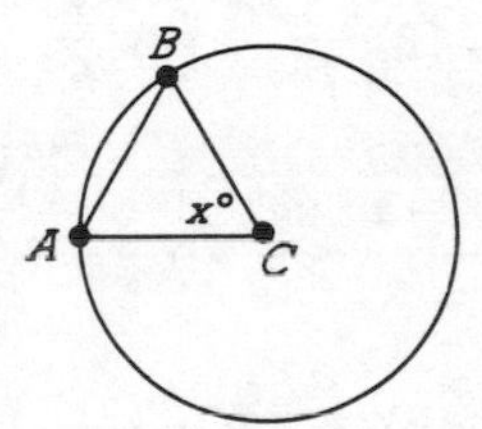

C is the center of the circle.

$x \neq 60$

19. $\frac{AB}{BC}$ | 1

20. 1^k | 1^{2k}

Car	Speed (Kilometers per hour)	Time (Minutes)	Distance (Kilometers)
X	88 k.p.h.	x min.	1 kilometer
Y	90 k.p.h.	y min.	1 kilometer
Z	95 k.p.h.	z min.	1 kilometer

Each of the experimental cars X, Y, and Z maintains the constant speed indicated in the table above for the distance and time indicated.

21. x | z

	Column A	Column B

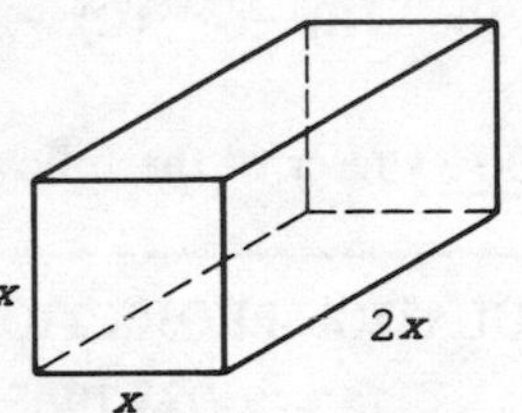

22. Total surface area of the rectangular solid shown | $10x^2$

23. The area of a right triangle with sides of lengths 3, 4, and 5 | The area of an isosceles triangle with two sides of length 5

$y = x + 1$

24. The average (arithmetic mean) of 7, 9, and x | The average (arithmetic mean) of 2, 13, and y

$-1 < x < 1$

$x \neq 0$

25. $\frac{1}{x}$ | x

n is an odd integer greater than 125.

26. The remainder when $85n$ is divided by 2 | 1

$x < y < z$

27. xy | yz

Solve each of the remaining problems in this section using any available space for scratchwork. Then indicate the one correct answer in the appropriate space on the answer sheet.

28. A right angle is bisected and each of the two resulting angles is trisected. Which of the following could NOT be the degree measure of an angle formed by any two of these lines?

(A) 15 (B) 30 (C) 50 (D) 60 (E) 75

29. If the product of 4 consecutive integers is zero, what is the least possible sum of these integers?

(A) −10 (B) −6 (C) −2 (D) −1 (E) 0

Questions 30-31 refer to the following table.

POPULATION PROJECTIONS BY REGION
1975-1985
(Thousands)

Region	1975 Population	Projected Population Change Between 1975 and 1985
P	2,671	202
Q	3,011	162
R	2,934	761
S	2,744	1,226
T	2,133	−134
U	2,210	631

30. What is the difference between the projected 1985 populations for regions T and U ?

(A) 497,000 (B) 574,000 (C) 765,000
(D) 842,000 (E) 923,000

31. Which of the six regions show(s) a projected population change for the period 1975-1985 of less than 10 per cent of the 1975 population?

(A) Q only
(B) P and S only
(C) Q and R only
(D) P, Q, and T only
(E) S, T, and U only

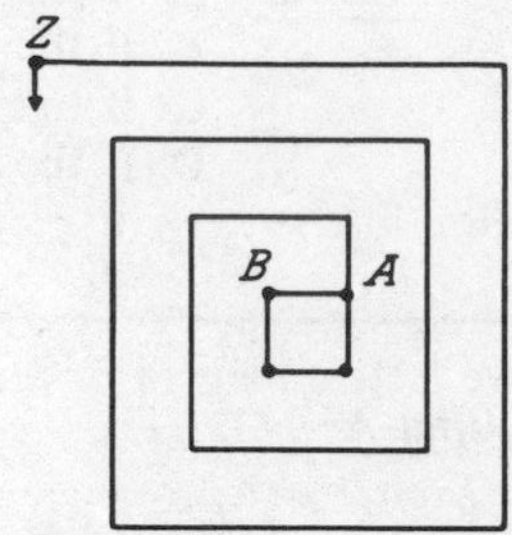

32. In the figure above, any two intersecting segments meet at right angles and any two adjacent parallel segments are a distance of 1 centimeter apart. What is the length of the solid-lined path from A to Z through B ?

(A) 40 (B) 41 (C) 42 (D) 43 (E) 44

33. In a certain factory, $\frac{3}{4}$ of the workers are married and $\frac{3}{4}$ of these married workers have children. What fraction of the workers in the factory are married without children?

(A) $\frac{1}{16}$ (B) $\frac{3}{16}$ (C) $\frac{1}{4}$ (D) $\frac{1}{2}$ (E) $\frac{9}{16}$

34. If $x + y = k$ and $x - y = \frac{1}{k}$, then when $k \neq 0$, $x^2 - y^2 =$

(A) $\frac{1}{k}$ (B) k (C) k^2 (D) 2 (E) 1

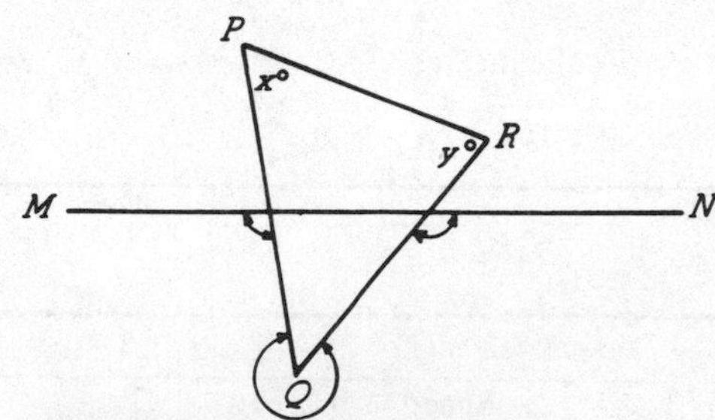

35. In the figure above, what is the sum of the degree measures of the angles marked with arrows?

(A) $540 - 2x - 2y$
(B) $360 - 2x - 2y$
(C) 360
(D) 450
(E) 540

S T O P

IF YOU FINISH BEFORE TIME IS CALLED, CHECK YOUR WORK ON THIS SECTION ONLY. DO NOT WORK ON ANY OTHER SECTION IN THE TEST.

SECTION 4

Time—30 minutes

45 QUESTIONS

For each question in this section, choose the best answer and blacken the corresponding space on the answer sheet.

Each question below consists of a word in capital letters, followed by five lettered words or phrases. Choose the word or phrase that is most nearly opposite in meaning to the word in capital letters. Since some of the questions require you to distinguish fine shades of meaning, consider all the choices before deciding which is best.

Example:

> GOOD: (A) sour (B) bad (C) red (D) hot (E) ugly
>
> Ⓐ ● Ⓒ Ⓓ Ⓔ

1. RUMPLED: (A) smooth (B) plentiful (C) recurrent (D) diverse (E) commonplace

2. CALAMITY: (A) pleasure (B) virtue (C) good fortune (D) suspicion (E) firm belief

3. OUTSPOKEN: (A) perceptive (B) reserved (C) ineligible (D) unnecessary (E) triumphant

4. REPRESS: (A) distract (B) annoy (C) borrow (D) release (E) miscalculate

5. CELESTIAL: (A) sectional (B) rational (C) earthly (D) realistic (E) feeble

6. TAPER: (A) make wider (B) make difficult (C) contradict (D) strengthen (E) remove

7. HUMID: (A) autumnal (B) polar (C) overcast (D) insipid (E) arid

8. DISBURSE: (A) oversee (B) proceed (C) collect (D) praise highly (E) gain weight

9. PRESTIGE: (A) lack of skill (B) lack of money (C) lack of influence (D) lack of ambition (E) lack of pride

10. ASCETIC: (A) parasitic (B) erratic (C) sensual (D) deleterious (E) merciless

11. RECANT: (A) avow (B) curse (C) restrain (D) deflate (E) compensate

12. TENUOUS: (A) endless or boring (B) extreme or excessive (C) firm or substantial (D) noisy (E) controlled

13. BILK: (A) banish fear (B) show respect for (C) portray faithfully (D) enforce strictly (E) deal honestly with

14. LACHRYMOSE: (A) dry-eyed (B) warmhearted (C) high-minded (D) sharp-sighted (E) wide-awake

15. COMMENSURATE: (A) unequal (B) stringent (C) improvident (D) inadvertent (E) immutable

Each sentence below has one or two blanks, each blank indicating that something has been omitted. Beneath the sentence are five lettered words or sets of words. Choose the word or set of words that best fits the meaning of the sentence as a whole.

Example:

> Although its publicity has been ----, the film itself is intelligent, well-acted, handsomely produced, and altogether ----.
>
> (A) tasteless. .respectable (B) extensive. .moderate (C) sophisticated. .amateur (D) risqué. .crude (E) perfect. .spectacular
>
> ● Ⓑ Ⓒ Ⓓ Ⓔ

16. Even though mistletoe berries are ----, they do contain medicinal properties and have been refined into a useful drug.

    (A) scarce (B) hardy (C) colorful (D) poisonous (E) beneficial

17. In a sense, technology always ---- traditional social forms and creates a crisis for contemporary culture.

    (A) underlies (B) disrupts (C) presupposes (D) delineates (E) facilitates

18. Maria's quick mind and ingenious imagination were evident in her ---- performances.

    (A) reticent (B) marginal (C) banal (D) impromptu (E) stultifying

19. He was the scapegoat, by whose ---- punishment all the other transgressors in the group were, it is supposed, sufficiently ----.

    (A) vicarious. .amused
    (B) undisclosed. .avenged
    (C) undeserved. .implicated
    (D) sacrificial. .disillusioned
    (E) public. .chastised

20. People of intemperate minds can never be free, for their passions ---- their fetters.

    (A) forge (B) sever (C) shackle (D) tarnish (E) dissolve

Each passage below is followed by questions based on its content. Answer all questions following a passage on the basis of what is stated or implied in that passage.

(The passages for this test have been adapted from published material. The ideas contained in them do not necessarily represent the opinions of the College Board or Educational Testing Service.)

Sometimes as I sit communing in my study I feel that death is not far off. Death neither alarms nor frightens one who has had a long career of fruitful toil. The knowledge that my work has been helpful to many fills me with joy and great satisfaction. Sometimes I ask myself if I have any legacy to leave. Truly, my worldly possessions are few. Yet, my experiences have been rich. From them, I have distilled principles and policies in which I believe firmly, for they represent the meaning of my life's work. Perhaps in them there is something of value. So, as my life draws to a close, I will pass them on to blacks everywhere.

I leave you the challenge of developing confidence in one another. Black banks, insurance companies, and other businesses are examples of successful economic enterprises. These institutions were made possible by vision and mutual aid. Economic separatism cannot be tolerated in this enlightened age, and it is not practicable.

I leave you a respect for the uses of power. We live in a world which respects power above all things. Power, intelligently directed, can lead to more freedom. We must select leaders who are wise, courageous, and of great moral stature and ability. We have great leaders among us today. We have had great men and women in the past: Frederick Douglass, Harriet Tubman, and Mary Terrell. These are people who worked not for themselves, but for others.

I leave you faith. The measure of our progress as a race is in precise relation to the depth of the faith in our people held by our leaders. Frederick Douglass was spurred by a deep conviction that his people would heed his counsel and follow him to freedom. Our forefathers struggled for liberty in conditions far more onerous than those we now face, but they never lost the faith. We must never forget their sufferings and sacrifices, for they were the foundations of the progress of our people.

I leave you racial dignity. We must recognize that we are the custodians as well as the heirs of a great civilization. We have given something to the world as a race and for this we are proud and fully conscious of our place in the total picture of mankind's development.

If I have a legacy to leave my people, it is my philosophy of living and serving, my vision of a world of Peace, Progress, Brotherhood, and Love.

21. The best title for the passage would be

(A) Thoughts of My Approaching Death
(B) A Legacy of Guiding Principles
(C) The Contributions of Black Leaders
(D) The Uses of Collective Power
(E) A Vision of Worldwide Peace

22. Which of the following statements is most compatible with the author's principles as presented in the passage?

(A) Too many leaders have rallied to wrong causes and destructive movements.
(B) Justice will prevail only in a world of cooperation and brotherhood.
(C) Stubborn perseverance sometimes hampers negotiations for liberation.
(D) Each individual must work for an abundant, secure personal life.
(E) Great leaders of the past could not have succeeded without formal education.

23. The author is primarily concerned with

(A) emphasizing the need for idealistic leaders
(B) exploring the possibilities of human nature
(C) portraying the present position of blacks in the United States
(D) presenting her life convictions to provide inspiration
(E) stating her views on the role of blacks in American history

24. It can be inferred from the passage that Mary Terrell (lines 28-29) was which of the following?

I. An intelligent and able leader
II. A pioneer in the use of economic power
III. An example because of her personal economic success

(A) I only (B) I and II only (C) I and III only (D) II and III only (E) I, II, and III

25. With which of the following statements regarding black leaders would the author be most likely to agree?

(A) Attempting to emulate past leaders is difficult because the times have changed greatly.
(B) Only leaders who have avoided personal fame should be held up as models.
(C) Past leaders provide more inspiration than present leaders.
(D) Only leaders who have achieved a measure of economic success should be imitated.
(E) If today's leaders lose faith in their race, our progress will be difficult or impossible.

GO ON TO THE NEXT PAGE

A characteristic of modern science is that it prefers to tackle well-defined, finite problems that appear to be soluble with the methods and evidence available. This often means eschewing the more fundamental, the more "metaphysical" issues, in the belief that the cumulative result of solving many smaller and more manageable problems will ultimately throw more light on the larger issues than would a frontal attack. One of the paradoxes of modern science has been that the greater its success in a pragmatic sense, the more modest its aims have tended to become in an intellectual sense. The goals and claims of modern quantum theory are far more modest than those of Laplace, who believed that he could predict the entire course of the universe, in principle, given its initial conditions.

The aim of science has changed from the "explanation" of reality to the "description" of reality—description with the greatest logical and aesthetic economy. The claims to universality of nineteenth-century physics have been replaced by a greater awareness of what still remains to be discovered about the world, even "in principle." The day of global theories of the social structure or of individual psychology seems to have passed. Experience has taught us that real insight has often been achieved only after we were prepared to renounce our claim that our theories were universal. The whole trend of modern scholarship has been towards greater conservatism in deciding what can be legitimately inferred from given evidence; we are more hesitant to extrapolate beyond the immediate circumstances to which the evidence applies. Even in art criticism, we are quicker to recognize a greater diversity in the influences playing on an artist, a greater ambiguity in his or her motives or artistic intentions.

The emphasis on finite aims in scientific and scholarly inquiry has been paralleled by the extension of scientific and scholarly attitudes to practical affairs. The preoccupation of science with manageable problems has a close analogy in the decline of ideology and the growth of professional expertise in politics and business. One of the most striking developments of the postwar world has been the increasing irrelevance of political ideology to political decision-making. One sees the influence of the new mood in the increasing bureaucratization of government and industry and in the growth of "scientific" approaches to management and administration. The day of the intuitive entrepreneur or the charismatic statesman seems to be waning.

26. The passage primarily concerns the

(A) diversity of issues for which modern scientists are seeking explanations
(B) means by which modern scientists have discredited nineteenth-century theories
(C) trend of modern scientists and scholars to focus on limited and manageable problems
(D) application of scientific methods to problems in political science and business
(E) challenges faced by modern scientists who are attempting to explain reality

27. The author's use of the phrase "a frontal attack" (line 9) could best be interpreted to mean which of the following?

(A) Finding practical applications for theories
(B) Questioning the validity of the available evidence
(C) Criticizing widely accepted theories
(D) Devising global theories of explanation
(E) Applying scientific methods to other fields of scholarship

28. According to the passage, modern scientists are more willing than their predecessors to

(A) recognize the limits of their knowledge
(B) find explanations for fundamental issues
(C) dismiss unresolved complexities and misunderstandings
(D) apply scientific methods to problems in other disciplines
(E) predict the future on the basis of the pattern of past events

29. The author sees a similarity between the concerns of modern science and which of the following trends in politics?

(A) A preoccupation among politicians with scholarly issues
(B) The reluctance of politicians to focus on practical issues
(C) Governmental resistance to the influence of industry
(D) The decreasing importance of political ideology
(E) The unpopularity of bureaucratic decision-making

30. The author apparently believes that the aim of science has changed from that of

(A) solving problems to that of devising questions
(B) analyzing causes to that of describing effects
(C) studying specific issues to that of inferring general solutions
(D) accepting experience to that of disregarding experience
(E) observing reality to that of interfering with reality

GO ON TO THE NEXT PAGE

4

Select the word or set of words that best completes each of the following sentences.

31. Virginia Woolf wrote fiction in which sensitive, ---- reactions to experience were objectified and patterned in a manner both intellectually exciting and aesthetically ----.

(A) impartial. .complete
(B) precise. .tranquil
(C) observant. .conclusive
(D) indefinite. .theoretical
(E) personal. .satisfying

32. Having lived in the public eye for years, the ex-mayor cannot believe that from now on he will live in ----.

(A) adulation (B) controversy (C) anonymity (D) agitation (E) veneration

33. Unlike Professor Stark, who is openly ---- about the value of the cell research, Dr. Gorman favors ---- the already sizeable funds allotted to the project.

(A) dubious. .trimming
(B) ecstatic. .donating
(C) enthusiastic. .endorsing
(D) skeptical. .augmenting
(E) curious. .scrutinizing

34. People were tired of what human ---- could provide; the invisible, the ---- were the need of the time.

(A) intellect. .irrational
(B) belief. .mysterious
(C) strength. .constructive
(D) beauty. .unheard
(E) beings. .traditional

35. Where one advances, hundreds ---- ; and the balance is always in favor of nearly universal ----.

(A) retreat. .peace
(B) battle. .weakness
(C) retrogress. .deterioration
(D) subside. .conflict
(E) stagnate. .subjugation

Each question below consists of a related pair of words or phrases, followed by five lettered pairs of words or phrases. Select the lettered pair that best expresses a relationship similar to that expressed in the original pair.

Example:

YAWN : BOREDOM :: (A) dream : sleep (B) anger : madness (C) smile : amusement (D) face : expression (E) impatience : rebellion

Ⓐ Ⓑ ● Ⓓ Ⓔ

36. CAPTAIN : TEAM :: (A) manager : responsibility (B) shortstop : basketball (C) teacher : book (D) administrator : staff (E) catcher : winner

37. INVITATION : SUMMONS ::
(A) procrastination : urgency
(B) action : thought
(C) request : demand
(D) suggestion : reminder
(E) telegram : cable

38. UNMASK : IDENTITY :: (A) concoct : plot (B) decode : message (C) escape : prison (D) submerge : emotion (E) exaggerate : truth

39. TADPOLE : AMPHIBIAN :: (A) lizard : insect (B) minnow : dolphin (C) lamb : mammal (D) branch : tree (E) rooster : chicken

40. GLOAT : SATISFACTION :: (A) gape : wonder (B) solve : mystery (C) glimpse : dismay (D) inspect : damage (E) disappear : surprise

41. DOMINEER : TYRANT :: (A) overrule : delegate (B) admire : champion (C) sympathize : victim (D) purchase : salesman (E) protect : guardian

42. CRIME : FELONY :: (A) worth : respect (B) wealth : gem (C) impiety : blasphemy (D) accident : injury (E) inferiority : rejection

43. STRIDENT : EAR :: (A) supple : skin (B) acrid : tongue (C) honeyed : lip (D) hypnotic : eye (E) saccharine : nose

44. GENRE : LITERARY :: (A) planet : astronomical (B) fallacy : philosophical (C) painting : artistic (D) phylum : zoological (E) plant : botanical

45. CULPABLE : CENSURE :: (A) moral : penance (B) meritorious : reward (C) laughable : abuse (D) admirable : judgment (E) affable : praise

S T O P

IF YOU FINISH BEFORE TIME IS CALLED, CHECK YOUR WORK ON THIS SECTION ONLY.
DO NOT WORK ON ANY OTHER SECTION IN THE TEST.

SECTION 5

Time—30 minutes

25 QUESTIONS

In this section solve each problem, using any available space on the page for scratchwork. Then indicate the one correct answer in the appropriate space on the answer sheet.

The following information is for your reference in solving some of the problems.

Circle of radius r: Area $= \pi r^2$; Circumference $= 2\pi r$
The number of degrees of arc in a circle is 360.
The measure in degrees of a straight angle is 180.

Definitions of symbols:

$=$	is equal to	$\leq$	is less than or equal to
$\neq$	is unequal to	$\geq$	is greater than or equal to
$<$	is less than	$\parallel$	is parallel to
$>$	is greater than	$\perp$	is perpendicular to

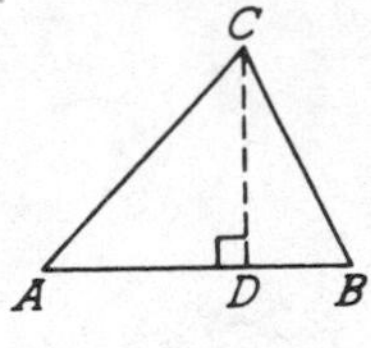

Triangle: The sum of the measures in degrees of the angles of a triangle is 180.

If $\angle CDA$ is a right angle, then

(1) area of $\triangle ABC = \dfrac{AB \times CD}{2}$

(2) $AC^2 = AD^2 + DC^2$

Note: Figures which accompany problems in this test are intended to provide information useful in solving the problems. They are drawn as accurately as possible EXCEPT when it is stated in a specific problem that its figure is not drawn to scale. All figures lie in a plane unless otherwise indicated. All numbers used are real numbers.

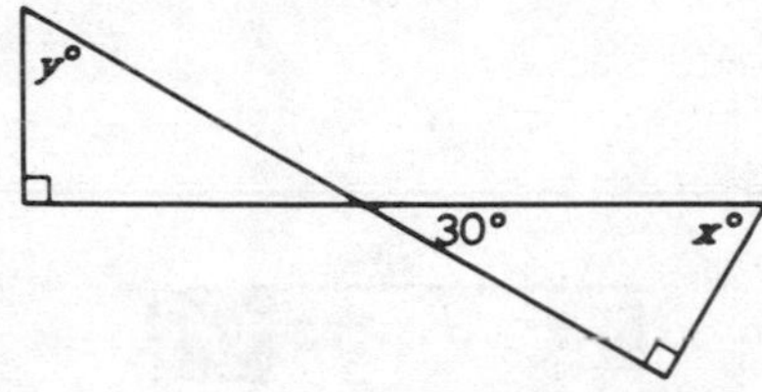

1. In the figure above, $x - y =$

(A) 0 (B) 10 (C) 15 (D) 45 (E) 60

2	3	5	8					

2. The boxes above show part of a sequence of numbers in which each number after 3 is the sum of the two numbers immediately to the left of it. If one number goes in each box, what number goes in the shaded box?

(A) 13 (B) 21 (C) 31 (D) 34 (E) 65

3. What is 99 per cent of 2 ?

(A) 0.0198
(B) 0.198
(C) 1.80
(D) 1.98
(E) 1.99

4. What is the result when $6 + 2x$ is subtracted from the sum of $2 - x$ and $3x^2 + 3x + 4$?

(A) $-3x^2$
(B) $-3x^2 - 2x + 4$
(C) $3x^2$
(D) $3x^2 + 2x + 6$
(E) $3x^2 + 6x + 8$

5. If $x^2 - 4 = 14 \cdot 18$, then x could be

(A) 12
(B) 14
(C) 16
(D) 18
(E) 20

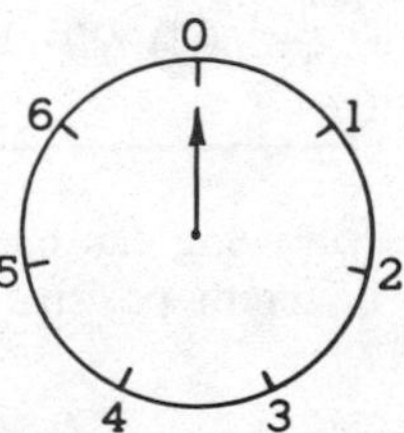

6. A 7-hour clock is shown above. If at 12 noon today the pointer is at zero, where will the pointer be at 12 noon tomorrow?

(A) 0 (B) 2 (C) 3 (D) 5 (E) 6

GO ON TO THE NEXT PAGE

5

7. Of the following, which is greatest?

(A) $\frac{4}{7}$ (B) $\frac{3}{8}$ (C) $\frac{1}{3}$ (D) $\frac{2}{5}$ (E) $\frac{1}{2}$

8. If the average of the first 6 integers on a list is equal to the average of the first 5 integers on the list, then the sixth integer must be equal to

(A) the average of the first 5 integers
(B) an odd number
(C) a negative number
(D) the product of 5 and an integer
(E) the product of 6 and an integer

9. If $\sqrt{16} = x$, then $\sqrt{64} =$

(A) $4x$ (B) $2x$ (C) $x + 2$
(D) $2\sqrt{x}$ (E) $\sqrt{x}$

10. A worker is paid D dollars per hour per week for the first 40 hours worked and $2D$ dollars for each hour over 40. If a worker earns $360 for one week's work, what is the value of D ?

(A) $3 (B) $5 (C) $6 (D) $9
(E) It cannot be determined from the information given.

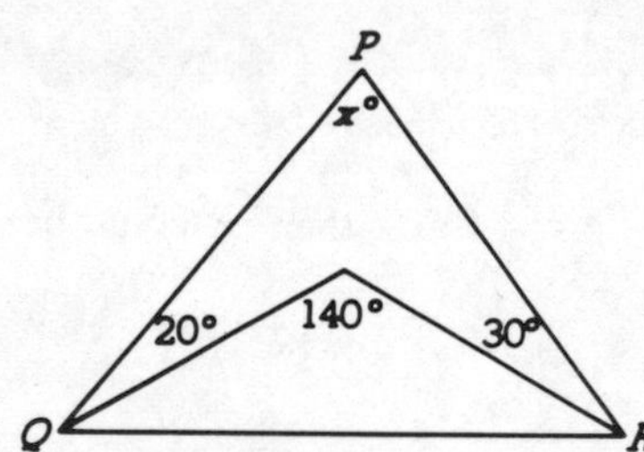

Note: Figure not drawn to scale.

11. In $\triangle PQR$ above, $x =$

(A) 40 (B) 50 (C) 90 (D) 100 (E) 130

12. Which of the following can be expressed as the product of 3 different positive integers, each unequal to 1 ?

I. 24
II. 42
III. 45

(A) I only (B) I and II only (C) I and III only
(D) II and III only (E) I, II, and III

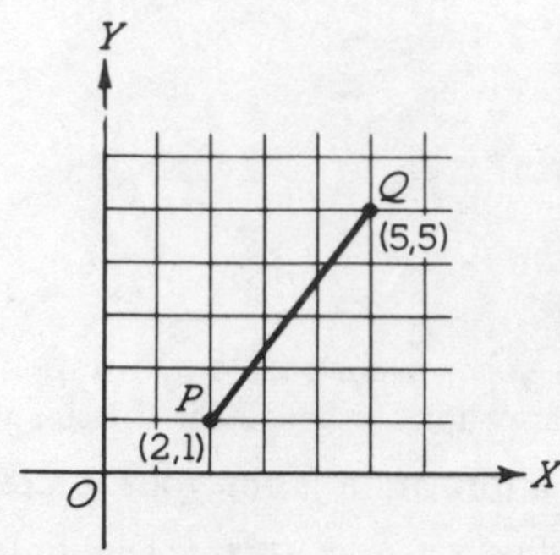

13. In the figure above, what is the length of PQ ?

(A) 13 (B) 7 (C) 6 (D) 5 (E) 3

14. Of the following values of N, $\left(-\frac{1}{3}\right)^N$ will be greatest for $N =$

(A) 2
(B) 3
(C) 4
(D) 5
(E) 6

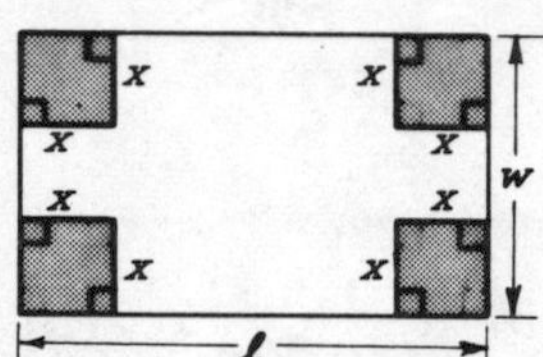

15. In the figure above, the area of the unshaded region of the rectangle is

(A) $\ell w - 4x^2$
(B) $(\ell - 2x)(w - 2x)$
(C) $(\ell - x)(w - x)$
(D) $\ell x + wx$
(E) $(\ell - 4x)(w - 4x)$

GO ON TO THE NEXT PAGE

16. What is the diameter of a circle with circumference 1 ?

(A) π

(B) 1

(C) $\frac{1}{2}$

(D) $\frac{1}{\pi}$

(E) $-\pi + 1$

$$X = 1 - \frac{9}{10}$$

$$Y = 1 - 0.99$$

$$Z = 1 \div 9$$

17. If X, Y, and Z have the values indicated above, in which of the following are X, Y, and Z in order from least to greatest?

(A) X, Y, Z
(B) X, Z, Y
(C) Y, Z, X
(D) Y, X, Z
(E) Z, Y, X

18. A two-digit number has a tens' digit x and a units' digit y. What is the product of this number and the number 5, in terms of x and y ?

(A) $5x + y$
(B) $5x + 5y$
(C) $5x + 50y$
(D) $50x + 50y$
(E) $50x + 5y$

19. A 20-centimeter wire is cut into exactly three pieces. If the first piece is 3 centimeters shorter than the second piece and the third piece is 4 centimeters shorter than the second piece, what is the length in centimeters of the shortest piece?

(A) 5 (B) 6 (C) 7 (D) 8 (E) 9

20. If $0 < N < 1$, which of the following must be true?

I. $N > N^2$

II. $N > \frac{1}{N}$

III. $N > \frac{1}{\sqrt{N}}$

(A) I only (B) II only (C) III only
(D) I and II (E) I and III

21. A game board is made up of X rows of X squares. The squares of the board alternate in color from black to white and the corner squares are all white. If there are W white squares and B black squares, what is the value of $W - B$?

(A) -1
(B) 0
(C) 1
(D) 4
(E) It cannot be determined from the information given.

22. A child built a tower with a set of cubic blocks. If the first block had an edge of $2\frac{1}{2}$ inches and each block added had an edge which was $\frac{1}{4}$ inch less than the preceding block, what is the ratio of the volume of the fifth block to the volume of the first block?

(A) $\frac{1}{8}$

(B) $\frac{27}{125}$

(C) $\frac{9}{25}$

(D) $\frac{3}{5}$

(E) $\frac{125}{27}$

GO ON TO THE NEXT PAGE

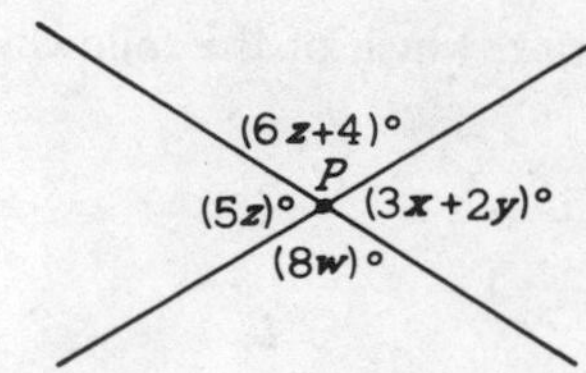

Note: Figure not drawn to scale.

23. If the two straight lines in the figure above intersect at P, what is the value of w ?

(A) 10

(B) $12\frac{1}{2}$

(C) $17\frac{1}{2}$

(D) 20

(E) It cannot be determined from the information given.

24. If for all numbers n,

$\#n = n(n+1)(n+2)$, then $\dfrac{\#8}{\#4} =$

(A) #1 (B) #2 (C) #3 (D) #4 (E) #6

25. In a certain bookcase 50 per cent of the books are math textbooks, 80 per cent of the books are over twenty years old, and 40 per cent of the books over twenty years old are history books. What is the maximum per cent of books in the bookcase that could be math textbooks over twenty years old?

(A) 28%
(B) 32%
(C) 40%
(D) 48%
(E) 50%

S T O P

IF YOU FINISH BEFORE TIME IS CALLED, CHECK YOUR WORK ON THIS SECTION ONLY.
DO NOT WORK ON ANY OTHER SECTION IN THE TEST.

Correct Answers for Scholastic Aptitude Test Form Code 0B023

VERBAL		MATHEMATICAL	
Section 1	**Section 4**	**Section 2**	**Section 5**
1. E	1. A	1. D	1. A
2. C	2. C	2. A	2. D
3. B	3. B	3. E	3. D
4. D	4. D	4. B	4. C
5. C	5. C	5. B	5. C
6. C	6. A	6. B	6. C
7. A	7. E	7. A	7. A
8. C	8. C	*8. A	8. A
9. B	9. C	*9. C	9. B
10. A	10. C	*10. C	10. E
11. E	11. A	*11. A	11. C
12. E	12. C	*12. B	12. B
13. D	13. E	*13. B	13. D
14. B	14. A	*14. D	14. A
15. C	15. A	*15. C	15. A
16. C	16. D	*16. A	16. D
17. B	17. B	*17. A	17. D
18. A	18. D	*18. B	18. E
19. D	19. E	*19. D	19. A
20. D	20. A	*20. C	20. A
21. C	21. B	*21. A	21. C
22. B	22. B	*22. C	22. B
23. A	23. D	*23. D	23. B
24. A	24. A	*24. C	24. A
25. E	25. E	*25. D	25. D
26. A	26. C	*26. C	
27. B	27. D	*27. D	
28. E	28. A	28. C	
29. C	29. D	29. B	
30. B	30. B	30. D	
31. E	31. E	31. D	
32. D	32. C	32. D	
33. C	33. D	33. B	
34. C	34. A	34. E	
35. A	35. C	35. E	
36. B	36. D		
37. E	37. C		
38. D	38. B		
39. D	39. C		
40. E	40. A		
	41. E		
	42. C		
	43. B		
	44. D		
	45. B		

*Indicates four-choice questions. (All of the other questions are five-choice.)

The Scoring Process

Machine-scoring is done in three steps:

- *Scanning.* Your answer sheet is "read" by a scanning machine and the oval you filled in for each question is recorded on a computer tape.
- *Scoring.* The computer compares the oval filled in for each question with the correct response. Each correct answer receives one point; omitted questions do not count toward your score. For each wrong answer, a fraction of a point is subtracted to correct for random guessing. For questions with five answer choices, one-fourth of a point is subtracted for each wrong response; for questions with four answer choices, one-third of a point is subtracted for each wrong response. For example, the SAT-verbal test has 85 questions with five answer choices each, and if a student has 44 right, 32 wrong, and 9 omitted, the resulting raw score is determined as follows:

  $$44 \text{ right} - \frac{32 \text{ wrong}}{4} = 44 - 8 = 36 \text{ raw score points}$$

  Obtaining raw scores frequently involves the rounding of fractional numbers to the nearest whole number. For example, a raw score of 36.25 is rounded to 36, the nearest whole number. A raw score of 36.50 is rounded upward to 37.
- *Converting to reported scaled score.* Raw test scores are then placed on the College Board scale of 200 to 800 through a process that adjusts scores to account for minor differences in difficulty between different editions of the test. This process, known as equating, is performed so that a student's reported score is not affected by the edition of the test taken nor by the abilities of the group with whom the student takes the test. As a result of placing ATP scores on the College Board scale, scores earned by students at different times can be compared. For example, an SAT-verbal score of 400 on a test taken at one administration indicates the same level of developed verbal ability as a 400 score obtained on a different edition of the test taken at another time.

How to Score the Test

You can verify the College Board SAT scores reported to you recently by using the information in this booklet along with the copy of your answer sheet. *Before you begin, check that the form code you marked in item 3 on your answer sheet is the same as the one printed on the front of this booklet.* Compare the responses shown on the copy of your answer sheet with the list of correct answers.

SAT-Verbal Sections 1 and 4

Step A: Count the number of correct answers for *section 1* and record the number in the space provided on the worksheet on the opposite page. Then do the same for the incorrect answers. (Do not count omitted answers.) To determine subtotal A, use the formula:

$$\text{number correct} - \frac{\text{number incorrect}}{4} = \text{subtotal A}$$

Step B: Count the number of correct answers and the number of incorrect answers for *section 4* and record the numbers in the spaces provided on the worksheet. To determine subtotal B, use the formula:

$$\text{number correct} - \frac{\text{number incorrect}}{4} = \text{subtotal B}$$

Step C: To obtain C, add subtotal A to subtotal B, keeping any decimals.

Step D: To obtain D, your raw verbal score, round C to the nearest whole number. (For example, any number from 44.50 to 45.49 rounds to 45.)

Step E: To find your reported SAT-verbal score, look up the total raw verbal score you obtained in step D in the conversion table on the back cover.

SAT-Mathematical Sections 2 and 5

Step A: Count the number of correct answers and the number of incorrect answers for the *four-choice questions (questions 8 through 27) in section 2* and record the numbers in the spaces provided on the worksheet. To determine the subtotal A, use the formula:

$$\text{number correct} - \frac{\text{number incorrect}}{3} = \text{subtotal A}$$

Step B: Count the number of correct answers and the number of incorrect answers for the *five-choice questions (questions 1 through 7 and 28 through 35) in section 2* and record the numbers in the spaces provided on the worksheet. To determine the subtotal B, use the formula:

$$\text{number correct} - \frac{\text{number incorrect}}{4} = \text{subtotal B}$$

Step C: Count the number of correct answers and the number of incorrect answers for section 5 and record the numbers in the spaces provided on the worksheet. To determine the subtotal C, use the formula:

$$\text{number correct} - \frac{\text{number incorrect}}{4} = \text{subtotal C}$$

Step D: To obtain D, add subtotal A, subtotal B, and subtotal C, keeping any decimals.

Step E: To obtain E, your raw mathematical score, round D to the nearest whole number. (For example, any number from 44.50 to 45.49 rounds to 45.)

Step F: To find your reported SAT-mathematical score, look up the total raw mathematical score you obtained in E in the conversion table on the back cover.

SAT-Verbal Worksheet

A. Section 1:	______ no. correct	− ¼ (______ no. incorrect)	=	______ subtotal A
B. Section 4:	______ no. correct	− ¼ (______ no. incorrect)	=	______ subtotal B
C. Total unrounded raw score (Total A + B)				______ C
D. Total rounded raw score (Rounded to nearest whole number)				______ D
E. Reported SAT-verbal score (See the conversion table on the back cover.)				[ ] SAT-Verbal

SAT-Mathematical Worksheet

A. Section 2: Questions 8 through 27 (4-choice)	______ no. correct	− ⅓ (______ no. incorrect)	=	______ subtotal A
B. Section 2: Questions 1 through 7 and 28 through 35 (5-choice)	______ no. correct	− ¼ (______ no. incorrect)	=	______ subtotal B
C. Section 5:	______ no. correct	− ¼ (______ no. incorrect)	=	______ subtotal C
D. Total unrounded raw score (Total A + B + C)				______ D
E. Total rounded raw score (Rounded to nearest whole number)				______ E
F. Reported SAT-mathematical score (See the conversion table on the back cover.)				[ ] SAT-Math

If you have any questions on these scoring instructions, you may call the phone number below.

If, after following the above scoring directions and checking your work carefully, your results disagree with the verbal or mathematical score reported on your ATP Student Report, you may request a hand scoring of your answer sheet by writing or calling:

College Board ATP
Box 592
Princeton, NJ 08541
Attention: Rescore Request
Telephone: (609) 883-8500

Please indicate whether it is your verbal or mathematical score, or both, that you want to be rescored. When you write, please include a copy of the scoring worksheet in this booklet on which you did your calculations.

Score Conversion Table
Scholastic Aptitude Test
Form Code 0B023

Raw Score	College Board Reported Score		Raw Score	College Board Reported Score	
	SAT-Verbal	SAT-Math		SAT-Verbal	SAT-Math
85	800		40	470	610
84	790		39	460	600
83	780		38	460	590
82	770		37	450	590
81	760		36	440	580
80	760		35	430	570
79	750		34	430	560
78	740		33	420	550
77	730		32	410	540
76	730		31	410	540
75	720		30	400	530
74	710		29	390	520
73	700		28	390	510
72	690		27	380	500
71	690		26	370	490
70	680		25	360	490
69	670		24	360	480
68	660		23	350	470
67	660		22	340	460
66	650		21	340	450
65	640		20	330	440
64	640		19	320	430
63	630		18	320	430
62	620		17	310	420
61	610		16	300	410
60	610	800	15	300	400
59	600	790	14	290	390
58	590	780	13	280	380
57	590	770	12	270	380
56	580	760	11	270	370
55	570	750	10	260	360
54	570	740	9	250	350
53	560	730	8	250	340
52	550	720	7	240	330
51	550	710	6	230	330
50	540	700	5	230	320
49	530	690	4	220	310
48	520	680	3	210	300
47	520	670	2	210	290
46	510	660	1	200	280
45	500	650	0	200	280
44	500	640	−1	200	270
43	490	640	−2	200	260
42	480	630	−3	200	250
41	480	620	−4	200	240
			−5	200	230
			−6	200	230
			−7	200	220
			−8	200	210
			−9 or below	200	200